Sociology as Everyday Life

Sociology as Everyday Life

Voices from the Field

Edited by Robert McNamara

The Citadel

Bassim Hamadeh, CEO and Publisher

Jennifer McCarthy, Field Acquisitions Editor

Michelle Piehl, Senior Project Editor

Christian Berk, Associate Production Editor

Emely Vilavicencio, Senior Graphic Designer

Stephanie Kohl, Licensing Coordinator

Natalie Piccotti, Senior Marketing Manager

Kassie Graves, Vice President of Editorial

Jamie Giganti, Director of Academic Publishing

Dedication

THIS BOOK IS dedicated to the approximately ten thousand students whom I have taught over the course of my career. I have learned far more from you than anything I may have imparted, and I am grateful to everyone who has spent time with me in some way.

This book is also dedicated to my old friend and professor, Dr. Eugene Fappiano, a wise scholar and kind friend, who taught me that the students come first. Thank you, Gene, for everything.

Contents

Preface

I HAVE ARGUED for years that sociology impacts people's behavior, be it their interpersonal relationships, family of origin dynamics, or large-scale problems like poverty and racism. Sociology also helps us to understand how our culture shapes our attitudes, values, beliefs, and behavior.

On college campuses, sociology helps us to understand how and why universities operate as they do. It also helps us to understand things like why college football is so popular and the many rituals and practices found on particular campuses related to it. Sociology is also helpful in giving students insights into their professors' idiosyncrasies, which are often a consequence of their training and experiences, and it offers faculty members a way to understand the changing learning styles of generations of students and their behavior in the classroom.

In my own case, the time I have spent with students has been the most valuable and rewarding part of my career. Almost daily, we laugh together, we learn something new together, and we often lament the complexity of the problems that face our society. I have been extraordinarily blessed to have had such a remarkable group of students over the years—each providing their own unique contribution to my development as a scholar, mentor, and educator. Not only are they extraordinarily talented and thoughtful individuals, they are some of the best people I know. They come from a variety of backgrounds, but what ties them together is a clear understanding of their purpose in society and their role in helping others. Many former students have become sociologists, physicians, attorneys, counselors, and pastors, or have answered a call to serve others in their communities.

It is fitting, then, that as I celebrate my thirtieth year of teaching, and the number of students I have taught approaches upwards of ten thousand, this project serves as a testimony to the enormous talent and expertise of many former students. In this collection of readings, they offer their own insights about the challenges they face in their given professions. In addition, as former sociology majors, they offer theoretical or conceptual insight into these observations, thereby giving students a unique glimpse of sociology from a practical point of view.

I have also tried to address one of the most significant issues in higher education—the escalating cost of textbooks. Some students avoid purchasing textbooks because of their exorbitant cost, thereby risking their success in a given course due to financial reasons. As someone who has written multiple textbooks, I can tell you that authors do not profit greatly from the books they write, and at some point common sense has to prevail over this problem. The publishing company producing this textbook has attempted to address this issue in a meaningful way and all royalties from this book are donated to charity. Hopefully this project is a step in the right direction and allows students a chance to gain as much from their courses as possible. I call your attention to the following articles, written by brilliant and thoughtful people, who understand how sociology has impacted their perceptions of the world as well as their place in it.

Introduction

HAVE YOU EVER heard of sociology? While a few students might have taken a sociology course in high school, most have a very limited exposure to the field or how it relates to their lives. Some students likely have a fairly clear understanding of psychology, and while there are parallels between psychology and sociology, there are also a number of fundamental differences.

A standard definition of sociology might say something like sociology is "the scientific study of society, culture, and group behavior," such a definition is of little help in providing any significant insight into the discipline or how it relates to people in general. The basic insight into sociology is that it tries to understand why people act a certain way. In that respect it is a lot like psychology, which also tries to predict people's behavior. The difference between the two is that psychology attempts to understand and predict people's behavior by attributing the causes to internal traits: personality, genetic predisposition, etc. Sociology, in contrast, attempts to explain and predict human behavior by examining external factors, specifically the groups to which people belong and the interactions that take place within those groups.

Think about it; you act differently depending on where you are and the people you are with—when you are with your closest friends you likely act one way, but while in church or with your parents, you may act very differently—why? This is a key insight into sociology.

In the following articles, we explore the role of theory in understanding complex human behavior, and we also explore a bit about how social scientists conduct research. This may be a bit different than what most students understand about science and theory, but both are critically important in helping scientists learn more about people's behavior. Remember that both are simply tools—even theory is ultimately designed to help us understand phenomena that occur around us. As Kenny Schmitt points out in his article in this section, sometimes theory seems intimidating, but it does not have to be—in fact, it can be similar to jazz improvisation in music. Similarly, Carrie Coward Bucher points out some of the challenges of conducting research on people in their natural environment. While most people are familiar with survey research, this technique doesn't always work depending on the topic a researcher wishes to explore. Field research, or ethnographic research, tries to understand a given group of people as they go about their lives. Researchers conduct systematic observations, interviews, and informal conversations as a way to understand a group's way of life and why certain things are so important to them.

Research Methods

How Do Sociologists Conduct Research?

The Basics of Social Science Inquiry: Who Is Homeless?

Carrie Coward Bucher, PhD

The function of sociology, as of every science, is to reveal that which is hidden.

(Bourdieu, 2012)

THE FUNDAMENTAL CALLING of the sociologist is the rigorous exploration of the social roots of the human condition. C. Wright Mills described this calling as the sociological imagination, which "enables its possessor to understand the larger historical scene in terms of its meaning for the inner life and the external career of a variety of individuals" (1939). By that he meant that the sociologist uses scientific methods to understand the ways in which individual lives and opportunities shape, and are shaped by, social institutions. Many introduction to sociology readers are filled with poetic treatises on the passion of sociology; Berger (1963) likened it to spiritual possession while Schwalbe (1998) extols sociological mindfulness as a life philosophy. However you conceptualize the sociological imagination, in order for it to be insightful it must be valid and reliable in its assertions about the causes and consequences of structure and culture.

Research in the social sciences follows the scientific method, with some unique challenges in terms of isolating and accurately measuring the complex social world. Overcoming these challenges requires identifying the appropriate method of analysis for your question, measuring and analyzing your variables accurately, and completing your work in an ethical manner. It is this rigorous methodology, however, that separates the social scientist from the casual observer of everyday life. This article will use a deceptively simple topic, homelessness in America, to illustrate the challenges associated with sociological research.

The Department of Housing and Urban Development estimates that on any given night 553,742 people are homeless in the United States. Approximately 35 percent of them are living without shelter, while the rest are in emergency or transitional living spaces. The majority—61 percent—are male and forty thousand of them are veterans. About 20 percent of this population is under the age of eighteen, some homeless with their families and many homeless on their own as either a runaway or a child who does not have family to care for him. While the overall number of homeless has declined over the past decade, there has been a recent uptick in people who are chronically homeless, or those who are living on the street for extended periods of time (HUD 2017). Understanding this population is essential to reducing the emotional and physical trauma that homelessness inflicts on its victims.

CHOOSING A METHODOLOGY

Understanding the extent and experience of homeless people in America presents meaningful challenges to the sociologist. One challenge centers around determining what it is you would like to know about the homeless. Are you interested in how they became homeless? Or what factors contribute to rehousing them? If so, do you want to understand the lived experiences that brought people to and from the street or the broader social forces that constrain their options? Both are valid avenues of inquiry that will provide important insight. Sociologists label these two approaches as microsociology and macrosociology.

Macrosociology is interested in large-scale social institutions, such as the criminal justice system or urban planning. Some authors have approached the issues of understanding homelessness through these institutions. Talmadge Wright (1997) understands homelessness as a consequence of capitalist labor relations, wherein people who exist outside of the chain of production interact with a system of institutions designed to make them invisible. For example, the homeless are subjected to city ordinances meant to push them away from centers of economic production (such as downtown areas) to the outskirts of cities where they are not seen and do not "impede" commerce. Herring and Lutz (2016) find this alienation is accomplished through an intersection of institutional systems (city planning and policing) whereby urban planners build anti-homeless technology (such as spikes in the ground in building enclaves or benches with multiple armrests to deter sleeping) into the city and police selectively enforce loitering laws in commercial centers while ignoring those same behaviors when they occur in parks and neighborhoods at the edge of town. People using a macrosociological lens would consider the homeless as people caught in the crosshairs of economic, political, and law-enforcement institutions that constrain their opportunities.

Microsociologists, on the other hand, are more concerned with the study of interpersonal interactions and the creation of meaning. This approach acknowledges that broad institutions influence our opportunities, but it is the process of meaning making within those institutions that drives our behavior. Snow and Anderson (1986), for instance, found that homeless men define themselves in very different terms. Some distance themselves from the homeless stereotype by claiming they aren't a "typical homeless person" while others frame their role as knowledgeable and free from the constraints of society. For homeless youth, Roschelle and Kaufman (2004) found that they employ a complex process of passing and covering to manage the stigma caused by their social location.

Researchers must also decide if their question is best addressed by a numerical representation, which may be more generalizable, or interviews and observations that can provide rich, contextual data. Quantitative data is the numerical sort, where variables are represented in number form. These data are excellent for questions that can be answered through surveys, such as the census. For example, the US Department of Housing and Urban Development (2017) completed a point-in-time survey of homeless people and extrapolated to conclude that 553,742 people experience homelessness on any given night. Two-thirds of those people were in shelters and one-third were on the streets or in a habitat not meant for living (tent cities or abandoned houses). Qualitative data, on the other hand, gives voice to the subjects and can provide rich contextual understanding to the researcher through interviews or participant observation.

Taken together, this research provides us with a more complete and nuanced understanding of homelessness. We know which social factors push people to marginalized spaces where opportunity for employment and access to resources is limited. We also know that once in that space, people respond very differently to the strain of their homelessness. This provides insight not only for future research but also for those interested in serving this population.

THE SCIENTIFIC METHOD

Once researchers have determined the correct approach, we must generate a research question and operationalize our variables. To begin this process researchers engage in an extensive literature review, where we read the significant, scholarly research on our topic. Reading the previous literature guides us to a theory, or a series of logical assertions about how the social world operates. We will use that theory, then, to generate a new hypothesis, or a testable statement of the relationship between independent and dependent variables. An independent variable is the factor that we think causes a change in the dependent variable. Lastly, we operationalize the variables, which means we need to decide how precisely to measure each one.

Applying the scientific method to understanding homelessness in the United States is deceptively complicated. First, the literature tells us that there are three forms of homelessness: people who have a temporary experience and quickly become stably rehoused, people who are episodically homeless and spend extended periods cycling between having shelter and being homeless, and those who are chronically homeless for an extended period (Culhane et. al 2007). Then there are questions of definition: are you homeless if you are sleeping on a friend's couch? In a short-term motel? In a shelter? How long do you have to be on the street or in temporary housing to count as homeless? Is twenty-four hours sufficient? A weekend?

Second, researchers may also struggle to determine causality among a variety of health related issues and homelessness. It is well documented that the homeless have worse health than their housed peers (Haddad et al 2005, Lee & Grief 2008,). This is particularly true in regard to mental health and substance abuse, which can be found in nearly 85 percent of the adult homeless population (Toro et al. 2014). While that is certainly higher than the housed population, it is difficult to establish which came first, the illness/addiction or the homelessness? We know that with the deinstitutionalization of state mental health hospitals there was an increase of people suffering from mental illness who were not treated effectively and became homeless (Snow et al. 1986). However, we also know that living on the street is rife with stress and trauma, which can contribute to the incidence of addiction and mental illness.

Third, the researcher will be challenged to generate a generalizable sample of homeless people. Generalizability is the extent to which we can take the findings of one study, which includes a small sample of the homeless, and draw conclusions about the behavior of those not in the study (i.e., all the homeless). Generalizability is difficult to determine for homeless populations because they are heterogenous, or comprised of different kinds of people living in very different situations, and by definition hard to count. Most often people count the homeless through a point-in-time study, wherein they survey people on the streets and care providers, such as shelters or soup kitchens, to determine how many people are homeless. This is how the Department of Housing and Urban Development came to their number of 553,742 homeless individuals on any given night (HUD 2017). While this number is useful for service providers, it does not give us an understanding of the rate of homelessness among all Americans. One way to address this issue is to ask housed people if they have ever been homeless. Bruce Link (1995) and his colleagues did just this, and discovered that 14 percent of Americans have had a homeless episode in their lifetimes. This number is much higher than the point-in-time-study (extrapolating out to 26 million Americans) and provides us with a more comprehensive understanding of how homelessness impacts a much larger proportion of the country than previously thought.

ETHICALLY ANSWERING SOCIOLOGICAL QUESTIONS

Lastly, researchers are challenged to develop an appropriate and ethical approach to exploring their issue. Ethical sociological research includes informed consent and the work must not harm the subject physically, emotionally, or reputationally. This is especially important with people who are not housed, as a major part of the experience of homelessness is deindividuation, or being made to feel that your humanity is not valued. Think of all the times people in society avoid the homeless, refuse to make eye contact with people who are panhandling, or step over someone sleeping in the doorway ... these experiences may result in homeless people feeling alienated from mainstream society. Sociologists are tasked with recording the necessary data for their project without using and abusing their subjects like lab rats. Approaching your respondents respectfully, with warmth and professionalism, without judgement or bias, is essential to not only getting reliable data but also making all participants feel valued.

CONCLUSION

As an undergraduate I always found the methods section of research articles and books intimidating. The numbers and regressions figures were, at best, boring and, at worst, full of statistics that were as complicated as they were esoteric. It wasn't until I began working with homeless youth that I developed an intense appreciation for methodologically sound social research. After graduating with a bachelor's degree in sociology, I worked for a wonderful organization serving homeless youth, between the ages of twelve and eighteen, who were living on the streets independently. It was in this environment that I realized the research on best practices was not esoteric or overly complicated, but rather essential to helping the complex system of addiction counselors, police officers, social workers, and support staff make the most effective choice for the children sitting right in front of us.

Indeed, as my passion for those kids—who deserved far better than the trauma they had endured—grew, so did my desire to return to graduate school for a Ph.D. in sociology. I became convinced that the hands-on work I was doing was only one part of an important system of care for these children. The other part was to develop a larger understanding of the causes and consequences of adolescent homelessness and how we can prevent the next generation of children from having to suffer. That research has identified that only 18 percent of runaway youth are adequately treated by the current system of interventions and that far more comprehensive services are needed to effectively reduce the impact of running away from home (Coward Bucher 2008).

Bibliography

Berger, Peter. (1963) 2004. *Invitation to sociology*. New York: Anchor Books.

Bourdieu, Pierre. *On Television*. Hoboken: John Wiley & Sons, 2012.

Culhane, Dennis, Stephen Metraux, Jung Min Park, Maryanne Schretzman, and Jesse Valente. "Testing a typology of family homelessness based on patterns of public shelter utilization in four U.S. jurisdictions: Implications for policy and program planning." *Housing Policy Debate* 18, no. 1(2007): 1–28.

Coward Bucher, Carrie. "Toward a Needs-Based Typology of Homeless Youth." *Journal of Adolescent Health* 42, no. 6 (2008): 549–554.

Haddad, M.B., T.W. Wilson, K. Ijaz, S.M. Marks, and M. Moore. "Tuberculosis and Homelessness in the United States, 1994–2003." *Journal of the American Medical Association* 293, no. 22 (2005):2762–6.

Herring, C. and M. Lutz. "The roots and implications of the USA's homeless tent cities." *City* 19, no 5 (2015): 689–701.

Lee Barrett A. and Meredith J. Greif. "Homelessness and hunger." *Journal of Health and Social Behavior* 49, no. 1 (2008): 3–19.

Link B.G., J. Phelan, M.Bresnahan, A. Stueve, R.E. Moore, and E. Susser. "Lifetime and five-year prevalence of homelessness in the United States: new evidence on an old debate." *American Journal of Orthopsychiatry* 65 (1995): 347–54.

Mills, C. "The Sociological Imagination." *The American Catholic Sociological Review* 20, no. 3 (1959): 249.

Roschelle, A. and P. Kaufman. "Fitting In and Fighting Back: Stigma Management Strategies among Homeless Kids." *Symbolic Interaction* 27, no. 1 (2004): 23–46.

Schwalbe, Michael. *The Sociologically Examined Life*. Mountain View, CA.: Mayfield Publishing, 1998.

Snow, D. and L. Anderson. "Down on Their Luck: A Study of Homeless Street People." *Contemporary Sociology* 23, no. 1 (1994): 42.

Snow, D., S. Baker, L. Anderson, and M. Martin. "The Myth of Pervasive Mental Illness among the Homeless." *Social Problems* 33, no. 5 (1986): 407–423.

Toro, P., K. Hobden, K. Wyszacki Durham, M. Oko-Riebau, and A. Bokszczanin. "Comparing the Characteristics of Homeless Adults in Poland and the United States." *American Journal of Community Psychology* 53, no. 1–2 (2014): 134–145.

US Department of Housing and Urban Development. *The 2008 Annual Homeless Assessment Report to Congress*. Office of Community Planning and Development: Washington, DC, 2009.

US Department of Housing and Urban Development. *The 2016 Annual Homeless Assessment Report to Congress*. Office of Community Planning and Development: Washington, DC, 2017.

Wright, Talmadge. *Out of place*. Albany: State University of New York Press, 1997.

Theories and Analogies, Jazz and Creativity

Kenny Schmitt, PhD

A BLIND MAN introduced me to Sociology. I was a high school senior on a campus visit at Furman University. I had a friend who was a sophomore there, and he invited me to hang out for the weekend. We were set to meet on a Saturday morning outside the main library. And as I waited at the main entrance, two guys approached me. One was apparently blind, wearing dark sunglasses and walking with a cane. The other held the blind guy's elbow, gently guiding him along. When they began approaching me, I did a double take—the blind guy had the size and build of my friend. No sooner, the elbow-supporting guy inquired, "Hey, are you Kenny?" I said yes. Then the blind guy spoke. I recognized the voice immediately—it was my friend.

As I stood there aghast, I asked what had happened. My friend explained that he had been in an accident in his chemistry class. Acidic chemicals splashed in his eyes and blinded him. But his doctor said he was hopeful the blindness would only be temporary. I felt terrible. He assured me he had deliberately concealed the news because he didn't want me to cancel my visit. About this time, my friend's elbow-clutching companion began to giggle. "What could possibly be funny about this?," I asked. Before the question was out of my mouth, they were both laughing hysterically—clearly, the joke was on me. They eventually calmed down and explained that they were taking a sociology class.

Their assignment was to develop an experiment to test social theories about how people responded to the blind in public. Apparently I was their first unwitting participant. I asked how long the study would last and my friend said the next two days. "What?," I interjected, "You're going to go around like this all weekend?" He nodded with a grin smeared across his face—Yep. So that whole weekend, there I was on my college visit, walking around holding my friend's elbow as he shuffled along with his cane and dark sunglasses. And you may think I was annoyed by this; I wasn't—I totally loved it. He invited me to join him in making observations about people's responses and developing social hypotheses as he bumped into them (sometimes literally) on campus and throughout the city. Looking back, the theories we developed may be better understood as elaborate excuses to act sophomoric in public. Even so, I left Furman that weekend with a crazy idea in my head—that social theory was fun and relevant.

In this article I want to explain how social theory can help you—how you can work with it in ways that are fun and relevant. I want to dispel the fear that most students have when they first encounter the arcane writing of pipe-smoking French, German, and Ivy-League intellectuals. If you stop thinking about your own suicide every time you hear the name Emile Durkheim ([1897] 1951), I have succeeded. I will also explain how your life experiences and personal interests are the best resources you have for understanding social theory. I give a few pointers on how to harness your own creativity, too. And while you may never spend a weekend accompanying your sunglasses and cane-clad friend as he bumps into random people on the street, I'd like you to finish this article with ample permission to connect your lived experiences and personal interests to social theory.

Here's what you need to understand right at the start: social theory is about analogies. An analogy is a comparison between two things—thing X is like thing Y in some meaningful way. And for all its insights, theories, and books, that's what sociology is about. Sociology asks one basic question over and over again—what is society like? The question itself begs an 'analogy-like' answer, right? What is society *like*? Society is like a _____. And when you fill in that blank, you have an analogy. Society is like a network or web, for example, where people connect with one another in different ways. That's an analogy. What comes to mind when people talk about networks and webs? Maybe the internet. Maybe spiders. Maybe Facebook, the social 'networking' site. The analogy is simple—society is a web of social relationships, crisscrossing and connecting all over the place. But before I bore you with things you already know since Facebook and the Internet are old news, let me point out that social theory has a whole subdivision called social network analysis (Scott 2017). And if you started reading it, you would be amazed how far sociologists have taken it. This analogy is well known and easy to grasp. Let's take a harder one.

Pierre Bourdieu is a famous social theorist. He developed a thing called field theory (1992, 1977) and his ideas have been quoted and requoted throughout the social sciences. But Bourdieu has one problem: his writing is dense and turgid, almost impossible to grasp. He basically assumes you're an expert in what he's talking about. He uses words like *habitus*, *doxa*, and *reflexivity*—words that no average English speaker has ever heard (much less used in everyday speech). But students and scholars alike bang their heads against his writings because, in them, he has profound social insights. I recall being in graduate school, thinking I had to relearn English to understand him. Whenever it took me more than twenty minutes to understand a page, I quit. One day, however, I had a eureka moment.

I was lamenting my disdain for Bourdieu to a friend, and he told me to imagine a soccer field—think of people passing balls, opponents, strategies, jerseys, teamwork, and players. Call to mind, he explained, everything that soccer involves and then you'll understand Bourdieu's field theory. After this, all Bourdieu's convoluted writing was clarified—ok, not entirely—but I did have an analogy to guide me. His theory was much easier to understand after that. I then mentally renamed Bourdieu's field theory—the soccer field theory. That was all I needed. I now enjoy reading Bourdieu and understand why so many academics quote him—his work is brilliant.

Here's another example. Erving Goffman wrote a book called *The Presentation of Self in Everyday Life* ([1956] 1990). And like Bourdieu, he's at the summit of sociological coolness. He argued that society was like a drama—a theater or play—and he used the analogy to explain people's face-to-face interactions. In the drama of life, there are frontstages and backstages, audiences and actors. Each part is involved in the performance. People take on various roles and participate in different ways. Actors use the backstage to prepare for their performances; they put on makeup and rehearse. They don't intend for the audience to see these backstage activities.

When actors go frontstage, they perform. They act their parts, conveying meaning, emotion, and excitement to the audience. People often say that good actors and actresses 'step into' the role they play. They get into their character so well they develop feelings and emotions that match their characters. You may recall, for example, when Heath Ledger played The Joker in the movie *The Dark Night*, he killed himself while they were filming the movie. Why? He got too into his role. His colleagues said he had gotten into his character so much that he became dark and depressed. He couldn't step off stage—he became the character he played. Acting became his reality, and he killed himself.

That's why Goffman says society is like a drama—we are all acting, putting on faces, trying to get the approval of audiences while we act frontstage. People's feelings and emotions—their sense of identity and self—get wrapped up in the characters they play whether they are students, lawyers, mothers, doctors, teachers, or social workers. That's Goffman's analogy—social interaction that occurs in society is a drama.

With these three examples—the web, soccer field, and drama—I've given you a taste of the analogies social theorists use to explain how society operates. I could have used penitentiaries (Foucault 1977), religion (Durkheim [1912] 1995), or McDonald's (Ritzer 1993) to explain society, too. And that's only the beginning of the list. Analogies are important because they give people ways to understand and relate. When your professor assigns some dense reading in social theory, keep the analogy question in mind—What analogy is the author using to explain society? Social theory is the art of analogy.

After you've grasped this point, the second thing you need to realize is that you already have many insights about society. Your life experiences and personal interests are the best tool you have for learning how to work with social theory. You have seen, done, and observed things your professor and fellow students have never experienced, and each one of these things is relevant to your sociology class. Here's the goal: figure out how your life experiences relate to society and use them. I'll illustrate this point with my own experience. I entered university with a piano performance scholarship. I was invited for my skills playing Beethoven, Mozart, and Rachmaninoff.

But when I heard an upperclassman improvise a piano solo to the tune "On Green Dolphin Street" with the jazz combo, my musical trajectory changed course. I began studying to become a jazz pianist. Over the next four years, I learned to imitate the jazz-greats—Davis, Coltrane, Corea, and others. My improvisations became more creative and unique as I learned to emulate their styles and solos. I played in the jazz combos and big-bands for the university—and loved it! And as my skills developed, the experience became more rewarding.

Fast forward fifteen years and I became a doctoral student, studying for a PhD in Arab and Islamic Studies. I lived in East Jerusalem, working on a project about Muslim religious practices in the city. And since Jerusalem is home to Judaism, Christianity, and Islam, the city often filled with conflict and tensions. I wanted to understand how the conflict influenced Muslim religious practices (Schmitt 1017). After much experience in the city, I started drafting my dissertation. While I had sufficient data and personally understood my observations, I struggled to explain my findings in a way that others could relate. Then, one day as I was discussing this frustration with my advisor, he told me to think about my data with analogies. He said he often has images in mind when he writes.

And since his hobby is farming, his mind is often filled with images from the pasture—trees, birds, and barbed wire. His best ideas come when he's pulling weeds. This comment permitted me to start thinking—What analogy could explain the connection between Muslim religious practices and the conflict? One came immediately: Muslim religious practices in Jerusalem were like broken bones—the conflict breaks the practices, and they heal improperly because the wounds were not treated. My advisor liked where I was going and suggested I discuss the metaphor with a physician. If the doctor saw the connection, he could help me find the right vocabulary to make the analogy useful for my study. Or, alternatively, he may help me realize that the analogy broke down and was better to abandon. Before our conversation ended, I realized that the broken-bone analogy wasn't quite right, but it had been a good first try.

A few weeks later I was writing at a coffee shop, blasting jazz through my headphones (as was my custom). I was writing a section of the dissertation about how people's religious practices changed according to the physical environment where they were performing. And as I fought to organize my thoughts, I kept puzzling about why people saw no tension between the adaptations they made and what they perceived as the right way to practice Islam. How could a religious practice change and be perceived authentic simultaneously? The adaptations were not so different that they seemed un-Islamic to those performing them, but I wondered if they were different enough that other Muslims may say these Muslims were practicing their faith incorrectly. How could I explain this—and clearly? Even reading the last three sentences, you may have thought—yep, this is abstract and difficult to understand. As I strained to grasp the abstraction, I began zoning out, listening to the jazz in my headphones. Then a random thought came to me—What if religious rituals were like jazz improvisations?

I started to daydream about my experience as a jazz musician. I pictured myself performing solos—what I did was creative and spontaneous, but it was also practiced and learned. I imitated Handcock and Coltrane so I could expand my creative capabilities. I practiced deliberately so I could improvise spontaneously. And when I was performing with the band, I also responded actively to what the other musicians were playing—my performances were always influenced by the environment. This was Muslim religious practices in Jerusalem—they were like jazz improvisations.

And there it was; I had my analogy. Muslims drew from a practiced repertoire of themes that they called Islam. But on account of the conflict, they were also forced them to make adaptations. What they were doing was practiced and learned, creative and spontaneous. I had a clear way to explain how religious practices were changing and people still experienced them authentically. Right then, I stopped fighting the failing paragraph I had been writing and began brainstorming all the ways the analogy could relate. I filled several pages. I left the coffee shop a few hours later fully energized—I was groovin' with the vibe.

Over the next few days, I tested the analogy with my advisor and several friends. Everyone liked it. And since I was a Jazz musician, I didn't have to find a specialist (like a physician) to get the right vocabulary. Improvising jazz solos with the jazz combo was all the experience I needed for the analogy to flow. To do my due diligence, I also began thinking about how the analogy might relate to other social theories I knew. I remembered Erving Goffman's society-is-drama analogy, for example. His insights aligned well with the jazz analogy—religious practices and jazz improvisations were specific types of performances. Other theories helped me fill out the analogy. After that, jazz piped through my headphones whenever I wrote. My writing gained momentum and focus. I had the most productive season of writing I'd ever had. And I loved it! I submitted the dissertation several months later, and the feedback from examiners was exceptional. They told me I was smart and creative and all those things.

This is why your life experience is extremely important. I realize that you might not be able to improvise jazz solos, but you have other interests and experiences that are massively relevant to social theory. You might know about dance and rock climbing, or growing up in poverty. You may be a second-generation immigrant or the child of a well-to-do family. What are your hobbies and interests? What intrigues you? Thinking about these is your first and best step to succeeding in sociology. Everything is fair game. Your life experience and personal interests are first-rate resources for relating to social theory in meaningful ways. The analogies you develop to explain social phenomena may change the way others relate, too. This is where learning how to harness your creative potential enters the discussion.

Many people think they are not creative. They have picked up this nonsense idea that other people have a knack for clever ideas and that they simply don't. I disagree completely—creativity is a learned skill. Ok, yes, people do have different aptitudes, but that doesn't change the fact that creativity can be developed and practiced. Harnessing your creativity is like learning jazz improvisation (here I go again)—you work at the craft deliberately so the music can flow naturally and spontaneously. Your ability to be creative is linked to your willingness to practice. And when jazz musicians practice, they learn certain tricks and tactics. Here's my number-one trick for practicing creativity: I write down all my ideas—even the bad ones, especially the bad ones! I usually have twenty to thirty bad ideas before I have one with potential. I keep a note on my iPhone called "genius ideas," and whenever an idea comes to mind, I write it down.

Recently, for example, I was walking in the woods with my family and I was thinking about forest fires and how park rangers have difficult jobs—How can they be everywhere at once, making sure people don't set the trees ablaze? Then I started thinking about drones—What if forest rangers had drones? Rangers could fly their drones everywhere, checking for forest fires, or people littering at campsites, or grizzly bears crossing streets. Cool, right? Maybe. Maybe not. I don't know. Perhaps forest rangers already have drones. Maybe forest fires would burn drones. I have no clue. That's not the point. The point is that I captured the idea—I wrote it in my iPhone. And until someone tells me otherwise, I will think it's genius. That, by the way, is my next trick: I try out my ideas on friends. It's the way I discover whether or not they are good. After sharing, most of the ideas seem silly and amount to nothing. Occasionally I have the funny experience of discovering my idea was not truly original—someone else had it first. And I'm never discouraged by this—it shows me the idea was good. The experience also reminds me that creativity takes work—someone else not only had a good idea, they did something with it. That's an essential tip for creativity, too—if you don't put work into your ideas, nothing will come of them.

Then—every so often—an idea comes that's genuinely creative. I'll never forget the first one I had that related to sociology. I was a junior at Furman and, by that time, a sociology major. I was taking two required courses that fall: social deviance and British literature. In the literature course, the final assignment was writing an eight-page critical analysis of a novel we read for the class. Since the main character of the book I picked was wicked, I kept thinking about what I had learned in my deviance course and how those theories explained his vile, self-destructive behavior. I went to my literature professor and asked if I could analyze this character through the lens of social deviance theory. He said yes. Later, when he returned the graded papers, below the exemplary mark he gave me, he scribbled a note: "Please come see me in office hours." Several days later, I stepped into his office with hesitation. He invited me to sit and asked me to elaborate on the links I saw between the novel and the sociology of deviance. Still uncomfortable, I shared several additional thoughts, and he asked a few follow-up questions. Then, to signal my exit, I thanked him for the excellent grade. He expressed his gratitude that I stopped by and then told me that the paper was the best he had graded in several years. The comment gave me chills. In the days following, as I reflected on the experience, I was perplexed by his very positive reaction. All I had done was connect the dots between his literature course and my fascination with theories of deviance. Apparently that was creative and interesting.

Years later, I understand completely that that is precisely what makes social theory so fun and relevant—it allows people to make meaningful connections with their lived experiences and personal interests. With social theory, people can see their lives—or the lives of others—from different perspectives and in new creative ways. On the specific topic of university assignments, by the way, new research has shown that when professors assign writing projects that incorporate students' life experiences, students get better grades. And they enjoy the assignments more (Eodice and Geller 2017). This means that if you can make connections between social theory and your life experiences—even if it's not asked for directly in the assignment—you will be more successful.

Now, having read this chapter, you have several tools to get started with social theory. First, you can search for (and think through) the analogies social theorists draw from to explain society. You may resonate with viewing society as a web, a drama, a soccer field, or something else. Understanding these analogies will help you survive the dense and verbose literary style of those pipe-smoking social theorists. Second, you can begin drawing from your life experiences and personal interests to create your own social theories. I used jazz improvisation to explain Muslim religious practices in a conflict zone. How might your fascination with horse racing or skateboarding give you insight into the ways other people relate to the world? Finally, you know that creativity is a learned skill. Write down your ideas and share them with friends. Share them with your professors, too—you never know when the connections you make will resonate and lead to excellent grades. You may even find a connection between sociology and your career, as each author in this book has done.

Bibliography

Bourdieu, Pierre. The Logic of Practice. Stanford, CA: Stanford University Press, 1992.

———. Outline of a Theory of Practice. Cambridge Studies in Social Anthropology 16. New York: Cambridge University Press, 1977.

Durkheim, Emile. The Elementary Forms of Religious Life. New York: The Free Press, 1995.

———. Suicide: A Study in Sociology. New York: The Free Press, 1951.

Eodice, Michele and Anne Ellen Geller. The Meaningful Writing Project: Learning, Teaching and Writing in Higher Education. Logan, UT: Utah State University Press, 2017.

Foucault, Michele. Discipline and Punish: The Birth of the Prison. New York: Pantheon Books, 1977.

Goffman, Erving. (1956) 1990. The Presentation of Self in Everyday Life. New York: Penguin.

Ritzer, George. The Mcdonaldization of Society. London: Pine Forge Press, 1993.

Schmitt, K. "Ribat in Palestine: The Growth of a Religious Discourse Alongside Politicized Religious Practice." Jerusalem Quarterly 72, (2017): 26–36.

Scott, John. Social Network Analysis, 4th ed. Los Angeles, CA: Sage, 2017.

Culture

How Do Values Shape Us?

CULTURE

The topic of culture can be a bit tricky to understand. When asked to describe a given culture, most people can give examples of rituals practiced in that culture or perhaps even the reason for the ritual, but culture as a general concept is abstract—we can't really get our hands on culture as a tangible thing. More often we identify examples of culture, like the American flag, and the meaning behind them, but the flag is not all there is to American culture. When you think about culture, it is sometimes helpful to think of it as a collection of attitudes, values, beliefs, and behaviors that characterize a group of people who feel a sense of belonging to that group. Culture can be understood, then, by examining its component parts. Even that is not a good definition, because we have not defined what we mean by attitudes, values, or beliefs. Language is also a key element to culture, since it is the way information is passed on from one generation to the next. This is what prevents us from having to reinvent the wheel every generation and allows society to grow and develop a level of sophistication.

A key element of language, of course, as with culture in general, is that participants understand the meaning behind the ideas. Language, after all, is a symbolic form of communication, but to communicate, each party must know the meaning of those symbols. In fact, most of the problems people have in their interactions with others are based on differing interpretations of meaning. For example, take the letter A. What does it mean? In an academic setting, it is a form of evaluation of performance, but in music it is a note to be played. In grammar, it is part of a sentence, and so on. In order for people to interact and communicate effectively, each person must know the meaning of the symbol and how the other person is using it. Understanding culture in general is based on the same idea.

Our society is diverse and contains a wide range of groups, each with its own culture, with some integrated into the larger societal culture while other groups are in opposition to it. Therefore, if someone wants to understand the behavior of a group of people, they must know and understand the many different ways culture influences behavior. In fact, some behaviors often get misinterpreted as offensive in part because of a lack of understanding of the meaning of a particular ritual. An example of this occurred recently in the National Football League, where players got down on one knee during the playing of the National Anthem before the start of games to protest the mistreatment of minority groups. Many military veterans and other supporters were offended by what they perceived as an action invalidating the sacrifices of soldiers who gave their lives to defend the United States. In fact, some people refused to watch NFL football games because of these actions, thereby causing a host of problems for the league, television networks, and the entire football industry. But the protests were not designed to insult the flag or the sacrifices of soldiers and their families—the players were protesting against something else. However, those reasons were lost in all the shouting and protesting, invalidating what might otherwise be a noble objective.

Thus, the study of culture in society, and what each group values, is an important element in understanding how culture shapes and influences individuals' behavior. In this section, Rebecca Swift offers us a glimpse of life as a refugee, which can be difficult even for those who have made it safely to the United States. The cultural challenges refugees face, and the potential backlash against them, create a host of problems. In an article about a rather obscure population, I explore the culture of male prostitutes in the Times Square section of New York City. Drawing from a study conducted twenty-five years ago, I conclude that the consistency and stability of the community of hustling remains despite dramatic physical changes to the area. Finally, Shelvis Smith-Mather offers a rather unique perspective about immersing oneself into a culture vastly different from one's own. As a missionary, he straddles several different cultures in an effort to make a difference in the lives of others.

The Difficulties of Life as a Refugee

Rebecca Swift, LCSW

THE REFUGEE CRISIS in our world today is catastrophic. More people are displaced from their homes and countries than at any other time in our history. According to the United Nations High Commissoner for Refugees (UNHCR), there are 65.6 million displaced people in the world today, and of that amount, 22.5 million are refugees. (Figures at a Glance n.d., UNHCR) The 1951 Geneva Convention defines a refugee as "someone who has been forced to flee his or her country because of persecution, war, or violence. A refugee has a well-founded fear of persecution for reasons of race, religion, nationality, political opinion, or membership in a particular social group. Most likely they cannot return home or are afraid to do so" (What is a refugee? 2017).

In addition to refugees, there are also internally displaced peoples. The UN reports that there are currently 40.3 million people who are internally displaced (What is a refugee? 2017). This means that they are forced to flee, but they do not cross any country border. These persons may live in the remains of schools, buildings, or in makeshift camps but stay within the borders of their homeland. Unfortunately for these people, they remain under the domain of their country's leaders and cannot access all international aid services as they would if they were designated as refugees and living in a refugee camp. The UN reports that the countries with the most displaced persons are the Democratic Republic of the Congo, Nigeria, South Sudan, Iraq, and Syria (Internally Displaced People n.d., UNHCR).

There are many precipitating events that result in people fleeing their homeland. Violence and war are the main causes of people and families fleeing for safety. In the last ten years, we have seen more movement of people fleeing war and violence than at any other point. The news has shown us many of these groups including those fleeing the war in Syria, Iraq, and Afghanistan. In addition, we have seen continued ethnic violence in Myanmar, DRC, and South Sudan. All of these world conflicts have resulted in thousands of lives lost and thousands of lives uprooted.

One of the countries most often discussed regarding the refugee crisis is Syria. While we cannot expect to unravel the conflict in Syria in this brief space, it is possible to discuss the major points that have led to such a massive group of people and families fleeing. The UNHCR reports that since 2011, over five million Syrians have fled into neighboring countries seeking safety. Pro-democracy protestors began clashing with the Assad dictatorship in early 2011, which later resulted in many people arming themselves for war. What may have initially appeared to be a debate about the effectiveness of the current administration is now multifactorial and involves many different sectarian groups. Per BBC, "A UN commission of inquiry has evidence that all parties to the conflict have committed war crimes—including murder, torture, rape and enforced disappearances. They have also been accused of using civilian suffering—such as blocking access to food, water and health services through sieges—as a method of war" (Rodgers et al. 2016). These factors have resulted in a massive movement of people fleeing from violence, war, chemical weapons, rape, torture, and lack of human necessities—now they have become refugees.

Most recently the Rohingya people of Myanmar have been in the news. At this point, the UNHCR estimates that 624,000 refugees have fled to Bangladesh since August 25, 2017 (Rohingya Emergency 2017). The Rohingya people are a stateless Muslim minority, unwanted and unrecognized by the government of Myanmar, who in recent months have been fleeing in massive numbers into Bangladesh. A United Nations top human rights official called this attack "ethnic cleansing," meaning "using a pretext of rooting out Islamist insurgents, Burma's military, together with Buddhist villagers, is terrorizing the Rohingya, emptying and razing their villages, and attempting to hound them out of the country" (Bearak, Karklis, and Meko 2017). The Buddhist government and other villagers are attacking, killing, burning, shooting, and threatening the Rohingya people. The individuals arriving at the refugee camps in Bangladesh are mainly women with small children who have fled with only the clothes on their backs, and the UNHCR is having to provide shelter, food, and provisions for this ever-increasing group of people. Just as the conflict in Syria is not easy to capture in a brief space, the background on the Rohingya people and their place in the history of Myanmar is not easy to summarize.

One final example of the current refugee crisis in our world today is the conflict in South Sudan. According the UNHCR, since December 2013, the conflict has resulted in the deaths of thousands of people and driven millions of people to neighboring countries out of fear for their safety (South Sudan Emergency 2017). The UN also reports that Uganda, Ethiopia, and Sudan have taken in the majority of the refugees from the South Sudanese crisis.

South Sudan gained its independence from Sudan in July 2011, but there has been so much difficulty along the way for this small new country. According to Mercy Corps, an organization doing humanitarian work in South Sudan, the current refugee and internally displaced people (IDP) crisis is due to many factors, including broken peace agreements from a civil war that broke out in 2013 and continues to erupt periodically, the decrease in the currency rate of the country, and severe famine (Quick Facts 2017). People are fleeing to find food for their families and safety. Once again, the conflict in South Sudan is complicated, multifactorial, and not able to be fully summarized in this brief space.

THE REFUGEE CRISIS AND ITS IMPACT ON HOST COUNTRIES

It is important to remember that the refugee crisis is not just detrimental to the country from which the refugees are fleeing, but it can be incredibly straining on the economy, resources, and government of the host countries. These host countries are not resettling the refugees; rather, they are simply providing a temporary place for them to stay, receive aid, and find safety. Most of these countries are simply host countries by means of proximity to the fleeing people. The Syrian people are fleeing to neighboring countries like Turkey, Jordan, and Lebanon. The Rohingya people are fleeing to Bangladesh. The South Sudanese are fleeing to Uganda, Ethiopia, Kenya, DRC, CAR, and Sudan (Quick Facts 2017).

What is it like for Turkey, for example, to have so many Syrian refugees fleeing to join its population? According to an article in the *Economist*, compared with other countries, Turkey has done an excellent job of looking after the three million refugees who have poured in since the start of Syria's civil war in 2011. President Erdogan's Islamist government says it has spent $25 billion managing the two dozen camps near the Syrian border, home to 250,000 people, and providing aid to refugees outside of camps in other parts of the country. That cost, and the strain on public services (Syrians in Turkey receive free health care), will likely continue, particularly since the refugee population is growing much faster than Turkey's native population. For instance, at the Kahramanmaras camp, the refugee population is set to double in under ten years (The New Neighbors 2017).

There is another conflict that could result in problems in Turkey. The majority ethnic group of the Syrians in the Kahramanmaras camp have different religious views than the Turkish people who live nearby. Some Turkish people are fearful that the camp is housing radical terrorists, while the refugees fear that the locals are supporting the Syrian regime. More and more conflict is presenting itself, because the refugees fleeing do not have a way to fully integrate into Turkey, and the Turkish people are not sure that they really want the refugees to become part of their country.

What is it like for Bangladesh? According to Joehnk (2017), the influx of so many refugees has created a humanitarian emergency and created security concerns for refugees. The Rohingya refugee crisis is also having an impact on Bangladesh's political structure, where concerns have been raised that the crisis may result in a transition to a more authoritarian form of government. Joehnk (2017) also points out that the people in Bangladesh support their government's decision to shelter these refugees even though they know that it will be very costly and troublesome to do so. Nothing is simple about helping refugees who are considered stateless and unwanted by their own country.

What is it like for Uganda to absorb one million South Sudanese refugees? According to the UN, "Over the past 12 months, an average of 1,800 South Sudanese have been arriving in Uganda every day," said the Office of the UN High Commissioner for Refugees in a statement to the press. "More than 85 percent of the refugees who have arrived in Uganda are women and children, below age 18 years" (UN News Centre 2017). The sheer number of people flooding into the country seeking safety is severely taxing the resources available through aid agencies. Moreover, Uganda has been a source of refuge for people fleeing from many other wars in the area, so accepting those fleeing into the country from South Sudan is an additional burden.

LIFE IN A REFUGEE CAMP

Life in a refugee camp is not easy. Many of these individuals and families have fled violence and live in fear, but instead of finding peace, they find different problems when they arrive in the camps. In my work, I've spoken with Bhutanese refugees who have been living in the Nepali refugee camps for over twenty years. They have endured fires and flood, which rip through the camp destroying their few personal belongings. Even if their home isn't destroyed in the camp, they see the destruction of their neighbor's property, and this is traumatizing. I spoke with a man who survived the earthquake in Nepal in April 2015. He had been vetted and was in Kathmandu preparing to come to the United States after being cleared by the necessary agencies for resettlement. While waiting there, an earthquake struck and a building collapsed, killing his brother who had come to see him off. Can you imagine the trauma of this for him— living in a refugee camp for over twenty years after fleeing persecution from the Bhutan government, and thinking you have made it through the worst that could happen, only to lose your brother in a random earthquake? He was not able to stay to participate in the burial or family grieving because he had to be on a flight to his new home in the United States.

I've had other refugees living in Kenya or Rwanda who have fled Somalia or DRC who tell me that the overcrowding in the camp and the lack of enough food to provide for their family is incredibly difficult. They are so happy to be away from the war in their country, but they continue to be traumatized by the circumstances of living in a refugee camp. One Congolese father told me that they never had enough food in the camp to feed his family, and this was such a deep source of pain for him as a provider. Another family told me of the fear they felt in the refugee camp because so many different ethnic groups were staying in the same area, and there were tensions between the groups that resulted in fights and assaults. It may be easy for some people to perceive that when individuals and families finally are able to get to a refugee camp, they have a much easier life. However, I would disagree.

RESETTLEMENT CHALLENGES FOR REFUGEES

For those refugees to register, complete the vetting, and decide to apply for resettlement, what is it like for them to come to a new country? Many of them have been living outside of their homelands for many years—either in the city or in a refugee camp. Many of them have experienced war, violence, fear, death, and not having enough of the basic human necessities. Many have gone without medical care or schooling. Many have lost their jobs, careers, and even family members. When they arrive in the country where they are being resettled, this is a vastly different experience than living in a refugee camp.

Which countries in the world provide resettlement to the most number of refugees? According to the UNHCR,

> resettlement is the transfer of refugees from an asylum country to another State that has agreed to admit them and ultimately grant them permanent settlement. UNHCR is mandated by its statute and the UN General Assembly Resolutions to undertake resettlement as one of the three durable solutions. Resettlement is unique in that it is the only durable solution that involves the relocation of refugees from an asylum country to a third country. There were 16.1 million refugees of concern to UNHCR around the world at the end of 2015, but less than one percent were resettled that year. (Resettlement n.d., UNHCR)

According to the UNHCR (Resettlement n.d.), there were only fourteen resettlement countries in 2005, but since 2016 the number has grown to thirty-seven.

THE ROLE OF THE UNITED STATES IN THE REFUGEE CRISIS

The United States has resettled about three million refugees since 1980, which is more than any other country (Conner 2017). However, over the past few years, the number of refugees resettled in the United States has not kept up with the growth of so many international conflicts that have resulted in a massive refugee crisis:

> In 2016, for example, out of approximately 1 million eligible refugees identified by UNHCR, an estimated 189,000 were resettled worldwide, with more than half (51%) of these ending up in the United States. Between 1982 and 2016, the U.S. admitted more than two-thirds (69%) of the world's resettled refugees, followed by Canada (14%) and Australia (11%). (Conner 2017)

One of the Executive Orders signed by President Trump at the beginning of his presidency limited the number of refugees who would be allowed into the United States and banned other immigrants from certain nations from coming to America. This action has reduced the number of refugees proposed for 2018 to forty-five thousand, a historic low (Conner 2017). Many Americans feel that refugees are the cause of many problems and should not be allowed to come to the United States. Many Americans don't understand or know about the horrors that refugees are fleeing and their desire to simply live in peace with their family in a new country.

I have been working with refugees and immigrants as a social worker for the past six years. I have heard many difficult stories straight from the mouths of individuals who have lived them. When you hear the story directly and are not simply reading a statistic on a website or seeing a story on the news, everything becomes much more real. I have heard these stories from individuals and families from Afghanistan, Burma, Burundi, Bhutan, Cuba, DRC, Egypt, Eritrea, Ethiopia, Iran, Iraq, Nepal, Pakistan, Russia, Rwanda, Somalia, South Sudan, Sudan, Thailand, and Uganda. It is because of these stories that I celebrate the resilience of the human spirit and the hope that comes out of ashes.

"Ahmed" told me that he gave up his great career in Iraq to bring his family to safety in the United States, knowing that by doing this, he would not be able to practice law again. "Amina" told me that she fled Somalia after seeing her family members' body parts in the trees. She only wants to find a place where she can find safety. "Li" told me that when she hears a police siren here in the United States, she is afraid because back in Malaysia the police targeted the Burmese people who were living there. "Ms. Rai" told me that even though she never had the chance to go to school in Bhutan, she is hopeful that her children will have a good education here in the United States. "Omar" told me that he just wants to be able to walk to work without being afraid of bombs exploding like he feared in Afghanistan. "Celeste" told me that she was raped during the war in Congo and contracted HIV. She wants her children to have a chance to succeed in the United States and to receive the medicine she needs so that she does not die from AIDS like so many back in Congo. "Juan" told me that because he spoke out against the government in Cuba, he was not able to keep his job and he was detained in jail for a month.

These individuals have shown me the same human spirit that so many Americans have—a desire to see their children succeed, a desire for good health for themselves and their families, and a chance to live in safety. However, even when they arrive in the United States, there are many barriers to that American dream—learning English, learning how to drive, setting up a bank account, enrolling your children in school, learning to parent without your extended family, learning to pay bills, and figuring out how to help your children with their homework. While refugees resettled in the United States have the help of a resettlement agency that assists refugee families, this help only lasts a few months. After that, many of these families are on their own.

ADJUSTING TO A NEW LIFE FOR REFUGEES

How long does it take for refugees to feel like this is their new home? How long until the honeymoon period wears off? Part of what I educate our newly arrived refugees about at my job is the U-Curve of adjustment (Cultural Adjustment Toolkit n.d.). Teaching them what to expect is a good way to help them lower or normalize their expectations. The Cultural Resource Orientation Center (http://www.culturalorientation.net) explains that there is a honeymoon phase for refugees when they first arrive in the United States, where they feel that everything is perfect and wonderful. I had one Iraqi man tell me one time that "America is heaven." I understand that he was trying to express the joy he felt in living here, being safe, and having his family together again. However, I ache for him because I know very well that America is nowhere close to heaven.

The next phase is cultural shock where the refugee may feel worry, concern, and confusion about adjusting to the differences between life in the United States and what they experienced back home. I had a refugee explain to me that he did not want a life that required his wife to work, as she needed to here in the United States, because in his native country she would be able to stay home and care for their children. However, he had come to the realization that in order for them to pay their bills and buy the things that they needed, his wife was going to have to work too.

Following this culture shock is the adjustment phase when refugees may feel settled in and more aware of what it takes to live in their new city. One refugee explained to me that he had finally learned how to balance his work and family time. His family had found a park in the city that was a little further away, so he had to drive them there instead of walking. He was so proud of himself for being able to navigate this and to relax with his family instead of being so focused on work.

The mastery phase is the final phase of the U-Curve of adjustment where the refugee has a feeling of comfort with the new life and culture (Cultural Tool-kit n.d.). An Iranian woman talked to me about this because she had learned to adjust to life in her city and had begun to adopt certain American customs (like celebrating Christmas) that she would not have done back home. She and her elderly mother have begun to blend their cultural celebrations in a way that makes them feel comfortable and at home. In this phase, although the shock of the new environment has worn off, there are times when people can still feel out of place, isolated, and alone.

Many of the refugees I have worked with have experienced this U-Curve of adjustment. Those refugees from DRC fled to other surrounding countries hoping for safety and they had to experience the difficulties of adjustment in a refugee camp. Now they are experiencing the difficulties of adjustment again in the United States.

I've had some of my patients express their desire to be more integrated into American culture and have more American friends. Some are able to do this easily through their jobs or neighborhoods. However, I've had other refugees express to me that American people have not treated them well. One Somali woman had someone yell at her to "Go back to your country!" while she was walking from her car into a store.

One Afghani lady told me that someone came up to her at the grocery store while she was waiting on a prescription for her sick child and yelled "BOOM!" in her face. She knew that they were mimicking a bomb exploding, and they were trying to scare her. They did. She was terrified. Unfortunately this ignorant person did not realize that this woman and her husband came to the United States through a special Visa program designed to resettle the men and women who work side by side with American troops as interpreters, security guards, or other personnel.

Her husband has worked as an interpreter for ten years in Afghanistan, putting his life on the line along with our troops. Without his help, important dialogue and meetings would have not been possible between Afghani personnel and American military leadership. It seems that whatever this woman and her husband do, there are still some Americans who will never accept them as part of the American culture simply because of their ethnicity and religion.

UNDERSTANDING THE REFUGEE EXPERIENCE SOCIOLOGICALLY

How can sociology help to understand the refugee crisis? What about refugees who have "made it," meaning they have successfully resettled in the United States, the land of opportunity? Is America really "heaven," as one refugee described it? As was mentioned, the transition from one culture to another can create a host of challenges and problems for families, particularly when the cultures are quite different in attitudes, values, and beliefs. What many of the people I have worked with describe in their experiences in the United States can be understood sociologically through a concept known as anomie, a concept most associated with the work of Emile Durkheim, considered by some to be the father of sociology.

At the most general and inclusive level, Durkheim's great concern was with the declining strength of the common morality in the modern world (Coser 2014). Durkheim felt that the social order existed because of a common set of moral beliefs. This, he argued, allowed social contracts and economic relationships to form. A special type of common moral beliefs is what Durkheim called the collective conscience. A collective conscience involves a shared sense of belonging to the larger community and a moral obligation to live up to the demands of society. Durkheim argues that when people are focused on the same things, a sense of moral obligation develops. That is, repeated social interactions result in certain rituals that translate into these needed moral agreements (Durkheim 1997).

Durkheim demonstrated his concern with the problems of a weakened common morality in his conceptualization of anomie. This occurs when people are left without a clear idea about the consistency and predictability of the rules that guide behavior. Anomie tends to occur when the rules or norms that guide behavior are broken or do not apply. When these types of situations occur, and the rules governing social interaction have not been reestablished, the individual experiencing them is likely to have significant levels of anxiety and fear (Durkheim 1897).

Understanding the impact of anomie is relatively easy when negative events occur. A natural disaster, a divorce, or being immersed into a new culture can create a situation where people can become disconnected from the things that keep them grounded to the larger society. Without these social and emotional anchors, anomie is far more likely. At the same time, Durkheim argues that positive events can also result in the effects of anomie. Winning the lottery, having sudden success in the stock market, or acquiring a large inheritance could easily result in recipients making significant life changes that disconnect them from those same anchors (e.g. career or job changes, leaving one's social circles). Changes like these negatively influence the framework that provides the individual with a level of safety, security, and regulation in their lives. This sudden success, then, removes the norms that keep one's aspirations under control. If the sky appears to be the limit and there are no constraints, all the anchors normally working to keep the person grounded are removed. Thus, anomie is a response to situations that occur when the norms that provide stability and predictability to social life are either disrupted or are no longer relevant. These situations can have an extraordinary effect on the person's ability to navigate life and the culture in which they live (Durkheim 1897).

Clearly the refugees who find some level of safety and security in refugee camps likely experience a form of anomie; not to mention while they have fled one type of extreme situation, their circumstances are only slightly better in the camps. Similarly, even those refugees who have made it out of the camps and have resettled in other countries still experience a significant amount of anomie as they attempt to transition and assimilate into their new surroundings. While it may be easy to discount the adversity experienced, particularly if the refugee comes to a country like the United States, one should be careful to understand the enormity of the changes that have occurred in those families' lives and the difficulty involved in becoming a part of the new culture. This is particularly true if the members of the new country are not welcoming of immigrants.

Bibliography

Bearak, Max, Laris Karklis, Tim Meko. "The 'ethnic cleansing' of the Rohingya." *Washington Post* September 18, 2017. www.washingtonpost.com.

Connor, Phillip. "U.S. Resettles Fewer Refugees, Even as Global Number of Displaced People Grows." October 12, 2017. pewglobal.org

Coser, Lewis. *Masters of Sociological Thought.* New York: McGraw-Hill, 2014. "Cultural Adjustment Toolkit." Center for Applied Linguistics/Cultural Orientation Resource Center. www.culturalorientation.net.

Durkheim, Emile. *The Division of Labor in Society.* New York: Simon and Schuster, 1997.

———. *Suicide.* New York: The Free Press, 1897. "Figures at a Glance Statistical Year-book." UNHCR. www.unhcr.org.

"Internally displaced people." UNHCR. www.unhcr.org.

Joehnk, Tom Felix. "How the Rohingya Crisis Is Changing Bangladesh." *New York Times.* October 6, 2017. www.nytimes.com.

"Resettlement." UNHCR. www.unhcr.org.

Rodgers, L., D. Gritten, J. Offer, and P. Asare. "Syria: The Story of Conflict." BBC News. March 11, 2016. www.bbc.com.

"Rohingya Emergency" UNHCR. 2017. www.unhcr.org.

"Quick Facts: What You Need to Know About South Sudan." Mercycorps. 2017. www.mercycorps.org

"South Sudan Emergency." UNHCR. 2017. www.unhcr.org.

"The New Neighbors: Turkey is taking care of refugees, but failing to integrate them. Economist. 2017. www.economist.com.

UN News Centre. "South Sudan Refugees in Uganda Exceed One Million; UN Renews Appeal for Help." United Nations. August 17, 2017. www.news.un.org.

"What is a Refugee?" UNHCR. 2017. www.unrefugees.org

The Times Square Hustler Twenty-Five Years Later: A Community

Robert H. McNamara, PhD

ABOUT TWENTY-FIVE YEARS ago, I conducted an ethnographic study of male prostitutes in the Times Square section of New York City. The study originated from an interest in HIV/AIDS issues and risk-taking behavior, where I was primarily interested in what hustlers knew about the disease, and the steps they took to prevent getting infected. Only a few researchers had studied this population and none had really examined the topic in New York City. Once there, however, I realized there was a great deal more to the story of hustling than simply the risks of infection with HIV.

Unlike virtually all other street populations, there existed a sense of community among most of the hustlers in Times Square, and this connectedness resulted in a relatively organized and stable set of relationships between the hustlers and clients, between the hustlers and the police, and among the hustlers themselves. However, significant changes were occurring during the 1990s in Times Square and other parts of the country, including the crack epidemic, efforts to educate sex workers about the risks of infection of HIV/AIDS, and historic redevelopment efforts in Times Square, which were dramatically changing the physical and social environments. The study ended with lingering questions about what might happen to the hustling community, its culture, and the sex trade in general in the future.

Of particular note in the study of the hustlers of Times Square were the unspoken and informal rules that drove much of the predictability to the sex trade in the area. These norms regulated social life in all sorts of ways, including negotiations and transactions with clients, but they also provided an element of safety to the hustlers and others who worked in the area. The following is a description of those norms as an illustration of what can occur in an otherwise desperate and selfish existence for street people.

OVERVIEW OF HUSTLING

Historically, male prostitution has taken many forms, including "escort boys," those who worked in brothels, and even "kept boys," who served more as a companion to a client than a prostitute (Coombs 1974; Drew and Drake 1969; Weisberg 1985).

While research on the subject of male prostitutes is still relatively sparse, there have been a few attempts to examine this population. For instance, the now classic study by Reiss (1961) found that most of the boys view prostitution as a job or simply a means of making money. He also found that many boys limit the scope of their activities, which allows them to retain a sense of identity and control over their lives.

Other studies have attempted to identify common characteristics and describe the various motivations for becoming involved in prostitution (Weisberg 1985; Butts 1947; Jersild 1956; Ross 1959; Luckenbill 1986a, 1986b, 1985; Lloyd 1983; Campagna and Poffenberger 1988; James 1982; MacNamara 1965; West 1991; Bracey 1989). Most of the recent research has focused on the risks of AIDS and on the runaway population (Ross 1988; Elifson, Boles, and Sweat 1993; Calhoun and Pickerill 1988; Morse et al. 1991; Pleak and Meyer-Bahlburg 1990; Borus-Rotheram and Koopman 1991).

Thus, while it appears there is a body of AIDS related literature on this population, little is known about hustling in Times Square and even less is known about the ways in which hustlers develop a sense of cohesion as they share similar experiences. Part of the explanation is found in the way in which prostitution is practiced. In Times Square, male prostitution is more of an entrepreneurial activity occurring in an organized market area than is generally the case elsewhere. It is referred to colloquially as "hustling," a term whose meanings can include the activities of confidence men, drug dealers, those who deal with stolen merchandise and, in general, individuals who engage in a variety of illegal activities. However, the label "hustler" is also applied to males who engage in various sexual activities with other males for money, illegal drugs, or some other form of payment. Hustling is incorporated into the definition of prostitution since the person seeks out and attempts to entice as many clients as possible without the benefit of a broker, client list, or other type of intermediary.

THE MARKETPLACE

Times Square possesses certain characteristics and institutions that facilitate prostitution. For instance, the peep shows, porno shops, hotels, bars, and the Port Authority Bus Terminal not only offer a centralized locale for the sex market, they also provide places for hustlers and clients to meet and carry out their transactions. Additionally, the influx of people who use the terminal and peep shows produces a steady supply of patrons to the market.

Virtually all of these organizations are profit making, and the economic benefits they derive from hustling foster their acceptance. This is especially true of the hotels and peep shows, which have strong economic links to the sex trade. Consequently, the nature of hustling is predicated on the existence of these types of organizations as well as the manner in which they allow this type of activity to occur.

Moreover, the Port Authority Bus Terminal provides the market with a diurnal quality. In many ways, hustling is dependent on the work schedule of commuters and its frequency coincides with rush hours: hustlers are very busy early in the morning, as people make their way to work, and in the early evening, as they return home. There are also a number of older men who reside in the Times Square area who are either retired or living on public assistance. They, too, regularly solicit hustlers and know that the terminal serves as a central meeting place.

Another feature of the hustling market involves the activity's occupational structure. Because the vast majority of hustlers have few, if any, other means of economic support, hustling in Times Square is viewed as an income-producing activity. For most, it is a full-time job. While some are receiving public assistance, which would normally reduce participation in the trade, these hustlers usually have wives and children to support. Thus the need to earn a living from hustling remains important.

In this way, hustling can be seen as an occupation for almost all the participants. Another illustration of this occupational role is demonstrated by the fact that most of the hustlers do not reside in the market area. In fact, many live outside Manhattan and, like so many other workers, must commute to Times Square every day. Additionally, part of the market is organized for the hustlers themselves. For instance, there are certain bars or parks where hustlers meet to socialize only with friends and colleagues.

In sum, there is a local market in which hustling exists, and it has a certain organization. There is a sense of territoriality in that it is found in a relatively small geographic area; it is organized along ethnic lines to the extent that most hustlers are Hispanic while almost all clients are Caucasian; there is a social class dimension, because it is an income-producing activity rather than a recreational one; most of the hustlers work in the area and live elsewhere; the market depends to some extent on repeat clients, who either travel through on their way to work or reside in the area; and there are institutions and organizations that either facilitate hustling or provide places where hustlers can gather on their own. This article, based on a two-year ethnographic study of hustling in Times Square, and consisting of numerous interviews and conversations with hustlers and those involved in the life, describes the nature of this market and its participants, as well as some of the important events that have affected it.

In addition to the organizational qualities of hustling, perhaps the most important contribution of this study may be to offer a way of thinking about hustling in Times Square. I view the hustlers of Times Square as a community within a structured marketplace. Moreover, the community's existence is due in part to the organizational features of the hustling market. The hustling community has been affected by a number of changes that occurred in Times Square over the last twenty-five years. Urban redevelopment, the emergence of crack, and an increased impact of AIDS, among other factors, have affected virtually every aspect of hustling in Times Square and each member of the population.

But what is life as a male prostitute like? Since this is a street-level activity, one might think that everyone is concerned only with their own sense of survival. Being on the street usually connotes a desperate situation: one in which altruism and abiding by the rules do not apply. However, among the hustlers in Times Square, something unusual occurs. There are norms that regulate the trade and the boys' behavior, as well as various types of social control, which are understood and practiced by everyone involved. Because this is a rather unusual phenomenon, allow me to describe what the life is like and then demonstrate how this high-level of social organization results in a predictable type of interaction whereby everyone involved in the trade comes away from the interaction achieving their objectives.

DO THE HUSTLE

A typical day for a hustler begins early, often as early as seven o'clock, and ends as late as two or three the next morning. The weekend schedule is different, beginning and ending later and sometimes involving overnight stays with clients. The excitement of the weekend contrasts with the idleness of the remaining days of the week.

The Port Authority Bus Terminal is a special place for many hustlers. Much of the hustling in Times Square occurs either in the Terminal or in the peep shows. Both offer anonymity for the client because of the great deal of human traffic through both places. The exodus of commuters from the City, for example, especially at rush hour, offers clients the opportunity to lose themselves in the throng of people making their way home and to carry out transactions with hustlers without attracting much attention.

One particular area in the Terminal is known among hustlers and clients as the "Meat Rack." This is an area near some of the departure gates where the majority of hustling takes place. When the two parties reach an agreement, they go to a variety of places: the peep shows, a local hotel, the client's apartment or car, or one of the restrooms inside the Terminal. However, the latter are now considered less of a sanctuary for hustlers as a result of an aggressive police presence, which includes undercover operations. These areas are now used sparingly or for limited activities such as what Lite describes:

> I don't do nothin' that I... I don't do nothin'....the farthest thing I did was to jerk another man off you know what I'm sayin'? But I never sucked a dick, never fucked another person. I tell them straight up you know, like they say "yo you wanna come with me? You know I'll give you seventy dollars." But then when we start walkin' I'll say stop and what you all about man? What you want me to do? I'll say 'listen, I don't get fucked and I don't fuck nobody.' The only thing I do is jerk off and I will let them watch. I'll strip for them too and let them look at my body. But no kissing, I don't kiss no men. Sometimes you can catch the tricks early in the morning too. Like I had this trick at nine o'clock in the morning. You can catch them before they go to work or sometimes a trick will get them when they goin' into the bathroom. That's another kind of trick. You only get five dollars for the bathroom. You go to the bathroom and make like you peein' and somebody's watchin' the door. You get it hard and then you jerk off and then they get off but you don't do nothin' though. You don't want to come, you definitely don't want to come. Cause then you can't make no more money. If you gonna come, it's gotta be a real expensive trick or the last one you gonna do that day, and even then you charge him extra for that.

As Lite mentioned, hustling activities are marked by their diversity. A group of hustlers explain further:

> **Smokealot:** It depends on who the trick is and what they want you to do. Like some guys will just come up to you and say how much? Right then you know they be Five-0 [the police] because they got to get you to admit the price first. But some of the tricks will come up to you and ask you what your name is, what you like to do, if you wanna get high or somethin' like that. We work out an arrangement depending on what the trick wants. I only go with tricks I know so I ain't gonna get picked up [arrested]. But other guys will pick up anybody. And usually, depending on what they want, you can make anywhere from thirty to forty dollars a trick. See it depends on a lotta factors like what they want, how long they wanna go. It's just like females youknowhatI'msayin? But like for an average, it's about

thirty dollars. But you always gotta be clockin' [observing or watching him closely] the man to make sure he ain't Five-0.

Canno: Well a lot of it depends on how long it takes them to come. Also you gotta know what kind of things that get them off. So you gotta have the knack. Sometimes they get off by watching you come. I mean I have a trick that wants me to come in, take my clothes off and pose for him, flexin' and shit you know. Sometimes there are people that can't come, you gotta make 'em come, that's your job. Then there's overnights. I tell them straight up. Fifty dollars alone for me just to go to your house. Then there's another fifty dollars to do anything, and another fifty dollars to stay over. So it's like a hundred and fifty dollars. And like different guys work out different arrangements. Like this one john he'll take a twenty-dollar bill and rip it in half. He'll give you half and take half. So if he feels he's satisfied, he'll give you the other half and you just tape it and spend it. But if he's not happy, we both lose.

It appears then that hustling can consist of simply voyeurism, posing nude, masturbating clients, or sadomachoism, in addition to oral and anal sex.

The frequency with which the boys hustle also varies considerably. Some hustle every day, turning as many tricks as possible, while others are satisfied with one or two per day. The deciding factor, obviously, is how much money the boy needs to make. Those with drug habits, especially those addicted to crack, need to hustle as much as possible. Family men need a steady income, but since their income is supplemented by public relief, they usually hustle less frequently than other hustlers

Lite: I hustle at least once a day. The most people I picked up in a day? Seven. I usually pick up like three or four. And if I get like thirty dollars each time then I chill for the rest of the day. Maybe I don't come back here for two or three days.

Apache: I come down here a good four times a week and most of the time I'll pull in two tricks a day. I could pull more, but I'll just pull two tricks. The average hustler around here? He'll pull I guess five to seven tricks and make himself a good three to four hundred dollars in like five hours.

Dead Head: Like I gotta go with as many guys as I can cause I ain't got no money and no place to stay. Some days I'll do good and get four or five, which is maybe like a hundred and fifty bucks. That's cool cause then I can eat and stuff and maybe go to a movie, buy some pot or whatever. But I gotta do more than most of these guys cause I'm broke. [what is your average number for a day?] The average? Well, I guess it's probably like two a day. Yeah... probably one or two a day. But some days, just like anybody, I get skunked and nobody comes around.

Obviously, the amount per trick varies according to what the client requires, but the amount can also be determined by the talents of individual hustlers. For instance, some hustlers, such as Apache, are better negotiators and often convince clients to pay more than the usual fee.

THE NORMS OF HUSTLING

A pattern to hustling exists to which all the participants respond. There are agreed-upon locations, a familiar dialogue, and a roughly established pricing policy for the various activities. This pattern fosters stability in hustling. For the most part, very few problems occur between the hustler and the client or among the boys themselves. In the vast majority of cases, the activities are completed without incident. These patterns of behavior can be seen as a normative system that regulates the boys' behavior. One extremely important norm is that once a hustler and a client begin a conversation, another hustler should never intervene. This serves as a territorial marker that is not to be encroached upon. Violation of this norm can lead to severe and violent retaliation.

> **Flacco:** You see that's one thing among hustlers. You don't go and ask nobody, even if you are asking the hustler for money, you don't do it in front of the trick. You don't do that. You don't do that. This one kid caught a serious beat down from me around the corner for that. I had this one trick he was gonna give me seventy-five dollars just for hangin' out with him and man, he was about to step off and get into the van to go to New Jersey. This hustler walks up and asks the guy for fuckin' ten dollars man. In front of me! And I looked at him and said 'Yo you should have never done that.' And the trick got all roust and this and that and he said to me 'Look I'm sorry I just don't like people asking me for money.' And he stomped away all pissed off. I turned around and said 'Listen, first of all, you need money you come and see me. But don't you EVER EVER get in front of one of my tricks.' And then I kicked the shit outta him so he would never forget that.

Another related norm involves time and etiquette. There are times when a hustler and a trick cannot complete a transaction either because of price, type of activity, or some other reason. When this occurs, another hustler may offer his services to the man, provided he waits until he is certain this initial conversation has ended. This is often referred to as being a "free agent." Playboy explains:

> Yeah, well it's like this. See if Flacco is talking to this guy but they can't work it out, the guy or Flacco starts to leave. As long as he is far enough away so that everybody knows he ain't goin' with him, then he's a free agent and can negotiate whatever deal he wants with anybody else. I can go up to him now and there's no problem 'cause Flacco ain't got no claim on him see? That's what we mean by free agent. But I gotta make sure the guy ain't comin' back to Flacco before I approach him else I'm gonna get my ass kicked. I do that by waitin' until he is far enough away and then maybe I ask Flacco what's up?

Parenthetically, no one can give an exact time or distance that a client must be from the hustler in order to qualify as a free agent. There seems to be an implicit understanding about how far is "enough." In all likelihood, the longer another hustler waits and the further the client is from the initial contact, the less likely the norm will be violated.

Another important norm has to do with preserving and enhancing one's reputation within the community. While one's street reputation is always important in these circles (e.g. being able to handle one's self, showing courage, bravery, etc.), one's hustling reputation is quite important since it has far reaching implications. A cardinal rule among the boys is to never allow a client to publicly humiliate or insult him in front of his peers. This leads others to believe that the particular hustler is weak (which can lead to a loss of status and a violent retaliation by the group), and it serves as a reminder to other hustlers that they too can be treated that way. Additionally, an incident such as this sends a message to the clients that public humiliation of the boys is acceptable behavior. Thus, if a hustler does not respond to a challenge to his reputation, it has serious ramifications for him, his social standing, and it threatens the very structure and social order of the community.

> **Canno:** See around here your reputation isn't everything, it's the only thing. If I let some fuckin' trick come in here and take advantage of me in front of everybody, then I'm lettin' myself down and I'm lettin' everybody else down too. They be thinkin' I'm nothin' but a punk and now I got to deal with them tryin' to get over on me. And every

trick that sees this happen starts thinkin' 'hey why don't I do that too. He got away with it so why can't I?' So everybody has got to get involved now if I don't deal with it first. But it's better just to not let it ever come up in the first place.

Watchdog: I'm gonna tell you a little story. This is a story about a guy, I ain't gonna tell you his name. He likes to go out with guys and screw them and then gives them twenty dollars. So he walked up to me this morning, he never walked up to me before. He come up to me and asks me what I like to do. So I said 'Listen, first of all, you see me this morning, I cost a hundred dollars. Second of all this morning, I don't get screwed, I don't get screwed, I never got screwed by no asshole like you.' So he starts talkin' all this shit. So I tell him Listen... and before he even told me about the twenty dollars... so I told him 'if you think you gonna pay me twenty dollars for me to get screwed you must be outta your mind.

He gets all offended and starts talkin' shit to me about how he could do what he wants to me and all this shit. Then he called me a motherfucker. Well, that was it. He did this right in front of everybody thinking everybody gonna be laughin' and shit and on his side. Well it got real quiet all of the sudden up here. So I walk up to him and get right in his face and ask him real quiet what he said. He looks around and now everybody be lookin' real pissed off at him and he got scared. He be like 'nothin' I didn't say nothin' I was just fuckin' around you know.' And I said 'Listen, don't be fuckin' around like that around here. So don't say shit like that unless you lookin' to back it up.' So now he's real nervous and he apologizes and walks real quick to the escalators. We ain't gonna see him for a while now. But he can't be doin' that shit especially right in front of everybody.

The relationships that exist among the boys also plays an important role in the hustling culture. Some, such as Apache, look upon the hustling community as one big family. He says,

It's really like a family here. Everybody knows everybody else, everybody is basically friends with everybody else and there's kind of a support group you know. But it's like any big family of boys: you gonna have arguments and fights and people gonna get pissed off at each other, but basically we all know what we're about and if somebody needs something and we know them, we help them out. The New

Jacks (new hustlers) are different cause we don't know what they about yet. But after you been here a while and you straight up, you added to the family.

Like brothers, hustlers usually pair off and hang out together, sharing drugs, money, or other incidentals. Moreover, a sense of loyalty and responsibility develops between each boy and his partner whereby each boy tries to protect the other. When one goes with a client to a hotel for example, his partner will usually wait for his companion either outside the room or at the entrance to the hotel. In some cases, however, a hustler's partner is not always available. In those instances where a hustler has been picked up by an unknown client, there is an understanding among the members of the community that the boy will not go with him alone. There is usually someone who is hanging out or has just returned from a sexual exchange who will accompany the hustler. What is significant about this norm is that it also includes those situations in which a hustler would sacrifice his own trick to protect his comrade. While I believe this norm emerged as a result of survival rather than altruism, it is an important element in the nature of the trade.

Admittedly, I had some initial difficulty understanding this rule. The streets are such a desperate place, and this particular type of street life seemed, at first glance, to be particularly problematic for the participants. However, one must recognize that many hustlers engage in the trade to supplement their income. As a result, a number of hustlers are not involved in the mad scramble to earn every single dollar they can. In fact, in some cases, their situation allows them to forego the economic advantages in the name of maintaining strong social ties.

Consider Eddie and Jose's relationship. Eddie always goes with Jose when he takes a client to a nearby hotel. He waits outside the main entrance to ensure that Jose comes out safely. Jose, in turn, does the same thing for Eddie.

> **Jose:** This thing? It's a job, a constant job. You eat off it, you get clothes off it, you get drugs off it, you meet a lotta people, but you gotta know what you doin' or else you gonna get hurt. Every day somethin' happens... Every day me, him, everybody runs into somebody. Either 'Yo you wanna get high, you wanna make a few dollars, you wanna go eat and make a few dollars, let's go.' It happens, it happens. I turned Eddie on to a steady of mine. And every time the steady sees him, he throws me some money, maybe five or ten dollars. We know which ones pay more than others. Like if a guy wants me and he looks at me, and he looks at him I know him, I tell him 'Yo that guy is thirty-five dollars take him.' Or he'll tell me 'Yo what is that date like, no that

nigger fucks you,' or I'll tell him 'No don't go with him he wants you to suck his dick.' So, Boom I'll let him know.

Eddie: You gotta be careful of tricks though. They be like 'No you didn't do the job right' so you gotta get really really uptight sometimes and perform in there, 'I'm gonna beat the shit outta you you're not leavin' this room.' I usually bring him with me. He gets picked up and I see him go into a hotel, I'll wait in front of the hotel. Like if you go to their apartment and they do somethin' there, some of these guys they gotta realize they gotta pay. Like this one Japanese guy I had the other day. We were in the booth, you can go in the booths with these guys. Well this guy didn't think he had to pay cause we went in the booth together. I took this guy and lifted him up by his neck in the booth and took his money.

He didn't think he had to pay. So for not payin' me the twenty dollars you owe me, I'm takin' your wallet. That was a hundred and fifty dollars, his quarters, and a lottery ticket. He was cryin' over that. I took his phone card too and brought it to the Port and sold it for thirty-five dollars. And where was my boy? He was right outside the booth waitin' to see if I needed him. We got high that night. [high fives partner]

This issue of loyalty also emerges when conflict arises. For instance, when conflicts and fights occur, it is expected and even demanded that a hustler's friends, and, especially his partner, come to his defense. The issue of who's right is irrelevant; the only concern is how many friends will be fighting along side of him when fists fly.

For instance, one day Angel began arguing with another male in front of the bus terminal. As is often the case, the situation escalated into a brawl in a matter of minutes. The other young man had three associates with him, whereas Angel had but one companion, Nelson. Given the high police presence in and around the area, the fight began and ended quickly. Yet Nelson failed to join in and support Angel. Raul and I were walking down 8th Avenue when we saw what was happening. Running to the scene, Raul became furious when he learned Nelson did not react:

Raul: That stupid son of a bitch! What is this bullshit about bein' on parole? That's fuckin' bullshit! If I see my boy is gettin' a beat down, and that's my real boy, you think I'm on parole I can't do nothin'? I'm gonna jump on the motherfucker even faster cause I know I'm a go back upstate. He's talkin' about bein'on parole. I be like 'Yo man what's up I thought you were one of my boys man?'That's when he be getting' a serious ass beatin' I should kick his ass now in front of everybody just to teach him a motherfuckin' lesson. I'm gonna get you man! You and me man!

Thus, the relationships between hustlers have far reaching effects. Most maintain close ties with one other hustler while being a part of the larger collectivity. The trade norms include personal protection from tricks as well as other outside threats, and a standing rule involves sharing drugs or money. If a hustler has one or the other, he is expected to share with his friends and associates. This allows everyone to endure and pass the time. Additionally, as Eddie mentions, there is an unwritten "book" about clients. Hustlers will share information on clients in terms of what is expected in terms of payment or any particular preferences the trick may have.

Judging from what the hustlers, clients, and others associated with the trade say, as well as my own observations of events, it seems clear that the sense of cohesion among the hustlers is quite strong. There is a sense of community felt among this population and this degree of social organization allows the trade to operate with a type of rhythm and flow. As long as everyone understands and abides by the rules, there are few problems. There is even a mechanism in place to socialize new hustlers to the rules of the trade.

Finally, a clearly defined mechanism of informal social control also operates within the hustler community. The threat of punishment has been a clear deterrent to those who might consider deviating from the norm. In fact, one could even argue that the hustlers of Times Square are a good example of a consensus model of society: as a group and as individuals, the hustlers believe that following the norms of the trade is in everyone's best interest.

However, having said this, a number of social, political, and economic changes have taken place in Times Square that have posed threats to this established system. The emergence of crack cocaine as well as the massive redevelopment efforts in the Times Square area have caused more than a few problems for the community, both in terms of opportunities to hustle as well as the nature of social interaction between the participants.

❊ ❊ ❊ ❊ ❊

In the years since that initial study, there have been no studies conducted of the hustlers in Times Square and very few studies of male prostitution in general (See for example, Finlinson et al. 2006; Weitzer 2009; Morrison and Whitehead 2007; Lee-Gonyea et al. 2009). The research that has been done typically focuses on the public health approach, which is understandable, and the role of the

Internet in prostitution. While the changes to the physical landscape in Times Square have not removed the marketplace completely, much of the activity has gone underground and is less visible than in the past. Still, if one goes to Times Square and knows what to look for, evidence of the trade remains.

Bibliography

Borus-Rotheram, Mary, and Cheryl Koopman. "Sexual Risk Behaviors, AIDS Knowledge and Beliefs about AIDS among Runaways." *American Journal of Public Health* 81, no. 2 (1991): 206–08.

Bracey, Dorothy. *Baby Pros: Adolescent Prostitution*. New York: John Jay Press, 1989.

Butts, William Marlin. "Boy Prostitutes of the Metropolis." *Journal of Clinical Psychopathology* 8, (1947): 673–81.

Calhoun, Thomas, and Brian Pickerill. "Young Male Prostitutes: Their Knowledge of Selected Sexually Transmitted Diseases." *Psychology: A Journal of Human Behavior* 25, no. 3/4 (1988): 1–8.

Campagna, Daniel J., and Donald L. Poffenberger. *The Sexual Trafficking of Children*. South Hadley, Mass: Auburn House, 1988.

Coombs, Neil. "Male Prostitution: A Psychological View of Behavior." *American Journal of Orthopsychiatry* 44, no. 5 (1974): 782–89.

Drew, Dennis, and Jonathan Drake. (1969). Boys for Sale. New York: Brown Book Company.

Elifson, Kurt, Jacqueline Boles, and Michael Sweat. "Risk Factors Associated with HIV Infection Among Male Prostitutes." *American Journal of Public Health* 83, (1993): 79–83.

Finlinson, H. A., H.M. Colón, R.R. Robles, and M. Soto. "Sexual Identity Formation and AIDS Prevention: An Exploratory Study of Non-Gay-Identified Puerto Rican MSM from Working Class Neighborhoods." *AIDS & Behavior* 10, no. 5 (2006): 531–39.

James, Jennifer. *Entrance into Male Prostitution*. Washington D.C.: The National Institute of Mental Health, 1982.

Jersild, Jens. *Boy Prostitution*. Copenhagen, Denmark: C. E. Gad, 1956.

Lee-Gonyea, J. A., T. Castle, and N. E. Gonyea. "Laid to Order: Male Escorts on the Internet." *Deviant Behavior* 30, no. 4 (2009): 321–48.

Lloyd, Robin. *For Money or Love*. New York: The Free Press, 1976.

Luckenbill, David. "Dynamics of the Deviant Sale." *Deviant Behavior* 5, no. 1 (1985): 131–51.

———. "Deviant Career Mobility: The Case of Male Prostitution." *Social Problems* 33, no. 4 (1986): 283–96.

———. "Entering Male Prostitution." *Urban Life* 14, no. 2 (1986): 131–53.

MacNamara, Donald E. J. "Male Prostitution in American Cities: A Socioeconomic or Pathological Phenomenon?" *American Journal of Orthopsychiatry* 35, (1965): 204.

Morrison, T. G., and B. W. Whitehead. "Male Sex Work: A Business Doing Pleasure." *Journal of Homosexuality* 27, no. ½ (2007): 318.

Morse, Edward, Patricia Simon, Howard Osofsky, Paul Balson, and Richard Gaumer. "The Male Street Prostitute: A Vector for Transmission of HIV Infection into the Heterosexual World." *Social Science and Medicine* 32, no. 5 (1991): 535.

Pleak, Richard R., and Heino Meyer-Bahlburg. "Sexual Behavior and AIDS Knowledge of Young Male Prostitutes in Manhattan." *Journal of Sex Research* 27, no. 4 (1990): 557–87.

Reiss, Albert J., Jr. "The Social Integration of Queers and Peers." *Social Problems* 9, no. 2 (1961): 102–20.

Ross, Laurence H. "The Hustler in Chicago." *Journal of Student Research* 1, (1959): 13–19.

Ross, Michael. "Social and Behavioral Aspects of Male Homosexuals." *The Medical Clinics of North America* 70, no. 3 (1988): 537–47.

Weisberg, Kelly D. *Children of the Night*. Mass: Lexington Books, 1985.

Weitzer, R. "Sociology of Sex Work." *Annual Review of Sociology* 35 (2009): 213–34.

West, Donald J. *Male Prostitution*. New York: Harrington Park Press, 1991.

Through the Eyes of Others: A Reflection on Identity by an American Living in South Sudan

Shelvis Smith-Mather

MY MOTHER ENGAGED in a fierce tug-of-war over my identity in my formative years. I didn't notice at first, but as I grew older her struggle became clearer. On one end of the rope, the forces of ignorance band together. Their strong arms contracting as biceps tumble backwards to reel in the rope. Their presence is daunting and their power unmistakable. On the other end of the rope, an outmatched mother clings. The cord wound around her wrists and firmly held in her palms, knuckles taut. Her body craning back, every fiber of her being strains to redirect the efforts of the other side. The rope tightens arounds her wrists, bruising, and splitting her skin, but she will not let go.

My mother struggles because there are young men in our country...black young men...who are desperate and unhinged, abandoned and misguided. Our society often fears them and quickly cages them. She also knows there are young men in our country...black young men...who strive to offer brilliance and beauty to this world. The latter group is often mistaken for the former, and the consequences are devastating. Terrified by the fate which might await me, my mother pulls with wild fury against those vying for my identity.

[PULL] "Keep your hands out of your pockets, people might think you are stealing in stores," she would tell me. [PULL] "Don't walk in large groups [with other black boys], people might think you are a gang." [PULL] "Don't let anyone stand in the way of your dreams." [PULL] "Work hard and believe in yourself."

My mother resisted the forces of ignorance. For her, seeing me through the eyes of others translated into a call to action: be aware of the world's perception of you, consider the stereotypes and the historical backdrop of the scene, and at the same time, know who you are and live a contrary narrative. Use your God-given talents, in the midst of your circumstances, to transform the storyline, for yourself and for the larger society.

The stereotypes associated with African American young men were important for me to know as I navigated life within the United States in my youth. I did not fall into the behaviors the prejudices expected, yet the simple awareness of the biases influenced my understanding of myself. As I grew up, I discovered more of the parts that make me. Some elements I could control, some I could not.

Through encounters with various people from around the world, my perspectives on my race, nationality, and privilege increased in complexity, becoming much more nuanced. While sharing how these encounters broaden my perspective, I will also name ways in which my previous perspective was limiting and incomplete. Finally, I will express renewed understandings of my own identity and ways these understandings might help me better engage others. As you read this article, I hope you consider how others see you and how you see yourself. From a place of self awareness, you are better situated to honestly study and profoundly engage the world around you, as a sociologist or as simply a member of the global family.

WHEN PERSONAL EXPERIENCE IS NOT ENOUGH

I have engaged in reconciliation efforts for the last ten years in Africa. For most of this time, I have lived in South Sudan—a country plagued by civil war, ethnic division, political upheaval, and an alarming history of oppression. During this time, I have conducted research on forgiveness and identity. I have lived amongst people whose resilience inspires me and actions encourage me to better understand my own struggles and bias. As such, I enter each exchange with something to offer, and much to learn. One of my first significant encounters occurred during my first few weeks in South Sudan.

"You will be the first white to preach in our church," my friend says to me with a hint of pride. Like many in East Africa, he is deeply honored when foreigners visit. As such, Bakata has been exceedingly hospitable to my family since our arrival in South Sudan. For three weeks, he has escorted my family through his community introducing us to dozens of neighbors and important area leaders. In addition, he has invited us into his home, fed us, and shared genuine hopes for his war-plagued country. In spite of his gracious generosity towards my family, I sense an argument brewing.

Did he just call me white? I silently ask myself in disbelief. *What?* His words leave me confused and a bit conflicted. My arms fold and eyebrows descend into thought as I begin nibbling on my lower lip. *Should I press my arm against his arm: his brown skin next to mine to remind this brother of my skin color?* My skin-to-skin comparison method was used earlier this week to try to convince a coworker about my race. During this previous discussion, the coworker explained the term *white* refers less to skin color and more to a person's country of origin. Foundational to his argument are two inherent assumptions: First, Africans are black. Second, non-Africans are white. I, therefore, am considered white in this community regardless of my mocha brown skin and almost forty years of an American understanding of the black/white binary. To be fair, Bakata's perspective arose from his almost forty years of life experience as a black person and his South Sudanese understanding of the black/ white binary.

Growing up black in a racially divided part of the United State, marrying interracially, and having biracial children prepared me for many discussions on race within the American context. My discussion with Bakata, however, was a bit disorienting. We both based our arguments on our experience with race, but our personal experiences were simply insufficient by themselves.

Although my conversation with Bakata is just beginning, I sense resentment invading my calm, in the same ways I have experienced in years past in the United States. I take a deep breath, then another, then another, hoping the unwanted feelings will retreat quickly. I speak, hoping not to offend him, but needing to respond: "Bakata I am *not* white. I am black just like you." Much like a head juror announcing the verdict of a court case, I assume the decision is final. This, however, was only the start to our conversation about identity—a conversation leading him to a better understanding of me and me to a better understanding of him.

As I become better acquainted with Bakata and the culture in which we live, I learn most foreigners are referred to as Khawajas. Khawaja is a Juba Arabic term, borrowed from another language, meaning "Master" or "Lord." The word was once used to refer to wealthy European foreigners who were in positions of economic or military power. As time passed, the term was used more and more to refer to all European and western foreigners in this region, many of which had wealth and power. Eventually Khawaja was used interchangeably with white to refer to most non-African foreigners believed to be in this elite group.

Bakata's reference to me as white is disturbing; nevertheless, his words are worth consideration. I *am* foreign, western, wealthy[1] and considered a person of power. In South Sudan, my maleness, role as a father, exposure to formal education, status as clergy, position as head of an institution, and citizenship to a world power all contribute to my "power." In many ways, I have overlooked or ignored these dynamics since arriving to South Sudan. Rather I chose to believe Bakata and other South Sudanese considered themselves to be "black just like me." This conversation revealed a valuable perspective I had previously failed to see in Africa's youngest nation. Bakata was *not* black just like me. Unlike many black people raised in America, he is not familiar with or vaguely aware of America's racially laden history of inequity. This is simply not his experience, much like I am unfamiliar with the deep wounds still present between he and other tribes in his country. This is simply not my experience.

---

1 Wealthy compared to most South Sudanese who live on less than two dollars a day.

Bakata does, however, have a distinct history with elite westerners. My birth in America connects me to this category. To ignore his perspective of my identity would be to ignore a vital part of *his* story. A story that informs the way in which we interact but doesn't have to define it. Ultimately, by better understanding his perspective, I gain a more comprehensive understanding of the power dynamics at play each time we interact. As a result, I can be intentional about responding to negative assumptions. As we better understand our stories, we recognize our identity is not static. It does not form once and remain the same forever. No, it changes again and again. By learning the stories of others, we are better able to understand our own story and the new chapters we form together.

In many ways, my family story mirrors the reality faced by many people of color trying to escape the shadowy legacy of slavery and Jim Crow in the American south. I was born in Atlanta, Georgia, a major Confederate railway and military point during the Civil War. Union soldiers found the city so vital to the success of the South that they seized it and set it ablaze. One hundred years later these battlegrounds were repurposed by a young pastor named Martin Luther King Jr. He and several other leaders seeking racial progress established Atlanta as a headquarters during the Civil Rights Movement. Within Atlanta's segregated communities, leaders of historically black churches and colleges spoke out against racial injustice and taught their members to be agents of resistance. My father's sister, Ruby Doris Smith Robinson, was one of those members. She entered Spelman College at the age of sixteen and left shortly afterwards to be a leader in the movement. As one of the founding members and senior leaders in the Student Nonviolent Coordinating Committee (SNCC), she organized demonstrations across the nation addressing racial discrimination. In fact, her role as one of the original Freedom Riders led to the integration of buses nationwide.

My mother was one of the beneficiaries of Ruby Doris and the Freedom Riders' actions. The wheels of those integrated buses carried my mother out of her segregated farm town in search of educational and economic opportunities in Atlanta. She left behind her mother and grandmother, who were sharecroppers, and her great-grandmother, who was a former slave. While in Atlanta, she earned several graduate degrees and developed a career in education spanning more than three decades. Moreover, she married her college sweetheart and had two children. Even with all she accomplished, the pains of discrimination continued to find and wound her. She stored her lessons learned in our family culture.

Just as my family and national history shape me, issues of ethnic/racial difference influence and shape my South Sudanese sisters and brothers. The categories are different—not black and white, but various ethnic groups or tribes who all self-identify as black. The context is different, but the hurt is similar. The expressions of hurt are also similar: distrust, anger, guilt, and lack of forgiveness, etc. Nevertheless, tension and frustration around ethnic identity—if handled well—may lead strangers to become friends and friends to become more aware of each other. As relationships deepen, we better understand the uniqueness of our stories and those in the world around us.

EXPLORING NATIONALITY BESIDE BEES, BUCKETS, AND A PILE OF FLOUR

In the town's open-air market, somewhere past the gold and auburn mangos, but before the leafy green piles of kale and stacks of overripe banana, sits a woman. She, and several other ladies selling flour, squat on white buckets turned upside down. "Where are you from?" she asks while digging a plastic cup deep into a mound of flour. As she draws out eight ounces, a host of spirited bees circle her flour-powdered forearms occasionally dipping into the green cup she holds.

"From America," I answer, with a southern accent and fear of bees too obvious to conceal.

"From America?" The woman nudges her friend who nudges *her* friend and the ladies lean in to hear my story. "*You* are from America?"

Sensing their puzzlement with my odd accent and unexpected home country, I say more, "Yes, I am a black person from America."

"You are from Kenya?" she questions, still in disbelief that I am not African. Kenya is often the first option South Sudanese think of when guessing where I am from.

"No, I'm from America."

"You are from Nigeria?" she makes another attempt. Nigeria is usually the second option. After all, Nigeria's citizens have accents which sound quite odd to many South Sudanese.

"No, I am a black person from *America*."

"Black American!" she exclaims, tickled by the notion. Unsure of whether I was telling the truth or prolonging a joke, she responds with laughter. The woman nudges her friend who nudges *her* friend and the ladies laugh and laugh and laugh. They rock back and forth on their upside-down buckets. Puffs of flour swell and fade into the air as they high five eachother with amusement. "Black American!" they exclaim. The scene feels comical although I am not sure what is happening. She high fives me as the celebration continues. I chuckle, a bit unsure of whether they are laughing at me or excited for me, but nevertheless, I enjoy the moment. I draw my Georgia driver's license from my unzipped side pocket to provide them with evidence of my nationality. My name, picture, and former US home address are on the card. The card's silver emblem catches the sun's light and sparkles into the faces of the women searching for my identity.

Exhausted from laughing, the woman extends her hand to thank me for the moments of delight. Our conversation ends without a decision regarding my identity but rather with an appreciation for my unique story. Several months after our first encounter, her eyes still curl with laughter when she sees me in the open market. We greet each other with a tamed chuckle and she says, "Black American."

Each of us has a story to share—a dynamic, vibrant, colorful tale which weaves together the strands of our lives. The ladies in the market remind me to celebrate the peculiar tapestry of my own story, yet I am mindful of many whose nationalities are not celebrated. A person's country of origin is assigned at birth yet brings scorn or praise for a lifetime. While we cannot choose our place of birth, we can choose how we respond to others from different countries. My encounter in the market led me to reflect on my own bias towards nationality and led me to think about how my nationality has influenced my thoughts about other nationalities.

Indeed, I am not only an American but a child of the 1980s, an era marked in America by Michael Jackson, Pac-Man, and strained relations with the Soviet Union. The two countries once allied to end the Holocaust, but during the 80s their relationship faced significant turmoil. Diverging political, economic, and military ideologies caused President Jimmy Carter to boycott the 1980 summer Olympics in Moscow and President Ronald Reagan to reference the USSR as the "Evil Empire." In many ways, Reagan's words and Carter's actions were representative of a growing anti-Soviet sentiment in our nation. This contempt was evident during the 1980 winter Olympics in Lake Placid, New York, when our nation's most celebrated gold medal came after our unexpected defeat of the Soviet Hockey team. This victory was famously known as the "Miracle on Ice," and many Americans felt the triumph was a foretaste of future "God-given" victories over the Soviets. This contempt grew during the 1984 summer Olympics in Los Angeles, when the USSR refused to compete. American scorn was not only expressed among presidents and elite athletes, it was infused into our entertainment. Movie goers across the nation were delighted when Rocky Balboa defeated Russian nemesis Drago in the box office smash *Rocky IV*. Crowds again celebrated when Rambo overcame his Russian nemesis Colonel Podovsky in the war movie series *Rambo*. Over time, a general disdain of Soviets stained the fabric of the American conscious. Our Presidents said it,

Olympians endorsed it, and Hollywood cast it before us in brilliant color.[2] Like many, I accepted the message. I accepted the message until I met a profoundly different reality.

At the age of twelve, I traveled with the Atlanta Boy Choir to sing in an international music festival in Russia. During the trip we formed deep friendships with the Glinka Boys' Choir from St. Petersburg, Russia. We spent the day practicing music together, playing soccer, and enjoying food. In the evenings we performed before packed concert halls and cathedrals with audiences excited to see the musical union of American and Russian children. Each new encounter with another boy or affectionate parent forced me to rethink my negative perceptions of Russians. I made assumptions about Russians based on national politics, media images, and my own limited experiences. Those assumptions, however, were ultimately overcome by several genuine encounters with others. We repeated the tour the following year, and I continued to rethink my assumptions.

Much like my South Sudanese sisters and brothers, race and nationality are formative in my understanding of self. The two are not the only influencers of my identity, but they certainly are essential to it. My encounters with Bakata and the woman in the market are fresh reminders of the central role of these definers for each of us. For example, if I stated Bakata was a member of the majority Dinka tribe instead of his minority Mundu tribe, he might have been the one conflicted, feeling the need to quickly set the record straight. Or if I suggested the vendor in the market was Sudanese instead of *South* Sudanese, then she might have grown a bit frustrated. Their responses would be drawn from their own personal experiences of interethnic relations in their country and a painful history with the neighboring country, Sudan.

As I entered into my work in South Sudan, it was important for me to know the stereotypes of foreigners in general and specifically of Americans. Based on the US government's support of South Sudan's independence, there is generally a positive feeling towards and warm hospitality offered to Americans visiting the country. After living in South Sudan for a time, however, I had the privilege of also hearing the stories of the ways individual US citizens or organizations, often with the intention of helping a developing nation, interacted with locals in harmful ways. Taking charge, not honoring local traditions, looking past the talents and skills of indigenous leaders, and operating with an air of superiority not unlike that of colonial times, all created baggage that the South Sudanese, like my friend Bakata, may carry into a new relationship with an American.

---

2   To be fair, President George H. Bush improved ties with the Russian government at the end of the decade, but the general perception of the country remained quite negative.

Again, my mother's advice rang true and helped me see the opportunity in front of me: be aware of their perception of you, keep in mind the stereotypes and the historical realities present, and at the same time, know who you are and be a part of creating a new historical context for those who will come after you.

FINDING PRIVILEGE IN UNEXPECTED PLACES

Until I lived abroad, I underestimated one major part of my story: privilege. As the son of public school teachers and the grandson of sharecroppers, I rarely considered myself privileged. After all, where was the opulence, affluence, grandeur, and excess in my life? Nowhere. My experiences in the majority world tell me differently. Privilege is having access to clean drinking water. Or rather, privilege is drinking water without fear of becoming sick from life-threatening diseases. I am privileged. Privilege is having access to medical care. My friend Bakata died three years after we met. He passed away from an inability to get good treatment for malaria, a curable illness, which is common to his region. I have been treated for the same sickness several times since his death. I am privileged.

Privilege is the ability to receive care for unborn life. At one time, the United Nations named South Sudan "the worst place in the world to have a baby" because of the lack of medical care available to mothers. Five years ago, our family experienced this reality. Our son was born two months prematurely and days before my wife's flight back to the United States. My son, Jordan, was unable to breathe properly, maintain a healthy body temperature, or nurse sufficiently. The medical equipment was not working, and the medical team was unsure of whether they could care for the fragile life. The child needed neonatal intensive care, and we needed to be medically evacuated to a hospital in another country. The medical team used the only incubator in town to stabilize the baby. After the child's breathing steadied, a chain of colleagues from my sending organization in the United States helped secure an air evacuation plane holding a nurse, a doctor, and all the medical equipment needed to care for our baby. They flew into South Sudan, landed on the dirt airstrip, fixed the incubator into a Land Cruiser, transferred the baby into their medical equipment, and flew us to Nairobi, Kenya. Once we arrived in Nairobi, an ambulance met us on the runway and hurried us to a top-notch hospital where the child was admitted immediately into neonatal ICU. Miraculously our son lived, and my family is forever grateful. Nevertheless, we are sadly aware many families do not have health insurance to pay for such care. I am privileged.

Many of my conversations in South Sudan remind me of privilege being an undeniable aspect of my life. This fact was most evident when violence erupted in our town in January 2014. My family was in the country when the fighting initially began in the capital city, yet we were able to cross the border by road for safety. We later flew back to the United States, to raise support and awareness for the crisis. My friend Hilary Adeba is a South Sudanese Episcopal Bishop. He had the option to leave but chose to stay and used his privilege to address the crisis from within the country. The following is a reflection detailing my conversation with him while he was in Yei, South Sudan:

My search for the phone numbers of South Sudanese contacts leads me to the information for Bishop Hilary Adeba. He is a trusted friend and Chairman of the Board of RECONCILE International. If anyone knows the status of Yei, our town, he does. I dial the number, and a weary yet appreciative voice greets me. His smile reaches across the phone line to welcome me.

"Shelvis, I am so happy you've called me all the way from the United States of America."

"Of course, Bishop, of course. How are you doing? How is Yei?"

"Well Shelvis, we are not doing well." He goes on to explain hundreds of families are entering Yei in search of refuge. The families are gathering on the grounds of an abandoned UN compound. In a matter of days, the numbers swell from two hundred fifty internally displaced people (IDPs) to more than five thousand IDPs in our town. In the upcoming weeks, the total number of internally displaced people within the entire country passes one million. Over time, the number exceeds more than two million.

Old disasters complicate new disasters in South Sudan. While many residences want to help the displaced families, food and shelter are not readily accessible for their own families. For example, many communities in South Sudan live on less than a dollar a day and must travel significant distances to reach water points. Therefore, the masses seeking refuge within the country are causing an immeasurable strain on people who already suffer from limited resources like clean drinking water.

In our phone conversation, Bishop Hilary talks about his initial response when families began to arrive in Yei. He states quite humbly, "God has sent us these people, but we have nothing to give them." I could hear the weariness in his voice … the longing to make a difference and its sobering collision with the reality facing him. Tears brim in my eyes as we sit together, yet at a distance, in silence.

"Shelvis," the Bishop goes on to tell what happened next, "I recently met with the church leaders in this town. We prayed and decided we will lead our congregations in a fast once a week. The money which we use for our breakfast, tea[break], or lunch will be set aside for the people who have come to our town. And let me tell you, Shelvis, we collected more than two truckloads of supplies during our first week of fasting: two truckloads of food, firewood and water. We will continue to fast for the people in need." In the months that followed, the churches continue to fast for one meal a day, and Bishop Hilary solicits the help of others. He presents their story to humanitarian organizations in the international community and many respond with relief.

While Bishop Hilary chose to stay, and our family chose to leave, we both had the privilege to choose. Many displaced South Sudanese seeking refuge within the country did not have these choices. I am privileged.

Bishop Hilary has given me a gift. He uses his privilege to honor the community he encounters. He inspires, intrigues, encourages, and amazes me. He reminds me that each time I sit in an empty room with my laptop and thoughts, I too can make a difference.

CONCLUDING THOUGHTS

All three encounters help me understand my own identity a little bit better and the ways in which I might more meaningfully interact with those around me. My discussion with Bakata encourages me to push back against racial assumptions and consider alternative perspectives. My exchange with the women in the market challenges me to rethink belonging and citizenship. My phone call with Bishop Hilary makes evident my privilege and the way it can be used to make a difference.

Again and again, our everyday lives offers clues as to how we might better define or redefine ourselves and our relationships with others. In this space, familiar understandings are confronted by unfamiliar realities: our perspective is challenged and our imagination ignited. In this space, the world as we know it is turned on its head. Race is confounded, privilege is rethought, and the essence of who we are is revealed. This space cannot be created without the invaluable exchange of others and the willingness to be vulnerable and moldable.

So, let us courageously embark on the adventure of understanding ourselves and those with whom we share this global home. Let us remain open to profound meaning in ordinary encounters. Let us handle with care the lens through which others see us, knowing their insights help us reflect thoughtfully, critique constructively, and make a difference. It is a humbling enterprise, yet proper understanding of ourselves and mindful navigation of our lives together is essential for every responsible global citizen.

Groups

Why Are They So Important?

GROUPS

The discussion of groups speaks to the heart of what sociologists examine—the impact of groups on a person's attitudes, values, beliefs, and behavior. A discussion of the sociological influence on groups typically includes a micro-level analysis: how and in what ways do groups shape an individual's behavior, but it also includes a macro-level understanding of large scale organizations. We can think of bureaucracies as an example of this type of organization and the impact it can have on an individual's assessment of their place in society. We can also study the day-to-day operations of how large scale groups function, where informal norms often drive behavioral expectations far more frequently than formal policies and procedures which purportedly dictate how the organization functions.

At the micro level, much of the discussion is often driven by social psychological research, where experiments have been conducted on individuals to see when and under what circumstances a group norm can influence a person's decision to act. Some of the classic experiments, such as those by Solomon Asch, provide us with important clues as to exactly what causes people to adopt group norms, even when they do not believe in them. The need for social acceptance is a powerful influence on people's decision making and it can change their worldviews as well as their actions in a given situation.

Much of the discussion about groups also focuses on how people identify and affiliate with others who have similar characteristics and to exclude others who are very different from themselves; what sociologists often refer to as in-group/out-group dynamics. While American society claims to embrace and celebrate diversity, with assertions that we enjoy and appreciate the uniqueness of others, the realities are that we tend to be attracted to people that are a lot like ourselves and tend to distance ourselves from those who are different from us.

In this section, several articles offer insight into the nature of group dynamics and the interactions that occur in groups. For instance, Carrie Coward Bucher offers insight into how groups serve as the foundation of society, offering insight into life as a high school student as an illustration. Christina Franks Hasselbrock draws from her experiences in working with young women in transitional housing to provide insight into how living in a positive group setting can make a significant difference in a patient's overall recovery from experiencing trauma. Finally, one other example offered about the impact of groups is found in an article about rodeo clowns. While most people outside the rodeo have little idea of what life is like as a rodeo clown, there is a strong sense of solidarity and cohesion among this group of individuals, largely based on the enormous risks they take to protect bull riders.

Residential Group Homes: How Labeling Theory Can Impact Female Youth and How They Broke Those Labels

Christina Hesselbrock, LCSW

RESIDENTIAL GROUP HOMES were developed to house youth who need psychological, psychiatric, and behavioral support. The existence of group homes dates back to the late 1890s, when children were placed in orphanages (Fruendlich, Morris, and Blair 2004; Lee and Thompson 2008). During the early 1900s there was concern about the institutionalization of youth, and therefore social and legislative reform was put into place to decrease the number of orphanages and find more conducive living environments for youth. With the closing of the orphanages, more group home facilities were created. There are various types of group home settings and they can range from residential placements, youth survival training in more remote settings, and school-based placements (Freundlich, Morris, and Blair 2004). The continuation of the group home development spanned into the 1960s and 1970s in response to the deinstitutionalization of hospitals. The idea was to move youth to an environment that was less restrictive and where they could learn the skills needed to become more independent. The hope was that these youth would be provided with more opportunity to grow and have the chance to accomplish more with their lives.

Group homes today frequently offer a combination of treatment to youth. They mainly focus their intervention strategies on mental health and substance abuse. The mental health treatment focuses on providing therapy, working on behavior modifications, and having the youth meet with a psychiatrist for psychotropic medication review. The youth live in an environment that is structured and where supervision is provided all day and night to ensure they are kept safe. However, group homes are usually a less restrictive environment than being placed in a lockdown facility or psychiatric hospital, where there is constant supervision and patients cannot leave unless formerly discharged (Bettman and Jasperson 2009). The group homes also meet the basic needs of the individual by offering food, housing, and sometimes education. They also offer therapy services to support youth with emotional and physical abuse that they may have encountered in their past (Bates, English, and Kouidou–Giles 1997). They are typically nonprofit and receive funding through the state. In a report provided by the Office of Juvenile Justice and Delinquency Prevention (OJJDP) in 2011, over nine hundred facilities identified themselves as residential treatment centers. Out of these, about half reported providing counseling services. The counseling services provided were both group and individual therapy for the youth. Unfortunately, the number that also provided family therapy was much lower. This may be due to the family issues that led to placing the child in a group home setting. Further, the youth that are placed in group homes are considered to be problematic and exhibit higher rates of defiant behaviors (Breland-Noble et al. 2005).

Due to these challenges, much of the research conducted on group homes has focused on their success with handling youth with problematic behaviors. There have been few studies that look at the actual development and challenges youth face while growing up, with most focusing on managing maladaptive behaviors (Lee, Chmelka, and Thompson 2010). There is also little in the way of outcome measures about how youth have done after leaving the group home setting, particularly the work needed to prepare them in their transition to adulthood. This is particularly the case for the females that were interviewed for this article. Some reported learning basic life skills while in the group home setting, while the others shared that they had to learn these skills on their own. The research has shown that group homes are most often used to help youth who are at more risk of being placed in the juvenile justice system, abusing drugs, becoming pregnant, and/or dropping out of school. Since these factors come into play and are true for some of the youth in group homes, a stigma attaches itself to the youth and they are seen as being troubled or deviant.

A sociological perspective that explains the idea of youth in group home settings being described as problematic or continuing to engage in maladaptive behaviors is labeling theory. During their time at the group home there would be many labels given to the youth, including the women described in this article. The world outside the group home saw these youth as deviant and troublemakers and kids that would not amount to much or do too much with their lives. Even within the group home setting, the staff would often talk about the girls as if they were bound for lives that would be spent in jail. These thoughts fall in line with labeling theory and can be viewed as a way to keep these youth in the potential continuum of a downward spiral, keeping the negative perspective alive that they will not succeed. When given this label at an early age, it can make things even more difficult for youth who are trying to break it.

Labeling theory posits that people will come to behave and act in the ways that people label them. If someone is labeled a deviant then this label will propel them into further deviant behaviors. Labels are given to people every day, and in a society filled with constant and easy access to social media, labeling is even more prevalent. Further, the more dominant a group is in society, the more they will provide labels to less dominant groups. As it relates to this article, the more dominant group were those not exposed to living at a group home. This dominant group then labels those that live in the group home as being deviant. A primary concept of labeling theory is that once a youth has been defined as deviant, they will adhere to this role, and it can become a self-fulfilling prophecy (e.g., Matsueda 1992). The individuals with these labels then begin to build and organize their lives around this status (Becker 1963; Schur 1971). The women in this article shared that while living at the group home they had lower self-esteem and felt that they did not measure up to other youth who were living with their families. They knew that this living situation was atypical and were witness to many other youth at the group home who had significant behavior problems. They found it was easy to adhere to the negative labels that they were given, since the other youth there were frequently in trouble and they wanted to fit in. At that time, it was easier to be caught up in the negative behavioral momentum than to work to make positive decisions and be an outcast from their peer group.

The literature above gives a brief overview of group homes and their development, as well as how the youth living in these settings can be labeled as deviant. However, the information does not provide the insight and level of understanding of what a group home is really like for the youth that live there. Of particular interest is how youth feel about being removed from a home setting and being placed in an atmosphere where all activities are monitored. During my career, I had the opportunity to work for a few years at a residential group home. During this time, I met several young females who had been placed there for a variety of different reasons. Some had been removed from home due to abuse issues, some did not have a parent(s) healthy enough to take care of them (mainly because the parent was a chronic substance abuser), and some had become wards of the state at birth and had been bounced around from foster homes to group home settings. In this article the perspectives of four different women will be incorporated. The women whose thoughts are described in this article all spent time as youth in a residential group home setting. Most spent several years in these settings, and some did not leave until they were emancipated from them as adults. Although they each had different ideas on their time spent in group home care, they all shared that the time at this setting had an impact on their life.

The youth in group homes come in with significant histories of abuse, out of home placements, and varying degrees of emotional and behavioral traumas (James 2011; Lee et al. 2010). While it is also true that some of the youth that live in group homes do not have this type of history, most do. Since these issues are prevalent, the youth in group homes are labeled as problems and as youth that will have a challenging time when they then get out into the real world. Many of the youth and the women who were interviewed for this article felt this and also reported feeling a secondary label when they were given a mental health diagnosis. They shared that these labels would make them feel inferior and that they should live up to them. When the women would find out their mental health diagnosis, they reported that they would find themselves behaving in a way similar to the diagnosis. One woman shared that she felt the diagnosis was a way for the group home to "push more meds." These women would meet with a psychiatrist one time per week to discuss medication management. Since they had already been labeled as troubled and deviant youth the mental health diagnosis served as a way to compound their belief that something was wrong with them. Many of the youth at the group home would then use their diagnosis as an excuse to act out and get into trouble. This made things easier for them rather than dealing with the actual emotional trauma.

One concern that arises when these youth are all placed together in group home setting is that they will then feed off each other in the form of deviant behaviors. The term for this manifestation of negative behaviors and acting out is called peer contagion (Dishion, McCord, and Poulin 1999; Lee et al 2009; Robst et al. 2011). For example, youth who had initially come into the group home with fewer negative behaviors showed an increase in problematic behaviors and delinquency when around youth who were already at higher levels of behavioral problems.

This shift from less to more negative behaviors exposed the concern of living in a group home setting. One woman shared that she could be easily influenced into negative behaviors from her peers. This negative influence came in the form of drug use and also making poor decisions that affected her safety. One woman described making a decision to run away from the residential site. She said:

> The most-crazy time I ran away was when me and two other girls got ahold of the group home suburban truck, and we planned this amazing escape, but it didn't go as planned—we ended up crashing before even making it out of the gate. The girl that was driving braked and panicked and lost control of the wheel and we flipped three times. By the grace of god, we weren't hurt badly— the only girl who had her seat belt on got a broken arm.

Some of the other women described sneaking out of their cottages to meet up with the boys that were living there. They would also describe getting involved in alcohol or drug use. At the time, these behaviors were not seen as atypical since their peers were also doing it, and it was an easy way to escape some of the real emotions that they had to deal with given the hardships in their own lives. Further, there is not enough research to show that if these youths did have the appropriate supportive intervention while at the group home setting, they would not end up leading productive and successful lives.

My experience working at a group home setting began in September 2003. At this time, I spent three years employed at a residential group home that was located in the mountains of San Fernando Valley in Sylmar, CA. This group home was a licensed level twelve nonprofit organization that supported youth from as young as five up to seventeen years of age, at which point they could emancipate out. It was a ninety-eight-bed facility that provided care for boys and girls with behavioral, social, and emotional difficulties. It is important to note that there is no clear and consistent definition of a group home. This is because group home care varies widely, from highly structured facilities to unstructured homes where youth are afforded more freedoms (Friedman et al. 2006). For purposes of this article, group home is defined as a nonsecure out-of-home placement. A place where youth under the age of eighteen years receive supportive services to meet their basic needs and psychological services to help with trauma. The state of California issues "rate classification levels," which establish the monthly payments for residential placements based on the amount of onsite services provided. The higher the level, the more services are provided by the placement (e.g. onsite school, therapist, psychologist, psychiatrist, etc.). The higher levels are also considered more restrictive, because youth have less access to the community. However, a level twelve is not considered a lockdown facility, and youth can walk away any time.

At this group home, there were several buildings on the property and they housed around sixteen youth each. The group home called each of the housing units cottages. Each cottage had a central meeting area and the rest of the unit was divided in two, where there were four to five bedrooms which roomed two youths each. The cottages also had a staff office and a kitchen. The cottage I was working on was for adolescent females from the ages thirteen to seventeen years. Although this article will focus on four different female perspectives in the group home setting, the Child Welfare League of America (2005) reported that a little more than half of the group homes population is male. This is significant because a common theory among the researchers is that the higher rate of males in group home settings may result in more attention to the challenges males face in group homes, while neglecting some of the factors that are typically known to adversely affect females. Examples include body image issues, pregnancy, self-esteem, and female peer bullying. Unfortunately, the research does not provide a lot of information on females in group home settings or on outcome measures after females leave group home placement.

In the female cottage at the group home, each girl would share a room and each room had two twin beds and a closet. The girls would decorate their side of the room with mementos that they had from home or that they had collected from living in various foster homes over the years. Typically, the girls were sent to the group home due to abuse or neglect and/or not having any other place to go. Their behaviors were not severe enough to warrant being placed in a hospital setting, but they were also too severe to be placed in a foster home. The cottage also had a communal bathroom on each side and the girls would have to share time in the bathrooms. Further, each cottage was managed by a head cottage supervisor who would work with the direct staff and ensure that things on the cottage were running smoothly. Many of the girls would refer to this head supervisor as "mom" since she was the one who took on a parental role and helped take care of the girls. She would help with the girl's basic needs or with daily emotional problems. There were also direct staff that worked around the clock to ensure that the girls were always supervised. The women shared that the staff played a role in their lives by being a source of support. They said that a lot of the staff were "cool" and "had an important impact on my life." As shown in the research, the direct staff would be the front line and manage any problem behaviors, and they would also be the ones to set up a reinforcement system based on how well the youth behaved (Stroul and Friedman 1986). The cottages became like home for the girls that lived there and the staff became secondary guardians.

Since this group home was located in the mountains, there were not a lot of things nearby and access to stores in the nearby community required about a twenty-minute drive down the mountain. Due to the degree of isolation from others, the girls would be exposed to the same people and activities for the majority of their time there. They would report that this would make things tough on them, and they shared that it would cause problems since they 'could not get away' and had to be around the same people all the time. This was also true of the school setting, although some youth from outside of the group home did attend school on the group home campus. The girls would also attend school on site while living at the group home. The school had all grade levels and provided a supportive atmosphere for the girls who were trying to work towards graduation. The class sizes were smaller than a public school and many of the girls had an individual education plan (IEP) to help support their needs in the classroom.

The women shared that they could not get away from the drama or a peer they had an issue with. They would see them at school and then again when they went back to their cottage. This would sometimes lead to arguments and fights between the girls. When this occurred, the staff would step in to break up the altercation. All the women in this article shared that living in an all-female cottage would at times lead to heated arguments and fights. One female shared, "I would say one thing that bothered me was living with all the girls. Hormones fly and it is very noticeable when living with 14 other girls where many of them came from a broken home, plus being teenagers and going through puberty!" They reported that living in such close quarters with so many other girls could be challenging but that they could also lean on each other for support, and many built friendships with the other girls, who are still a part of their lives today.

The group home also had a requirement that the girls attend individual and family therapy with the hope to be placed back at home or in the least restrictive environment. My role while working at the group home was to provide therapy to the girls and family therapy when their families were involved. The girls were required to attend therapy at least once a week and family therapy once a month. The therapy sessions were to focus on supporting the girls in addressing the emotional and physical trauma that they may have experienced from their past, working on increasing skills and knowledge to live independently, and working towards reunification with their families. Due to the amount of trauma that the girls had experienced in their lives, bonding with and trusting a therapist was difficult. Some of the girls were resistant to receiving therapy. Many girls reported that they were reluctant to share their experiences because of the high turnover rate of therapists. They explained that when they finally did open up about difficult things, their therapist would leave and they would have to start over with a new therapist and go through their potentially painful stories again. They also shared that opening up in therapy was hard for them in general, as some had extreme cases of abuse from immediate family members. As a therapist working with these girls, I found it to be both rewarding and challenging. Building rapport and trust with these girls was vital in working with them in therapy. Once they did begin to open up and share what had occurred in their lives, they made the most amount of progress with moving forward and taking control back.

While I worked primarily with four to five girls in therapy, I had relationships with everyone, because I spent time each day with them and helped them with their daily activities. By doing this, I was able to learn more about them and hear about both the good and bad things that had occurred in their lives. One of the things many of the girls mentioned were comments about living in a group home. The group home is a unique and an atypical environment for youth to grow up in, and these girls developed opinions and spent time in situations that they most likely would not have encountered while living at home. Therefore, the time that the girls spent in the group home had an impact on them and on the lives they are living now.

The women noted in this article shared that they experienced an overlying stigma that labeled them as being someone who would not be successful in life, and they felt that they were looked down on.

Although the girls who lived at the group home were given these types of negative labels, many were able to rise above this and make decisions to succeed. Some admitted to having challenges along the way and having to endure some rough times in their lives before figuring out what was going to be best for them. When asked what they felt was positive about living at the group home, one woman shared:

> The staff at the vocational education department had the most positive impact on me. They helped me get my first California ID, create my first resume, my first volunteer position, and even helped me get my first real paying job! The staff taught me how to do my own laundry, how to cook and clean properly, they were there when we needed someone to talk to even during our darkest hours. The people at the group home helped mold some of us and, for me, helped me become the successful woman I know I am today. Without them I think I would still be lost and DEFINITELY not where I am today.

These women also shared a common thought that the group home was a place where they felt safe and had their needs met. Having the positive experiences at the group home helped in their determination to figure out what they wanted to do next in their lives. They also felt that the therapy component helped with some of the trauma they had gone through in their own families. One woman shared that she had a tough time connecting with her own family and, although the group home offered family therapy, she stated:

> My parents decided to stop coming after my third month there. They were supposed to join us once a month, but my mom disagreed with my therapist and me once and stopped coming. This made me feel like there wasn't much of a point to therapy anymore. However, I still continued to go, and my therapist was amazing and she helped me work out my feelings and resentment towards my mother.

All of the women that were interviewed felt that the therapy did help them in their lives and in working through some of the areas that they had problems. Another woman shared:

I got this one therapist that was different, that really took passion in her job and really cared about what I been through. I have to say she really helped me open up and try to express how I feel—till this day I have a problem with that. But she taught me how to cope with my emotions honestly. She was the best therapist I ever had. It didn't seem like we had a therapist and patient bond; it was more like a family bond.

The research on group homes shows that having consistent and collaborative services does help youth who are placed in a group home setting. However, for those that remain in the group home for a longer amount of time, they have to deal with the loss of therapists that they have connected with and, in turn, may not be willing to open up to new therapists, thus leaving them without as much support. The research has shown that consistent counseling can be correlated with higher rates of success once the youth leaves the group home. Being able to work through the emotional trauma they experienced can lay the foundation for success later in life, since youths will have developed coping skills to deal with challenges.

Although these women shared positives aspects about the group home placement, many also shared that there were also some negatives aspects. Most felt that it was somewhere they could not escape from. One woman shared that she felt that one of the negative aspects of the group home was "being restrained." She reported that when she did get into trouble the staff would step in and it would be "like five staff holding me down kneeing me elbowing me. Then we get thrown in a quiet room; it's a very small room with padding all over it, a small lil window with no access to get out from the inside." The girls would remain in the room until they were able to calm down and not injure themselves or anyone else. She shared that, "They think it calms you down; no, it makes you more amped cause you're stuck in that room, mad, banging on walls, screaming, till you're just too tired and pass out." Another negative aspect described by the women was a fear of abandonment. This underlying fear of abandonment stemmed from the girls getting to know the staff and other adults at the group home and then the staff leaving, which coincided with the same feeling of abandonment and being let down most had experienced within their families. For the girls who did get into trouble more often at the group home, the staff would label them as troubled or defiant, and they would tend to be the scapegoats for other kids who would then try and blame them for problems that came up. At the time, these girls shared that since they were given these labels as "the problem youth," they would live up to the label and get into trouble more often.

One of the overriding themes from the interviews with the women who lived at the group home was that they all felt that the group home did help teach them some life skills. Learning these skills helped to prepare them for things they would experience later in life. A few of the women shared that they learned how to cook and to do laundry. One woman shared, "We learned how to fill out important forms and documents, like applications for employment or DMV forms, and how to put together events. I was taught home duties and picking up after myself, living with family. I was taught how to cope with my feelings." Two other women shared that they learned how to budget their money and be creative with spending. Each month they would be given money from a social worker for things like clothes and other personal items. They shared that they would learn how to spend their money in creative ways in order to buy more things or buy items that they wanted. A couple of the woman felt that although they did learn things at the group home, they relied on themselves to teach them about the real world. One woman shared that once she left the group home, "I had to teach myself how to survive and be independent."

All of these women shared that, although the group home did help prepare them by teaching them simple life skills, they also had to rely on them and figure out how to navigate in a world that had already labeled them as being troubled. They had to work to prove these stereotypes wrong. It was not an easy thing to do for these women, and it took a lot of internal strength and perseverance to make a better life for them.

The perspectives of the above women show a variety of different thoughts and emotions based on their specific journeys while living at a group home. What I learned from each of these women is that, although things could be tough at times, their experience in a group home did help shape them into who they are today. Most shared that they would not change their time in the group home, although they may change some of the specific things that occurred. They have each moved on in their own lives now, and some have their own children, are married, and are working full-time jobs. Although the time spent in the group home was short in comparison to the time outside of it, it holds memories. While a couple of the women may credit some of their successes to things they learned while at the group home, most credit their inner perseverance and internal motivation to get them where they are today.

The group home setting where these women spent time and where I worked for three years may not have been perfect, but it did offer what they needed at that time. Research shows that youths who have an ability to create better interpersonal relationships and who do not have chronic behavioral problems tend to have better outcomes when leaving group home placement(Landsman, Groza, Tyler, and Malone 2001; Wilmshurst 2002). These women also had the advantage of specialized therapy, either in individual or family sessions, to help with problems that they had encountered in their lives. The success of these youths upon discharge from the group home setting can be correlated with consistent family therapy and supportive resources set up within the community (Hoagwood and Cunningham 1993; Larzelere et al. 2001). A prognosis of unfavorable outcomes is associated with a history of abuse (sexual or physical), substance abuse, and juvenile delinquency and/or time spent in juvenile hall (Peterson and Scanlan 2002). Some of these woman reported that it had been difficult when they left the group home placement and had to navigate society completely on their own. Unfortunately, some encountered life challenges, but they were able to overcome those obstacles and can now reflect on their current priorities. For some, the focus is on their children; for others, it is their career; for still others, it is in finding a partner who has fully supported them.

In conclusion, the research on youth and in particular females in group home settings is scarce. As mentioned above there are many reasons for this, including the lack of a clear definition of what constitutes a group home and a greater priority placed on services for males. What appears clear, however, whether from the existing research or the stories from the select group of women I worked with over the years, is that the time spent in the group home had an influence on their future lives. Positive variables like having supportive staff, receiving therapy, and being taught life skills, all contributed to a positive approach to success. However, not everyone succeeds and negative influences such as limited family involvement, poor relationships with peers and staff, and drug use on site, create problems. These women were able to break out of the labels that they had been given. They were able to take the positive things they learned and use them to make favorable decisions in their lives. While their lives have not been easy and each has experienced their own challenges, they have been able to move beyond their negative labels. The strength of these women and their ability to go through these challenges in their youth and become successful shows the importance of perseverance and internal motivation in overcoming conflict.

Bibliography

Bates, Brady C., Diana J. English, and Sophia Kouidou-Giles. *"Residential Treatment and Its Alternatives: A Review of the Literature."* Child & Youth Care Forum 26, no. 1 (1997): 7–51.

Becker, Howard S. Outsiders: *Studies in the Sociology of Deviance.* New York: Free Press, 1963.

Bettman, J. E., and R. A. Jasperson. *"Adolescents in Residential and Inpatient Treatment: A Review of the Outcome Literature."* Child and Youth Care Forum 38, (2009): 161–183.

Breland-Noble, A., E. B. Elbogen, E. M. Z. Farmer, M.S. Dubs, H. R. Wagner, and B. J. Burns. *"Use of Psychotropic Medications by Youths in Therapeutic Foster Care and Group Homes."* Psychiatric Services 55, no. 6 (2005): 706.

Dishion, T. J., J. McCord, and F. Poulin. *"When Interventions Harm: Peer Groups and Problem Behavior."* American Psychologist 54, no. 9, (1999); 755–764.

Freundlich, M., L. Morris, and E. Blair. *"A Return to Orphanages?."* Children's Rights, (2004).

Friedman, R. M., A. Pinto, L. Behar, N. Bush, A. Chirolla, M. Epstein, and C. K. Young. *"Unlicensed Residential Programs: The Next Challenge in Protecting Youth."* American Journal of Orthopsychiatry 76, no. 3 (2006): 295–303.

Hoagwood, K., and M. Cunningham. *"Outcomes of Children with Emotional Disturbance in Residential Treatment for Educational Purposes."* Journal of Child & Family Studies 1, (1993): 29–140.

James, S. *"What Works in Group Care?—A Structured Review of Treatment Models for Group Homes and Residential Care."* Children and Youth Services Review 33, no. 2 (2011): 308–21.

Landsman, M. J., V. Groza, M. Tyler, and K. Malone. *"Outcomes of Family-Centered Residential Treatment."* Child Welfare 80, (2001): 351–79.

Larzelere, R. E., K. Dinges, M. D. Schmidt, D. F. Spellman, T. R. Criste, and P. Connell. *"Outcomes of Residential Treatment: A Study of the Adolescent Clients of Girls and Boys Town."* Child and Youth Care Forum 30, no. 3 (2001): 175–85.

Lee, B. R., and R. Thompson. *"Comparing Outcomes for Youth in Treatment Foster Care and Family-Style Group Care."* Children and Youth Services Review 30, (2008): 746–57.

———. *"Examining Externalizing Behavior Trajectories of Youth in Group Homes: Is There Evidence for Peer Contagion?"* Journal of Abnormal Child Psychology 37, (2009): 31–44.

Lee, B. R., M. B. Chmelka, and R. Thompson. *"Does What Happens in Group Care Stay in Group Care? The Relationship Between Problem Behavior Trajectories During Care and Post Placement Functioning."* Child and Family Social Work 15, (2010): 286–96.

Matsueda, Ross L. *"Reflected Appraisal, Parental Labeling, and Delinquency: Specifying a Symbolic Interactionist Theory."* American Journal of Sociology 97, (1992): 1577–611.

Peterson, M., and M. Scanlan. *"Diagnosis and Placement Variables Affecting the Outcome of Adolescents with Behavioral Disorders."* Residential Treatment for Children and Youth 20, (2002): 15–23.

Robst, J., M. Armstrong, and N. Dollard. *"Comparing Outcomes for Youth Served in Treatment Foster Care and Treatment Group Care."* Journal of Child and Family Studies 20, no. 5 (2011): 696–705.

Schur, E. M. Labeling deviant behavior: Its sociological implications. Oxford, England: Harper & Row, 1971.

Stroul, B., and R. M. Friedman. *A system of care for children and adolescents with severe emotional disturbances, rev. ed.).* Washington, D.C.: Georgetown University Center for Child Development, National Technical Assistance Center for Children's Mental Health, 1986.

Wilmshurst, L. A. *"Treatment Programs for Youth with Emotional and Behavioral Disorders: An Outcome Study of Two Alternate Approaches."* Mental Health Services Research 4, no. 2 (2002): 85–96.

This Isn't My First Rodeo: The Social Organization of Rodeo Clowns

Robert Hartmann McNamara, PhD

A COUPLE OF months ago, friends of ours gave us tickets to a Professional Bull Riders Association event. While I had seen segments of bull riding on television over the years, I had never experienced it firsthand. I thought it was a nice gesture but wondered how many people actually would show up. While I live in the South, Charleston is likely known for its cosmopolitan flavor rather than its reputation for bull riding. Was I mistaken.

The local coliseum was packed—and the crowd was lively and loud. It was also quickly evident that this was a carefully orchestrated event, with loud rock music blaring enough to make me wish I had brought ear plugs, and enthusiastic and quick-witted announcers who dabbled in stand-up comedy. The entire event lasted a couple of hours from start to finish—even with a twenty-minute intermission. The event was polished, organized, and wildly entertaining.

Even from a distance the size of the bulls could easily be seen. As others pointed out to me, bulls in this event can be two thousand pounds or more. Given their size, I was impressed with their speed and agility: many a rider found himself on the turf within seconds of the gate's opening, despite hours of practice and carefully lashed hands onto the bull. Riding a bull for eight seconds is an extraordinary event.

As I took in this great example of American culture, the energy level from start to finish was extraordinary, and I couldn't help but notice one group of employees who were often overlooked (but a critical part of the success of the entire event): the rodeo clowns. These guys stand in the arena when the bull is released, and their job is to protect the rider from the charging bull when he is thrown off. Essentially, they attempt to distract the bull and have the animal chase them to allow the rider to get safely out of the arena. Let me say that again: their job is to stand between the bull and the rider and get the bull to chase them so the rider can safely get out of the arena. Wait, what?

Naturally, as a professional observer of human behavior, one who tends to focus on those who act outside the rules of acceptable behavior, my attention centered on the rodeo clowns. Who are these guys and why would anyone, anyone, purposely get in front of an angry animal that weighs two thousand pounds or more and has a set of horns that can gore a person to death?

SEND IN THE CLOWNS

The role of the rodeo clown is critical to the event—while the riders and others may garner a great deal of attention, along with the fame and fortune, it is the rodeo clown who allows all of it to occur and to keep the audiences and the bulls calm about what is going on in the arena. Interestingly, the person playing the role of rodeo clown is also sometimes known as a "Bullfighter" or a "Barrel Man." They don't fight the bull like the Matadors of Spain or Mexico, but they do engage the bull in meaningful ways. The term Barrel Man comes from one of the devices rodeo clowns use once they have the bull's attention. At times, they literally dive in a specially constructed barrel to protect them from the charging bull (Smith 2015).

Some evidence indicates that rodeo clowns are different from bullfighters, in that the former is really tasked with entertaining the crowd, similar to a clown in a circus, while the bullfighter/barrel man's job is to protect the riders from the bulls. The distinction dates back to an earlier time in the rodeo's history, when clowns originally were designed to provide entertainment to the crowd during intermissions or delays in the event. Rodeo officials noticed that during longer delays, patrons would leave the event early. In an effort to keep the crowd engaged, the role of the rodeo clown was created (Smith 2015).

At some point, arguably around the 1920s, rodeo began introducing more aggressive bulls, called Brahma bulls, which increased the risks of injury to the riders. These bulls tended to be much more aggressive and likely to chase after riders once they had been bucked off. It was at that point that rodeo clowns were given the responsibility of protecting the riders from the bulls in addition to maintaining their entertainment roles. This is why people still see rodeo clowns wearing makeup and goofy-looking outfits while they get the bulls to chase them. After rodeo clowns realized they were also facing considerable risks as a result of distracting the bulls, one enterprising individual brought a specially designed barrel that allowed him to jump into it if the bull gained the upper advantage. Years later this device has seen dramatic improvements and customization effort and has arguably extended the career of many rodeo clowns (Smith 2015).

WHO ARE THESE CLOWNS ANYWAY?

Maybe it was just me, but I knew very little about the rodeo in general or rodeo clowns in particular. Have you ever heard anything about rodeo clowns? Some people may have learned a bit about rodeo clowns due to a 2013 article that garnered national attention. In that article, readers learned about a rodeo clown who performed his duties at a rodeo while wearing a mask depicting then-president Obama. While the employee offered no real political commentary, his actions resulted in a lifetime ban from the Missouri Rodeo Association (Memott 2013).

Is this a high-risk/high-reward profession? The short answer is no—the available literature says that there are opportunities for rodeo clowns to work—there are dozens of rodeo shows during the spring and summer—but performers have to pay their own travel expenses and any equipment they might need. One crucial piece of equipment is the aforementioned padded barrel that allows clowns to jump in when a bull is chasing them. These barrels can cost up to a $1,000 or more. Additionally, any protective gear a clown might use, such as a Flak vest, shin guards, elbow pads, costumes, or any props they use as part of their act in entertaining the crowd, comes out of their own pockets. So there is a considerable expense involved.

The salary for most rodeo clowns ranges from $100-$500 per show, which, if calculated on a full-time basis, essentially pays about $50,000 per year. This does not include the costs of health insurance, which is also borne by the clown, or loss of work time due to injuries sustained on the job. Given that this is a high contact sport, the injury rate is quite high. Think about it: how likely is it that you would be injured if your job is to get an angry bull to chase you in a confined space? Given the broken bones, ligament tears, concussions, puncture wounds, and a regular diet of cuts, sprains, and bruises, being a rodeo clown is a high-risk profession. An added feature is the type of injury sustained by being "horned" by a bull. Despite the fact that the bull's horns are ground down and not pointed, at times they are still the size of silver dollars—getting hit with one of those, even though blunted, leaves a mark (Smith 2015).

So given the high expenses, low pay, lack of job security, and high injury rate, why would anyone take a job like that? Many rodeo clowns are former cowboys, which creates a familiarity with being around bulls and their temperament. Some rodeo clowns at one time attempted to make it as part of the bull riding profession, but because of injuries or other factors, became rodeo clowns in order to stay somewhere close to the profession. For others, the life involves associating with other like-minded individuals, many of whom have storied pasts and struggles with poverty, addiction, and even homelessness (Sommerville 2017; Smith 2015). For many, being a rodeo clown is a better job than the one they normally have, if they have one at all. Unfortunately, the shelf life of a rodeo clown is shorter than most professional athletes—the longer a clown works the rodeo, the more injuries they will collect—as Hansen (2009) points out, the bulls never really lose.

HOW DOES SOMEONE BECOME A RODEO CLOWN?

While it may seem like all rodeo clowns do is scramble around, wear outlandish outfits, and try to distract the bulls from the riders, there is actually quite a bit of strategy involved in their role. Part of the reason is that the job is multifaceted, because in addition to having the bulls chase them, clowns are also responsible for engaging with the crowd and entertaining them during intermission, any delays, or between riders.

Because of the many responsibilities, there are actually training programs for aspiring rodeo clowns. One example of such a program was described in an article in the *Chicago Tribune,* where reporter Eric Hansen visited the Lyle Sankey's Rodeo Clown School in Colorado to learn more about what occurs there and how clowns are trained. As Hansen (2009) describes it, this three-and-a-half day course taught him perhaps more about himself than about being a rodeo clown. One of the first lessons taught at the school is that there are essentially two elements to being a clown: the entertainer portion and the protecting the bull rider portion. For those clowns who have hung up their costumes and no longer challenge the bulls, the role played really involves that of an entertainer or emcee, where the objective is to keep the crowd engaged and entertained. This is usually a role reserved for older clowns who may have sustained a culmination of injuries and can no longer be effective interacting directly with the bulls—assuming the rodeo has that type of role for them in their event.

For others however, those who are literally in the trenches, the goals are rather simple. The first priority is to protect the riders. As the trainers teach prospective candidates, this is accomplished in a two-step process. First, the clown has to get the bull's attention. This is fairly easy since the bull is already quite animated—after all, the bull has its testicles squeezed via a rope wrapped around them (what, you thought the bulls just naturally disliked anyone riding them?), so that by the time they have thrown the rider, they are still looking for a target. Getting the bull's attention is accomplished by a clown waving his arms, shouting, and grabbing a horn. Contrary to popular belief, bulls respond to motion, not color (Smith 2015; Rodeo Clown School 2017).

Second, bulls are incredibly fast when running in a straight line, but they aren't particularly agile. This means once the clown has succeeded in accomplishing step one, they must run away from them and get away by dodging or cutting away from them at an angle. Thus, endeth the training. Again, think about this counter intuitive notion for a moment—the clown's job is to protect the rider by putting themselves in path of an angry and charging bull (Smith 2015; Rodeo Clown School 2017).

In describing his first day of training, Hansen (2009) noted that Bennie Bob, the owner/operator of the Rodeo Clown School, used a wheelbarrow with horns to chase students. As was mentioned, actual bulls can have horns as wide as the span of a person's arms, and the fact that the tips are blunted (or "tipped") does not mean contact with one fails to leave a mark—it does.

The advanced training involves using actual bulls for students to practice their techniques. The difference is the strap used on the training bulls is wrapped around their shoulders and not their testicles. This tends to make for a less angry bull—an important consideration since newly trained students are likely to make mistakes in judgement. As Hansen (2009) described, by the afternoon of day two in training, students advance to large and more aggressive bulls—in this particular case, a 1,500 pound behemoth named "Bodybag." As Hansen (2009) describes his experience:

> When Bodybag was fifteen feet away, he stutter-stepped. I assumed this meant he was planning to spring to the left, as I'd seen him do before, so I ran to the right. But instead he pounced like a cat with his front legs extended, diving at my shins. I backpedaled, one hand low on his forehead. It felt oddly warm. I looked left: horn. Right: horn. He pounced again. And again, steering me in an S as I swerved and stumbled backwards. Then he knocked me on my ass.

Most clowns attend a school like this one and then practice their newfound trade in unsanctioned events, on ranches, or in practice pens. Only a handful of clowns make a living in this profession, largely because of the risks and the assortment of injuries. While football players, hockey players, and others who engage contact sports have protective equipment, most rodeo clowns do not. Even rugby players, who are known for their toughness, don't have a two thousand pound angry animal with horns chasing them all night long. While riders only have to last for eight seconds, clowns have to handle all the bulls during the course of the night.

For some clowns, insurance is the only real solution to the threat of injuries; however, given how little rodeo clowns actually make, and given that they have to absorb all of their expenses, who can realistically afford insurance? According to sources in the insurance industry, the physical risks for rodeo clowns are significant. For instance, by some accounts rodeo is considered one of the fastest growing sports and carries with it one of the highest injury rates (The Trusted Choice 2017). While college football players have about a 47 percent rate of injury, meaning about half of them will sustain an injury while playing, rodeo athletes have an 89 percent chance of getting injured each year, nearly double the rate of football players. And among rodeo participants, which group do you think has the highest rate of injury? Rodeo clowns, who have about an 80 percent injury rate (The Trusted Choice 2017).

Such alarming figures should suggest that rodeo clowns have a good insurance plan, particularly for the wide range of injuries they are likely to sustain. There are insurance plans available, and some rodeos require that clowns sign a release stating they carry a minimum amount of accident insurance. This includes life insurance as well as health insurance for injuries (The Trusted Choice 2017). However, given how little rodeo clowns are paid, one has to wonder if releases are signed without having the insurance at all.

IS THIS A PROFESSION OR ARE THEY JUST A BUNCH OF CLOWNS?

Not only is there a high degree of respect offered to rodeo clowns by anyone knowledgeable about the rodeo, the members of this unusual group of athletes/ performers have organized in such a way to gain some professional credibility. In fact, within rodeo circles, rodeo clowns are highly respected for the role they play, particularly among the riders. Professionally, the Professional Rodeo Cowboys Association sponsors sanctioned events, and barrel men and clowns must be certified to participate in those particular rodeos. The process of becoming a member involves not only letters of recommendation but performance assessments at non-sanctioned events so that rodeo clowns are determined to be competent performers. Even after these assessments are completed, an evaluation committee issues a permit to perform in five sanctioned rodeos. After the completion of these events, the committee determines if the performer should be granted full membership with no limitations (Silver Spurs Rodeo Association 2017).

Granted, the logic behind these restrictions is to limit the number of individuals who wish to perform as rodeo clowns only to those who are deemed competent and fit to do so. However, efforts to professionalize the occupation inevitably make it less attractive, particularly given the absence of any meaningful benefits to the performers. After all, rodeo clowns take all the risks, pay all their own expenses, and have shortened careers simply by the very nature of what they do, all for very little in the way of salary and limited numbers of opportunities to perform. Added restrictions such as professional dues, membership requirements, and proof of competency, while important and necessary, only add to the costs of entering and remaining in the profession.

THE SOCIOLOGICAL SIGNIFICANCE OF RODEO CLOWNS

As was mentioned, among rodeo clown riders and others connected to the profession, rodeo clowns are highly valued for their contributions to the sport and to the safety of the riders. While the salary is meager and the working conditions have enormous risks, the rodeo clown community has a high degree of cohesion and solidarity. While many rodeo clowns contend that the adrenaline rush and excitement of the activity is the main draw to become a rodeo clown, there is a closeness among this group of performers that extends beyond the normal working group connection. While many rodeo clowns are poor and some even experience bouts of homelessness and alcoholism, coupled with the physical disabilities that stem from the culmination of injuries, one might think that the life of a rodeo clown is a challenging and discouraging one. However, most rodeo clowns talk extensively about their friendships and the loyalty found among their clown brothers. Some of this may be borne of the inherent risks in the profession, but some of it is likely also due to the time spent together facing those moments of adversity.

From a more global perspective, the work of Karl Marx provides insight into the nature of the profession. Briefly, Marx describes elements of capitalism, particularly its exploitative nature of workers at the hands of the elite—those who own the means of production. With the advent of the Industrial Revolution, and the primary goal of capitalism (profit), the elite attempt to pay workers as little as possible and gain as much productivity from them that they can. Such a strategy, in the end, maximizes their profit (Coser 1994).

As Marx describes it, for a time, workers in such a system accept the conditions in the factory as a feature of being employed—by accepting the wages, however meager, workers agree that the elite can use them however they like. Such a condition, however, is what Marx refers to as false consciousness. In Marx's view, workers do not realize the importance of their contribution to the creation of commodities and profit (Coser 1994).

After all, the elite own the means of production, which, by definition is everything needed to produce wealth except the labor. The workers, called the proletariat, only have their labor to sell. Both are needed to produce the commodity, which is then sold at market for a profit. But the benefits of such a model are only experienced by the elite, since all the profit goes back to them. Were this a fair exchange, workers would benefit either equally or in greater proportion than the current system allows, since they are integral to the process (Coser 1994). But they don't and the elite will not voluntarily give it to them—why?

Because the goal of capitalism is the pursuit of profit and any consideration given to the workers comes out of the profits gained. In fact, Marx argues that the only way this exploitation of workers occurs is when they develop what is known as class consciousness, or an awakening to the value of what they contribute to the process and the system (Coser 1994). Given that this has to occur not in one factory or country, but as an entire class of people—all workers everywhere—and given that the elite will resist such dramatic changes and use their power to keep the worker under control and powerless, the only way the situation is resolved in Marx's mind is through a revolution, where the workers rise up and take control of the means of production away from the elite and the workers then operate the system.

In such a model, everyone works, but everyone also benefits from the effort (Coser 1994). Of course, there is no guarantee that such a revolution will occur, or if it does, that the system will be improved and the solution offered by Marx would be implemented, but Marx argues that nothing will change under the current model since the workers have not leveraged their value to the elites in such a way that forces them to grant consideration to the workers.

If Marx sat with us that night at the professional bull riding event and learned more about rodeo clowns, he would likely agree that the circumstances under which rodeo clowns operate is similar to what workers in factories experienced at the turn of the century—where they are working long hours, for extraordinarily low wages, with high-risk conditions that virtually assure them that they will sustain a serious injury that will impede their ability to earn a living, with all of the profits of their labor going to the officials and organization that operates the bull riding event and tour.

By accepting these working conditions, including the absence of any type of paid health or disability insurance, rodeo clowns are engaging in a modern day version of false consciousness. By earning so little, paying for all their expenses, and taking such enormous risks with their bodies, the rodeo benefits greatly from their performances, but little comes back in the way of reward to the rodeo clowns. While professional bull riders can earn upwards of $150,000 per year riding for essentially eight seconds at a time, at best a rodeo clown, who protects those riders with their own lives, makes a fraction of that amount. Marx would also argue that the only way the situation will change is if rodeo clowns, as a class of workers, recognize their contribution to the event and develop a form of class consciousness that results in demanding better pay, working conditions, and benefits. And as long as rodeo clowns do not see the value in organizing, they will remain a valuable but unrewarded part of the process.

Bibliography

Coser, Lewis. *Masters of Sociological Thought*. Upper Saddle River, NJ: Prentice-Hall, 1994.

Hansen, Eric. *"Rodeo Clown School." Outside*. July 3, 2009. www.outsideonline.com.

Memott, M. *"Rodeo Clown Behind Obama Skit is Banned From State Fair."* NPR. August 13, 2013. https://www.npr.org/sections/thetwo-way/2013/08/13/211602534/rodeo-clown-who-wore-obama-mask-banned-from-state-fair

Smith, N. *"Bullfighters, Rodeo Clowns, and Barrel Men." SmithPro Magazine*. January 30, 2015. www.thelemonadedigest.com.

Sommerville, Jim. *"Rodeo Clown." Jim's Blog*. September 10, 2009. https://jimsomerville.wordpress.com.

"Rodeo Clown School." *Outside*. 2017. https://www.outsideonline.com/1892296/rodeo-clown-school

"The Roles and Responsibilities of Rodeo Clowns and Barrel Men." Silver Spurs Rodeo Association. www.silverspursrodeo.com.

"What Can Stop a Rodeo in Its Tracks?" The Trusted Choice. www.trustedchoice.com.

Groups: The Foundation of Society

Carrie Coward Bucher, PhD

A PRIMARY CONCERN for sociologists is understanding the mechanisms by which society is held together. Consider the social microcosm of high school. Since I graduated high school twenty-five years ago there have been important changes to the educational experience. The rise of the Internet, and its resultant social media trauma, and expanded learning opportunities, have genuinely changed important components of how students interact with each other and the broader world. I-gen students, born after 1995, are concurrently more connected via technology but more isolated physically and emotionally than past generations. This generation reports increased loneliness, social isolation, and disinterest in the typical teenage freedoms of driving and dating than past high school students (Twenge 2017). However, despite the intensity of these changes there are still consistencies from my pre-Internet adolescence and the current high school experience. High school students still attend classes and experience academic stress, they still separate themselves into cliques and use those groups as a basis for a social hierarchy, and there are still ritualistic activities such as sports events and pep rallies.

Fundamentally, students still learn formal and informal knowledge about how the world works that is used to frame their late adolescence and early adult experiences. High school is a space where a million larger social phenomena are maintained and passed to a new generation: the societal expectations of timeliness, appropriate classroom behavior, and other facets of social control; the mundane greetings and social exchanges of teens and authority; and the larger reproduction of a social hierarchy, which itself masks the recreation of class, race, and gender inequalities, and the resultant othering of those not in the privileged group. The cliques in high school lay a foundation for a sense of self, access to resources later in life, and understanding of the rules and norms of the social world.

As a sociologist, I am especially interested in how society can maintain consistency in normative expectations and social structures even in the midst of wild, manic, life altering social changes. One mechanism by which society maintains the status quo is that of social groups. Social groups, or collections of more than two people who share an identity, are the common phenomenon that guides our understanding of how individual behaviors are constrained in service to social cohesion. These groups, which vary in size and density, act as a foundation for larger social structures, a socializing agent for individuals, and a mechanism for connecting individuals to the larger resources in society.

GROUPS AS THE FOUNDATION OF SOCIETY

Georg Simmel (1898) identified groups as the smallest unit of any society: "I see society ... wherever a number of human beings come into reciprocity and form a transient or permanent unity" (664). These groups can be quite small, as few as three people with a common identity and frequent interactions. These may be friendship groups or an athletic team, where members are interacting casually without preassigned roles and have relative equality among them. They also may be large and formalized, with a hierarchy of specific statuses that individuals fulfill (Simmel 1902). A large group may be the student government, where there is a president and a treasurer and senators who interact with some frequency, and each is fulfilling the set expectations associated with their position. You can think of these groups (small and large) as circles within circles, i.e., that there are cliques of friends (a small group) within larger sororities or fraternities (a large group). Furthermore, we each belong to several small and large groups that vary in size, the extent to which we interact with other members, and the importance we place on our membership.

One function of the group is to socialize the individual, or provide them with the norms and values necessary to function in society (Cooley 1909). If you think back to your earliest playmates, the kids in your neighborhood or the ones in your family, they likely played a role in teaching you what it meant to be cool, or a friend, or smart, as well as helping you develop a commitment to them (the group) as important and worth caring for. The same socializing experience is replicated across neighborhoods, in families, or in elementary schools all over the country. Collectively, these primary groups teach each new generation norms and values consistent with past generations. Effectively, we all learn to participate in and value larger society because of the norms and values we learned in our primary groups.

Again, if you consider the social milieu of high school, it is in this environment that we learn to cultivate our community while conforming to the social expectations essential to successful adult functioning.

GROUPS AS A SOURCE OF SELF

A second function of groups in society is to provide individuals with a definition of themselves and others. If we continue with our high school example, students identify themselves and those they interact with according to informal status groups, like nerds or jocks or cool kids. These groups are not formalized, which is to say that there is no membership card, but membership in them tends to be clearly defined, be widely known, and come with certain expectations. These expectations, or stereotypes of behaviors and beliefs, are loose in nature but generally applied to all members of the group (Tajfel and Turner 1986). In fact, learning these unwritten group memberships and the associated expectations of behavior is an important task for any new student if they are going to navigate the social environment effectively.

As we navigate our social environment we separate the people we encounter into two groups: in-groups and out-groups. An in-group is simply a collection of people with whom we identify as having a shared connection. Each of us belongs to several in-groups at a single time; for example, you may include your friendship group, your family, your religious environment, the team you play on, and the summer camp you attend. When we identify these people as having a similarity to us, we are identifying behaviors and beliefs we think of as common amongst ourselves. In this way, we essentially apply the stereotype of group membership to both the self and others by saying "all of the people, including myself, who are in this group tend to have this set of beliefs or dress in this idiosyncratic way."

By necessity, the formation of an in-group includes the identification of an out-group. That is to say, we cannot have a sense of belonging to a group, with all of its stereotyped expectations of behaviors and beliefs, unless we are able to say which people do not belong to that group and, therefore, do not display the appropriate behaviors and beliefs. Out-groups, then, are simply the categories in which we lump together those who do not belong to our in-groups. Out-group categorization includes stereotyped beliefs for how others behave, and each social environment has numerous out-group categories. This is important, because we recognize that out-group members are different from one another at the same time that we recognize their difference from ourselves. In fact, we rank these out-group memberships on their level of difference from ourselves and how problematic we find those differences (Tajfel and Turner 1979). For example, members of one religious group (Lutherans) may recognize some important out-group differences from other Christian-based religious organizations (Catholics or Baptists), but find those differences less substantial to their differences from religious organizations that stem from different traditions (say, Buddhists or Muslims).

Once we have categorized ourselves and others into these group memberships, two concurrent social phenomena happen: we will adopt the norms of our group and cognitively seek to separate ourselves from others in a positive way. The first step is a result of the stereotypes that we have applied to group membership, i.e., as we identify the behaviors we associate with a particular group we will feel motivated to live up to those behaviors ourselves. In so doing, we signal, to both ourselves and others, that we are good group members worthy of the privileges of being in the in-group. The second process has to do with our self-esteem. No one wants to view their group identity as being lower than, or less acceptable, than the out-group. People will highlight characteristics of their group identity that they perceive in a positive light regardless of objective standards of group comparison. For example, if you strongly identify with your sports team and your team has just lost to your rival, you are likely to acknowledge their win while disparaging some other aspect of their team, such as their sportsmanship or your legacy of greatness.

These processes of self and other categorization can help explain how intergroup hostility, such as racism or classism, develops. To the extent that people categorize themselves as white or rich, for example, they are definitionally categorizing others as *not* those things (creating out-groups) and those others as not on the same level of worth (creating self-promoting distinction). In this sense, groups act as not only a source of your personal identity but also a source of societal-level conflict.

GROUPS AS A RESOURCE

Lastly, groups can operate as a mechanism by which individuals access resources. A social network is a set of connections between individuals that provide us access to the rewards and resources of society. Your social network consists of everyone that you know, and by extension, everyone they know. When you are seeking access to a resource in society, perhaps a job or internship, you may seek out connections in your social network. That is, you may ask your mom or your neighbor if they know anyone who needs an intern and use that connection to pass your resume around. The better connected you are, the more opportunities you have to leverage your social network for access.

We refer to this connectivity as the "strength of weak ties." Essentially, this concept argues that individuals with diverse social networks have access to a diversity of opportunities. More diverse opportunities result in an increase in your likelihood of landing a great job or internship. So while your close ties, the people to whom you are intimately connected, are important for daily support and encouragement, it is the diversity of your extended (or weak) ties that grants you access to a multitude of opportunities.

Pierre Bourdieu (1986) used the term *social capital* to highlight the way that individuals can leverage their social networks and weak ties to generate monetary value. Social capital is defined as "networks of connections with others whose collective resources can be mobilized to protect and assert individual and group interests" (Finn 2010). In this sense, the economic value of your social networks varies. If your network, including your weak ties, includes lawyers and doctors and other elite professionals, then that will provide you with access to resources not common in networks dominated by working class professionals like teachers or laborers. For example, doctors and lawyers are more likely to have other doctor and lawyer connections who may be able to provide you with an internship or volunteer opportunity that builds your resume. While working class people will have some elites in their networks, the collective resources are smaller and opportunities for leveraging them fewer. In this sense, economic inequality is recreated through social capital and your group ties.

Students who attend elite boarding schools have peers with access to elites in American society, including the Roosevelt family and other titans of finance and culture. The social capital they gain from those affiliations operates to generate a wealthy class solidarity, or a sense that they are members of the same in-group (Finn 2012). The benefits of this education extend past graduation, where post-graduate access to these elite webs of affiliation connects graduates to high status occupational spaces (such as boards of directors) which effectively sustains their class solidarity.

Indeed, C. Wright Mills (1959) argued that these schools were among the most effective socializing agents for teaching the normative expectations of the upper class. Students serve on disciplinary boards and student governments in such a way as to instill the values of effective exertions of power in order to maintain the status quo. In class and in their social environment they serve to teach students to conceptualize themselves as the future leaders of industry, government, and culture and regulate who is allowed access to those powerful circles. In addition to this self-categorization, the schools provide students with access to the movers and shakers in society who can make those dreams a reality. As such, this educational environment allows society to reproduce class inequality subtly, without making that the explicit purpose of the institution.

Cookson and Persell (2008) argue that elite boarding schools provide an environment for the children of wealthy parents to develop a sense of themselves as entitled to the rewards of their social networks. These schools have an annual tuition in excess of $55,000.

CONCLUSION

Understanding group level mechanisms is essential to understanding the larger processes that hold society together. It is at the group level that larger systems are created and recreated, seemingly without intention. For those interested in inequality or group animosity, group and network analysis are invaluable tools.

Bibliography

Bourdieau, P. "*The Forms of Capital,*" in J. G. Richardson (ed.) *Handbook of Theory and Research in the Sociology of Education,* pp. 241–258. Westport, CT: Greenwood, 1986.

Cookson, P. W. and Persell, C. H. *Preparing for Power: America's Elite Boarding Schools.* New York: Basic Books, 1987.

Cooley, C. H. *Social Organization: A Study of the Larger Mind.* New York: Charles Scribner, 1909.

Finn, J. *"A descriptive study of e-counselor attitudes, ethics, and practice."* Journal of Counseling and Psychotherapy Research, 10(4) (2010), 268–277.

Mills, C. W. *The Sociological Imagination.* New York: Oxford University Press, 1959.

Simmel, Georg. *"The Persistence of Social Groups."* American Journal of Sociology 3, no. 5 (1898): 662–98.

———. *"The Number of Members as Determining the Sociological Form of the Group."* American Journal of Sociology 8, no. 1 (1902): 1–46.

Tajfel, H., and J. C. Turner . *"An Integrative Theory of Group Conflict."* In The Social Psychology of Intergroup Relations, edited by William Austin and Stephen Worchel, 33–47. Monteray, CA: Brooks/Cole, 1979.

———. *"The Social Identity Theory of Intergroup Behaviour"*. In Psychology of Intergroup Relations, edited by Stephen Worchel and William Austin, 7–24.. Chicago, IL: Nelson-Hall, 1986.

Twenge, J. M. *I-Gen*. New York: Simon and Schuster, 2017.

Socialization

Learning Your Place

SOCIALIZATION

Sociologically, when we examine the topic of socialization, we often frame it by learning more about how people become members of particular groups. In a larger sense, however, sociologists ask questions about how people in society become socially human. In both cases, we are describing the process of socialization, which can be defined as the way in which people in a group learn the attitudes, values, beliefs, and behaviors of the larger collectivity. In occupations, for example, there is usually some type of formal training, where a new employee is shown how to perform particular tasks and exposed to the cultural climate of the workplace. Additionally, there is also an informal set of expectations among workers. In other words, there is often a prescribed way to do things and there is an informal norm that guides workers' behaviors. Those individuals that successfully adapt to the standards of the work group tend to be more highly regarded by their peers than those who take a strict or extreme position on what is expected of employees.

The process of socialization that answers the question about the development of the social self begins early in children's lives and progresses as they develop cognitively. This process involves being able to understand their place in society as well as the roles of other people around them. By understanding these roles, children begin to conceptualize their own place in society. In the following articles, we explore some examples of the socialization process. Carrie Flagler Whitney, for example, offers important insight into understanding how women, particularly those who are highly educated and career-minded, wrestle with the challenges of balancing their jobs with the demands of being a mother. The tension between wanting to be a successful professional often clashes with personal and societal expectations about the role of motherhood, something not usually found among men.

Similarly, in examining how and in what way women (and to some extent, men) are socialized into marginalized roles, Giovanna Gomez provides a fascinating description of how victims of domestic violence are perceived and the expectations for their behavior. While one might think that these individuals are only seen by society with sympathy and compassion, there is another element to the public perception of victims that can teach young women valuable lessons about their experiences.

Additionally, Robert McNamara has offered insight into the ways in which police officers are socialized into the culture of law enforcement, which can provide insight into the attitudes, values, and beliefs of members of that profession. As some experts have noted, society seems to be evolving into a tendency to withdraw from public interaction, where people are increasingly withdrawing from some types of social interaction. That is, regardless of the convenience of things like FaceTime or other electronic tools, there is also something to be said for the importance of interacting and relating to one another in public face-to-face. The challenge is found in generating enough of a benefit or advantage to this type of interaction since it can be time consuming and labor intensive. Allison Peck Lankford offers us a rather unique perspective on how public spaces are used to facilitate social interaction.

Women in the Workplace: Managing Changing Roles, Gender Differences, and Social Norms

Carrie Flagler Whitney, MPH

A DEGREE IN sociology exposes students to important principles and theories that are applicable in many life situations. The degree is broad in nature, but there are many avenues in which it can be used, both professionally and personally.

Upon graduating with such a degree, I took a job in the development department at a nonprofit rehabilitation hospital in Atlanta. After several years of fundraising, event planning, and managing hundreds of volunteers, I returned to school to get a master's degree in Public Health (MPH). This degree combined my interests in health care, helping others, fundraising, and program design. At a substance abuse and mental health facility in North Carolina, I was able to meld all these interests into one. I served as the only full-time development employee during a capital campaign. We secured funds for a new building, continued annual giving, and found new sources for ongoing programmatic funding, which seemed to decrease annually with waning government funding and reimbursement. Additionally, I utilized my MPH knowledge to start a diabetes education program for patients and also created the policies and conducted the staff training to take the campus tobacco-free, a hotly debated move in substance abuse and mental health treatment. It was the perfect combination of being able to write grants, secure funding, and then design, implement, and evaluate the programs.

Back in Atlanta, I settled into employment in a university setting where I focused on tobacco control research and writing. My number of publications increased significantly over the next few years as I found and fine-tuned a very specific research niche. One project I worked on allowed me to visit Singapore, where a book I helped edit was launched at the World Conference on Tobacco or Health. My crowning achievement in this position was taking a significant role in the organization, the writing and funding of a $19 million federal grant related to tobacco control research.

My next move was a bit of a career shift, as I became the CEO of a small start-up company. The days were longer (fifteen or more hours a day and weekends), and I was managing only four people. But in this position, I was truly able to meld all my interests—helping others, education, health, fitness, and being a leader. As a start-up, there were no sick days and the benefits were lousy in terms of vacation, health insurance, and retirement benefits. As expected, there were some tedious tasks, but someone had to do them. If I wasn't working, there was a risk that the whole thing would fall apart. In this particular job, I found my passion, and the hard work paid off in ways I could not imagine.

My sociology degree has served me well and has been extremely relevant to my professional and personal development over the past almost fifteen years. Are you inspired to believe that your degree can take you to places you never imagined? That you can build on your skills and over time achieve more and continue to grow, learn, and succeed?

My current position, the one that provides passion built on hard work and a constant search for balance, is that I am a stay-at-home mom of three children. That's right—I earned an undergraduate and then a graduate degree, and I contributed to the workplace in a meaningful and rewarding way. For a while I tried to balance home and work and be everything to everyone. And then there was a point where the balance tipped in favor of my family. As our family grew, childcare expenses were nearly more than I was making in terms of salary (fair warning about going into nonprofit work), and even the most lenient of employers would have questioned the number of sick days, holidays, and unexpected school closings. And on the weeks that school was in session and everyone was healthy, there were still appointments, school volunteer needs and opportunities, extracurricular activities, a household to manage, and lots of hungry mouths.

I could have written this article and started by blatantly saying I was a stay-at-home mom. I love the work I have done in the past, but I have decided, for personal and financial reasons, that it is best I stay at home for a few years. I have every hope and intention of returning to the workforce when I can, but for now I want to be valued for my role of raising the next generation—even if that means there are no sick days, my little people rarely seem to listen to me, and sometimes I wonder if I am making a meaningful contribution to society.

This brings to light questions about how our society values women, specifically moms, and the varying roles they hold in the workplace and at home. There are working moms, stay-at-home moms, work-from-home moms, and those who work part-time, etc. The introduction of this article could have been written from any of these standpoints. It could have been a story from an empowered working mom who never questioned her desire to work full-time. In today's society, more mothers are working than not. While this is the norm, there are times that the full-time working mom struggles with what to do with a sick child on the day of a big deadline and how to achieve a home/life/work balance.

There is also the perspective of a mom who works from home or works part-time. I am willing to guess (because I've been there and felt this too) that she enjoys her work and the balance that working and being at home brings. But I am also certain that finding balance seems impossible at times, that she works late into the night or early in the morning to get her hours in, and that she still feels guilty missing a school event that always seems to fall on a day she is scheduled to be in the office.

Over time, our society has changed how women in the workplace are valued. These shifting values have extreme benefits for and importance to women's rights and our abilities to achieve and succeed personally and professionally. Yet as these values have changed, so have the number of roles and types of employment that women might hold. Working moms represent the majority, but there are so many types of situations out there that sometimes even women don't understand where other women are coming from in regards to each person's individual work perspective and choice. But one thing is certain: all these women work hard, are doing the best they can for themselves personally and for their family, and are striving for a balance that may not be attainable.

I still consult and conduct project-based work in tobacco control, although my time dedicated to this is very minimal right now. For me, it is nice to have a foot in both worlds, but to be honest, I often feel I should be doing more to contribute financially to our family, to show my children that I am a strong, independent woman. Every day I perform one of the hardest and yet most rewarding jobs in our society. Every day I question myself or how a decision I make will impact my children.

Ultimately, I know I'm lucky to have this position and time with my family. But I do wonder where my career will go from here. How will I reenter the workforce with a resume with a huge glaring hole in it? How do I find balance in this home life? Since my current role is outside the norm, there are times I feel my contributions are not equal to full-time working parents. Would your opinion of my career path have changed if I'd fully disclosed my most recent job was at home rather than traditional employment? How can we, as sociologists, look at the roles women play in today's society, all the different jobs they hold, and ensure that all are treated equally, valued equally, and given the appropriate credit for a job well done, even if that job falls outside of the norm?

DEFINING CULTURE, VALUES, AND NORMS

At its most basic level, sociology is about the study of society, or the system of interrelationships created by humans that connects individuals in a common culture. There are several components of society that result from human inter-action, including culture, values, and norms (MIT 2005).

Culture is the set of symbols, language, beliefs, and rules that are enacted as thoughts, feelings, and behaviors within a group of people. Each culture has its own values or preferences. These overarching shared ideas of what is good or bad, desirable or undesirable, within that culture guide the creation of norms. Norms are concepts and behaviors considered acceptable or "normal." These behavioral concepts create the norms and rules for social interactions and guide individual behavior. (MIT 2005; UMN n.d).

The roles of women have changed with time in the United States. There was a time in our history, and this is still the case in many countries of the world, where women were not valued outside the home. Our culture valued the work of men over women, and this value created social norms that meant the place of a woman was primarily in the home. Fortunately the roles of women have changed significantly with time.

Yesterday's Norms—The Working Woman's Fight to Have a Place in Our Culture

Before World War II, women were most valued for their work at home, and the norm was that most married women, whether or not they had children, did not work outside the house. During the war, their value in the workplace was critical to support the war effort at home and abroad. Between 1940 and 1945, the percent of women in the workforce increased from 27 percent to 37 percent (History.com 2010). Additionally, 350,000 women served in the Armed Forces during World War II (History.com 2010). Following the war, there was societal conflict as men returned home to their jobs and society tried to readapt to a former way of life. But things were not the same and some women continued in the workforce and took important steps and action towards gender equality and shifting social norms. In the past few decades, the number of women in the labor force has continued to increase in general, although there have been some periods of slight decline, with social factors and the health of the economy playing into why shifts occasionally occur.

Today's Norm—The Working Woman's Place in Our Culture

Today the norm is that women work outside the house. This extends to mothers, with 64 percent of moms with children under the age of six in the labor force, of whom 72 percent are working full-time (US Bureau of Labor Statistics 2017). Our country has benefitted from decades of leaders and activists who have promoted and fought for gender equality. In recent years, women have been receiving and pursuing more equitable roles in our American culture and workforce—more women are more educated, more women work outside the home, and they hold higher-level jobs. These are all very positive cultural changes that allow women the more equitable roles in society that they deserve and have worked for, yet these changes are not without continued conflict and inequity.

In 2010, approximately 65 million women were part of the labor force. Over half (53 percent) of these working women held jobs related to three industries: education and health services; trade, transportation, and utilities; and local government (US Bureau of Labor Statistics 2011), indicating a lack of diversification of the types of jobs women hold and the industries they work in. Working women in the United States are still compensated less than men in the same position, bringing home approximately 80 percent of the pay that men in comparable positions earn (AAUW 2017). In terms of leadership positions, men still hold an exponential number of positions. In 2009, only 24 percent of CEOs in the United States were women, and these female CEOs earned 74.5 percent of the amount of their male CEO counterparts (US Bureau of Labor Statistics 2010). There are many examples of gender inequality in our culture today. A more subtle inequity lies in the choice to start a family, as the physical and biological burden lies on the female. This physical burden of growing and birthing a child does not end at birth or even at twelve weeks when the "fourth trimester" is over and women are expected to return to work from their often unpaid, or partially paid, maternity leave.

GENDER DIFFERENCES—SOME OF IT IS BIOLOGY

Women in the workplace should be treated equally to their male counterparts. Yet, if a woman decides to have a child or a family decides to expand, the physical burden falls significantly on the shoulders of the woman, and this can indirectly impact her work in regards to time off, distraction, and health issues, etc. There are laws and regulations to protect women and their jobs during maternity leave, but this is a burden that women exclusively maneuver. During pregnancy, there are countless doctor appointments, and there may be morning sickness or other complications or requirements for bed rest, which means a female employee may be distracted or missing work. Once a baby is born, there is a significant physical recovery, sleepless nights, and potentially around-the-clock nursing. Then enter the regular doctor appointments for the baby and the new mom's recovery.

There are federal protections for the jobs of women having children, but the process of actually gaining those protections varies by company, is often complicated, and unfortunately simply part of having a baby in today's world. The Family Medical Leave Act (FMLA) guarantees new moms up to twelve weeks of unpaid, job-protected leave (US Department of Labor n.d.). FMLA has some limitations, such as the size of the company (companies with less than fifty employees are exempt) and the length of employment (your job is not guaranteed if you have been employed less than twelve months).

Some employers may pay all, part, or none of the employee's salary during maternity leave, resulting in a significant financial burden for some single women or families. Some companies offer short-term disability or allow employees to use vacation and sick days as part of their maternity leave, and this can help keep income flow in the event of unpaid leave. This seems helpful, but it is hard for a new mom to return to work with no vacation or sick leave, as they will absolutely need that time for sick days or self-care.

Some working women may choose to go back to work before the twelve-week mark, which is unfortunate, as moms are still recovering themselves and important bonding is taking place between mom and baby. The benefits vary by employer, and there are a lot of details and complexities around understanding maternity leave at a company. These complexities are unique to women, since men, no matter how involved in the pregnancy and childbirth, do not need to understand the maternity benefits available at their company and do not have to consider maternity benefits when they take a new job, are considering a job change, or planning a family. This is not to say men are not affected by maternity leave and benefits, it just impacts them in a different, less direct way than women.

No Way Around It—Working Double Duty

Once a baby is born, the real fun begins—in more ways than one. Somehow the addition of just one child results in exponential increases in household chores and coordination and management of schedules; this is only compounded with the addition of multiple children. The amount of work required to run a family is reflected in the type of work commonly performed by stay-at-home parents (usually mothers in our society), who are essentially working a full-time job in childcare and home management. The average stay at home parent works more than ninety-four hours per week and the work is valued around $117,000 (in terms of how much it would cost to hire replacement workers should the stay-at-home parent not be performing the work) (Dean 2016). Each week, stay-at-home parents spend time performing the following functions (Salary. com n.d.)

TABLE 4.1

JOB FUNCTION/TITLE	HOURS SPENT WEEKLY
Housekeeper	14.8
Cook	13.9
Day Care Teacher	13.7
Facilities Manager	10.7
Computer Operator	8.9
Driver	7.9
Janitor	7.7
Psychologist	7.6
Laundry Operator	6.3
CEO	3.2
TOTAL	94.7

In 2012, 29 percent of women (or 10.4 million) were stay-at-home moms (Cohn, Livingston, and Wang 2014). Stay-at-home moms are providing an important service to their family and contributing much in terms of labor and finances saved. Yet no matter the work set up (both parents full-time, one part-time, or one as a stay-at-home mom), the household requirements are still present.

Families with two working parents (46 percent in 2015) likely outsource some of the tasks otherwise performed by stay-at-home moms, but there are still many aspects of running a household that have to be accomplished on a daily basis. Even if you have help with childcare (in-home or at a day care), there is driving, cleaning, cooking, laundry, scheduling appointments, and extracurricular activities, etc. (Pew Research Center 2015). As more working moms have reentered the workforce, there has been a shift in norms related to managing the household.

The men and fathers of today are far more involved in the day-to-day management of the house and children than they were a decade ago. In 2015 working fathers reported spending seven hours per week on childcare (a value nearly triple what fathers in 1965 spent on childcare) and nine hours a week on household chores (compared to four hours per week in 1965) (Parker and Livingston 2017). Despite this increase in the male's role, women still perform the majority of child management and scheduling. As a comparison, in 2015 mothers were spending fifteen hours per week on childcare and eighteen hours per week on housework (with men spending seven and nine hours on the same activities) (Parker and Livingston 2017).

Ultimately, the burden of home management and work disproportionately falls to women, and they feel this stress more than men. For example, 20 percent of full-time working moms say it is really difficult to balance family and work, compared to 12 percent of full-time working men stating the same. While men and women nearly equally share the burden of household and child management when both parents are working, this is not the case when one works part-time or not at all, with mothers performing the vast majority of household management and childcare. No matter how jobs are split up and who is working, all families have a hard time finding balance. In 2015, 56 percent of all working parents with children under eighteen years of age said it was difficult to balance the responsibilities of job and family, with 42 percent saying it was somewhat difficult (Pew Research Center 2015).

FITTING IN—FINDING YOUR PLACE WHEN YOU AREN'T THE NORM

While we are fortunate to live in a country based on liberty and personal freedom, there has been a shift in the past fifty years in regards to the roles of women at home and in the workplace. Perhaps it is the changing aspect of women's role in our society that has complicated the understanding of the value of women at home and in the workplace. Women in the United States work outside the house and their positions and contributions are valued in real ways, although inequalities and obstacles still abound. Yet sometimes women make a choice to go against the norm and not to work outside the house. If norms are determined by our culture, then our culture is currently telling us that since over 60 percent of moms also work, that working is the norm. While there are many other work and stay-at-home and work-from-home scenarios, these remain in the minority and are not viewed the same as traditional, full-time employment.

The society of yesterday valued a mother's role at home. Today's society now values a woman's place in the workforce. Women having children today grew up learning about the years of activism, fighting, and pushing the limits that allowed women the chance to play an equal role in the workforce. These women have most likely been in the workforce for years before having a child, and they now are maneuvering how to manage a career, a family, and a household simultaneously. Quite often, as soon as life gets sorted out, something changes again—a career move or job change, having an additional child(ren), or day care and school considerations.

For a period of time, I have made the choice to push the "pause" button and seemingly go "backward" in my career so I can stay at home and raise my children. To be honest, I am fortunate to have this opportunity and to be able to make this choice, even if it is outside the norm. It works for me and my family, yet I occasionally question my choice and feel undervalued in society, especially compared to my full-time working counterparts.

What I should feel, what I want to feel, is that the fighters and activists before me have given me this chance to make this exact choice. I should feel empowered about my choice, yet I often question where I fit in a society that currently values the contributions of working women over those that stay at home. As I tell my kids regularly, it's hard to feel out of place, but it is important to stand by our choices and values—and most importantly to support rather than judge others who are different than us. I hope to take my own advice and live in a world where I value my contributions in the past, present, and future, whatever they may be, and, most importantly, a world where I support all mothers and their choices in pursuing the elusive life/work/home balance.

Bibliography

"American Women in World War II." History. 2010. http://www.history.com/topics/world-war-ii/american-women-in-world-war-ii.

"Basic Concepts from Sociology and Anthropology – Tools to Think With." Massachusetts Institute of Technology (MIT). https://ocw.mit.edu/courses/anthropology/21a-219-law-and-society-spring-2003/study-materials/hobasicconcepts.pdf.

Cohn, D'vera, Gretchen Livingston, and Wendy Wang. "After Decades of Decline, A Rise in Stay-at-Home Mothers." Pew Research Center. April 8, 2015. http://www.pewsocialtrends.org/2014/04/08/after-decades-of-decline-a-rise-in-stay-at-home-mothers/.

Dean, Ginger. "Stay at Home Mom vs. Returning to Work: A Cost Analysis." Forbes. March 31, 2016. https://www.forbes.com/sites/gingerdean/2016/03/31/stay-at-home-mom-vs-returning-to-work-a-cost-analysis/#3355256adc7d.

Parker, Kim., and Gretchen Livingston. "6 Facts About American Fathers." Pew Research Center. June 15, 2017. http://www.pewresearch.org/fact-tank/2017/06/15/fathers-day-facts/.

"Raising Kids and Running a Household: How Working Parents Share the Load." Pew Research Center. November 4, 2015. http://www.pewsocialtrends.org/2015/11/04/raising-kids-and-running-a-household-how-working-parents-share-the-load/.

"The Elements of Culture." In Sociology: Understanding and Changing the World. Minneapolis: University of Minnesota Libraries, 2016. http://open.lib.umn.edu/sociology/.

US Bureau of Labor Statistics. *"Highlights of Women's Earnings in 2009."* June 2010. https://www.bls.gov/opub/reports/womensearnings/archive/womensearnings_2009.pdf.

US Bureau of Labor Statistics. *"Women at Work."* BLS Spotlight on Statistics. March 2011. http://www.bls.gov/spotlight/2011/women/pdf/women_bls_spotlight.pdf.

US Bureau of Labor Statistics. *"Economic News Release: Table 5. Employment status of the population by sex, marital status, and presence and age of own children under 18, 2015–2016 annual averages."* Last Modified April 19, 2018. https://www.bls.gov/news.release/famee.t05.htm.

"U.S. Cities Reveal a Wide Range of Gender and Racial Pay Gaps." American Association of University Women (AAUW). December 11, 2017. https://www.aauw.org/article/u-s-cities-reveal-a-wide-range-of-gender-and-racial-pay-gaps/.

US Department of Labor. *"FMLA (Family and Medical Leave)."* https://www.dol.gov/general/topic/benefits-leave/fmla.

"What is a Stay-at-Home Mom Worth?" Salary.com. https://www.salary.com/stay-at-home-mom-infographic/

Using Public Space to Reshape Social Interaction

Allison Peck Lankford, J.D.

THIS ARTICLE EXPLORES the concept of social interaction in public spaces and the notion that the design, programming, and management of such spaces can lead to an increase in social capital. A proposed new public space project in downtown Lexington, Kentucky will provide a lens through which to examine this topic. The article will begin with an introduction to the Town Branch Commons project and an overview of its history. Following a literary review and synthesis of relevant academic research, it will return again to the scene in Lexington and examine recent projects undertaken to better understand the current landscape and improve future public space projects.

Lexington, a mid-sized city, provides an interesting laboratory, as it straddles the midwest and the south. The city is just one hour from Cincinnati, Ohio, and one hour from the heart of Appalachia, Kentucky. Despite its distinctive culture, Lexington is prototypical of many like-sized communities across the United States. Lexington is also an emerging city, as are many cities in the fastest-growing regions of the United States. These peer cities face many of the same challenges and are seeking the most effective and innovative ways to invest in the improvement of their built environments. Lexington provides a progressive and forward-thinking testing ground to explore these issues and serves as an example for communities around the country.

THE HISTORY OF PLACE

The Town Branch Creek in Lexington, Kentucky has a storied history dating back to the city's founding. Settlers seeking westward expansion came upon what is now Lexington in 1775. It would be three years before Lexington was permanently established when the first blockhouse was built on the banks of the Middle Fork of Elkhorn Creek, also known as Town Fork or Town Branch. The location was chosen for its plentiful springs, which provided fresh drinking water for the new settlement (Merkin 2001). Just as it influenced our early settlers, Town Branch would influence the layout and growth of this community for decades to come.

Early settlers seemingly understood the importance of public space. Strategically included among the original eighty-seven lots that would become Lexington was a dedicated open space called the Commons. Town Branch ran through the Commons and creek leisure activities—fishing and swimming—would soon become the main social activity or programming in that space (Merkin 2001). While this important little water body was once described as a "magnificent stream...whose green banks were hemmed with the brightest flowers," it was gradually polluted and plagued the City with flooding and sanitation issues (Ranck 2010, 23).

The Creek was ultimately covered by development, channeled into an underground culvert, and largely hidden from the public eye for the two and half miles that run through the heart of downtown (Pettit 2008). The idea of the Commons was soon forgotten and Water Street put in its place but not before standing witness to one of the darkest periods in Lexington's history and indeed, that of our country.

Any discussion of Town Branch Creek would be incomplete without the inclusion of its African American history. Lexington controlled Kentucky's largest slave population, and the Town Branch area, specifically, was the site of some of the most notorious slave traders, businesses, and pens (Wright 1992).

Even after the Civil War, Town Branch served as a settlement site for freed slaves. The lowest geographic point in downtown, the banks of the Town Branch were less than prime residential real estate but offered affordable land for newly freed slaves. The settlements were plagued by constant flooding and sanitation issues. Robinson's Row—a series of "negro dwellings" along the banks of Town Branch Creek—is today covered by the lower Rupp Arena parking lot, the future home of Town Branch Park—the signature public space of the Town Branch Commons Project (Appler et al. 2016).

This is barely a glimpse into the history of this space, but hopefully it sets the stage for a discussion of the topic at hand. While the Town Branch Creek is nowhere to be seen in downtown Lexington today, almost two hundred fifty years later it is once again having a significant impact on the design and growth of the City and reshaping how we think about social interaction in our public spaces through the Town Branch Commons project.

Town Branch Commons Project

Town Branch Commons is an ambitious public-private linear park system that traces the historic Town Branch Creek in downtown Lexington, Kentucky. Town Branch Park is the anchor of the overall system, as a new nine-acre signature park adjacent to the convention center and Rupp Arena, home to the legendary University of Kentucky Wildcats basketball team. The project also includes

3.2 miles of new protected bike and pedestrian paths through the heart of downtown, knitting together five existing public spaces and providing a missing link to 22 miles of existing trail.

This project will undoubtedly physically connect the urban core to Lexington's iconic countryside. The question is, can we do more than just physically connect our community? Can we design and program a space that actually encourages social interaction in downtown Lexington?

Social Interaction, Social Capital, and Public Space

"Since ancient Greece, public space has been vital to people and cities. The most notable example is the Athenian Agora, an open square that served as a place for political gatherings and public markets, religious services, athletic and educational events, philosophical discussions, and art displays" (Toloudi 2016, 2). While we are far removed from a time when city-centers served as the primary avenue for culture and politics, it is still generally agreed that a strong relationship exists between public space and social integration.

Social Integration

The term social integration was introduced through the work of Émile Durkheim, who first explored the concept in a book called *The Division of Labor in Society* in 1892 (Durkheim 1933). According to Durkheim, unlike the individual conscience, which is a person's understanding of society's morality and its impact on his behavior, a collective conscience is the sum of the aggregate of those attitudes, values, beliefs, and behaviors. As the name suggests, the collective conscience is the unfolding of society's morality in terms of people's behavior. When it is strong, the collective conscience has the benefit of improving the sense of social cohesion of a group of people (Allan 2005).

Durkheim believed that society existed because unique individuals feel a sense of solidarity with each other because of this collective conscience. He believed that in earlier times, when most people in communities spent a lot of time together—they performed similar tasks, they understood the world in the same way, they engaged in leisure activities together—this shared time led to a high degree of social integration. As a result of the Industrial Revolution, the dramatic social changes that occurred decreased the impact of this integration. As such, Durkheim was concerned with how modern society could hold together given that it would increasingly be composed of many individuals, each acting in an individual and autonomous manner, with separate, distinct, and different interests. In short Durkheim was concerned that these societal changes would cause a disruption in the social cohesion of society (Allan 2005).

Social Capital

From Durkheim's work, one can see the beginnings of the concept of social capital. While the idea goes back further still, the works of Pierre Bourdieu and James S. Coleman can be credited with introducing the term *social capital* to sociology (Bartleby.com). The term gained prominence only recently and even moved into the mainstream through the work of Robert Putnam (Smith 2007).

Putnam (2000) argues that social capital, as distinguished from physical and human capital, is the connections among individuals that in turn forms social networks. Within these networks, the critical norms of reciprocity and trust arise and establish the foundation for a cohesive society:

> Whereas physical capital refers to physical objects and human capital refers to the properties of individuals, social capital refers to connections among individuals—social networks and norms of reciprocity and trustworthiness that arise from them. In that sense social capital is closely related to what some have called 'civic virtue" [i.e. standard of righteous behavior in relationship to a citizen's civic involvement]. The difference is that 'social capital' calls attention to the fact that civic virtue is most powerful when embedded in a sense of networks or reciprocal social relations. A society of many virtuous but isolated individuals is not necessarily rich in social capital. (19)

In *Bowling Alone*, Putnam (2000) started with the premise: "quality of public life and the performance of social institutions are...powerfully influenced by norms and networks of civic engagement" (16). Putnam identified a considerable decline in social capital in the United States since the 1950s and interpreted this as a consequence of the individualization process, citing mass media entertainment, increased spatial mobility, and work pressure as among the reasons for the decline.

As an illustration, Putnam examined how the social factors relating to changes in bowling in the United States occurred. He notes that while bowling as an activity increased, participants did not compete against one another in bowling leagues. Rather, people increasingly engaged in bowling as an individual act. As the title of the book suggests, the networks that existed that facilitated bowling as a group activity came as a result of the decline in social capital (Putnam 2000).

Public Space

Despite current trends, can public space serve as an avenue to rebuild social capital and reshape our social interactions? To further explore this notion, it is important to unpack the idea of public space. Each discipline seems to have a slightly different definition. Sociologists tend to focus on the accessibility of the space—both physically and psychologically. This moves beyond the traditional urban planning definition that includes streets, city parks, plazas, and other publicly owned and managed outdoor spaces, to "any space accessible to individuals, provided access is not based on some membership" (Tonnelat 2010, 1).

Historically, public spaces, by their very nature, have provided opportunities for all residents and visitors to use that space for a common purpose. But, to be certain, there has been an erosion of public space in America. In part this decline is a result of the shift to the privatization of activities traditionally occurring in public spaces. For example, our kids play on personal playsets in fenced-in backyards instead of the public playground. We get our books on Kindle or e-book instead of the public library and we connect with our friends on social media instead of face to face. Overall, people in the United States are more suspicious of others, due in part to the fact that they are less likely to interact in public with others and most certainly spend less time with people who have different life experiences from their own (Cortright 2015). In Joe Cortright's (2015) *City Report: Less in Common*, he argues that given these changes in society—a decrease in face-to-face social interactions and a decline in social capital—public space needs to adapt and reinvent itself to reclaim its full civic potential, but how?

For public spaces to really reshape social interactions in such a way as to build social capital in modern society, a strategic focus on the design and programming of the space is critical. We must reverse the trend of users abandoning the public realm for private, pay options and challenge the status quo by delivering experiences in public assets that the private alternatives cannot. Public spaces must "become a place where people enjoy spending their free time and sharing their common interests with others in that space" (Ijla 2012, 49).

This brings us to the concept of placemaking. This idea originated in the 1960s when Jane Jacobs and William H. Whyte introduced the idea that the design of cities and spaces should facilitate social interaction. That is, architectural designs go beyond simply the construction of buildings and highways and must include the creation of social spaces where people can gather and interact (Jacobs 1968; Whyte 2001) In its simplest form, placemaking is both a process and a philosophy related to the design, programming, and management of public space ("What is Placemaking" n.d.).

The authors of *Public Space* explored the idea of placemaking and social interaction: "In well designed and well-managed public space, the armor of daily life can be partially removed, allowing us to see others as whole people. Seeing people different from oneself responding to the same setting in similar ways creates temporary bonds" (Carr et al. 1993, 344).

Jan Gehl, the founder of Gehl Architect Studios in Copenhagen, Denmark, whose team led a Public Space Public Life Study in Lexington, has spent his career exploring this concept. He states:

> In a society becoming steadily more privatized with private homes, cars, computers, offices and shopping centers, the public component of our lives is disappearing. It is more important to make the cities inviting, so we can meet our fellow citizens face to face and experience directly through our senses. Public life in good quality public spaces is an important part of democratic life and a full life. (Gehl 2013, 288)

As a young architect married to a psychologist, Gehl and his wife had many discussions about why the human side of architecture was not more thoughtfully considered. He set out to study the intersection of sociology, psychology, architecture and planning. In his book, *Life Between Buildings*, he argued that success of the place depends on the nature of the activities undertaken. He characterizes outdoor activities into three categories:

1. Necessary activities involve everyday tasks a person carries out, usually with no other choice, and so such tasks are only slightly influenced by the physical quality of the space. This includes things such as going to work or school, waiting on a bus, or shopping for food.

2. Optional activities, by contrast, only take place when conditions are optimal and are therefore a direct barometer of the quality of the space. These include taking a walk through the park or sitting at a cafe.

3. Social activities occur as a result of the first two activities and are dependent on the presence of others in the space. This includes activities such as children playing at the playground, casual greetings, and communal activities (Gehl 2011). Gehl (2011) argues that some activities will occur regardless of the conditions of the physical environment, but in other instances it very much depends on the configuration of the physical environment and how the use of that space makes people feel—the better the space, the more it is used. The more it is used, the greater opportunities for social interaction.

In the realm of public spaces, parks are uniquely situated to encourage social interaction, and specifically, interactions among individuals not otherwise likely to interact relative to their social groups. In a recent article in the *Journal of Sociology and Anthropology*, Akram M. Ijla (2012) recognized imaginative leaders across the United States that understand the importance of great parks:

> McCoffin of San Franscisco, Johnson of Cleveland, Lawrence of Pitts-
> burgh, Clark and Dilworth of Philadelphia, La Guardia and more
> recently Lindsay in New York and Daley in Chicago were Mayors
> who understood the vitality of the city was related to parks. They
> each urged and supported innovative designs for open space so that
> residents would have opportunities to find and build a sense of unity
> across age groupings, economic classes, nationality and race. (50)

One might add Mayor Jim Gray of Lexington to that list, who has been a passionate advocate for the Town Branch Commons project. Lexington's own data
supports this idea of parks as important spaces for social connection. In a recent
public input event called "On the Table," more than eleven thousand citizens came
together to give feedback for city plans. Forty-three percent identified parks as
a primary site of connection to others (On the Table 2017).

SOCIAL INTEGRATION AND SPECIFIC PUBLIC SPACE AMENITIES

As explored above, public space promotes positive social interactions, which
contribute to social integration, cohesion, and community building. Can certain
amenities within the space contribute to social interaction in different ways and
either encourage or dissuade social engagement? In this section, we will explore
a few amenities uniquely positioned to contribute to positive social interaction.

Technology

Web access and technology are expanding and absorbing much of the social and
political dialogue that once took place in the public realm. As the authors of *The
Role of ICTs in Creating the New Social Public Space of the Digital Era* state:

> The continuous advancements of this information age and the rev-
> olution in mobile phones, wireless internet, Bluetooth, GPS and all
> their associated applications have influenced the way people interact
> with each other and with their surrounded physical space which raises
> questions about the impact of these technologies on the usage and
> act of communication within public space. (Abdel-Aziz, Abdel-Salam,
> and El-Sayad 2016, 488)

This section will explore the impact of the digital era on social spaces and in
turn, its effects on social interaction.

An interesting study found that contrary to prevailing assumptions, the
overall increase in the use of technology has not had a substantial impact
on social interaction in public space. Keith Hampton used time-lapsed video

observations from the 1980s and compared them to contemporary observations in the same space at Bryant Park. In the last thirty years, it turns out Americans have become less socially isolated, even as people leverage technology as a form of communication. As it turns out, the space is occupied by mobile users less than 10 percent of the time and often it was because they were waiting for someone to join them.

Rather than fighting against the technology wave, the design of public spaces should embrace technology as here to stay. While some amenities actually encourage people to remain in public spaces, such as water fountains and park benches, new designs of public space should also include power outlets and charging stations and seating arrangements that facilitate online and offline interactions (Technology Brings People Together 2014).

That said, the idea of technology in public space should go beyond the design. While Hampton's conclusion that technology did not have a negative impact on social interaction is helpful, it leaves the question: is it possible that technology could have a positive effect on social interaction if thoughtfully applied to the programming of the space?

Interactive technology—between people and/or between people and a physical object—can be incorporated into a variety of programming areas: (1) culture and art, (2) history of place, (3) education, (4) games and entertainment, and (5) information and communication (Abdel-Aziz, Abdel-Salam, and El-Sayad 2016). In so doing, can we encourage more people to visit the space and create a more sociable environment where people stay longer and have more social interactions while there?

Playgrounds

Playgrounds in the United States were originally inspired by the social reform movement of the industrial revolution and were directed at providing children with venues and modalities for play. Originally playgrounds were found in schools and supervised by adults, typically teachers, with a goal of cultivating civic behavior and social control. In the 1950s, the demand for playgrounds increased and funding shifted largely to municipal governments (Bennet, Yiannakoulias, Williams, and Kitchen 2012).

Research has shown that play is critical to intellectual and physical development, as well as important for interaction among children. "The kind of chance interactions that take place in public space also provide a context where children can develop and refine the principles of civility and good citizenship" at an early age and carry it with them into adulthood (Corcoran et al. 2009, 39). As Bennet, Yiannakoulias, Williams, and Kitchen (2012) note, while playgrounds are spaces designed to facilitate the play and interaction of children, certain features may also contribute to the interaction of parents or adult caregivers.

Newer literature in the field of the sociology of childhood has challenged a more passive view of children and argues that children are active agents who can help create and sustain social bonds and social cohesion: Corsair (2005) points out that, "Children are active, creative social agents who produce their own unique children's cultures while simultaneously contributing to the production of adult society" (3).

From this perspective, can we improve social interaction in public space by designing and programming the space to attract some of our youngest citizens? As noted above, the connection between social interaction and the use of public space has been well documented; however, little research has sought to understand the role of children's play in public spaces in facilitating social interaction between parents. Arguably, as children play, parents talk to other parents about ready-made topics of conversation—their children—and a vast amount of shared experience. Studies have demonstrated that positive social relationships are based partly on frequency of face-to-face contact (Bennet, Yiannakoulias, Williams, and Kitchen 2012).

As a result of the interaction between their children, parents have repeated opportunities to meet at these playgrounds and develop relationships not otherwise available to them. While more research needs to be done on this topic, spaces conducive to children's play could be particularly fertile areas in bringing together people from diverse backgrounds and places, potentially increasing social capital and reshaping social interactions.

Dogs and dog parks within public spaces may similarly increase the likelihood of social interaction. According to the Trust for Public Land, the number of dog parks—essentially playgrounds for dogs—grew by close to 90 percent across the United States from 2007–2015, making them the fastest growing type of park in American cities (Dog parks lead growth 2016).

APPLYING THE RESEARCH: A CASE STUDY

Today Downtown Lexington is the economic and cultural center of Central and Appalachian Kentucky, with a reviving art scene, new restaurants and businesses, modern homes, and renovated historic buildings. In the 2017 US Census Estimate, the city's population was 325,813, anchoring a metropolitan area of 506,751 people and a combined statistical area of 723,849. Lexington is the self-proclaimed Horse Capital of the World and a true university city with 43,000-plus students within blocks of downtown. Yet, despite a flurry of downtown development, the downtown corridor remains car centric and, like most of its American peers, it has seen a downward spiral of audiences in its public spaces.

Public Space Public Life Study

In the Spring of 2015, Gehl Arhitect Studios conducted a Public Space Public Life (PSPL) survey to observe and measure public life in downtown Lexington. They looked at where people were staying versus moving through the city, including where they stay, for how long, and what were they doing, and ultimately asked what Lexingtonians want in the public realm.

During weekdays, unlike typical business districts, Lexington has a sociable downtown that sees its highest concentration of people out walking during lunch and after work, rather than the more typical morning and evening rush hours. The weekends see similar rhythms in pedestrian activity with sharp increases in activities around events like the Farmer's Market, followed by stretches of quiet. Overall there is a buzz of activity in downtown Lexington—up to one thousand people an hour on Short Street, comparable to Philadelphia's famous Market Street. But the study found that people were not staying downtown or, as the report noted, people did not stick, particularly in Lexington's public spaces. The study concluded that there are reasons to visit downtown Lexington, but the city should focus on creating reasons for people to stay.

The PSPL study also examined the qualities Lexingtonians cherish most in public space. Distilled from hundreds of pubic responses the following rose to the top, forming the ten core values Lexingtonians aspire for their public spaces: spending time, greenery and trees, family- and kid-friendly environments (less than 5 percent spending time in the downtown are under fourteen years old), opportunities to socialize, quiet and peaceful, spontaneous and unexpected, everyday bicycling, walkability, recreation and play, and hidden gems and discovery.

splashJAM

The City, with the leadership of local nonprofit partners, set out to further explore these ideas through a series of temporary pilot projects. Gehl Studios describes one such project, splashJAM:

> In this sociable city, tuned for college students and young professionals—with great events, an elite basketball team, and a burgeoning restaurant and bar scene—what we heard and observed was a clear need for family-friendly invitations in the city. In particular: there was a latent demand for play and water. The splashJAM—a temporary splash pad in the East End, at the nexus of several neighborhoods, and the gateway to the city—aims to fill this demand, while testing how water-play can bring families together in the public realm, from all parts of the city. (GehlInstitute.org)

Overall splashJAM was resoundingly positive. What started as a forgotten public park became a regional destination, as well as a neighborhood hotspot cherished by families through thoughtful design and programming. The results:

- 85 percent increase in the amount of people walking in the area per hour
- 1000 percent increase in the people staying in the park by hour (from eight people all day to over twenty-three people per hour)
- The stickiness of the park increased from 3 percent to 60 percent (those walking through the park versus staying), with 70 percent spending an hour or more in the space
- The income levels represented ranged from well above the average, to well below, with a great mix of educational attainment, as well.

One in five people visiting the temporary installation said that they interacted with someone they did not plan to meet at the park, and when people had interactions with people they did not plan to meet, the most common connector was their kids. In short, when the kids splashed and played, the caretakers interacted.

The concept was simple: get in, cool off, and splash around for free. That was the inspiration, which soon became a communal spot where parents came to interact while their kids splashed in the water or played on the once deserted playground. Projects like splashJAM show us that programming and design are crucial to making public space inviting, dynamic, and fun. In turn, an inviting, dynamic, and fun space encourages social interaction.

Town Branch Park

Armed with its history, relevant data and a wealth of information, Lexington sets out to create a new public space. The new space will undoubtedly be an improvement over the nine acres of pavement and concrete now occupying prominent real estate in Lexington's urban core. The real question is: Can we also reshape our social interactions and thereby improve the quality of life in Lexington? Through thoughtful design, strategically planned programming, and exceptional management, it aims to try. To achieve this goal, a multidisciplinary team is in place.

Design

SCAPE Studios, a landscape architecture and urban design studio, won the international design competition for Town Branch Commons in 2013. Kate Orff, SCAPE's founder and lead designer, was named a 2017 MacArthur Fellow ("Genius Award"), in large part due to her work on Town Branch Commons. She is the first landscape architect to win this prestigious award. SCAPE's winning proposal is more than just a beautiful new pubic space in downtown Lexington—it revives the hidden ecological system underlying Lexington and honors its geographic heritage. As Orff explained: "Rather than treat landscape as a passive backdrop, I'm trying to design frameworks of engagement that connect people and ecosystems in an immediate and direct way" (MacArthur Foundation 2017). In essence, Orff is using science and sociology to inform the design of the Town Branch Commons.

Programming

Biederman Redevelopment Ventures (BRV) is assisting with a comprehensive programming plan for the park that complements the design, honors the history of the space, and ensures the park attracts varied users every day of the year. The goal is to overlay the design with a comprehensive plan for active and interactive programming that brings life to the space and invites everyday users to stay. Dan Biederman, president of BRV, is best known for turning around Bryant Park, New York's most desolate and dangerous park of the 70s and the front door of the New York Public Library. Now one of the most actively used parks in the world, Bryant Park has become an international model of urban revitalization, catering to visitors twelve months a year.

Governance

This is Lexington's first venture into a public-private partnership of this magnitude. The City is leading the trail portion of the project, which is fully funded with construction scheduled to begin in 2018. On the private side, the local community foundation and a number of civic leaders and philanthropists joined together to create Town Branch Fund, which oversees the fundraising, design, and programming plan for the park. The Fund's Board of Advisors and staff are working to transform a nine-acre parking lot into Town Branch Park and incubate a nonprofit that will ultimately operate and manage the park. Public-private partnerships such as that proposed for this park are a proven model used by some of our nation's most prominent parks, but it will require a community effort, the likes of which have never been seen in Lexington, and a keen focus to ensure the space is designed, programmed, and managed in a way that invites all of Lexington to come visit and stay in the park.

Equity

Town Branch Park, like similar public space projects across the country, will bring lasting physical enhancements to Lexington's urban core, but will these changes come at a price for those living in its surroundings? Successfully creating a vibrant sense of place that encourages social interaction and increases social capital will require that the intended improvements are sensitively designed, programmed, and managed so that citizens from all over the city and beyond feel the park is inviting, safe, and accessible.

To this end, Town Branch Fund launched the Town Branch Partners, a dedicated group of local leaders in their respective professions serving as advisors to the Town Board and staff. By developing a set of shared principles, Town Branch Partners will review the park design, programming, and operations through the lens of equity, fairness, compliance, and inclusion.

Fundraising

Designing, building, and managing a world class park will require substantial private investment. In 2016, Town Branch Fund completed an extensive fundraising feasibility study that showed Lexington has the affinity and capacity to build a $31 million park. Private donations will complement the City's public investment of the land and the federal, state, and local grants of approximately $35 million already in hand to build the trail section, allowing the Fund to finalize the design and engineering and construct Town Branch Park.

CONCLUSION

The Town Branch Commons Project has been built on public input, and the Town Branch Fund will continue to seek insight from residents in all corners of Lexington as it furthers the design and programming plan. As a collective effort, it became apparent that the Park could be more than just a new public space. As part of a much larger effort involving multiple stakeholders, Town Branch Fund is changing how urban development occurs. In addition to creating a world-class space, the Town Branch Commons project seeks to transform the way Lexington designs and programs new and existing civic infrastructure, always with a goal of increasing social interaction and thereby improving the quality of life in Lexington.

Bibliography

Abdel-Aziz, A. A., H. Abdel-Salam, and Z. El-Sayad. *"The Role of ICTs in Creating the New Social Public Place of the Digital Era."* Alexandria Engineering Journal 55, no. 1 (2016): 487–93.

"A Comparison of Theories of Social Capital by Pierre Bourdieu and James Coleman." Bartleby. Last accessed January 26, 2018. https://www.bartleby.com/essay/ A-Comparison-of-Theories-of-Social-Capital-PK9UHNZTC.

Allan, Kenneth. *Explorations in Classical Sociological Theory: Seeing the Social World.* Pine Forge Press, 2005.

Amin, Ash. *"Public Space: Collective Culture and Urban Public Space."* public space. 2006. Last accessed January 29, 2018. http://www.publicspace.org/en/text-library/eng/b003-collective-culture-and-urban-public-space.

———. *"Collective Culture and Urban Public Space."* City 12, no. 1 (2008): 5–24.

Appler, Douglas., James Allen, Anton Fatah, Juan Fernandez-Cantero, Thomas Grubbs, Hyo Lee, Jennifer McCabe, Katie McNamee, Alexis Peneff, Christina Sabol, and Katie Wilborn. *"Interpreting Downtown Lexington's Town Branch History."* University of Kentucky's Historic Preservation Planning Class. 2016. https://www.town-branchcommons.org/wp-content/uploads/2017/07/History-of-Town-Branch.pdf

Bennet, S. A., N. Yiannakoulias, A.M. Williams, and P. Kitchen. *"Playground Accessibility and Neighbourhood Social Interaction Among Parents."* Social Indicators Research 108, no. 2 (2012): 199–213.

Carr, Stephen, Mark Francis, Leanne G. Rivlin, and Andrew M. Stone. *Public Space.* Cambridge: Cambridge University Press, 1993.

Cole, P. N. "Understanding Emile Durkheim's *"Collective Consciousness."* Last accessed January 29, 2018. https://www.thoughtco.com/collective-consciousness-definition-3026118.

Corsaro, William. *The Sociology of Childhood*, 2nd ed. Thousand Oaks CA: Pine Forge Press, 2005.

Corcoran, Mary, Jane Gray, and Michel Peillon. *"Making Space for Sociability: How Children Animate the Public Realm in Suburbia."* Nature and Culture 4, no. 1 (2009).

Cortright, Joe. "City Report: Less in Common." City Obervatory. June 2015. Last accessed January 29, 2018. http://cityobservatory.org/wp-content/files/CityObservatory_Less_In_Common.pdf

"Dog Parks Lead Growth in Urban Parks." The Trust for Public Lang. April 25, 2016. https://www.tpl.org/media-room/dog-parks-lead-growth-urban-parks/

Durkheim, Emile. *The Division of Labor in Society.* New York: Macmillan, 1933.

Gehl, Jan. *Cities for People.* Washington, D.C.: Island Press, 2013.

———. *Life Between Buildings: Using Public Space.* Washington, D.C.: Island Press, 2007.

Ijla, M. *"Does Public Space Create Social Capital?"* International Journal of Sociology and Anthropology 4, no. 2 (2012): 48–53.

"Landscape Architect Kate Orff, 2017 MacArthur Fellow." MacArthur Foundation. October, 11, 2017. https://www.macfound.org/videos/557/.

Merkin, Zina. *"The Disappearance of Town Branch."* November 2001. Last accessed January 29, 2018. https://www.townbranch.org/doc/The-Disapearance-of-Town-Branch.pdf.

"On the Table: Fact Sheet." Blue Grass Community Foundation. 2018. https://www.bgcf.org/onthetable-fact-sheet-2018.pdf

Pettit, V. M. *"Founding of Lexington along the Elkhorn Creek."* Town Branch Trail. February 13, 2008. http://www.townbranch.org/info/2008/02/13/founding-of-lexington-along-the-elkhorn-creek/.

Putnam, R. D. *Bowling Alone: The Collapse and Revival of American Community.* NewYork, NY: Simon & Schuster, 2000.

Ranck, G. W. *History of Lexington, Kentucky.* New York: Nabu Press, 2010.

Smith, M. K. *"Robert Putnam, Social Capital and Civic Community."* infed. February 4, 2013. Last accessed January 22, 2018. http://infed.org/mobi/robert-putnam-social-capital-and-civic-community/.

"SplashJam as a Catalyst for Play." Gehl Institute. https://GehlInstitute.org/work/splash-jam-pilot/.

"Technology Brings People Together in Public Spaces After All." pps. 2014. Last accessed January 26, 2018. https://www.townbranch.org/doc/The-Disapearance-of-Town-Branch.pdf.

Toloudi, Z. *"Are we in the Midst of a Public Space Crisis?"* The Conversation. June 7, 2016. https://theconversation.com/are-we-in-the-midst-of-a-public-space-crisis-56124.

Tonnelat, S. *"The Sociology of Urban Public Spaces."* In Territorial Evolution and Planning Solution: Experiences From China and France : Proceedings of The First Sino-French Urban, Regional and Planning Symposium, edited by Hongyang Wang, Michel Savy, and Guofany, Zhai. Paris: Atlantic Press, 2010.

"What is Placemaking?" Project for Public Spaces. https://www.pps.org/article/what-is-placemaking.

Wiesemann, Lars. *Public Spaces, Social Interaction and the Negotiation of Difference.* Amsterdam, 2011.

Wright, J.D. *Lexington: Heart of the Bluegrass.* Lexington, KY: University Press of Kentucky, 1992.

Surviving Domestic Violence from the Survivor's Perspective

Giovanna Gomez Collins, LCSW

*Of all the things trauma takes away from us, the worst
is our willingness, or even our ability to be vulnerable.*
—Brené Brown

AMELIA AND HER husband have been married for eleven years. By her account, the early part of her marriage had been like a fairy tale. Roberto was her high school sweetheart and was the kindest, most attentive, and most protective guy she had ever dated. When they first started dating, Roberto was fond of telling her she was the most beautiful, sexy, and wonderful girl in the world. He proposed to her on the day of their high school graduation and they married six months later. Shortly after they got married, Amelia and Roberto immigrated to the United States from their home town of Veracruz, Mexico. Despite the difficulties they had when they first moved to the states, Roberto spoke English well and found a good job. Amelia hoped that she would learn English and get a job as well so that they could buy a home together someday.

Amelia had always wanted a family, and her dream was coming true. Their first son, Hugo, was born almost exactly on their one year anniversary, and Daniel was born two years later. However, Amelia's dream life became more stressful than she had ever imagined. Roberto started coming home later than usual. One day Amelia smelled alcohol on his breath. Roberto knew Amelia was not a fan of alcohol. Drinking quickly became a daily occurrence, a habit that he had picked up seemingly overnight. "Why was he drinking all of a sudden?" she wondered. Amelia observed Roberto's attitude begin to change.

He no longer wanted to spend time with her after work. He went straight for the living room to watch the sports until dinner time. Roberto used to appreciate Amelia's cooking, until one day when he came home noticeably drunk, and he said dinner tasted awful. Amelia was perplexed. She started to wonder if she had forgotten to add a key ingredient to the meal. Roberto had never criticized her that way. For the next three years, Amelia worked hard to ease the growing tension between them by only preparing meals she knew he liked and staying quiet until he was sober again.

Roberto used to adore her, even idolize her. He told Amelia he could not bear to let her be swept up by another man; he would need to catch her before anyone else could. Amelia was overwhelmed with Roberto's romantic gestures. He brought her flowers every week and bought her expensive gifts when they were dating. Amelia thought to herself, "He is the man of my dreams. He wants me with him all the time, and he treats me like a queen." Soon after the wedding, Amelia was spending all of her free time with Roberto, so much so that she missed out saying goodbye to much of her family and friends when they moved to the United States.

Once they arrived in the United States, there was little time to make new friends. Roberto also convinced Amelia to stay home with him instead of going to church on Sundays by using passages from the Bible, telling her it was her duty as a wife to honor his wishes. Amelia was homesick, and had no one to talk to, but told herself she was happy with the way things were as long as Roberto was happy. Once both kids started school, Amelia started working at a restaurant, but Roberto told her to quit weeks later because he said too many men frequent that restaurant. Although Amelia thought they could use the extra money for savings and for the kids, Roberto assured her he would provide for all their needs and she would never need to work. Amelia was a little disappointed because she liked her job, but thought it was for the best.

Slowly the flowers and gifts became less frequent. Amelia didn't mind. She was sure of Roberto's love for her. She also knew that Roberto was stressed at work. Roberto started complaining of frequent headaches. Amelia did her best to make him comfortable while at home, but the heavy drinking bothered her. One night she decided to have a talk with Roberto to ask him to drink a little less. Before they were married, Amelia had never seen him drink, and she remembered distinctly telling Roberto she did not want to marry someone who drinks. She was so surprised when he started smelling of alcohol that she was not sure what to do. With all the stress from work over the years, Roberto had become very cranky and irritable, often yelling at her and the kids for no reason. Amelia wanted to make sure to broach the topic gently to avoid upsetting him. Amelia practiced what she would say a few times before dinner and then decided to talk to him while they were getting ready for bed.

As soon as Amelia opened her mouth to speak, Roberto turned over on the bed facing away from her. Amelia felt ignored but immediately dismissed her thought. "Maybe he's just really tired and didn't realize I wanted to speak," she thought. But the tension at home was becoming unbearable, and she knew she had to say something. As she leaned closer and said his name, Roberto suddenly turned around and slapped Amelia on the face. He said to her, "How dare you wake me up, you stupid bitch! Don't you know I have to work tomorrow? Of course not; you do nothing all day. You have no idea what's it is like."

Amelia's tears streamed down her face and the shock lingered for several minutes. Nothing like this had ever happened to her. "What just happened?" she thought. She wasn't sure if it really happened or if it was her imagination. Amelia felt the sting on her face for what felt like hours. She tried to sleep but instead was sobbing softly into her pillow. She woke up the next day and looked in the bathroom mirror; there were no marks on her face, but her eyes were puffy from crying and lack of sleep. This was not the man she had married. He was not his usual self. Amelia thought for sure it was because of alcohol that he was behaving this way. Amelia thought, "I have to find a way to encourage him to stop drinking."

It was Amelia's next-door neighbor, the only friend Roberto allowed her to have, who encouraged her to seek help. Amelia called the number to the county government's domestic violence services program, hoping for marriage counseling. The office assistant explained that the program was for victims of domestic violence only and that for safety reasons, the program did not offer marriage counseling. The word, "victim," gave Amelia pause. "Victim?" she thought. "I didn't know I was a victim." Although hesitant, she decided to attend her first appointment. It was a struggle to make it there on time, all the way across town, but she managed to get there. Amelia sat in the waiting area for a few minutes and filled out the application as best as she could, unsure how to answer some of the questions.

A bilingual licensed clinical social worker offered to help Amelia with the application in her office. The social worker's first question was, "What brings you here today?" Amelia, unable to maintain her composure, started to cry: "My life is falling apart. My marriage is not what it used to be and I don't understand why." The social worker provided a brief silence and then stated, "Tell me whatever you feel comfortable telling me. What we discuss in here is confidential." The social worker then explained the limits to confidentiality and her rights as a client of the agency.

Amelia soon started sharing details of the disturbing changes in her husband, and as she sat in the room, she wondered, "Is it true that because my husband slapped me that I am a victim? Didn't I upset him? Wasn't I at least partly responsible for what happened? Then she said to the social worker, "Honestly, I don't think my husband is abusive. He only hit me once. If he would just stop drinking, I know he would come to his senses and stop treating us badly." The social worker listened carefully, stating, "I hear you. I think this program will help you understand what is going on and how to work through your situation."

Amelia immediately felt calmer. For some reason, she worried that if she stated her husband was abusive, that would backfire on her in some way. Amelia felt better during that conversation than she had felt in several months. After a few more questions, the social worker asked Amelia if she had any safety concerns, if it was safe to call her, and if she was experiencing thoughts of harming herself or anyone else. Amelia stated she felt sad at times but would never harm herself or anyone else, because she loves her children and she could never abandon them. Amelia also had strong faith in God and prayed that He would either help her get through this situation or help her husband change. The social worker recommended brief individual therapy for Amelia and scheduled her first counseling session for two weeks later.

When Roberto came home that day, he told Amelia his boss was having a party at his home for the employees and their families. That weekend, they all went to the party. Amelia noticed that Roberto had no alcohol to drink that night, perhaps because he wanted to be on his best behavior in front of his boss. Roberto was pleasant the entire evening and the children had a great time. It was the first time in months that the whole family had fun together. Amelia thought, "Thank you, Lord. Perhaps he will change after all." Amelia felt so happy and told Roberto, "We had such a good time tonight, didn't we? Like old times. I really wish you wouldn't drink. You really upset me the other night." Roberto put his arm around her and held her, saying, "I was stressed that day. I didn't mean to hurt you. I drink to take the edge off. I promise I'll never hurt you again." Amelia was overjoyed to hear those words from her husband. She thought, "If Roberto keeps up this attitude, I won't need counseling services. I'm not a victim. We just had one incident, an argument. Married couples argue, don't they?" Amelia missed her first counseling appointment.

As the weeks progressed, Amelia's hope diminished. Roberto went back to drinking daily, even more than before. Any noise the children made angered him. The children started spending more time in their room to avoid their dad. Amelia was heartbroken. Her dream life was becoming a nightmare again. Amelia started researching stress management and encouraged Roberto to try those methods instead of drinking. Roberto reacted to Amelia with comments like, "Are you a doctor now? What makes you think you know anything? You don't even know how to raise your own kids. Stop trying to tell me how to live my life!" After weeks of insults from Roberto, Amelia's hurt turned into anger. She decided to store his beer in the garage so that it would be warm and maybe he would choose not to drink the next day.

Roberto was enraged to see his beer missing from the fridge. Roberto started smashing things in his path and yelled at the top of his lungs, "You whore! You stole my beer! Who the f**k do you think you are? This is my house. You can't just take whatever you want. Since you have no respect for my things, you can leave! Get out of my house now!" Roberto shoved Amelia out of the apartment and locked the door. Amelia knocked on the door vigorously, begging Roberto to let her inside. The neighbors could hear and some looked on and said nothing. Amelia's next door neighbor walked outside and asked what was going on. Amelia wiped her face and said, "I had just stepped out to get something from the car and didn't see when Roberto got home. He locked the door out of habit and now he can't find where he put the keys. He'll open the door soon." Amelia's account made no sense to her neighbor, but she sensed Amelia did not want any help, so she went back inside. Amelia prayed Roberto would open the door before dark. She wished he had her phone so that she could at least call a locksmith or something, but she would just have to wait.

About an hour later, Roberto unlocked the door and said firmly, "Let that teach you a lesson. Never grab my things without permission. I found where you hid the beer. That was a stupid thing to do. Hurry up and make dinner." After that day, Amelia kept her phone in her pocket at all times. Roberto continued to threaten Amelia with kicking her out of the house. He locked her out three more times and never gave a reason. Each time Amelia had her phone, and each time, just as she was about to dial 911, Roberto would open the door. The fifth time was the final straw. She waited for hours in the car with the boys. Roberto had never kicked out the children until now. Amelia knew she had to call the police for her children.

One January morning, I, the bilingual clinical social worker, received a referral from the local domestic violence shelter. I scanned the form and noticed a familiar name—the client who missed her first counseling session the previous month. She and her two sons were now living at the shelter. I called the number on the form and immediately recognized her voice. Amelia, a mother of two young boys, had been locked out of their home. Her voice was trembling and almost inaudible. She said she and her sons slept in the van that night. Amelia said she called 911 the next morning to see if the police could convince her husband to let her and the kids back in the house. Instead, the police arrested her husband and encouraged her to pack an overnight bag and go to the shelter. Amelia's fatigue and embarrassment were evident in her voice. She was not prepared for the police to arrest her husband or live in a shelter; she knew she needed help to process what had happened and to figure out what to do next.

DISCUSSING DOMESTIC VIOLENCE WITH SURVIVORS

Like many in her situation, Amelia did not know that her problem had a name. For many people, domestic violence, domestic abuse, or intimate partner violence are familiar terms, but most lack knowledge and understanding of what those terms mean. Many organizations, human services agencies, advocates, and survivors have called for the use of the term intimate partner violence, which more closely describes the issue of mistreatment of an intimate partner, such as a boyfriend/girlfriend relationship, spouse, ex-spouse, or date.

Although there are certain distinctions among the terms, depending on the legal definition and the jurisdictions in which they are used, for the purpose of maintaining clarity throughout this article, I will use the term domestic violence. Although the criminal nature of domestic violence is not the focus of this article, it is important to note that throughout the United States and many other nations, domestic violence is considered a crime. Although laws and protections for victims of violent crime vary among jurisdictions, United States federal laws, such as the Gun Control Act and the Violence Against Women Act of 1996, outline protections and rights of all victims of domestic violence (U.S. Department of Justice).

Domestic violence refers to any intentional act used to maintain power and control over a current or past intimate partner. Examples of intimate partners include boyfriend/girlfriend relationships, partners who live together, spouses, or persons who have children together. Intimate partner violence is a learned pattern of behavior. The Power and Control Wheel (Duluth Model) illustrates the tactics and behaviors used by abusers to gain and maintain power and control in the relationship. In the case example above, the perpetrator used virtually all of the tactics of the Power and Control Wheel: coercion and threats, intimidation, economic abuse, emotional abuse, privilege, use of the children, isolation, and minimizing, denying, and blaming (theduluthmodel.org).

As a social worker in the mental health field, part of my role is to provide psycho-education, which refers to the information clients and their families use to empower themselves to deal with their presenting problem. Learning these concepts is often very eye-opening to clients. For Amelia, and many other clients, realizing that she was in an abusive relationship was a process. At first Amelia denied that her relationship was abusive. Part of the reason many survivors do not recognize an abusive is relationship is lack of information. Many people believe domestic violence only involves physical or sexual abuse. In nearly every case of domestic violence, abuse escalates gradually and starts with emotional abuse (insults, criticism, withdrawing, name-calling, etc.) Usually the abuse is subtle at first and often dismissed as a joke or playfulness.

Then a pattern of escalation develops that is no longer easy to ignore. The wounds from emotional abuse usually last much longer than the ones from physical abuse. There is also limited awareness about what constitutes abuse. For instance, Amelia did not consider shoving, being locked in a room, or being restrained to be physical violence until we had our first counseling session together. Even lack of affection can be considered a form of physical abuse if the non-offending partner identifies it as pattern of behavior by the offending partner to gain power and/or control (refuge.org).

Another essential part of my job as a clinician working with survivors of domestic violence is using a trauma-informed approach to unpacking the issues of domestic violence, known as trauma-informed care. Understanding the impact of trauma on survivors and providers is crucial to providing quality services to clients. Domestic violence is a traumatic experience that can lead to mental health conditions associated with trauma, such as anxiety, depression and posttraumatic stress disorder. Many clients have reported feeling depressed, sad, lonely, confused, disillusioned, angry, guilty, and ashamed. Many clients also report having nightmares, flashbacks, reduced sleep quality, changes in diet, lack of interest in activities once enjoyed, memory loss, trouble concentrating, and hyper arousal, all of which are symptoms associated with trauma and PTSD (National Center on Domestic Violence, Trauma and Mental Health 2011).

Trauma-informed care involves not only knowledge and understanding of trauma and its effects on survivors but also the use of culturally-sensitive and empathic language. Amelia did not identify with being a victim. In society, the term *victim* has negative connotations. Many people think victims, particularly women who are victims of crime, are considered fragile or helpless. Nothing was further from the truth for Amelia. She endured a vicious pattern of abuse for years driven by the belief that she needed to save her marriage. She loved and believed in her husband. She was a religious woman who believed marriage was forever, and she thought she was doing the right thing for her children.

She believed that separating from her husband would cause financial strain that her children did not deserve. They were used to a certain lifestyle that they no longer had at the shelter. Amelia was angry at herself for calling the police. She thought if she could have tolerated the abuse just a little longer, she could have found a way to convince her husband to change. For this reason, I avoid the term *victim* and prefer a strengths-based approach with clients. I call them survivors, because survival is a better reflection of their experience. The term *victim* is commonplace because of the criminal aspect of domestic violence but often fails to validate the clients' traumatic experience.

Amelia had no prior experience with domestic violence before she met her husband. She had grown up with both parents and four siblings. All of Amelia's basic needs were met growing up. She had never been abused as a child. Roberto, however, had witnessed domestic violence. Roberto's father was an alcoholic who beat his mother mercilessly as Roberto and his brothers watched in fear, helpless to do anything. Witnessing domestic violence as a child is a risk factor for becoming either a victim or a perpetrator of abuse. Brown et al. (2009) found through the Adverse Childhood Experiences Study conducted from 1995–1997 that the extent to which a person is exposed to abuse, or household dysfunction, during childhood increases the risk of several leading causes of death in adults. Roberto had not been a heavy drinker in his youth, but his life experiences and high levels of stress may have lead Roberto to use alcohol to escape his problems.

After discussing what domestic violence is, it is important to also address what domestic violence is not. Although many factors can contribute to the perpetuation of violence, many misconceptions exist about what causes and perpetuates domestic violence. In the case of Amelia, she believed wholeheartedly that drugs and alcohol caused domestic violence. While it is easy to understand why Amelia would associate substance abuse with domestic violence, drinking is not the reason Roberto abused Amelia.

I began exploring with Amelia moments in the patterns of abuse in the relationship to help her understand the relationship between substance abuse and the abuse she was experiencing. Amelia began to understand that domestic violence is learned behavior, and it is a pattern. Drinking may have influenced Roberto's behavior, but Amelia soon realized that ultimately abusing an intimate partner is a conscious choice, and the purpose of abuse is to gain power and control of one's intimate partner. An additional myth many people believe is that survivors stay in abusive relationships because they chose to stay (refuge.org).

Others believe only men are perpetrators of domestic violence. All of these myths serve to blame survivors of domestic violence and rationalize the behaviors of the perpetrators. Fallacies such as these are well documented throughout history and continue to spread to this day. The social media, news, films, music, and pop culture we consume are infused with messages of gender-based violence, classism, racism, homophobia, and other forms of systemic and structural injustice. Domestic violence, after all, stems from a history of oppression. Any form of injustice that exists will continue to justify and perpetuate domestic violence, as they are all have the same goal: to gain power and control (refuge.org).

As Amelia completed more therapy sessions, she learned gradually to recognize the types of abuse she was experiencing, the patterns of the abuse, how the abuse escalated over time, the characteristics of abusers, and the reasons why she stayed. Amelia had been feeling extremely guilty for separating her children from their father by going to the shelter. However, Amelia remembered how scared and withdrawn her children had become at home. At the shelter, the children did not want to socialize with other children, Hugo's grades were slipping, and he was becoming more irritable.

Daniel was becoming hyperactive and getting in trouble at day care. Amelia understood that sometimes a situation gets worse before it gets better. She started putting the pieces of the puzzle together. She was beginning to accept that she is a survivor of domestic violence. She concluded for herself that going to the domestic violence shelter was the right decision for her family, as difficult as it was to admit. For Amelia and the kids, life at the shelter has been very stressful. She contemplated going back home to reconcile with her husband many times. During a recent session, I asked her what she wanted for her future, and she responded, "a violence-free home."

Amelia is now working a full-time job and is saving money to get a place of her own. She requested counseling services for her children, as she could see that they needed help as much as she did. With therapy Amelia is working through some grief and loss of the hopes and dreams she had for her family. She is also learning healthy ways to cope and relaxation skills, working to increase her self-esteem, learning how to advocate for herself, and working on her safety plan continually. Amelia is not interested in starting a new relationship anytime soon, but she is learning about how to establish healthy boundaries with others so that she can have healthy relationships in general. Committing to therapy, starting a new job, searching for a new home, and adjusting to life at the shelter, all while trying to manage mixed emotions has been extremely challenging for her. Nevertheless she has persisted. Amelia would do anything for her kids, and she is learning that her safety and her well-being are the best gifts she can give them.

Despite the prevalence of domestic violence, each survivor has a unique story to tell. Each survivor deserves to be heard, and each one is worthy of vulnerability. When a person lives in fear or is under the threat of danger for any length of time, they are no longer free to be vulnerable. They must adapt to their environment in whatever way they can to survive in it. By providing a compassionate, nurturing, secure space, I hope to help Amelia and many others regain their sense of self by channeling their vulnerability. I intend to help them to close the chapter of past abuse and open a new chapter of hopes, dreams, and possibilities.

Bibliography

Brown, D. W., R. F. Anda, H. Tiemeier, V. J. Felitti, J. B. Croft, and W. H. Giles. *"Adverse Childhood Experiences and the Risk of Premature Mortality."* American Journal of Preventive Medicine 37, no. 5 (2009): 389–96.

"Tip Sheet." National Center on Domestic Violence, Trauma, and Mental Health. 2011. https://www.nationalcenterdvtraumamh.org/wp-content/uploads/2012/01/Tipsheet_T1-DV-Advocacy_NCDVTMH_Aug2011.pdf.

"*Myths About Domestic Violence.*" Refuge.org. https://www.refuge.org.uk/our-work/forms-of-violence-and-abuse/

U.S. Department of Justice, Bureau of Alcohol, Tobacco and Firearms. *Gun Control Act.* Available at: https://www.atf.gov/rules-and-regulations/gun-control-act

_____. Office of Violence Against Women. *Violence Against Women Act.* Available at: https://www.gallaudet.edu/title-ix-at-gallaudet-university/violence-against-women-act

"*What is the Duluth Model?*" https://www.theduluthmodel.org/what-is-%20the-duluth-model/

The Socialization of the Police

Robert H. McNamara, PhD

THE CONCEPT OF socialization has been subjected to extensive analysis with the definitions of the concept varying widely. Generally speaking, we can say the term socialization is used to describe the ways in which people learn to conform to their society's norms, values, and roles. Many sociologists contend that people develop their own unique personalities as a result of the learning they gain from parents, siblings, relatives, teachers, and all the other people who influence them throughout their lives (Elkin and Handel 1989). What is important about socialization is that people learn to behave according to the expectations of their culture and transmit that way of life from one generation to the next. In this way, the culture of a society is reproduced (Parsons and Bales 1955; Danziger 1971).

It is also important to note that socialization occurs throughout an individual's life as he or she learns the norms of new groups in new situations. Generally speaking, there are three categories of socialization: primary, which involves the ways in which the child becomes a part of society; secondary, where the influence of others outside the family becomes important; and adult socialization, when the person learns the expectations of adult roles and statuses in society. This latter socialization includes learning the standards set by one's occupation.

THE SOCIALIZATION PROCESS IN OCCUPATIONS

Of the many roles that a person is called upon to perform, few surpass the importance of possessing the skills and attitudes necessary for one's occupation. This is especially true in modern society where occupation has a central place in the life of the vast majority of adults. In fact, occupation is challenged only by the family and the peer group as the major determinant of behavior and attitudes (Moore 1969). To the degree that adequate socialization occurs to permit one to adequately perform in an occupation, an individual's worldview, attitudes towards others, and general well-being are influenced.

Interestingly, occupational socialization has not elicited the kind of scholarly interest that one might expect. While there are many studies on this topic, academic interest in socialization traditionally focused on infancy and childhood. It has only been within the last thirty years or so that research-ers have become keenly interested in occupational socialization, or what is sometimes referred to as the sociology of work (Erikson 1995). And the topics seem to focus on the normative dimensions of occupations—that is, the rules relating to the proper conduct and attitudes of an individual in a particular job or career occupation.

For instance, in a classic study of socialization into an occupation, Becker, Greer, Hughes, and Strauss (1961) examined the process by which medical stu-dents are socialized into their profession. At the University of Kansas Medical School, Becker found that lower-class medical students, by virtue of their under-graduate education and commitment to becoming successful physicians, had clearly assimilated middle-class norms and values. Becker also found that first year medical students had idealistic reasons for becoming a physician: helping people was more important than making money. In the beginning of their profession, then, there is a strong sense of idealism and many students felt that medical school would give them the opportunity to develop the skills needed to further that goal.

However, the process of medical training caused the students to alter their views. Early on, they adapted to the expectations of medical school and devel-oped a strong appreciation of clinical experience (working with patients rather than reading about disease and studying it in the laboratory). They also learned to view disease and death as medical problems rather than as emotional issues. Additionally, despite their idealism, students in medical school quickly learned that they could not learn everything they need to know to practice medicine and soon directed their efforts toward finding the most economical way of learning. Generally this meant guessing what their faculty wanted them to know so that the material could be studied for the examinations.

During the course of their medical training, idealism was replaced with a con-cern for getting through the program. Becker observed that medical students may in fact become cynical while in school, but he pointed out that these attitudes are often situational. As graduation approached, idealism seemed to return once the students were no longer under the intense pressure to perform. The immediate problem of completing their studies had passed. The lesson then is that, when isolated in an institutional setting, the students adjusted to immediate demands. Once released from that setting, their attitudes changed to again conform to their new surroundings.

The broader implications of Becker's work are that individuals will be socialized to meet the expectations that important institutions or organizations place on them. Their attitudes, values, and beliefs will become centered around fulfilling those expectations. In the case of the physician, where there is a great deal of autonomy, the original ideological concerns reemerge at the end of their training, largely because they have the ability to determine what type of medicine they will practice and under what circumstances. In those professions where there is an intense training period, less autonomy, and greater internal control by the organization, the more the individual is greatly influenced by the members of that organization.

In other words, where there is greater freedom to practice one's profession, there is less of an impact in terms of the socialization process. However, in those professions where the individual is constrained by organizational rules and regulations, the more influential other members are on the thoughts and actions of the individual. This is exacerbated in professions that actively promote a sense of camaraderie and solidarity among their members.

Resocialization

Perhaps the most significant aspect of the socialization process is that members within an organization (or, more broadly, within a society) internalize a set of norms that dictate appropriate behavior. When this fails to occur, the organization is forced to employ corrective methods to ensure conformity. Examples include deviants or criminals. Other people are resocialized because of a decision to join a new group. A good example of this occurs when an individual selects a particular career, such as soldier or police officer. It is here that the work of Erving Goffman plays a significant part in our understanding of resocialization. In his now classic *Asylums*, Goffman (1961) contends that the resocialization of individuals often occurs in what he calls total institutions.

These are places where the individual's physical and social freedom are constrained and channeled in a certain direction. Goffman describes resocialization as a two-step process. First, there is what he calls *the mortification of the self*, where the attitudes, worldviews, and behavior patterns of the individual are stripped away. This paves the way for the second step in resocialization, where a new set of attitudes, values, and beliefs are provided. For instance, in the case of the military, the new recruit or civilian is brought to a camp and stripped of any individual characteristics: clothes are taken away, haircuts are given, and rules on every aspect of life in the institution are explained.

It is during this process that the sense of self gives way and the individual becomes a cog in a much larger machine. Only after this process is complete can the organization implement the second part of the resocialization process. Upon completion of boot camp, the recruit has a different sense of self, along with a new set of attitudes and behavior patterns. A similar process occurs in law enforcement. After selection, the police academy (also often considered to be a type of total institution), represents the first overt process of socialization.

In addition to the skills and techniques needed to become an effective police officer, recruits are indoctrinated and exposed to the vernacular used by members and the cultural norms dictating acceptable and unacceptable behavior, as well as the worldview from the law enforcement perspective. In addition, these values, attitudes, and beliefs are reinforced informally as new officers interact with more experienced ones outside of the classroom. The "war stories" told by more seasoned officers reinforce the point made by the formal classroom lessons. Over time, recruits develop attitudes and behaviors that provide a consistent framework in which to understand the role of the police and the individual officer (Radelet 1986).

This process continues after the academy, when the officer is usually assigned some sort of field training. The time spent in this phase of training varies by department but can be up to six months. The field training officer (FTO) is responsible for teaching the new officer how to apply lessons from the academy to the tasks on the street. There is also an evaluative component to the process in that the FTO is charting the progress (or lack thereof) of the recruit. The style of the FTO, as well as the way in which the FTO interacts with citizens, will tend to be reflected in the recruit's behavior. In this way, FTO training is a part of the socialization process even though it may not be a conscious process (Radelet 1986).

After FTO training, the officer remains on probation for a period of time, usually one year. During this time, a supervisor evaluates the officer in terms of progress and overall performance in the job. As described by Becker, Greer, Hughes, and Strauss (1961), most recruits will admit that part of the learning process involves knowing the unique expectations their supervisor/teacher has for them. When this is learned, the officer will modify his or her behavior to conform with that of the supervisor (Becker, Greer, Hughes, and Strauss 1961; Radelet 1986). If, for instance, the officer learns that the sergeant places a great deal of emphasis on police-community relations, the officer will, in turn, have more community contacts. These learned behaviors are part of what Goffman (1961) refers to as working the system. More importantly, these behaviors are the essence of occupational socialization.

For the most part, this is a normal part of the learning process. In order to be an effective police officer, the rookie officer must first learn the tricks of the trade and the most knowledgeable officers should impart their wisdom on their less learned colleagues. However, there is also the potential for various forms of misconduct to be taught in addition to the proper procedures and attitudes.

NATURE VS. NURTURE

In 1991 Los Angeles police officers shocked the American public with the beating of Rodney King. In 1996 a South Carolina state trooper assaulted a motorist while she attempted to exit her vehicle after a traffic stop. Also in 1996, Los Angeles area officers were accused of assaulting Hispanic motorists after a prolonged pursuit. In more recent times, there have been a host of incidents, some of which have been captured on video, where officers have used excessive force on suspects. Notorious cases include the Michael Brown case in Ferguson, Missouri (USAtoday. com 2014), the Eric Garner case in New York (Apuzzo, 2018), the case of Freddie Gray in Baltimore, Maryland (Rector, 2017), and the Laquan McDonald incident in Chicago (Husain, 2017). Incidents like these raise many questions concerning the attitudes, values, and behavior of police officers around the country. Social scientists have offered differing and sometimes conflicting explanations for police use of authority and misconduct.

Some contend that police officers have very different personalities than people in other occupations. Others maintain that there is a cultural distinction that separates law enforcement from other occupations. Still others contend that officers have neither personality nor cultural differences from other occupations. In sum, what we know about the police culture and personality is dependent on how one views police behavior. While no single perspective provides a complete understanding of the varieties of police behavior, there is a long history of debate as to whether they have unique personalities or whether socialization and subcultures play a significant part in the behavior of police officers. What can be said with some confidence is that the roles and functions of the police set officers apart from other members of society (Radelet 1986).

THE SOCIALIZATION ARGUMENT

A number of researchers argue that personality is not fixed and rigid and is subject to change based on different personal experiences and socialization. This school of thought focuses on the role of the police in society and how professionalization, training, and socialization influence an individual's personality and behavior. Researchers operating from this paradigm study how the work environment, peers, and academy training shape and affect a police officer's personality and behavior. Many of these researchers, such as Adlam (1982), still focus attention on an individual's unique experiences and the development of individual personalities.

A somewhat different approach contends that socialization occurs, but it is more of a group experience than an individual one (Stoddard 1968; Van Maanen 1978).

For example, Van Maanen (1978) disagrees with the idea that police officers have certain personality characteristics, such as authoritarianism. He argues instead for a perspective based on both group socialization and professionalism. The latter is the process by which norms and values are internalized as an individual begins his or her new occupation. In this way, just as attorneys and physicians learn the values endemic to their profession, so too do police officers.

This perspective assumes that police officers learn their social personality from training and through exposure to the demands of police work. It follows then that if police officers become cynical or rigid, it is not because of their existing personality or individual experience, but because of the demands of the job and the shared experiences of others. Some research supports this idea. For instance, Bennett (1984) found that while probationary officers' values are affected by the training process, little evidence is available that personalities are shaped by their peers in the department. Part of this explanation involves the legitimacy of newly hired officers, who do not become 'real' police officers until they are accepted as a member in standing of the police subculture.

Other studies, such as Putti, Aryee, and Kang (1988) find that there may be a temporal factor at work in the socialization of police officers. That is, socialization into the subculture of police may occur at different points in the officers' careers. There is little evidence concerning the extent of how reference groups affect the personality of older officers, but it seems that in the beginning of their careers, officers' occupational values are shaped during the training and probationary process.

Still another model is offered by Kappeler, Blumberg, and Potter (1993) who contend that there is an acculturation process whereby the beliefs and values of police work are transmitted from one generation of officers to the next. In effect, the group socializes the individual officer into ways of acceptable and unacceptable behavior. This perspective draws heavily from an anthropological point of view and introduces the concept of the police subculture more concretely.

The Authoritarian Personality

Many researchers adopting this perspective feel that personality is fixed and does not really change by choice of occupation or experience. In other words, each person has a fixed personality that does not vary during the course of his or her life (Adlam 1982). This does not imply that personality is inviolate or does not have some degree of malleability, but generally speaking, it stays the same. As it applies to the police, most of the research in this area focuses on the personality characteristics of people who choose to become police officers. This perspective assumes that people with certain types of personalities enter law enforcement as an occupation and behave in certain ways.

One of the most influential experts in this area is Milton Rokeach. In comparing the values of police officers in Michigan with those of a national sample of private citizens, Rokeach (1971) found that police officers seemed more oriented toward self-control and obedience than the average citizen, and officers were more interested in personal goals, such as "an exciting life." Officers were also less interested in larger social goals, such as "a world at peace." Rokeach also found evidence that the experiences as police officers did not significantly influence their personalities. He concludes that most officers probably have a unique value orientation and personality when they embark upon their careers in policing.

In a similar study, Teevan and Dolnick (1973) compared values of officers in the Cook County, Illinois Sheriff Department with those Rokeach encountered in Lansing, Michigan. The findings suggest that the values of police officers in a large urban department are also far removed from those of the general public. Some of the reasons, according to Teevan and Dolnick, are that officers are isolated within society, they are required to enforce unpopular laws, and there is a sense of self-imposed segregation as officers think of themselves as a last bastion of middle-class morality.

In describing the authoritarian personality, Adorno (1950) characterizes it in part by aggressive, cynical, and rigid behavior. People with these characteristics are said to have a myopic view of the world and see issues, people, and behavior as clearly defined: good or bad, right or wrong, friends or enemies. They also tend to be very conservative in their political orientation (Niederhoffer 1967; Bayley and Mendelsohn 1969). Levy (1967) proposes that certain personality traits established early in life were clues to whether a person would be more likely to find policing attractive as a profession.

On the other hand, some researchers have pointed to a few positive aspects of this type of personality in police officers. For instance, Carpenter and Raza (1987) have found that police applicants as a group are less depressed and more assertive in making and maintaining social contacts. Additionally they find that police officers are a more homogeneous group, which may be based on their similar interests in becoming police officers as well as sharing similar personality traits and worldviews.

Ultimately, many develop an occupational working personality, characterized by authoritarianism, suspicion, and cynicism (Rubenstein 1973; Van Maanen 1978; Alpert and Dunham 1992; Neiderhoffer 1967). Skolnick (1966) provides perhaps the best description of the police personality:

> The policeman's role contains two principal variables, danger and
> authority, which should be interpreted in the light of a "constant"

pressure to appear efficient. The element of danger seems to make the policeman especially attentive to signs indicating a potential for violence and lawbreaking. As a result, the policeman is generally a "suspicious" person. Furthermore, the character of the policeman's work makes him less desirable as a friend, since norms of friendship implicate others in his work. Accordingly, the element of danger isolates the policeman socially from that segment of the citizenry which he regards as symbolically dangerous and also from the conventional citizenry with whom he identifies. (p. 43)

An integral part of the police personality is cynicism: the notion that all people are motivated by evil and selfishness. Police cynicism develops among many officers through the nature of police work. Most police officers feel they are set apart from the rest of society, because they have the power to regulate the lives of others. Moreover, by constantly dealing with crime and the more unsavory aspects of social life, their faith in humanity seems to diminish.

Probably the most well-known study of police personality was conducted by Arthur Neiderhoffer (1967). In *Behind the Shield*, Neiderhoffer builds off the work of William Westley (1970) that most officers develop into cynics as a function of their daily routines. Westley had maintained that being constantly faced with keeping people in line and believing that most people intend to break the law or cause harm to the officer led officers to mistrust the people they are charged to protect. Neiderhoffer tested Westley's assumption by distributing a survey measuring attitudes and values to 220 New York City police officers. Among his most important findings were that police cynicism did increase with length of service; that patrol officers with college educations become quite cynical if they were denied promotion; and that military-like academy training caused recruits to become cynical about themselves, the department, and the community. As an illustration, Niederhoffer found that nearly 80 percent of first-day recruits believed the department was an "efficient, smoothly operating organization." Two months later, less than one-third professed that belief. Similarly, half of the recruits believed that a supervisor was "very interested in the welfare of his subordinates," while two months later, those still believing so dropped to 13 percent.

THE SUBCULTURE OF POLICING

Occupational socialization creates occupational subcultures (Radelet and Carter 1994). The idea of the police being a subculture is not new and has been well documented (Westley 1970; Rokeach, Miller, and Snyder 1971; Kirkham 1976; Bittner

1970). For our purposes, subculture may be defined as the meanings, values, and behavior patterns unique to a particular group in a given society. Entry into this subculture begins with a process of socialization whereby recruits learn the values and behavior patterns characteristic of experienced officers.

The development and maintenance of negative attitudes and values by police officers has many implications. Regoli and Poole (1979) found evidence that an officer's feeling of cynicism intensifies the need to maintain respect and increases the desire to exert authority over others. This can easily lead to the increased fear and mistrust of the police by the general public. This, in turn, can create feelings of hostility and resentment on the part of the officer, creating what is sometimes known as police paranoia (Regoli and Poole 1979, p. 43). Regoli and Poole also found that these negative attitudes result in conservative attitudes and a resistance to change among the officers.

As was mentioned, the creation of the police subculture also stems from this unique police personality. However, despite the evidence, many researchers disagree with the notion of a police subculture. Tifft (1974) argues that while the attitudes of officers may be influenced by their work environment, the idea that officers maintain uniform personality traits developed through socialization or innate drives is fallacious. Thus, he argues that the activities and responsibilities most officers engage in have a role to play in how they see the world, but in many ways this is symptomatic of many other occupations.

Thus, the debate over whether or not officers possess a distinct working personality, as well as whether or not the subculture of policing is pervasive, continues and no attempt will be made to resolve it here. What is important to remember is that the nature of police work remains complex and the issues surrounding law enforcement have not been completely understood.

Bibliography

Adorno, T. *The Authoritarian Personality*. New York: Harper Row. 1950.

Adlam, K. R. "*The Police Personality: Psychological Consequences of Becoming a Police Officer.*" Journal of Police Science and Administration 10, no. 3 (1982): 347–48.

Alpert, Geoffrey, and Roger Dunham. *Policing Urban America*, 2nd ed. Prospect Heights, IL: Waveland Press, 1988.

Apuzzo, M. "*Charges Sought in Eric Garner's Death, But Justice Officials Have Doubts.*" New York Times, April 20th, 2018. Available at: https://www.nytimes.com/2018/04/20/us/politics/eric-garner-charges-recommended.html

Balch, R. "*The Police Personality: Fact or Fiction?*" Journal of Criminal Law, Criminology and Police Science 63, (1972):117.

Bayley, D. H., and H. Mendelsohn. *Minorities and the Police: Confrontation in America.* New York: The Free Press, 1969.

Becker, Howard, Blanche Greer, Everett Hughes, and Anselm Strauss. *Boys in White: Student Culture in Medical School.* Chicago: University of Chicago Press, 1961.

Bennett, R. R. *"Becoming Blue: A Longitudinal Study of Police Recruit Occupational Socialization."* Journal of Police Science and Administration 12, no.1 (1984):47–57.

Bittner, Egon. *The Functions of Police in Modern Society.* Chevy Chase, MD: National Clearinghouse for Mental Health, 1970.

Brown, Emily. *"Timeline: Michael Brown Shooting in Ferguson, MO."* USA Today. August 10, 2015. http://www.usatoday.com/story/news/nation/2014/08/14/michael-brown-ferguson-missouri-timeline/14051827/.

Carpenter, B. N., and S. M. Raza.*"Personality Characteristics of Police Applicants: Comparisons Across Sbugroups and with Other Populations."* Journal of Police Science and Administration 15, no. 1 (1987):10–17.

"Chicago Police Officer Jason Van Dyke Charges with 1st Degree Murder in Laquan McDonald Shooting" ABC News 7. November 24, 2015. http://abc7chicago.com/news/cop-charged-with-1st-degree-murder-in-laquan-mcdonald-shooting/1097312//

Danziger, Kurt. *Socialization.* Harmondsworth, England: Penguin, 1971.

Elkin, Frederick, and Gerald Handel. *The Child and Society: The Process of Socialization.* New York: Random House, 1989.

Erikson, K. and Vallas, P. (eds.) *Sociology of Sociological Perspectives.* Washington, D.C.: American Sociological Association, 1995.

Goffman, Erving. *Asylums.* New York: Anchor, 1961.

Husain, N. *"Laquan McDonalt: Timeline, the Shooting, the Video and the Fallout."* Chicago Tribune, October 20, 2017. Available at: http://www.chicagotribune.com/news/laquanmcdonald/ct-graphics-laquan-mcdonald-officers-fired-timeline-htmlstory.html

Kappler, Victor E., M. Blumberg and Gary W. Potter. *The Mythology of Crime and Criminal Justice.* Prospect Heights, IL: Waveland Press, 1993.

Kirkham, George. *Signal Zero.* New York: Ballentine, 1976.

Levy, R. *"Predicting Police Failures."* Journal of Criminal Law, Criminology and Police Science 58, no. 2 (1967): 275.

Moore, W. *"Occupational Socialization."* In Goslin, D. (ed.) Handbook of Socialization Theory and Research, edited by D. Goslin, 861–84. New York: Rand McNally, 1969.

Neiderhoffer, A. *Behind the Shield: The Police in Urban Society.*Garden City, NY: Doubleday, 1967.

Parsons, T. and R. F. Bales. *Family, Socialization, and Interaction Process.* New York: The Free Press, 1955.

Putti, J., S. Aryee, and T. S. Kang. *"Personal Values of Recruits and Officers in a Law Enforcement Agency: An Exploratory Study."* Journal of Police Science and Administration 16, no. 4 (1988): 245–249.

Rector, K. *"Freddie Gray Case: DOJ Won't Charge Baltimore Police Officers."* Baltimore Sun, September 13, 2017. Available at: http://www.baltimoresun.com/news/maryland/crime/bs-md-ci-doj-decline-charges-20170912-story.html

Radelet, Louis. *The Police and the Community*, 4th ed. NewYork: Macmillan, 1986.

Regoil, R., and Poole, E. *"Measurement of Police Cynicism: A Facto Scaling Approach,"* Journal of Criminal Justice 7, (1979): 37–52.

Rokeach, M., M. Miller, and H. Snyder. "The Value Gap Between Police and Policed." *Journal of Social Issues* 27, (1971): 155–71.

Rubenstein, Jonathan. *City Police*. New York: Farrar, Strauss, and Giroux, 1973.

Skolnick, Jerome. *Justice Without Trial: Law Enforcement in a Democratic Society*. New York: John Wiley and Sons, 1966.

Stoddard, E. R. *"The Informal Code of Police Deviancy: A Group Approach to Blue-Collar Crime."* Journal of Criminal Law, Criminology, and Police Science 59, no. 2 (1968): 201–03.

Teevan, J., and B. Dolnick. *"The Values of the Police: A Reconsideration and Interpretation."* Journal of Police Science and Administration 1, (1973): 366–69.

Tifft, L. *"The Cop Personality Reconsidered."* Journal of Police Science and Administration 2, (1974): 268.

Westley, William. *Violence and the Police: A Sociological Study of Law, Custom, and Morality*. Cambridge, MA: MIT Press, 1970.

Van Maanen, J. *"On Becoming a Policeman."* In Policing: A View from the Street, edited by P. Manning and J. Van Maanen. Santa Monica, CA: Goodyear, 1978.

Deviance

Who are the Rule Breakers in Society?

DEVIANCE

As was mentioned in the discussion of culture, norms are a component of a society's culture, which guide people on how they should act in a given situation. This is also part of the socialization process, where people learn what is expected of them as part of their roles in society. But what happens when people depart or deviate from those norms? What happens when they either do not learn what is expected of them or decide not to adhere to norms? The study of deviant behavior is a fascinating area for sociologists, because it offers an understanding of how rules are created within a group of people or society and explains how the larger group attempts to control the behavior of others, something often referred to as social control.

Some people think that because norms are dynamic and change over time, there is some variation in what is considered deviant behavior. In other words, deviance is simply a matter of opinion. It is to some extent, but deviance is also objectively real—there are norms and expectations for behavior, and there are actual violations that occur when offenders commit deviant acts and actual sanctions that offenders experience as a result of those acts.

Thus, deviance is a very complex phenomenon, which offers an important interplay between a society's views on what types of actions are acceptable and unacceptable. But remember, deviance changes over time, making the study of deviant behavior a bit of a moving target and anything but a simple process. Some types of deviance are clearly out of bounds and are violations of the law. These activities are what we think of when we consider crimes, but one can engage in deviant behavior without breaking any laws.

In the following articles, contributors provide several examples of deviant behavior and the notion of deviance. For instance, in one article I examine the notion of tattoos as a form of deviance. This topic raises interesting questions about how and when certain acts are no longer considered deviant. At what point does something like a tattoo, which has historically been considered linked to deviant groups, become socially acceptable? Thus, tattoos present a fascinating illustration of the social construction of deviance.

As was mentioned, a discussion of deviance often leads to one about crime. Given that race can serve as a form of stigma, Linda Henry offers insight into how artificial intelligence and technology are informing our decisions about sentencing offenders and predictive policing strategies. Finally, another type of criminal activity involves fraud. In an article that explores the world of chiropractic medicine, traditionally thought of as a deviant profession because of its questionable past, Robert McNamara examines the extent to which chiropractors have engaged in dubious billing practices under Medicare. In examining this phenomenon, efforts are made to understand the rationalizations and justifications used by chiropractors to explain what are either errors in billing or misrepresentation of the facts in order to be reimbursed.

Getting Ink Done: Tattoos as a Form of Deviance?

Robert McNamara, PhD

DEVIANT BEHAVIOR IS generally described as those acts that depart from a societal norm or expectation. However, the definition of deviance is anything but simple or easy to grasp. Because norms are dynamic, meaning they change over time, usually as a result of changes in the preferences and needs of a given society, so too do acts that are considered departures from those norms. In other words, what constitutes deviance can change over time and those who engage in it can be perceived differently. What complicates things somewhat is the fact that the same act can be perceived as acceptable during one period and then it can be considered inappropriate, deviant, or scandalous, in another. In those situations, what happens to those who engage in the behavior once it is no longer considered acceptable? Similarly, how are offenders perceived once a previously inappropriate act is no longer considered deviant? Does their standing in society change or are they still perceived as deviant because the acts were understood to be unacceptable in a previous circumstance?

Thus it is not always simply a matter of changing the way a behavior is perceived that results in social acceptability or some type of stigma. Rather, there are many facets to understanding how people are given a deviant label based on their actions. A good illustration of this dynamic can be seen in the growing popularity of tattoos in the United States. At one point in time, tattoos were considered deviant, as were those who wore them. Some even considered getting tattoos a form of taboo behavior. Tattoos became associated with criminals, vagrants, and the outcasts of society. As a result, not only were they symbols of the socially unacceptable, many proudly displayed them as a badge of honor of their unwillingness to accept mainstream cultural values that dictated appearance norms.

An important question is whether societal reactions to tattoos have changed, particularly in the United States. In other words, as they become more popular, do they become socially acceptable? Are the reasons for getting a tattoo changing as well? In the past it was understood that acquiring a tattoo was either a form of involuntary association with a group, such as in slavery, or it was done voluntarily to demonstrate allegiance and group unity—as in the case of gang members or others who wish to show their affiliation with a deviant segment of society. What does the research tell us about tattoos, their social standing, and the people who acquire them? To gain a greater understanding of this phenomenon, as well as to develop a clearer understanding of the nature of deviance in general, a look back at the history of tattooing is necessary.

HISTORY OF TATTOOS

Tattoos have been around for centuries and while some of the reasons for their popularity may have stemmed from misguided therapeutic reasons, other explanations for tattoos have been noted in anthropological and historical documents as far back as five thousand years ago. While all of the reasons for tattoos are not known, the fact that they have existed in various cultures for so long suggests a kind of social acceptability across societies (Lineberry 2007).

In the late eighteenth century, the Maori were one of the first documented groups of people encountered by the West that displayed body tattoos (Rubin 1988). The Maori used facial tattoos to indicate both social status and group membership. As DeMello (2000) points out, additional discoveries brought exposure of tattoos from Tahitians, Hawaiians, and the Polynesians. These experiences created the perception that tattoos were part of uncivilized tribes. The exposure to various tribes during the early years also exposed the practice of tattooing to sailors, who shared their tattoo designs and methods with native tribesmen. These designs and developments led to the more common practice of tattooing among sailors in the Western world.

In the United States, tattooing became popular around the mid-1840s, in New York, when Martin Hildebrandt opened a permanent tattoo business (Blanchard 2003). Hildebrandt's shop became a popular business for sailors and soldiers. At that time, tattooing was popular among military personnel because many viewed it as a way to show loyalty and devotion, to commemorate a great feat in battle, or to beautify the body with distinctive markings (Blanchard 2003).

Tattoos remained popular during this period with this segment of the population in part because the process was time-consuming and painful. Thus, acquiring a tattoo was a demonstration of courage and an ability to withstand pain. However, in the late 1800s the first electric tattooing machine was invented, which simplified the process and made it more palatable for the general public to consider tattooing. As its popularity grew, in part because of the famous tattooed attractions in P.T. Barnum's circus acts, the perception of those who acquired tattoos began to take on a deviant label (Blanchard 2003).

During World War II, even more soldiers acquired tattoos and soon they became associated with the lower and working classes. According to Blanchard (2003), by the 1950s tattooing was generally viewed as socially inappropriate, particularly by the wealthy and members of the aristocracy. Ward McAllister, "a self-styled spokesman for New York high society," declared of tattooing: "It is certainly the most vulgar and barbarous habit the eccentric mind of fashion ever invented. It may do for an illiterate seaman, but hardly for an aristocrat" (Cavanaugh 2016, 21).

In the 1960s an outbreak of hepatitis further solidified the deviant status of tattoos. Media reports of blood poisoning, hepatitis, and other diseases created a climate in which tattoos and tattoo parlors were considered socially unacceptable. The public health concerns led the state of New York to ban tattoos and tattoo parlors, driving the process of acquiring a tattoo underground. Even in places where tattoos were still legal, such as New Jersey and Pennsylvania, the public health issue decreased the demand for them (Silver, Silver, Siennick, and Farkas 2011). During this period, clients of illegal tattoo parlors primarily consisted of ex-convicts, criminals of various types, and gang members, all of whom contributed to the public's association of tattoos with deviants and deviant behavior.

The Relationship Between Tattooing and Deviance

The social scientific research on tattoos demonstrates a connection to deviance, both in the past as well as in the present. For instance, the first connection of tattoos to crime and deviance was discovered by Cesare Lombroso. Lombroso connected personality traits to subjects based on their tattoos (Lombroso 1911).

Lombroso's theory is generally based on the idea that criminals and deviants could be identified through their physical characteristics (Lombroso 1911). For example, although labeling does not typically occur in a physical manner, the social stigma tends to remain. As a result, the offender is excluded from full participation in society. Some experts have argued that the historical association of tattoos with deviants may be one reason why the public sees tattooing as a form of deviance.

More importantly, there appears to be a connection between tattooing and some forms of deviant behavior (Post 1968; Braithwaite et al. 2001; Koch et al. 2005). The findings of these studies show that deviant behavior is linked to tattoos. While not a causal link, meaning acquiring a tattoo does not result in these behaviors, a tattoo can serve as a form of self-labeling and result in a social stigma by society (Adams 2009; Braithwaite et al. 2001; Deschesnes, Fines, and Demers 2006; Dhossche, Snell, and Larder 2000; Koch et al. 2005; Kosut 2006).

At the same time, however, there is other evidence to indicate that the perception of many tattoos was not considered deviant (Koch et al. 2005; Deschesnes, Fines, and Demers 2006; Kosut 2006; Adams 2009; Swami and Furnham 2007).

Tattooing as a Form of Self-Expression

In recent decades, the reasons for acquiring a tattoo seem to have changed. Instead of showing allegiance to or affiliation with deviant subgroups, people have begun to acquire tattoos as a form of self-expression. Of course, along with such body art, there may be secondary benefits, such as commonality with others who have similar ideas about self-expression or for whom the tattoo is a political statement. Examples might include a tattoo that symbolizes support of gay rights, support of a particular sports team, or as part of membership in some other group. While acquiring a tattoo might have collateral social benefits, the research suggests it is not the primary reason for getting one. Rather the main reason appears to be individual expression. Further adding to the popularity of tattoos are celebrities, who are generally considered part of the elite and ruling class, who willingly display their tattoos in public. These individuals essentially use their societal status to give tattoos a form of social acceptability or at least use tattoos to demonstrate an unwillingness to follow the status quo.

As is often the case with the prohibition of certain acts in society, which typically limits the supply of the item or service in question, during the period where tattoos were considered illegal in some states, a form of tattoo renaissance began to emerge. In other words, it was the lack of social acceptability that led many to realize that there was something fascinating about the idea of tattooing one's body. This renaissance period lasted through the 1980s and 1990s, when tattooing began to gather greater social acceptability by the general public (Hewer 2014). In fact, as Hewer (2014) points out, mainstream American society began to see tattoos as a symbol of individuality that was to be celebrated. As they became more popular and socially acceptable, their deviant status was also altered; they were seen as a more common feature of middle-class America in the twentieth century, no longer just popular among the socially unaccepted. In fact, the rise in popularity of tattoos among the middle class made tattoos into a form of fashion and a stylistic accessory.

In other words, the popularity of tattooing coincided with a greater level of understanding of how one can use their body, particularly the exposed skin, to celebrate people's ideas about individuality, to champion social causes, or to send social messages as a form of social interaction with others. In a person's "presentation of self," as sociologist Erving Goffman (1969) pointed out, a wide assortment of social and symbolic messages is communicated by the actor to the audience. As the person uses his or her body to convey messages about life, relationships, or important statements about social life, tattoos have increasingly become venues of communication, a purpose that had not been considered in previous eras. That is, the symbolic and social value of tattoos has evolved from traditional motivators, such as loyalty, dedication, courage, or to commemorate a battle, to include social messages about being a part of the larger collectivity. And while some tattoos are still considered out of bounds, particularly as they relate to where they are placed on the body or the actual messages contained within them, there appears to be some evidence that some segments of the population no longer consider them inappropriate (Shilling 2012; Pitts 2003; Williams 2004; Fenske 2007).

As Bell (1999) points out, while the act of acquiring a tattoo has remained the same, the symbolic meaning attached to the experience has been transformed by the recipient from one of self-marginalization to that of one involving spiritual enlightenment, deep personal meaning, or embracing the freedom of expression.

A Profile of Tattoo Owners

There is growing evidence that whatever the reason for acquiring one, tattoos are becoming more popular. As Shannon-Missal (2016) points out, about 30 percent of Americans have at least one tattoo, which is approximately a 30 percent increase from five years ago. And like potato chips, the data appears to suggest that people cannot simply stop at one: among those with any tattoos, about 70 percent have two or more.

According to Heimlech (2010) about half (47 percent) of tattoo owners are millennials and about one-third are Gen Xers. In comparison, only about 13 percent of baby boomers and only about 10 percent of matures (the generation prior to baby boomers), report having a tattoo. Moreover, millennials and Gen Xers are much more likely than any other group to have multiple tattoos. The data also suggests that those living in rural and urban areas (35 percent and 33 percent respectively) are more likely to have a tattoo than someone living in a suburban area. Further, adults with children in the household are more likely than those without them to have at least one tattoo (43 percent vs. 21 percent).

The Pew Center data also shows that there are approximately twenty-three thousand tattoo parlors in the United States, and the average cost of a tattoo is about one hundred dollars an hour. Not everyone likes the idea of tattooing and some research shows that of those who did not wish to acquire one, about half refrained from doing so because they don't want one (45 percent) while others (36 percent) do not find them attractive. About 20 percent are afraid to get a tattoo because of the pain, while another 18 percent are concerned about buyer's remorse (statistica.com 2015).

ARE TATTOOS REALLY SOCIALLY ACCEPTABLE?

Though it may seem that society appears to be becoming more comfortable with the idea of people having tattoos, some indicators suggest they are not completely supportive. Some data shows that in 2015, only about one-third of those surveyed had very favorable or somewhat favorable attitudes about tattoos, with another third having no opinion about them. This means about as many people had unfavorable or very unfavorable ideas about tattoos (statistica.com 2015).

In fact there is a growing concern for the health and safety of the younger generation. Newman (2017) points to a recent report by the American Academy of Pediatrics, which offered insight into the trends in tattooing and piercings for adolescents and young adults. Several concerns about health implications were explored, along with guidelines for physicians in discussing the safety measures for those considering a tattoo or piercing. The report cited a Pew Research Center study that said about 38 percent of young people ages eighteen to twenty-nine have at least one tattoo and nearly three-quarters of them were covered and not visible.

Interestingly, some data suggests that about a quarter of people who have a tattoo wanted it removed. Additionally, the vast majority of people who have a tattoo hide or cover it up. According to a 2015 survey, only about 20 percent of Americans visibly display their tattoos (statistica.com 2015). There may be many reasons why people want a tattoo removed or want to hide it from public view. The most logical explanation is that those people who want it removed or who hide it are concerned about how they will be perceived if it becomes known that they have one.

So what do Americans think about those who have a tattoo? This is a fascinating question. One study in 2015 asked the question, "Compared to people without tattoos, which of the following characteristics to you think people with tattoos have?," and found that about 40 percent of respondents said they think people who have tattoos are more rebellious, while only 6 percent think they are less rebellious. (statistica.com 2015).

From this question, other characteristics were attributed to those with tattoos. For example, compared to people without tattoos, 16 percent of respondents said they think that people who have tattoos are less attractive and less sexy, and about 20 percent said they think those with tattoosto be less spiritual. About a quarter said they feel that people with tattoos are less intelligent, less respectable, and less healthy. It should be noted, however, that in responding to all of these questions, the vast majority of the responses were that there was no real difference between those with a tattoo and those without one (statistica.com 2015).

When asked if they thought that people with tattoos were more or less likely to engage in deviant behavior, about 24 percent stated they felt that those people who had tattoos were more likely than those without one to engage in acts that most people would consider deviant. Thus, the weight of the evidence seems to fall in the middle, meaning people either do not have an opinion one way or the other or they are not bothered by people with tattoos.

This same survey asked respondents if they were concerned about the credibility of people in certain occupations who also had tattoos. The data points out that most Americans have few problems with people in certain occupations (such as a professional athlete, chef, police officer, banker, attorney, physician, real estate broker, IT technician, teacher, judge, or the president of the United States having or displaying a tattoo in the workplace (statistica.com 2015).

In fact, while the percentages are highest for athletes, chefs, and IT technicians, most Americans say they are not concerned about tattoos in the workplace. Even 58 percent of respondents stated that they would feel comfortable with a tattooed presidential candidate. On one hand, then, it appears that there may be a growing level of support for the idea of people having tattoos. However, it is one thing to ask questions like this in a survey, it is another when the issue plays out in real life. It is also worth noting that those smaller percentages of people who do not like tattoos or who are not supportive of those who have them may be the very people that are in charge in the workplace. Remember, there are reasons why 70 percent of tattoo owners hide or conceal them. One of those reasons might be that they are concerned about how others, such as employers, might react to that information.

Can Tats Hurt Employment Opportunities?

The question about whether employers discriminate against those who have visible tattoos has become a thorny one in the world of employment law. In one study of human resources professionals, about 60 percent said they thought that visible tattoos could have a negative impact on an applicant's chance of being hired (Kennedy 2015). Interestingly, some employers do not wish to have their employees displaying tattoos in the workplace; as some believe tattoos create an uncomfortable work environment or, in the case where the employee interacts with customers, a tattoo may not be fitting with the image that the employer wishes to convey.

However, at what point does an employer cross the line between an employee's right to free expression and discrimination against them for doing so? While there are few laws regarding the prohibition of displaying tattoos in the workplace, there have been a few celebrated cases that outline the framework of acceptability on this issue (Kennedy 2015). What complicates the issue is whether the tattoo is part of observing the requirements surrounding a particular religion. Additionally, there is an element of tattooing that relates to race and ethnicity, where some evidence exists that about half of all Hispanics and about a third of African

Americans have body art, which is above national averages for tattoo owners. Policies prohibiting employees from displaying tattoos or using the presence of body art to exclude potential candidates can easily be seen as discriminating against protected classes of people.

How have the courts ruled in cases where tattoos or body art impacts an employee's standing in the workplace? While there is great variation in deciding cases like this, the courts have generally used what is known as the "reasonable business purpose" rule as guidance in deciding such cases. This rule states that in those cases where employers can show that the company's business plan attempts to promote a certain professional image, and that plan conflicts with the individual expression of employees who wish to display their body art, the employer is more likely to be successful in court.

Similarly, as a working rule to balance employee rights and company policies, in those instances where a reasonable accommodation can be made to allow the employee to conceal the body art rather than being terminated for it, the courts have generally been more flexible in their rulings. Related to this is the need for any policy that prohibits the display of tattoos to be equally applied to all employees. Similarly, the courts have sided with employers in those instances where policies relating to body art take into account coworkers and the work environment in addition to the image the company intends to present to its clients and customers (Kennedy 2015).

CONCLUSION

The available research suggests that tattoos in the United States are in a state of evolution in terms of their social acceptability. As people begin to acquire tattoos for reasons that stem more from artistic expression than affiliation or loyalty with deviant groups, mainstream society may begin to recalibrate its understanding of tattoos as a form of deviant self-labeling. As was mentioned, estimates show that about one-third of American adults are tattooed, and the most cited reason for being tattooed is individual self-expression. At the same time, however, most people conceal their tattoos, largely out of a concern that they will be discriminated against, either in the workplace or in other social settings. While celebrities may be more willing to expose themselves to that kind of potential social stigma, many recipients of tattoos remain mindful of the fact that not everyone considers tattoos a harmless form of body art (Roberts 2012).

In the larger sense, tattooing and its evolving nature are significant illustrations of the dynamic nature of norms, deviance, and social control. As more people find tattooing socially acceptable and the deviant label begins to fade, it may be that this form of self-labeling is considered no different than other forms of artistic expression (Greenblatt 2014; Roberts 2012).

Bibliography

Adams, J. *"Marked Difference: Tattooing and its Association with Deviance in the United States."* Deviant Behavior 30, no. 3 (2009): 266–92.

Bell, S. *"Tattooed: A Participant Observer's Exploration of Meaning."* Journal of American Culture 22, no. 2 (1999): 53–58.

Blackburn, Justin, J. Cleveland, R. Griffin, G. G. Davis, J. Lienert, and G. McGwin. "Tattoo Frequency and Types Among Homicides and Other Deaths, 2007–2008. A Matched Case-Control Study." *American Journal of Forensic Medicine and Pathology* 33, no. 3 (2012): 202–5.

Blanchard, M. "Skin Stories: History of Tattoos." Public Broadcasting Service. 2003. www.pbs.org/skinstories/history/beyond.html.

Braithwaite, R., A. Robillard, T. Woodring, T. Stephens and K. J. Arriola. "Tattooing and Body Piercing Among Adolescent Detainees: Relationship to Alcohol and Other Drug Use." *Journal of Substance Abuse* 13, (2001): 5–16.

Brooks, T. L., E. R. Woods, J. R. Knight, and L. A. Shrier. "Body Modification And Substance Use In Adolescents: Is There A Link?" *Journal of Adolescent Health* 32, (2003): 44–9.

Carroll, S. T., R. H. Riffenburgh, T. A. Roberts, and E. B. Myhe. "Tattoos And Body Piercings As Indicators Of Adolescent Risk-Taking Behaviours." *Pediatrics* 109, no. 6 (2002): 1021–7.

Cavanaugh, R. "O'Reilly's Tattoo Machine: Fine Art for the Masses." Irish America. 2016 http://www.irishamerica.com/2016/03/oreillys-tattoo-machine-fine-art-for-the-masses/.

Charlie, C. "Tattoo Statistics." *Inked Magazine.* April 10, 2017. http://www.inkedmag.com/tattoo-statistics/.

Lineberry. C. "Tatoos: The Ancient and Mysterious History." *Smithsonian,* January 1, 2007. Available at: https://www.smithsonianmag.com/history/tattoos-144038580/

DeMello, Margo. "The Convict Body: Tattooing among Male American Prisoners." *Anthropology Today* 9, (1993): 10–1.

———. *Bodies Of Inscription: A Cultural History of the Modern Tattoo Community.* Durham & London: Duke University Press, 2000.

Deschesnes, M., P. Fines, and S. Demers. "Are Tattooing And Body Piercing Indicators Of Risk-Taking Behaviors Among High School Students?" *Journal of Adolescence* 29, (2006): 379–93.

Dhossche, Dirk, K. S. Snell. and S. Larder. "A Case-Control Study of Tattoos in Young Suicide Victims as a Possible Marker of Risk." *Journal of Affective Disorders* 59 (2000): 165–8.

Fenske, Mindy. *Tattoos in American Visual Culture*. New York: Palgrave Macmillan, 2007. Goffmann, Erving. *The Presentation of Self in Everyday Life.* New York: Basic Books, 1969.

Greenblatt, Alan. "Job Seekers Still Have To Hide Tattoos (From The Neck Up)." NPR. Feb. 21, 2014. http://www.npr.org/2014/02/21/280213268/ job-seekers-still-have-to-hide-tattoos-from-the-neck-up.

Heimlich, R. "Tattoo Taboo." Pew Research Center. March 24, 2010. http://www. pewresearch.org/fact-tantk/2010/03/24/tattoo-taboo.

Hewer, Tony. "The Tattoos." Under the Skin. 2014. http://www.individual.utoronto. ca/antonygh/undertheskin/20thcentury.htm#.

Kennedy, G. "Tattooism: Where Body Art Meets Employment Discrimina- tion." The Labor Dish. June 22, 2015. https://www.labordish.com/2015/06/ tattoo-ism-where-body-art-meets-employment-discrimination/.

Koch, J. R., A. E. Roberts, J. H. Cannon, M. L. Armstrong, and D. C. Owen. "College Students, Tattooing, And The Health Belief Model: Extending Social Psychological Perspectives On Youth Culture and Deviance." *Social Spectrum* 25, no. 1 (2005): 79–102.

Kosut, M. "Mad Artists and Tattooed Perverts: Deviant Discourse and the Social Construction of Cultural Categories." *Deviant Behavior* 27, no. 1 (2006): 73–95.

Laumann, A. E., and A. J. Derick. "Tattoos And Body Piercings in the United States: A National Data Set." *American Academy of Dermatology* 55, no. 3 (2006): 413–21.

Lineberry, Cate. "Tattoos: The Ancient and Mysterious History." Smithsonian Institu- tion. January 1, 2007. www.smithsonianmag.com/history/tattoos-144038580/.

Litt, I. F. "Self-graffiti? Self-image? Self-destruction? Tattoos and Adolescents." *Journal of Adolescent Health* 15, (1994): 198.

Lombroso, Gina. *Criminal man: according to the classification of Cesare Lombroso*. New York: Putnam, 1911.

"Lyle Tuttle." *Illustration History*, Norman Rockwell Museum. 2015 www.illustra- tionhistory.org/artists/lyle-tuttle.

Michalak, Jodie. "What Is a Tattoo: The Story Behind the Ink." LiveAbout, July 14, 2017. http://www.liveabout.com/what-is-a-tattoo-3189418.

Newman, Meredith. "Report: More Young People Have Tattoos and Piercings than Ever Before." *USA Today*. September 20, 2017. http://www.usatoday.com/story/news/ nation-now/ 2017/09/20/ young-people-tattoos-and-piercings-report/686360001/.

"Perceptions of People with Tattoos." Statistica.com. 2015. https://www.statista.com/ statistics/512244/qualities-tattoos-acquired-usa/

Pitts, Victoria L. *In The Flesh: The Cultural Politics of Body Modification.* New York: Palgrave Macmillan, 2003.

Post, Richard S. "The Relationship of Tattoos to Personality Disorders." *The Journal of Criminal Law, Criminology, and Police Science* 59, no. 4 (1968): 516–24.

Rapp, Elizabeth. "Stigmatization or Decoration: Tattoo as Deviance, A Cross-Cultural Study." Academia.edu. 2017. www.academia.edu/1538291/Stigmatization_or_Decoration_Tattoo_as_ Deviance_A_Cross-Cultural_Study.

Roberts, D. J. "Secret Ink: Tattoos Place in Contemporary American Culture." *Journal of American Culture* 35, no. 2 (2012): 153–65.

Root, Damon. "The Rise and Fall of the New York City Tattoo Ban." Reason Foundation. March 8, 2014. http://www.reason.com/archives/2014/03/08/the-rise-and-fall-of-the-new-york-city-t.

Rubin, A., ed. *The Marks of Civilization: Artistic Transformations of the Human Body.* Los Angeles, CA: Museum of Cultural History, 1988.

Shannon-Missal, Larry. "Tattoo Takeover: Three in Ten Americans Have Tattoos, and Most Don't Stop at Just One." *Health & Life*, The Harris Poll. February 10, 2016. http://www.theharrispoll. com/health-and-life/Tattoo_Takeover.html.

Shilling, Chris. *The Body and Social Theory.* Los Angeles, CA: Sage Publications, 2012.

Silver, E., S. R. Silver, S. Siennick, and G. Farkas. "Bodily Signs of Academic Success: An Empirical Examination of Tattoos and Grooming." *Social Problems* 58, no. 4 (2011): 538–64.

Silver, E., M. VanEseltine, and S. J. Silver. "Tattoo Acquisition: A Prospective Longitudinal Study of Adolescents." *Deviant Behavior* 30, no. 6 (2009): 511–38.

Swami, V., and A. Furnham. "Unattractive, Promiscuous and Heavy Drinkers: Perceptions of Women with Tattoos." *Body Image* 4 (2007): 343–52.

Tate, J. C., and B. L. "Personality Correlates of Tattooing and Body Piercing in a College Sample: The Kids Are Alright." *Personality and Individual Differences* 45, (2008): 281–5.

"Tattoo Statistics, Facts, Stats and Trends 2016–2017." SkinTru. January 2, 2017. www. skintru.com/blog/tattoo-statistics/.

Tiggemann, M., and L. A. Hopkins. "Tattoos and Piercings: Bodily Expressions of Uniqueness?" *Body Image* 8, (2011): 245–50.

Williams, C. R. "Reclaiming the expressive subject: deviance and the art of non-normativity." *Deviant Behavior* 25, no. 3 (2004): 233–54.

Vail, D. "Tattoos are Like Potato Chips… You Can't Have Just One: The Process of Becoming and Being a Collector." *Deviant Behavior* 20, (1999): 253–73.

Medicare Fraud and Chiropractic Care: Accountability or Persecution?

Robert McNamara, PhD

FROM ITS VERY beginning, chiropractic medicine has faced challenges about the scientific validity of the treatment and the credibility of its practitioners. Since those early years, many of these criticisms have remained, but legislation, licensure, and litigation have created an environment where chiropractic care is allowed in all fifty states, and licenses are required of all chiropractors who wish to practice medicine (Singh and Ernst 2009). Despite becoming an increasingly popular alternative to traditional medicine, many critics contend that chiropractic care lacks scientific rigor and amounts to quackery, fraud, or simply is no more effective as a form of treatment than traditional remedies (Lisi and Brandt 2016; Manger and Barrett 1995; Long 2012).

Many experts also point out that medicine has transitioned away from the independent and autonomous profession it once was to one that is more responsive to the model of managed care, leaving physicians, and, in particular, chiropractors, facing a significantly different future than what many had perhaps expected (Cockerham 2017). As chiropractors and others feel the pressures of health care reform in their ability to provide treatment to patients, questions arise about the motives behind those who engage in dubious billing practices, particularly for Medicare patients. Thus, one of the research questions for this study was to examine how and why some chiropractors engage in questionable or outright fraudulent practices in billing to Medicare. The interviews and observations suggest that many chiropractors use a series of rationalizations to justify excessive or unnecessary billing based on the belief that they think insurance companies should not make decisions on patient care, that others are already engaging in similar practices, or that desperation to survive as a practice means taking risks and hoping to avoid discovery. Such justifications and excuses align with Sykes and Matza's techniques of neutralization (Sykes and Matza 1957).

METHODS

The basis for this study was to understand how and in what ways chiropractors are coping with the dramatic changes in health care in this country, particularly since most providers are solo practitioners who are struggling to maintain their practices in light of the declining reimbursements from insurance companies. In order to best understand how and in what ways a chiropractic office operates, as well as to gain insight into the nature of the relationship between patients and chiropractors, an ethnographic approach was used. This study used classic ethnographic techniques of systematic observation and unstructured and semi-structured interviews patients (Lecomte and Schensul 2012; Taylor 2002) of South Carolina chiropractors, their staff, and patients.

This allowed the researcher to gain an in-depth and comprehensive understanding of chiropractic medicine, how practices operate, and the relationships providers formed with their patients. It also allowed the researcher to inquire about more personal and private information regarding particular strategies used by chiropractors to remain viable. Such information would not have likely been revealed through the use of a survey.

Time was spent in numerous chiropractic offices learning about the procedures used in operating a practice, observing interactions between staff and patients, as well as examining the role of the chiropractor within the practice. Formal interviews were conducted with staff members, patients, and providers, along with informal conversations that occurred as a normal part of the ethnographic approach. Visits to various chiropractic offices occurred twice a week for approximately eighteen months, with each visit lasting approximately three to four hours, including the interviews.

Additionally, phone interviews were conducted with provosts, deans, and faculty at several schools of chiropractic medicine to learn more about the differences in the techniques and the training that students receive, as well as to gain insight into the presence of franchises such as the Joint in the marketplace. Numerous informal conversations also occurred with physicians, physical therapists, massage therapists, insurance providers, and others associated with medicine over the course of the project. In total, approximately one hundred interviews and conversations occurred from fall 2016 through fall 2017. No compensation was provided for participating in the study and efforts were made to ensure that anonymity and confidentiality of responses was maintained. To that end, all identifying characteristics of respondents and of their practices were concealed, and pseudonyms were used for any interview excerpt offered in the study.

CHALLENGES RELATING TO INSURANCE REIMBURSEMENT

The passage of the Affordable Care Act, also known as Obamacare, has impacted all medical providers as well as influencing how chiropractors operate. In fact, many public and private insurance companies have begun to reexamine how they reimburse medical treatment, and they are paying closer attention to chiropractors and the treatments they offer. In general, while most plans vary, chiropractic care is limited to a specific number of treatments for a given problem, and it will not cover what is known as maintenance care. The reimbursement rates for chiropractic treatments have also been reduced; the average Medicare payment per adjustment is less than $25 (O'Donnell, Hoyer, and Alcindor 2014). As one might imagine, these changes and reductions have had a significant impact on chiropractors. Steven, a chiropractor involved in the study, talks about how he sees treatment differently than insurance companies. He says:

> Listen, the insurance company tells me that this patient only gets twelve adjustments per year. Now I'll tell you, if a patient comes in to see me for an injury, twelve visits is plenty. I shouldn't say this because my colleagues will scream at me, but twelve visits is a lot of visits. If I can't fix that patient's problem in twelve visits, then I'm either doing something wrong, I don't know what's going on, or I'm just trying to make money off that patient. But the problem starts when that patient is taken care of, they go back to work or doing whatever they were doing, and then they injure themselves again. Then they come back to me, and in my mind, I start all over again, because that is a new injury. It's not the same problem, because I took care of that. But it's a new one…it could even be an overuse injury, but it's new. So in my mind, I should have another twelve or ten visits, or whatever the plan calls for. But then I usually get a call because I've seen this patient more than a dozen times and they go 'Hey, what are you doing with this patient?' And when I try to tell them it is a new injury, they are skeptical and think I'm trying to milk them or something. I tell them 'Look at my notes, look at the dates.' But a lot of times they give me grief about it.

The issue of maintenance care is a controversial one that continues to plague the profession. During the course of the study there were many providers who argued that regular adjustments are key to a patient's overall health. Like brushing one's teeth, these providers believe they are preventing injuries and illnesses from occurring by having patients regularly adjusted. The problem is that insurance companies do not see these types of treatments the same way.

Another challenge with insurance companies relates to the rate of reimbursements. As Doug points out, in the past, insurance companies would provide a greater percentage of reimbursement for treatment than they do under Obamacare. He says:

It used to be you'd get all you billed for—now? Sometimes I wonder if it is even worth the paperwork to get the $25 for an adjustment, especially since you have to call them up, fight with them over whether it was a legitimate treatment or medically necessary. And then you have to send over the documentation, then they may or may not approve it. Then next month, you have to do it all over again. It's crazy.

The general feeling by many chiropractors is that insurance companies, in an effort to cut costs, changed their view of chiropractic care as "medically necessary." While this is a critical term used in the industry to justify treatment, some chiropractors think insurance companies see it as a way to cut corners. As Jim, a chiropractor, points out:

Oh, I absolutely think insurance companies are seeing it differently. Nowadays, insurance companies are looking at chiropractic treatments as a luxury item that they can just eliminate among the many things they are cutting out of plans. So I end up having to use that term over and over again: it's medically necessary, it's medically necessary. That's the only way they'll pay and it's because they don't want to get sued. But insurance companies are doing everything they can to shortchange their customers and refusing to pay for chiropractic services is just another example.

Another area that troubles some chiropractors relates to patients experiencing greater out-of-pocket expenses for all types of medical treatment, whether it is at the chiropractor's office, the dentist's office, or with their primary care physician. What makes it a bit different with a chiropractor is that, while many patients see paying more out-of-pocket expenses as part of a growing trend in medicine, there can be an underlying question or even a suspicion about the motives of a chiropractor. As Theresa, a chiropractic patient, stated:

I don't know why, but when the chiropractor I used to visit told me this, I wondered if he was telling me the truth. I don't really know the details of my insurance plan, I don't think most people do. But I didn't have a problem when my dentist told me my insurance didn't cover a lot of the costs of my crown. And I didn't really think much about paying a lot out-of-pocket for my MRI last year. But for some reason, I had that little pause of disbelief when my chiropractor told me that my plan only covered a certain number of visits, and I had to pay for everything after that. Is that wrong? Is it because chiropractors have a reputation for being a little shifty and maybe a little desperate? I don't know, but I remember starting to question a lot more about what my chiropractor charged me for after that.

During the course of the study, such a response from patients was not uncommon—many expressed the same concerns as Theresa. Perhaps there is a question about the motives of chiropractors, which can be ignored as long as the patient's insurance covers the treatment. But when they are asked to pay for a greater portion of it, or the entire cost of the visit, patient concerns about a chiropractor's motives become tangible. Even if these suspicions are unfounded, where the chiropractor is legitimately providing services and reasonably expects to be paid for them, such questions can translate into a loss of business—either from losing patients if the mistrust is serious, or simply due to the loss of revenue related to reduced reimbursement rates and limits on visits by insurance companies.

MEDICARE FRAUD AND ACCOUNTABILITY

As several chiropractors in the study noted, the sense of desperation for revenue, along with the decline in reimbursement rates by insurance companies, have led many chiropractors to feel that they have to squeeze every dollar they can from each patient. It also creates a climate where questionable billing practices emerge and become justifiable. As more chiropractors push the boundaries of acceptable behavior, the entire profession has become more involved in audits by Medicare. One chiropractor, Joe, who says he has never been audited and has always under-billed for his services, nearly had an anxiety attack when he received a notice that he was being audited. He says:

> This is what I am dealing with now. I had a patient complain about paying for treatments he received like six months ago. I haven't seen the guy since then but he filed a complaint. Now Medicare wants to see my clinical notes for him and five other patients. I have heard about these audits and it scares the crap out of me! They can do anything they want and the fines are like $10,000 or more! I haven't slept in three days because of this—not only is it a pain to get all that information together, I am worried that they'll find some little thing wrong and then they'll want more information on more patients. I have heard this becomes a never-ending series of requests from them...and you can't really complain. I just don't know what I'm going to do. I treated this guy for his work-related injury and then he stopped coming. So I know I didn't do anything wrong.

During this conversation, Joe's wife, who works in the practice with him, offers her opinions about Medicare. She says:

> Of all the groups to go after with audits, they go after the little guys. The chiropractors. Why? Because they know we can't really fight them and they can do whatever they want to us. I don't see them going after doctors like they go after chiropractors. It's typical of how we are treated.

Joe's wife's comments are interesting, particularly because it reflects a theme among chiropractors in this study about feelings of being persecuted and singled out for unfair treatment. These feelings were commonly articulated by chiropractors about how insurance companies treat them, how the medical profession sees them, and even how others in the profession see each other.

What makes Joe's wife's comments even more interesting is how chiropractors see themselves in comparison to the data about how chiropractors bill for their services. In a recent report issued by the Office of Inspector General (OIG), a division of the Department of Health and Human Services, the agency responsible for overseeing health programs like Medicare and Medicaid, of all the providers who were cited for fraud, abuse, and errors in Medicare billing, chiropractors were overwhelmingly the largest set of offenders

THE OIG AND MEDICARE FRAUD

The OIG selected a stratified sample of 105 chiropractic services based on the services offered and the date of those services during the 2013 calendar year. In their analysis, the OIG found that most Medicare payments did not comply with the program's requirements. Of the 105 services sampled, only 11 were in compliance with Medicare requirements. In most cases, the documentation provided by the chiropractors did not support the medical necessity of the services and most were beyond the three-month time limit for services, which qualified as maintenance therapy. As it is defined by the Benefit Manual, maintenance therapy:

> ...is a treatment plan that seeks to prevent disease, promote health, and prolong and enhance the quality of life or (2) therapy that is performed to maintain or prevent deterioration of a chronic condition. Acute subluxation (e.g. strains or sprains) problems may require as many as three months of treatment but some require very little treatment...Chronic spinal joint condition[s]...may require a longer treatment time, but not with higher frequency. (Office of Inspector General 2016, 7)

The breakdown of the ninety-four chiropractic services that were not in compliance include subluxations of the spine that were not present, were not treated, or both; manual manipulations of the spinal subluxation that constituted maintenance therapy or was not appropriate for treatment of the patient's condition or both; and manual manipulations of the spinal subluxation that would not be expected to result in improvement within a reasonable and generally predictable period of time.

Extrapolating from the sample results, the OIG estimated that approximately $358.8 million or about 82 percent of the $438 million paid by Medicare for chiropractic services was inappropriately paid to chiropractors. The report stated that clearly the AT (Acute Therapy) modifier and the listing of the initial treatment dates did not prevent chiropractors from performing medically unnecessary chiropractic services on patients. Instead chiropractors routinely assign the AT modifier to virtually all of their patients, whether the treatment was for treatment of a subluxation or not. For example, the report stated that of the 17 million chiropractic services included in their review, less than thirty of them did not contain the AT modifier.

Additionally, while documentation was provided by chiropractors in the respective patient files, they did not typically document the medical necessity of the services as outlined in the guidelines by Medicare. The OIG report also noted that despite a great deal of effort to inform chiropractors of these requirements and how to properly submit claims for medically necessary treatment, many chiropractors bill for services that do not meet Medicare requirements. The high error rate (82 percent) indicates that chiropractors are billing inappropriately, whether intentionally with the hope of not getting caught, because of a belief that what they are treating is not maintenance therapy, or because they simply do not understand the coding and billing process.

This is not the first time that the OIG has discovered improprieties with the payment for chiropractic services. OIG conducted four separate reviews, with reports issued between 2013 and 2016, and consistently found that payments for chiropractic services were medically unnecessary, incorrectly coded, insufficiently documented, or not documented at all, resulting in overpayments in the millions of dollars. In 2005, for instance, the OIG issued a report that stated:

> As chiropractic care extends beyond 12 treatments in a year, it becomes increasingly likely that individual services are medically unnecessary. The likelihood of a service being medically unnecessary increases even more significantly after 24 treatments. (Office of Inspector General 2013, 9)

In 2013, the OIG analyzed claims totaling $502 million for chiropractic services and found that Medicare paid $76 million for questionable claims and nearly $21 million for claims that did not meet Medicare requirements. Each time OIG made recommendations to the Centers for Medicare and Medicaid Services (CMS) regarding a more reliable system of control and accountability to address the problem of maintenance therapy by chiropractors. In response, CMS initially attempted to implement a prior authorization medical review of services by certain chiropractors, but OIG disagreed with this approach and pointed out that it focused only on a small group of chiropractors who were repeat offenders for dubious billing practices, not the ones who are receiving payment for maintenance therapy.

Thus, while it is understandable that Joe's wife might feel a bit persecuted, as do many chiropractors about their scope of practice, their philosophy, and their inability to treat patients as they see fit, not everyone in the profession feels that the federal government is unfairly singling out chiropractors for audits. Jenny, a chiropractor involved in the study, noted:

> They (chiropractors) know what they are doing. They are just hoping they don't get flagged. These are not stupid people who can't figure out that they only get a limited number of treatments per patient. What they are trying to do is get as many treatments as they can before they get caught. Medicare has given them lots of information and shown them again and again that they can't bill for maintenance therapy. But these guys just keep doing it anyway. It's part of what's wrong with medicine in this country, so much money is spent on waste and improper payments to doctors.
>
> Chiropractors are getting a lot of attention because there are only so many things they can code for—whereas a primary care physician has a lot more codes to choose from, so it's a lot harder to spot those irregularities. But everyone is doing it. And since chiropractors feel they have to make as much as they can off every patient that walks in the door, they end up fudging the books by saying the treatments are for a new injury—that they're not doing maintenance therapy. That's a fine line because I can see what they are saying—if a guy gets treated for a back problem and then reinjures himself, that shouldn't count against the number of treatments for the first injury.
>
> But then again, ten or twelve visits is a lot of treatment time. I will get crucified by my colleagues for saying that, but honestly? That's a lot. I should be able to get you up and running in one or two

treatments if it's an injury. So even with another injury or the same one flaring up again, I should be able to stay within a twelve-visit limit, or I should be able to document what's happening and justify it that way. But like so many things in this profession, too many guys push the limits and then they make it hard for everyone, because now Medicare is suspicious of anybody doing chiropractic treatment. Let's forget for the moment that preventative care is cheaper in the long run for the government—but those are the rules of the game and we should be playing by them. But many of us are not, sad to say.

HOW MEDICARE HAS RESPONDED TO MISTAKES AND FRAUD BY CHIROPRACTORS

Consistent with the idea that there needs to be greater accountability in medicine, CMS has added programs and contractors to examine providers' claims, particularly chiropractors, to identify errors and overpayments. CMS contracted with what are known as Recovery Audit Contractors (RACs) to identify Medicare overpayments and underpayments. RACs review claims submitted by medical providers and attempt to identify instances where they were either overpaid for services or underpaid for them (Wachler and Associates 2017).

CMS has also created Medicare Administrative Contractors (MACs) who handle enrollment issues and claims processing. They are also responsible for addressing billing errors and incorrectly coded bills. MACs also review claims to determine if proper amounts were paid to providers and adjust or even deny payments that they deem unreasonable or not medically necessary for patients. For those providers who have excessively high error rates or those who have consistently been overpaid, they are put on a payment plan to reimburse Medicare.

One tool used by MACs is the Comprehensive Error Rate Testing Program (CERT). This program is designed to determine the reasons for claim errors and to develop a concrete plan to improve compliance by providers. The CERT contractor randomly selects a sample of Medicare claims and requests medical records and documentation from the provider who submitted those claims (Wachler and Associates 2017).

Given that there is a difference between mistakes and outright fraud, CMS has also created Zone Program Integrity Contractors (ZPICs), who are responsible for identifying suspected fraud. This program is different from MACs, which are designed to identify and correct errors in billing. ZPICs use a variety of proactive techniques, including computer-generated algorithms to identify providers who exceed an estimated rate of claims for a given code in a particular geographic region. This benchmark is then used to identify providers who exceed these expectations. ZPICs then issue a request for additional information about bills submitted for reimbursement. This can be a time-consuming process and often requires detailed information from the provider, which is then reviewed for accuracy and approval of the claim (Wachler and Associates 2017).

CHIROPRACTORS' VOCABULARY OF MOTIVES

While the topic of fraud is a common one in the deviance literature (Porchene and Evans 2004; Bryant 2010; Pontell 1999; Hobbs 2012; Elias 2013; Bergasma 2015; Gottschalk 2017; Trahan, Marquart, and Mullins 2005) and while fraudulent claims by medical providers are not a new or recent phenomenon (Graham 2015; Sausser 2017; National Health Care Anti-Fraud Association 2010; Porchene and Evans 2004), even in South Carolina (Sausser 2017), little or no empirical attention has been given to chiropractors. Because the structure of their practices is different from traditional medical providers, where chiropractors remain primarily solo practitioners who are reluctant to from larger medical groups, perhaps their participation in questionable billing practices is different from most physicians and health care providers.

To begin, not all mistakes or errors are intended to defraud the government—some are simply honest miscalculations or administrative errors in assigning codes or in explaining a particular form of treatment. Others, however, contain an intentional effort to either outright steal money for treatments not provided or bill based on some sort of philosophical stance about the course of treatments. In either case, providers know what they are doing and square their self-images with their actions.

In 1957, Gresham Sykes and David Matza offered a theory to explain delinquency that uses a set of justifications or rationalizations to explain offenders' behavior. The techniques of neutralization theory contain a variety of explanations that allow delinquents to square their self-images with their criminal or deviant behavior. Examples of these types of rationalizations include the denial of a victim, the denial of an injury, or an appeal to higher loyalties to justify criminal acts, meaning the offender feels that their allegiance to friends and colleagues justifies their behavior in some way.

Perhaps the most overlooked technique of neutralization is what Sykes and Matza refer to as condemning the condemners—where offenders justify their crimes because of some flaw in the structure or operation of the system or of society. An example might be to point out the inconsistency in the application of laws regulating alcohol use compared to marijuana use in those states where it remains illegal. Condemning the condemners provides perhaps the most insightful backdrop for understanding why chiropractors continue to engage in inappropriate billing or even outright fraud. The following section provides examples of rationalizations under this category.

Infringement Upon Expertise

Several chiropractors in the study took great exception to the fact that Medicare and other insurance companies refuse to pay for maintenance therapy, when the providers believe that such treatment is absolutely justified and appropriate. They resented the fact that the insurance industry is dictating the philosophy of treatment and a chiropractor's scope of practice when the industry has no real training or expertise to do that. In their minds, pushing the boundaries of appropriate billing is acceptable because of a much larger problem with the insurance companies. Cisco, a chiropractor involved in the study, says:

> I think it is completely inappropriate for an insurance company to determine what's in the patient's best interest. I believe in the idea of maintenance therapy, because I've seen it work. But when insurance companies, who have never been to chiropractic college, start telling me that they won't pay because they don't believe in the idea of maintenance therapy, I have to call them out on that. Who is the expert here? I've been audited several times and while I would like to be honest and describe exactly what I'm doing, I know that if I use the term maintenance therapy, I'm not going to get paid. So, do I game the system? Absolutely, and I don't think there is anything wrong with that. Are you going to tell me that doctors don't fudge the forms to fit the little box they need to get paid? Of course they do. But the problem isn't really about whether I'm gaming the system or not. The problem is that the insurance companies think they can practice medicine, because they hold the purse strings and we don't. So, if I am doing what I think is right for my patients but have to manipulate the process to do that, then I don't lose sleep at night over it. If I get caught, I get caught, but what I think you found is that most chiropractors feel like I do.

LACK OF COMPETENCY OF MEDICARE

As several chiropractors noted, many who engage in inappropriate or fraudulent claims either believe that insurance companies are inept or keep changing the rules to confuse the providers. As one provider pointed out, he made a good faith effort to follow the rules and they were changed without notice, and he was required to pay back some of the money. Jake, a chiropractor in the study, says:

> I can't seem to figure out what I'm doing wrong. Just when I get a clear answer from people about what it is I am supposed to be doing, I get notified that I have done something wrong. How can the rules change so quickly without notice and yet I'm getting hammered because I thought I was doing it properly?

Mike experienced an audit for the first time during the study. He says:

> Hey, I have been told this is no joke and the fines are like $10,000, even if you didn't do anything wrong. There are law firms out there that specialize in protecting chiropractors and doctors from these types of audits, but they're expensive too. So, either way it costs you a lot of money. I did my best to give them all the records and notes that I had, but sometimes they go after you for not having a signature on the form, or some other minor thing. That's not what this should be about. You should be going after the guys that are bilking the system and trying to defraud the taxpayer out of money, not for hitting the little guy hard for forgetting a signature or inadvertently putting in the wrong code. I'm going to give them everything they asked for, but I will tell you, this creates a lot of stress for me—I can't afford to take a hit like that or to pay back reimbursements on patients when I legitimately treated them. As it is, I'm already on the margins so I can't afford a major expense like this, or worse, be put on some list that flags me for more attention than other guys.

Dave talks about his experiences with an audit. He says part of the challenge involves Medicare not understanding that patients often come to see him for different injuries. He says:

> You get the letter every quarter that tells you the average patient visit is here and you've seen this patient x amount of times…and I'm like, 'yeah, I saw them in January and February for a neck problem and now I'm seeing him for a back problem.' Even though it is supposed to be visits per condition, they combine it to per patient per year, so it skews everything to make it look like I'm exceeding the number of visits allowed.

I've been audited two times by Medicare. And the first time it was because, for our adjustment codes, we have five regions of the body. And you bill based on one to two regions, three to four regions, or five regions. Right? So, what they did in each region of the state, they took the top 20 percent for each of these categories and asked to see their records. So I was selected because I have quite a few Medicare patients. So I sent it in and they sent it back, and I think my grade at that time was like a 74 percent or something like that. So I got that and called them up and asked the lady, 'So how did I end up with this percentage?' And she told me "Part of it was because you didn't have the specific level of what you adjusted." And I'm like, "It's right there in my notes, it's very specific. It's right there."

And she said, "Oh yeah, you're right. And that's a major thing right there." So I said, "Does that change the grade?" And she says, "Well it's too late." I'm like, "What do you mean it's too late?" And she's like, "Well it's already in the system." And then she says, "Listen, you got one of the highest scores. A lot of you guys are...most of the scores, and it should be an embarrassment for you guys, because most of the scores are in the 20–30 percent."

So about two years after that, I get audited again. I paid back Medicare like $250 or something and it was like twelve or twenty patients over a twelve-month period of time. But some got denied because I went over twelve visits, but others I sent in had twenty-one or twenty-two visits but they let them go through. So for me, it's like, as soon as you kicked that one out shouldn't all of those that followed get kicked out too? But no, it's just those on those dates. The visits before and the visits after were paid.

REDUCTIONS IN REIMBURSEMENT

Many chiropractors complain that the reduction in reimbursements hampers their ability to sustain a practice, and the heavy administrative responsibilities make it increasingly difficult to accept insurance. For some, the solution is to bill for more procedures or to capitalize on each patient's treatment. Many chiropractors point out that they cannot survive on how little insurance reimburses them, but they also do not feel comfortable asking patients to pay cash for their services. Steven offered perhaps the most candid account of the process. He says:

Hey, the reimbursement isn't like it used to be. Back in the 1980s, you got back what you billed for—today? It's next to nothing. Listen, I'm right on the edge here and a lot of people I know in this business are too. I have to make as much as I can off every person that walks through that door. I don't like it, and wish I had the luxury of not feeling so desperate, but when you can only make like twenty-five dollars per patient, unless you are doing other things, you aren't going to make it in a small practice. If I'm being honest, I will offer more treatments than are really needed, because I can bill for it—does that hurt the patient? No. But I wasn't the one who created this mess—I am the one, though, who has to find a way through it. And that means giving patients additional treatment or, as some of my colleagues inevitably do, billing for things they didn't provide. I haven't gone that far, but I'm not as desperate as some of those guys. But you can't expect me to survive on twenty-five dollars per patient when I only see a hundred patients a week and my overhead is 60 percent. The math just doesn't work. I have to really think if this year is going to be the year that I decide to do something else. I mean, I could make more money selling real estate and actually sleep at night than to do this.

DENIAL OF INJURY

While claims of a broken system could also be classified as a form of condemning the condemners, there is also something to be said for chiropractors who argue that additional treatments actually helped their patients' recovery. This is particularly true of those chiropractors who claim they simply added treatments, such as trigger point therapy or some other technique, as part of the overall treatment of an injury or condition. Questions arise about whether such a tactic is medically necessary or prescribed, but many chiropractors argued that these are clinical decisions that the provider must make. The fact that there is an economic incentive built into such a decision raises questions about the justification of such a course of treatment, however. Mike offers this as his explanation:

So if the only way I can make anything off of patients when they come in the door and use insurance is to bill for other services, then I'll do that. Besides, by giving patients additional treatment, I am facilitating their healing process. So I might normally give them an adjustment, but now in addition to that, I will bill for trigger point therapy, hydra therapy, or something else in order to give myself a bit of a cushion. This is especially true if I don't get reimbursed as much. The patient doesn't really know, and I am legitimately providing additional treatments to them that should help. Is that wrong? Would the patient mind that I gave them additional treatment to facilitate their problems? I don't think so. Should the insurance company mind that I got them back on their feet sooner than if I simply went the normal route? No, they shouldn't.

Tanya expresses concerns about the lack of anyone being really impacted by the unethical choices by providers. She says:

Even with all the controls in place, a lot of chiropractors feel like everyone has been asleep at the switch, so they just keep billing as they always have and hope they don't get caught. The secret to all of this is to know what data they are using and to fly under the wire. If you overbill or you always bill at the highest rate, you're going to get caught. But for the most part, no one really pays attention to what you submit if you say the right things on the charts and you don't try to take advantage of how the system works. It doesn't really work, but people have to game the system in order to survive.

As Mike points out, many chiropractors feel that the entire health care insurance industry is broken and is motivated only to reduce costs at the expense of patient care. Many chiropractors who have been involved in audits or requests for additional information complain that their stance is to continue billing out of compliance in the hopes that the problems in the system reach a critical stage that require reform. Such justification sounds like a noble and philosophical stance, but one has to wonder how such practices raise the public's awareness about the flaws in the system while not calling attention to the questionable actions of chiropractors at the same time. These chiropractors are not likely seen as conscientious objectors by the public, policymakers, insurance companies, or criminal justice agencies.

Finally, as Joe's wife points out, there is a segment of the chiropractor population who do not feel as though there is a problem at all—chiropractors are not engaging in inappropriate billing or fraud, or at least not on the scale that warrants such close monitoring of the profession. In fact, many providers believe that physicians and others are far more likely to inappropriately submit claims and do so far more frequently than chiropractors.

Thus, as these accounts illustrate, many chiropractors are anxious about the uncertainty of their place in medicine in the future, as evidenced by declining reimbursements and the number of patients, and this level of concern results in questionable acts with regard to billing insurance companies. It also explains how so many chiropractors can find a way to justify their actions in light of the clearly defined guidelines outlined by Medicare. For those who make an honest effort to comply but find themselves being identified for greater scrutiny, perhaps additional training is needed. Others who stubbornly cling to an ideology that is not supported by the insurance industry, or who seemingly take a symbolic stance against the ineffectiveness of the system, continue to bill for services that they know are not legal; additional training is not going to change their course of action. Instead, they will either hope they do not get caught or pay the fines and reimburse Medicare when audits reveal their lack of compliance.

LIMITATIONS AND FUTURE

This study consisted of interviews and observations of a select number of chiropractors and others related to the profession in one region of South Carolina. As is true with any ethnographic study, the generalizability of the findings is limited; what was discovered in this study may not be reflective of the issues and problems found among chiropractors in other states or countries. It could also be the case that another group of chiropractors within the same region or state might offer different perspectives than the providers in this study. That their comments are reflective of national trends in the profession is encouraging, but there is the possibility that the study involved an unusual segment of the population. Given that a sizeable portion of chiropractors are anti-science in philosophy, it may be a type of self-selection occurred by those willing to participate in the study.

In terms of future research, what is likely needed is a more systematic and in-depth examination of the findings of the OIG report and a nationwide sample of chiropractors, which may indicate if, like criminals in general, a small number of offenders are responsible for the majority of the fraud and inappropriate billing or whether it is an industry-wide problem. Given the magnitude of the problem, and given that most chiropractors are solo practitioners, this is unlikely, but confirmation of this would require a more elaborate and quantitative study. Also needed is a more detailed examination of those chiropractors like Cisco, who believe they are justified in the way they submit claims to insurance companies, arguing that there are fundamental problems with the way the system functions, which creates a climate in which many chiropractors feel the need to push the boundaries of acceptable behavior with regard to billing practices (Cressey 1972; Matza 1964; Sykes and Matza 1957).

Bibliography

Adams, S. "Why do so Many Doctors Regret Their Job Choice?" Forbes. April 27, 2012. www.forbes.com.

Bellamy, Jann. "The DC as PCP? The Battle Continues. Science-Based Medicine. January 24, 2013. https://sciencebasedmedicine.org/the-dc-as-pcp-the-battle-continues/

Bergasma, T. "General Strain Theory and Production of Occupational Fraud." Doctoral Dissertation, Walden University, 2015.

Bryant, C. D., ed. *Handbook of Deviant Behavior.* New York: Routledge, 2010.

———., ed. *Deviant Behavior: Readings in the Sociology of Norm Violations.* New York: Hampton Publishing, 2011.

Cockerham, J. *Medical Sociology.* 14th Edition. New York: Routledge, 2017.

Cressey, Donald. *Other People's Money.* California: Wadsworth Publishing, 1972.

Elias, S. M. *Deviance and Criminal Behavior in the Workplace.* New York: NYU Press, 2013.

English, C., and E. Keating. "Majority in U.S. say Chiropractic Works for Neck, Back Pain." Gallup. 2015. www.gallup.com

Gottschalk, P. "White Collar Crime Triangle: Finance, Organization, and Behavior." *Journal of Forensic Sciences and Criminal Investigation* 4, no. 1 (2017): 1–8.

Graham, D. "The True Face of Medicare Fraud. *The Atlantic.* June 19, 2015. www.theatlantic.com.

"Healthcare Audit Lawyers." Wachler and Associates. https://www.wachler.com/healthcare-audit-lawyers.html.

Hobbs, R. C. "Find Deviant Behavior, Find Fraud?" Association of Certified Fraud Examiners. 2012. www.acfe.com.

Lecomte, M. D., and J.J. Schensul. *Designing and Conducting Ethnographic Research.* New York: Rowman and Altimira, 2012.

Lisi, A. J., and C. A. Brandt. "Trends in the Use and Characteristics of Chiropractic Services in the Department of Veterans Affairs." *Journal of Manipulative Physiological Therapies* 39, (2016): 381–6.

Long, P. H. *Chiropractic Abuse: An Insider's Lament.* New York: American Council on Science and Health, 2013.

Magner, G., and S. Barrett. *Chiropractic: The Victim's Perspective.* New York: Prometheus Books, 1995.

Matza, David. *Delinquency and Drift.* New York: John Wiley and Sons, 1964.

McMillen, M. "Complementary and Alternative Medicine on the Rise." WebMD. 2011. www.webmd.com.

McNamara, Robert H. "The Joint as a Form of Disruptive Innovation in Chiropractic Medicine," *International Journal of Social Sciences and Business* 5, no. 2 (2017): 1–11.

O'Donnell, J., M. Hoyer, and Y. Alcindor. "Some Chiropractors Making Big Medicare-paid Adjustments." USA Today. April 29, 2014. https://www.usatoday.com/story/news/politics /2014/04/29/medicare-data-chiropractors-reimbursements/7720741/.

Pontell, Henry. *Social Deviance: Readings in Theory and Research*. New Jersey: Prentice-Hall, 1999.

Porchene, D. A., and R. D. Evans. "The Nature of Medicaid/Medicare Fraud and Neutralization Techniques Among Speech, Occupational, and Physical Therapists." *Deviant Behavior* 26, no. 3 (2004): 253–70.

Punke, H. "Survey: 42% of Physicians are Dissatisfied." Becker's Hospital Review. June 11, 2013. http://www.beckershospitalreview.com/hospital-physician-relationships/survey-42-of-physicians-are-dissatisfied.html

Rabin, R. C. "Burnt Out Primary Care Docs are Voting with their Feet." Kaiser Health News April 1, 2014. http://www.Khn.org/news/doctor-burnout/

Sausser, Lauren. "Medicaid Fraud in South Carolina Largely Tied to Health Care Providers." *Post and Courier*. September 4, 2017. https://www.postandcourier.com/health/medicaid-fraud-in-south-carolina-largely-tied-to- health-care/article_08618804-867c-11e7-b0d7-57e51c3606f0.html

Singh, Simon. and Edzard Ernst. *Trick or Treatment: The Undeniable Facts About Alternative Medicine.* New York: W.W. Norton and Company, 2009.

Sykes, G. M., and D. Matza. "Techniques of Neutralization: A Theory of Delinquency." *American Sociological Review* 22, no. 6 (1957): 664–70.

Taylor, Stephanie. *Ethnographic Research: A Reader.* Belmont, CA: Sage, 2002.

Trahan, A., J. W. Marquart, and J. Mullings. *Fraud and the American Dream: Toward an Understanding of Fraud Victimization.* San Francisco, CA: Stanford Center on Longevity, 2005.

US Department of Health and Human Services, Office of Inspector General. "Hundreds of Millions in Medicare Payments for Chiropractic Services did not Comply with Medicare Requirements." October 2016. https://oig.hhs.gov/oas/reports/region9/91402033.pdf

Automating Bias: The Role of Artificial Intelligence in Sentencing and Predictive Policing

Linda Henry, JD

FOR MANY PEOPLE, artificial intelligence (AI) conjures up images of futuristic robots taking over the world; however, AI has already transformed our lives and is reshaping how we make decisions on a daily basis. Whether picking a movie on Netflix, shopping on Amazon, asking Siri for a recommendation, or using Google Maps to pick the best route home, computer programs that mimic human intelligence routinely infiltrate our decision-making processes. In many areas of our lives, AI enhances our daily decision making and enables us to make better decisions. In addition, the risk-reward ratio is often favorable, since the consequences of relying on a bad shopping recommendation or erroneous prediction about the best route home are minor. What happens, however, when AI is used to make life-changing decisions?

WHAT IS ARTIFICIAL INTELLIGENCE?

AI is a branch of computer science devoted to the creation of intelligent machines that work and react like human beings. Artificial intelligence is a broad term that includes various processes, including natural language processing, cognitive computing, machine learning, and deep learning. At its most basic, AI involves computer programs that are designed to complete tasks that would typically require human intelligence.

Machine Learning and Deep Learning

Machine learning and deep learning are both subfields of AI. Arthur Samuel, a pioneer in the field of AI, coined the term *machine learning* in 1959 and defined it as the field of study that gives computers the ability to learn without being explicitly programmed. Through the application of machine learning, a machine is able to learn from data with minimal programming. Deep learning is a subset of machine learning and, in essence, takes machine learning to the next level. Deep learning modules attempt to replicate the web of neurons in the human brain, thus enabling the machine to learn how to learn. By using complex layers of algorithms called artificial neural networks, deep learning modules are able to analyze large data sets with a logic structure that is similar to humans (Metz 2016).

For example, when we log onto Netflix, the recommendations we see are neither the result of the software underlying Netflix being programmed to generate suggestions nor driven primarily by our individual past viewing habits. Rather, the individualized recommendations are the result of Netflix's proprietary neural networks, comprised of a complex set of algorithms that take into account feedback collected from the individual viewer, the historical viewing habits of over 250 million active profiles, and content tags generated by Netflix personnel that watch each minute of every available Netflix program and tag content to create a seemingly infinite number of mini subgenres (Plummer 2017). The Netflix neural network is constantly analyzing massive amounts of ever-changing data and training itself to provide better viewer recommendations.

Artificial Intelligence and Sentencing

The criminal justice system is another area in which AI, and more specifically, deep learning is being used to make predictions of future behaviors. Governments are increasingly using AI and deep learning, particularly in connection with creating risk-assessment profiles of defendants. For example, COMPAS (which stands for Correctional Offender Management Profiling for Alternative Sanctions) is a deep learning computer algorithm used to predict a defendant's risk of recidivism and is one of the risk-assessment tools most widely used by courts to predict recidivism (Angwin, Larson, Mattu, and Krichner 2016). COMPAS creates a risk assessment by comparing information specific to a defendant to large batches of historical data from groups of similar individuals (Citron 2016). Because COMPAS software is proprietary, however, outside parties have no visibility into how the COMPAS algorithms work. Consequently, some courts are basing sentencing decisions on recidivism predictions without knowing how the software arrived at such predictions.

COMPAS is only one example of proprietary software being used by courts to make sentencing decisions, and states are increasingly using software risk-assessment tools such as COMPAS as a formal part of the sentencing process. Because many of the algorithms such as COMPAS are proprietary, the source code is not published and is not subject to state or federal open record laws (Angelino, Larus-Stone, and Rudin 2017). As a result, the opacity inherent in proprietary programs such as COMPAS prevents outside parties from seeing the data and algorithms that impact sentencing decisions.

Because algorithms are often presumed to be objective and unbiased, the use of predictive analytics in risk assessments have been touted by some as a way to eliminate human bias in sentencing. Theoretically algorithms like COMPAS should "provide evidence-based reasons for sentences rather than 'ad hoc,' gut-based decisions by human beings beset with cognitive limits and implicit biases" (Citron 2016). However, recent investigations into algorithms used in the criminal justice system to predict recidivism have produced compelling evidence that such algorithms may be racially biased. Although COMPAS and other risk-assessment software programs use algorithms that are race neutral on their face, the algorithms frequently use data points that can serve as proxies for race, such as ZIP codes, education history, and family history of incarceration. In addition, critics of such algorithms question the methodologies used by programs such as COMPAS, since methodologies (which are necessarily created by individuals) may unintentionally reflect human bias (Hudson 2017). If the data sets being used to train the algorithms are not truly objective, human bias may be unintentionally baked into the algorithm, effectively automating human bias.

An investigation by ProPublica found that COMPAS risk assessments were more likely to erroneously identify black defendants as presenting a high risk for recidivism at almost twice the rate as white defendants (43 percent vs. 23 percent). In addition, ProPublica's research revealed that COMPAS risk assessments erroneously labeled white defendants as low risk 48 percent of the time, compared to 28 percent for black defendants. Black defendants were also 45 percent more likely to receive a higher risk score than white defendants, even after controlling for variables such as prior crimes, age, and gender (Angwin, Larson, Mattus, and Kirchner 2016). ProPublica's findings raise serious concerns regarding COMPAS; however, because the calculations used to assess risk are proprietary, neither defendants nor the court systems utilizing COMPAS have visibility into why such assessments have significant rates of mislabeling among black and white defendants.

In addition to the problem of biased data, AI programs used to make sentencing decisions may also eliminate individualized human judgment that is necessary to reach a fair sentencing decision. Unlike human beings, deep learning programs such as COMPAS are unable to take individual mitigating factors into account while making sentencing decisions. When determining sentencing, a judge has the benefit of being able to interact with defendants and consider material data points—such as a troubled childhood or disability—for which an algorithm may not account. Sentencing decisions based on predictive algorithms, however, eliminate the ability of judges to individualize justice (Israni 2017).

Examples of Artificial Intelligence in Sentencing

When Paul Zilly, a forty-eight-year-old construction worker, was arrested for stealing a push lawnmower and gardening tools, the prosecutor recommended that Zilly receive a year in county jail and supervision following release that would help Zilly, who had been working to overcome a meth addition, continue in his recovery. Zilly accepted the plea deal; however, at sentencing, the judge rejected the proposed plea deal based on Zilly's COMPAS risk assessment score and sentenced Zilly to two years in state prison and three years of supervision following release. Zilly's COMPAS risk assessment scored him as a high risk for future violent crime and a medium risk for general recidivism. At Zilly's appeal, the judge reduced Zilly's sentence after hearing the testimony of Tim Brennan, one of the creators of COMPAS, who testified that he never intended for the software to be used in sentencing. Although the judge did not address the validity of using risk assessments, the judge did note that had he not used the COMPAS risk assessment, it was likely he would have given Zilly a reduced sentence (Angwin, Larson, Mattus, and Kirchner 2016).

Legal challenges by individuals to the use of such algorithms in criminal sentencing have largely been unsuccessful. In 2017, Eric Loomis, a Wisconsin defendant, unsuccessfully challenged the use of the COMPAS algorithm as a violation of his due process rights. In 2013 Loomis was arrested and charged with five criminal counts related to a drive-by shooting. Loomis maintained that he was not involved in the shooting but pled guilty to driving a motor vehicle without the owner's permission and fleeing from police. At sentencing, the trial court judge sentenced Loomis to six years in prison, noting that the court ruled out probation based in part on the COMPAS risk assessment that suggested Loomis presented a high risk to reoffend (*State v. Loomis* 2016). Loomis appealed his sentence, arguing that the use of a proprietary risk assessment into which he had no visibility violated his constitutional right to due process. The Wisconsin Supreme Court ultimately affirmed the lower court's decision. In 2017 the US Supreme Court denied Loomis' petition for writ of certiorari, leaving unresolved the question of whether the use of proprietary algorithms in sentencing violates an individual's constitutional right of due process.

Artificial Intelligence and Predictive Policing

Predictive policing refers to the practice of using AI to predict where future crimes are likely to occur based on data from previous criminal activity. Just as AI-driven risk-assessment profiles used in sentencing may be problematic because of biased data, the data used to train predictive policing algorithms may also be biased, resulting in crime predictions that reinforce systemic bias.

Historical data based on police practices may reflect law enforcement biases as to which neighborhoods the police believe are good or bad. Civil rights organizations have also raised questions regarding the use of AI deep learning algorithms to make automated predictions based on potentially biased historical data (Reiland 2018). According to the ACLU, "the data driving predictive enforcement activities—such as the location and timing of previously reported crimes, or patterns of community- and officer-initiated 911 calls—is profoundly limited and biased" (ACLU 2016). The ACLU and other civil rights organizations contend that police crime statistics mainly reflect police *response* to situations rather than provide a comprehensive record of all crimes that have occurred. As a result, if the AI tools used to predict criminal activity rely on biased data that does not accurately reflect crimes that have occurred, then the use of such AI tools may "reinforce bias and sanitize injustice" (ACLU 2016).

In addition to the problem of biased historical data, various studies have also documented the problem of feedback loops with AI driven programs (Ensign 2017). When law enforcement is repeatedly sent to the same neighborhood, the volume of data that is collected regarding crime in a particular area may be disproportionate to the amount of actual crime that occurs. Yet, this skewed data will be used to further train the algorithm to predict certain neighborhoods as being bad, thus creating a problematic feedback loop (Ensign 2017).

CONCLUSION

When the technology developed to allow law enforcement and courts to make more accurate and fairer decisions is simply reinforcing systemic biases, how do we remedy this problem? Although increasing algorithmic transparency would seem an ideal first step, the right of companies to protect their intellectual property is in direct conflict with the need for visibility into how the predictive algorithms that make life-altering decisions work.

The increased public scrutiny of AI in the criminal justice system is prompting some legislators to acknowledge that a problem exists. In 2017 the New York City Council passed the first bill in the United States designed to address algorithmic discrimination in government agencies. The goal of New York City's algorithmic accountability bill is to create a task force to monitor algorithms used by municipal agencies and provide recommendations as to how to make the City's algorithms fairer and more transparent. Despite the task force's daunting task of tackling algorithmic bias, critics of the use of algorithms in the criminal justice system are hopeful that New York City's legislative acknowledgment of algorithmic bias will encourage other cities and states to address their own use of biased algorithms (Powles 2017). In addition, while this article only focuses on the problematic aspects of AI in sentencing and predictive policing, recent uses of deep learning technology to reform bail systems in New Jersey and Ohio offer evidence that with sufficient accountability and transparency, AI can work for the public good in the criminal justice system (Israni 2017).

Deep learning technology is still in its nascent stage and it remains unclear how to remedy the problems of bias that may arise from the use of AI in the criminal justice system. However, the fairness and accuracy of deep learning tools used in the criminal justice system may improve if more city and state governments are willing to acknowledge that data sets and algorithms may be biased and begin to utilize technology that is transparent about the underlying calculations and methodology.

Bibliography

Angelino, Elaine, Nicholas Larus-Stone, and Cynthia Rudin. "Learning Certifiably Optimal Rule Lists for Categorical Data." Nov. 30, 2017. https://arxiv.org/pdf/1704.01701.pdf.

Angwin, Julia, Jeff Larson, Surya Mattu, and Lauren Kirchner. "How We Analyzed the COMPAS Recidivism Algorithm." *ProPublica*. May 23, 2016. www.propublica.org/article/how-we-analyzed-the-compas-recidivism-algorithm.

———. "Machine Bias." *ProPublica*. May 23, 2016. https://www.propublica.org/article/machine-bias-risk-assessments-in-criminal-sentencing.

Citron, Danielle. "(Un)Fairness Of Risk Scores In Criminal Sentencing." Forbes. July 13, 2016. https://www.forbes.com/sites/daniellecitron/2016/07/13/unfairness-of-risk-scores-in-criminal-sentencing/#28fcc5f44ad2.

Ensign, Danielle, Sorelle A. Friedler, Scott Neville, Carlos Scheidegger, and Suresh Venkatasurbramanian. "Runaway Feedback Loops in Predictive Policing." *Proceedings of Machine Learning Research* 81, (2018): 1–12. https://arxiv.org/pdf/1706.09847.pdf.

Hudson, Laura. "Technology Is Biased Too. How Do We Fix It?", FiveThirtyEight. Juley 20, 2017. https://fivethirtyeight.com/features/technology-is-biased-too-how-do-we-fix-it/.

Israni, Ellora Thadaney. "When an Algorithm Helps Send You to Prison." *New York Times*. October 26, 2017. https://www.nytimes.com/2017/10/26/opinion/algorithm-compas-sentencing-bias.html.

Metz, Cade. "Microsoft Neural Net Shows Deep Learning Can Get Way Deeper."*Wired Magazine*. January 14, 2016. https://www.wired.com/2016/01/microsoft-neural-net-shows-deep-learning-can-get-way-deeper/.

Plummer, Libby. "This is How Netflix's Top Secret Recommendations Work." *Wired Magazine*. August 22, 2017. http://www.wired.co.uk/article/how-do-netflixs-algorithms-work-machine-learning-helps-to-predict-what-viewers-will-like.

Powles, Julia. "New York City's Bold, Flawed Attempt to Make Algorithms Accountable." *The New Yorker*. December 20, 2017. www.newyorker.com/tech/elements/new-york-citys-bold-flawed-attempt-to-make-algorithms-accountable.

Rieland, Randy. "Artificial Intelligence Is Now Used to Predict Crime. But Is It Biased?" *Smithsonian Magazine*. March 5, 2018. https://www.smithsonianmag.com/innovation/artificial-intelligence-is-now-used-predict-crime-is-it-biased-180968337/#WrWR2fUXqEbZWLRz.99.

"Statement of Concern About Predictive Policing by ACLU and 16 Civil Rights Privacy, Racial Justice and Technology Organizations." ACLU. August 31, 2016. https://www.aclu.org/other/statement-concern-about-predictive-policing-aclu-and-16-civil-rights-privacy-racial-justice.

State v. Loomis, 881 N.W.2d 749, 754–55 (Wis. 2016).

Social Inequality/Poverty

What Are the Consequences of Being Poor?

SOCIAL INEQUALITY/POVERTY

The discussion of social class is fundamentally a sociological explanation of society. When sociologists examine any issue or problem in society, they are likely to discover that there are elements of a person's social class at the root of some or even most of the behavior. The problem with examining social class, however, is that there is wide disagreement as to what constitutes a person's class standing. Instead, sociologists and other social scientists typically use what is known as socioeconomic status or SES. A person's SES is a product of their income, education level, and occupational prestige. This gets closer to a fair and equitable way of assessing something like social class by taking into account the fact that some careers generate a lot of income but are not generally considered high on the social status scale (think of a drug dealer as an example), while others may require a great deal of expertise but earn lower salaries (think of a priest or a teacher). Thus, when we talk about social class and social inequality, SES is the better marker for the discussion.

One of the challenges in having a discussion about social inequality or poverty relates to how people understand why it occurs. While conventional wisdom suggests that people are generally poor because they are lazy or lack a strong work ethic, the data suggests a far different picture. Part of the problem with discussing poverty is that the general understanding of why it occurs is often in conflict with the data on what actually takes place. In fact, the challenges relating to poverty are usually not a result of a lack of effort by people, although there are undoubtedly some people in every class who lack a work ethic. Rather, the data shows that most people who are poor already work full-time, and in some cases, have multiple jobs. The problem is that the wages offered, coupled with the extraordinarily high costs of living in this country, make the promise of achieving the American Dream virtually impossible. In all, the issues of poverty and inequality are real for millions of Americans, and the obstacles that are placed before them due to structural barriers such as low employment, declining wages, and the lack of affordable housing and rising costs of childcare, are not resolved by discipline or a strong work ethic. Effort and perseverance alone cannot overcome such formidable challenges, most of which are beyond the control of the individual. Thus, the study of poverty and what contributes to it is not a simple matter and requires the consideration of factors we normally would not include in the conversation.

The articles in this section explore some of the challenges poor people experience, particularly children. Amy Hauser examines the notion of homelessness, with an eye towards how we have shifted our focus from helping the homeless to criminalizing many of the behaviors they engage in as a consequence of their situations. Similarly, Shannon Woolf Connolly, in describing a broken system that attempts to help families in need, explores the challenges of training caseworkers who are helping poor mothers and families face the challenges of poverty and life on welfare. Finally, Brett Loftis examines life as a foster child, with an emphasis on what the experience in the foster care system does to a child and how to address the trauma these children have sustained.

A Look at the Laws in the United States: Legislation and the Ongoing Criminalization of the Homeless

Amy Presley Hauser, JD

ACROSS THE COUNTRY, laws have been enacted at all levels of government that affect homeless people directly and indirectly. The laws raise questions about the goals of the governing bodies in regards to the homeless. In 2017 the Department of Housing and Urban Development (HUD) reported the number of people experiencing unsheltered homelessness has increased (HUD Awards Record 2018). HUD found that 553,742 people were homeless on a single night in 2017. Those numbers work out to seventeen homeless for every ten thousand people in America. Emergency shelters housed approximately two-thirds of these individuals and the rest were occupying unsheltered locations. For the first time in seven years, HUD found that homelessness had increased (Annual Homeless Assessment Report 2017). As homelessness continues to be a crisis in America, we have to be aware of the legislation targeting the homeless and how it treats them as human beings and members of our communities. The solutions reflected by these laws, which are misdirected solutions, often work against ending homelessness.

FEDERAL LEGISLATION

In 1987, the Stewart B. McKinney Homeless Assistance Act, Public Law 100–77, was the first legislation passed evaluating and addressing the needs of the homeless population in America. It was signed into law by President Ronald Reagan. The Stewart B. McKinney Act has nine titles that range from establishing the US Interagency Council on Homelessness to authorizing the Emergency Food and Shelter Program and emergency shelter and transitional housing programs. The definition of a homeless person was provided as follows:

> An individual who lacks a fixed, regular, and adequate nighttime residence; and (2) an individual who has primary nighttime residence that is (A) a supervised publicly or privately operated shelter designated to provide temporary living accommodations (including welfare hotels, congregate shelters, and transitional housing for the

mentally ill); (B) an institution that provides a temporary residence for individuals intended to be institutionalized; or (C) a public or private place not designed for, or ordinarily used as, a regular sleeping accommodation for human beings. (McKinney-Vento Act 2000, section 103(a))

Through various amendments through the years, the Act maintained expanded programs and funding was increased sometimes and programs cut at other times. The McKinney Act, criticized by some, did aid many individuals. The Act was renamed the McKinney-Vento Homeless Assistance Act by President Bill Clinton in the year 2000. The fact that there is not a single or simple solution to homelessness was recognized in plain language in the Act (McKinney-Vento Act 2006).

Homeless children and youth were mentioned in the first version of the Act and it has been amended multiple times to include further provisions for these children and youth as the number of young people experiencing homelessness has grown (US Department of Education 2018). One of these amendments to the McKinney-Vento Act was the authorization of the Education for Homeless Children and Youth (EHCY) program. Under this program, each child and youth is guaranteed a free, appropriate public education. A homeless liaison is appointed for each public school district to assist in outreach, identification, and coordination with agencies (US Interagency Council on Homelessness 2015). The education of children and youth experiencing homelessness became front and center again in the Every Student Succeeds Act (ESSA) effective October 2016 (Part B 2015). The McKinney-Vento Act has not addressed all the problems facing homeless people and did not mention criminalization of homelessness.

An additional piece of federal legislation affecting the homeless that was passed is known as the Helping Families Save Their Homes Act of 2009. In this legislation, the Interagency Council on Homelessness was directed to figure out construction alternatives to criminalization measures that cities can employ across the country (NLCHP *Homes Not Handcuffs* 2009).

The 108th Congress was witness to a major piece of legislation known as the Bringing Home America Act. The intent of the legislation was to bring a permanent end to homelessness in America, and it was recognized as the most comprehensive initiative to address homelessness. Representative Julia Carson of Indiana introduced the legislation along with multiple cosponsors on July 25, 2003 as HR 2897. The Act recognized housing as a basic human right and detailed additional provisions for housing and related programs. The bill was also introduced again by Representative Carson in the 109th Congress as HR 4347. Representative Carson passed away before another version was introduced in the 110th Congress. The legislation as introduced addressed housing security, economic security, health security, and civil rights (H.R. 2897 2003; NCH Public Policy Recommendations).

Following this legislation, efforts have been made to end homelessness. According to the US Interagency Council on Homelessness, the definition of an end to homelessness is as follows: "every community will have a systematic response in place that ensures homelessness is prevented whenever possible or is otherwise a rare, brief, and non-recurring experience" (2015, 10). Some cities are taking on the challenge to end homelessness by developing plans. In Chicago, Illinois, the Interagency Homelessness Task Force was started in 2016 (US Conference on Mayors 2017). Under President Obama, a push was made through a program to end homelessness among veterans in 2015 (US Interagency Council on Homelessness 2015).

Though a slow start, steps have been taken by the federal government through legislation to recognize and address homelessness, from individuals to families. The same cannot be said for what has resulted from city council meetings and local governments across the country.

State and Local News: Criminalization of Homelessness

While there is limited federal legislation addressing homelessness, there are numerous laws affecting homeless individuals on a local level. The day to day lives of the homeless are directed by these laws. If you did not have a bed or a couch under a roof, where would you sleep? If you did not have a bathroom, where would you shower and use the toilet? If you did not have a home, where would you go during the day and night? What is criminalization of homelessness? It makes behaviors related to life-sustaining activities punishable under the law. As the National Coalition for the Homeless describes it, the homeless person who lives in public is forced to do in public what people prefer to do in private.

The most "fundamental defense" of the homeless is the right to exist (NCH *Criminalization of Homelessness*). If you think that homeless people want to be homeless, I challenge you to rethink that as you read about how these individuals are treated. Laws are in place effectively making it criminal for homeless people to do behaviors necessary to survive. These laws prohibit actions like "camping" or sleeping in public, begging in public, loitering, loafing and vagrancy, sitting or lying down in public, sleeping in vehicles, and food sharing.

Advocates for homeless individuals argue these laws are intended to remove the homeless from visibility within cities—so they cannot be seen in parks, streets, and other public places. There are not enough beds in shelters or affordable housing options yet individuals without homes cannot sleep outside and in some cases even be outside without the risk of arrest. The Western Regional Advocacy Project started collecting data from homeless people across the country in 2010. As to criminalization they had experienced, 80 percent of the 1,600 people interviewed reported harassment by police for sleeping in public (NLCHP *No Safe Place* 2014).

The criminalization of homelessness is not new. For a long time, groups that advocate for the homeless, a voiceless group in our society, have identified these laws and attempted to bring awareness and change. The National Law Center on Homelessness & Poverty (NLCHP) has studied certain cities for years to examine the laws being passed and enforced. Based on its study of 187 cities, NLCHP found that criminalization of homelessness is increasing and, while some laws on certain measures have decreased since 2011, more have increased substantially. For example, laws prohibiting sleeping in vehicles has increased 119 percent. NLCHP concluded that "homeless people are criminally punished for being in public even when they have no other alternatives" (2014). These laws are not a mere inconvenience to these individuals, the laws threaten their ability to do everyday actions to survive and effectively force them out of communities. As you read some of these laws, you may begin to wonder if those who pass the legislation even see the homeless as human beings.

A joint report by the National Law Center on Homelessness & Poverty and the National Coalition for the Homeless examined many laws criminalizing homelessness. Their research showed there was an increase in criminalizing homelessness since their 2006 report. The report even identified cities as "mean cities" where the most inhumane treatment of homeless people was occurring. Los Angeles, California was called out for its handling of the homeless population. A 2007 study showed that Los Angeles spent $6 million a year to pay for fifty extra police officers to try to bring down crime in the Skid Row area, yet only $5.7 million was in the city budget for homeless services. During an eleven-month period, twenty-four people were arrested 201 times, costing $3.6 million to pay for police, the jails, prosecuting attorneys, public defenders, and the court system. It was found that many of the citations given to homeless persons were for jaywalking and loitering, "crimes" that rarely resulted in written citations in other parts of the city. Homeless advocates asserted that the cost of these arrests could have provided supportive housing for 225 people (NLCHP *Homes Not Handcuffs* 2009).

Bans on camping and sleeping in public and living in vehicles are common. According to research by NLCHP, 34 percent of cities in their study had a city-wide ban on camping, representing a 60 percent increase since 2011. Approximately 57 percent of cities had a ban on camping in particular places which showed a 16 percent increase (NLCHP *No Safe Place* 2014). An Orlando ordinance provides as follows:

Sec 43.52 –Camping prohibited; exceptions. (1) For the purposes of this section, "camping" is defined as: (a) Sleeping or otherwise being in a temporary shelter out-of-doors; or (b) Sleeping out-of-doors; or Cooking over an open flame or fire out-of-doors. (2) Camping is prohibited on all public property, except as may be specifically authorized by the appropriate governmental authority. (3) Camping is prohibited on all property in the City used for residential purposes, provided, however, that camping is permitted on such property with the permission and consent of the property owner. (Ord. of 9–15–1980, Section 1; Ord of 12–8–1986, Doc. #20791) (Orlando 2017)

Research showed that 18 percent of the cities have bans on sleeping in public, which was consistent from previous reports. However, sleeping in public bans decreased by 34 percent, which could be attributed to the increase in anti-camping laws which could include the sleeping conduct (NLCHP *No Safe Place* 2014). In Myrtle Beach, South Carolina, Section 16–31 of the municipal code provides, "It shall be unlawful for any person to sleep in any motor vehicle in the city between the hours of 9:00 p.m. and sunrise" (Myrtle Beach 2017). Most people have heard stories of individuals who were homeless at one point, even sleeping in the family car for a period of time, and are now famous athletes, actors, and other successful persons (Smith and Walters 2015). Under these laws, those individuals would be subject to arrest for simply finding a place to sleep at night.

Other criminalization measures address begging, loitering, loafing and vagrancy, and even sitting or lying down in public. Some cities have laws making it illegal to panhandle in public places. There are degrees on the restrictions, from outright prohibition to prohibiting only vocal requests to prohibiting "aggressive panhandling." In its research, the NLCHP found a 25 percent increase in these types of laws since 2011, with 24 percent of the cities having bans on begging in public throughout the city (NLCHP *No Safe Place* 2014). A massive 76 percent of the cities banned begging in particular places, up 20 percent in such laws. These laws have not been shown to reduce panhandling (NLCHP *Homes Not Handcuffs* 2009). Some cities have tried something different—installing meters to accept money from people who would have given that change to those panhandling. The meters look like a parking meter and any proceeds are passed on to local groups providing services to the homeless. While this may be better than panhandling laws, it does not address the real problem and still has the effect of pushing out panhandlers.

Sitting and lying down are basic needs. The "sit/lie" laws criminalize resting in places usually available to the public. Of the cities surveyed, over half

(53 percent) have bans against sitting or lying down in particular places. That is a 43 percent increase since 2011 (NLCHP *No Safe Place* 2014). In Virginia Beach, Virginia, the ordinance addresses sitting, reclining, or lying down on streets or sidewalks. According to Section 33–10, "It shall be unlawful for any person to sit, recline or lie down on any street, sidewalk, alley, curb or entrance to any store or other place of business. Any person who violates the provisions of this section shall be guilty of a class 4 misdemeanor" (Virginia Beach 2018, Code 1965, section 23–36.3). Remaining in one place too long can be criminalized by loafing and loitering laws. It is asserted that these laws and vagrancy laws address suspicious behavior, but they essentially deal with a homeless person not having anywhere to go (NLCHP *No Safe Place* 2014). In Newport, Rhode Island, local ordinance 9.04.060 on loitering provides:

> A. As used in this section, 'loitering' or 'loiter' means remaining idly in essentially one location, including the concepts of spending time idly, loafing or standing about aimlessly, and also including the colloquial expression "hanging around." B. No person shall stand or loiter on any street, sidewalk, lane, parking lot or alley, or at the entrance to, or in the hallway, passageway or vestibule of, any church, hall, theater, place of entertainment or place of public assembly, or in and upon any parking lot, fence, stoop, sidewalk or platform attached to any dwelling house, store or other building or forming or being a part of a shopping center, so as to obstruct a free passage for foot passengers and/or vehicles, expect with the express permission and consent of the owner of the premises of which such parking lot , fence, stoop, sidewalk or platform is a part, and in no case after such dwelling house, store, shopping center or other building has been closed for the night. C. Any person loitering, as provided in subsection B of this section, shall immediately move on and away when requested to do so by any officer or member of the police division. (Newport, Prior Code section 660.02)

According to this law, hanging around in all these places is not allowed. The NLCHP found a 35 percent increase in city-wide bans on loitering in public since 2011, but a 3 percent decrease in bans of loitering in particular public places (NLCHP *No Safe Place* 2014). Laws such as these raise questions about what we expect homeless individuals to do. Where should they go when the reason they are outdoors is because they do not have a private place to go?

The homeless face other challenges, including storing their personal belongings. The belongings we have in our houses are essential to us personally. There are things of value that we would not want to part with, but we do not carry those things everywhere we go. Where can the homeless keep their personal items where the items will be protected? Instead of finding a safe place, homeless individuals have their personal belongings taken during "homeless sweeps" where government workers or law enforcement clear out an area and dispose of everything. This includes personal items, important papers, pictures, and even medicine (NLCHP *No Safe Place* 2014).

Laws like those described above have been justified for various reasons. It is commonly suggested that these laws are necessary to protect public interest. However, the downsides of these laws run deep and wide, as research shows they are costly to taxpayers while still being ineffective, and they violate the constitutional rights of the homeless. When these laws are broken and citations are issued or arrests made, the question can be asked who benefits from these practices? Once a homeless person is temporarily held, he or she still does not have a place to sleep and now has fines to pay without the means to do so. An arrest certainly does not assist the individual in finding a job or getting public benefits (NLCHP *No Safe Place* 2014).

BAN ON FOOD SHARING—RECENT TREND

Recent laws restrict the homeless and the people trying to help them. As early as 2007, the National Law Center on Homelessness & Poverty was reporting about laws prohibiting sharing food with the homeless. These ordinances existed in twenty municipalities, including Orlando, Florida; Las Vegas, Nevada; Wilmington, North Carolina; Atlanta, Georgia; Baltimore, Maryland; Dallas, Texas; and Denver, Colorado (Linnekin 2014). In 2014 NLCHP research identified 9 percent of the cities surveyed have food-sharing bans (NLCHP *No Safe Place* 2014).

Cities are using multiple means to deter groups from sharing food. For example, some cities are limiting the use of public property for designated purposes. The argument used by some law-enforcement agencies is that groups sharing food with homeless create a traffic hazard or fail to pick up the trash generated by their efforts. Legislation passed in Houston, Texas in 2013–2014 requires written consent to feed the homeless. Additional restrictions include the need to obtain permission from either the city, to occupy public space, or from owners, to use private property.

Some of the sanctions involved in serving meals in public places without these permits or permissions can result in a fine of up to $2,000. There are obvious effects from such legislation, including no food being served to the homeless due to the vigorous process of obtaining permission. Legislation in Manchester, New

Hampshire, directly states, "Organizations can no longer share food with people experiencing homelessness on public property in Downtown Manchester." In Olympia, Washington, the legislation says that now advocacy groups and other organizations must have a permit in order to share food with people experiencing homelessness in a public parking lot. In Lakeland, Florida, the law is worded as, "Sharing food with people experiencing homelessness is not permitted by a 'large-group' in a public park" (NCH *Share No More* 2014).

Another way to ban food-sharing with the homeless is to enact legislation that forces groups to adhere to food safety regulations. A law in Pasadena, California provides that hot meals can only be served to the homeless if the meals are prepared in approved locations. In St. Louis, Missouri, only prepackaged food is approved to be given to the homeless, unless an individual or group pays for a permit. There has been plenty of negative response to these laws. Some faith-based organizations, in furtherance of their commitment to serve underserved populations, have challenged such laws on the basis of a violation of their First Amendment rights. A food sharing ban in Albuquerque, New Mexico, was challenged on these grounds by three individuals in their suit against the city. The plaintiffs who had been arrested by an officer demanding to see a permit to feed the homeless claimed violation of First Amendment rights to exercise their faith freely and violations of their Fourth Amendment protections against unreasonable searches and seizures. The case was decided in their favor, which resulted in the city paying damages of over $40,000 to each individual (NCH *Share No More* 2014).

Have you heard the name Arnold Abbot? The topic of bans on food sharing made national news when Abbot, an advocate who founded a nonprofit called Love Thy Neighbor and who, at ninety years old, accompanied by two ministers of local Florida churches, was arrested for feeding the homeless. The ordinance in Fort Lauderdale restricting public feeding of the homeless became effective on a Friday and that Sunday, the men were arrested for handing out food to the homeless in a local park. As a result, the three men were each facing up to two months in jail and a $500 fine.

The advocate told the news that he was instructed by the police officer to "Drop that plate right now—as if I were carrying a weapon." (CBS News 2014). This ninety-year-old homeless advocate expects to be arrested again for feeding the homeless, because he does not plan to stop. The city's reaction to the news is telling as it indicated the belief that "the sight of the homeless is affecting tourism, nearby businesses and tarnishing the city's image." The story was given attention on multiple media outlets including, but not limited to, CNN, FOX News, and the Washington Times (Conlon and Shoichet 2014; Chasmar, 2014; Fox News 2014). At the city meeting where the new ordinance was passed, people in support of the law said things like "'Feeding people on the streets is sanctioning homelessness…Whatever discourages feeding people on the streets is a positive thing'" (Fox News 2014). Others argued that feeding the homeless is enabling them. In describing what happened, Mr. Abbot stated, "It's man's inhumanity to man is all it is" (CBS News 2014).

A recent article in *Newsweek* showed further results of these food-sharing bans. In El Cajon, California, twelve people were charged with misdemeanor offenses for giving food to homeless people (Guarnieri 2018). Mother Teresa said, "If you can't feed 100 people then feed just one." This seems like an honorable principle of doing the right thing, but some cities have made it a crime to do so. The laws in effect in many cities work in direct contradiction to this idea of helping others. At least positive attention has been given to people who refuse to comply with these local laws and ordinances and continue to provide food to those who need it most.

The National Coalition for the Homeless (NCH) found that some of these laws are based on myths about homeless people. One myth identified is that sharing food with homeless people enables them to remain homeless. Taking this a step further, some city officials have claimed that the homeless will disappear if you stop feeding them.

According to the NCH, the truth is that some homeless individuals rely on food-sharing programs to give them a healthy meal, because they do not have transportation or are ill or disabled. Further, people are homeless for reasons such as a result of a lack of affordable housing, a lack of job opportunities, or they are suffering from some other type of mental health disorder or disability. Another myth perpetuating these bans on food-sharing is there are enough meal programs already, and they waste unused food. According to NCH, the truth is that funding for federal food assistance programs, such as the Supplemental Nutrition Assistance Program (SNAP) have been cut since 2013, and as a result, the demand for meal programs across the country is higher (NCH *Share No More* 2014).

Advocates see these laws as un-American and mean spirited. It is certainly agreed that criminalization of homelessness is not making anything better, nor solving any problems, especially not in regards to addressing the causes of homelessness. According to the research done by the National Law Center on Homelessness & Poverty, the laws criminalizing homelessness are ineffective, expensive, and violate civil rights. Further, criminalization laws have been deemed a violation of the country's human rights duties by international human rights groups and the US government itself. The US Interagency Council on Homelessness (USICH) and the US Department of Justice (DOJ) agreed that criminalizing homelessness is a violation of basic human rights and international treaties signed by the United States. In looking at criminalization through a human rights lens, the USICH and DOJ pointed out that housing is a human right, human rights put people first, and homelessness has a human cost.

In 2014, the UN Human Rights Committee examined implementation by the United States of the International Covenant on Civil & Political Rights. The Committee recognized "steps taken by federal and some state and local authorities to address homelessness," but expressed concern "about reports of criminalization of people living on the street for everyday activities such as eating, sleeping, sitting in particular areas. The Committee notes that such criminalization raises concerns of discrimination, and cruel, inhuman, or degrading treatment" (NLCHP *No Safe Place* 2014, 28).

HOMELESS BILL OF RIGHTS

As discussed, the civil rights of homeless individuals are at risk due to the criminalization of homelessness. A Homeless Bill of Rights helps to ensure extra protections for these rights (NCH *Homeless Bill of Rights*). According to the National Coalition for the Homeless, homeless rights legislation currently exists in Maryland, Connecticut, Illinois, Wisconsin, Puerto Rico, Rhode Island, and Michigan. Twelve other jurisdictions are considering this type of legislation. The purpose of a Homeless Bill of Rights is to give protections against segregation, the use of public space, and laws targeting homeless individuals because they do not have homes. It is intended to also give them privacy and property protections, an opportunity to vote and to feel safe without fear or harassment, and broad access to shelter, social service, legal counsel, and quality education for children experiencing homelessness (NCH *Homeless Bill of Rights*).

Sometimes, litigation initiated by advocates for the homeless is the only way to challenge the ordinances that do not provide the homeless with these protections. As a result, the courts also contribute to the policy towards homelessness when they issue opinions on various laws and ordinances challenged in court. Anti-panhandling laws have been challenged on the grounds of vagueness, violation of equal protection, unreasonable exercise of police power, and a violation of free speech. Court cases have shown that it is a violation of a homeless person's constitutional rights to criminalize activities that they have to do in public (NLCHP *Homes Not Handcuffs* 2009).

THE FUTURE

There are alternatives to the criminalization of homelessness. Advocates for the homeless have many ideas, starting with the bigger goal of preventing and ending homelessness. Cities can dedicate the resources used to criminalize the homeless to affordable housing, permanent supporting housing, emergency shelters, and services for the homeless. Everyone will benefit if the cities work with the homeless and service providers instead of punishing them (NLCHP *Homes Not Handcuffs* 2009). Laws criminalizing homelessness are not a step towards working together. Additional laws criminalizing homelessness should not be enacted and current laws on the books should not be enforced. Another idea is to penalize cities enforcing these laws. We have a choice on where we are headed. The path we have been on for years includes punishing the homeless and pushing them aside, or we can pursue something new in hopes of change and progress. Some cities have been working towards a plan to end homelessness and that perspective is making a difference. In Salt Lake City, Utah, a ten-year Plan to End Chronic Homelessness came into existence in 2005. It has been highly successful by promoting a housing-first model, where housing is set aside for the homeless and an efficient process is in place to evaluate needs and meet needs. In Houston, Texas, the police department has a Homeless Outreach Team that combines services and resources with the goal of helping chronically homeless people find housing (NLCHP *No Safe Place* 2014).

There is no question that officials at the federal, state, and local levels have a voice in the treatment of homeless people. Will they use their power for good or evil? The federal government announced in January 2018 that a record $2 billion has been dedicated to state homeless assistance programs (HUD Awards Record 2018). This money supports over 7,300 programs helping the homeless. Advocacy groups for the homeless are adamant that the solution to this crisis starts with more affordable housing. The need for more affordable housing has been a constant through all the years that each of these laws has been introduced, debated, and ratified. If we are able to make progress on this issue, positive change will result for the homeless and their communities.

Bibliography

"90 year-old man, 2 pastors charged with feeding homeless in Florida."
CBS News. November 5, 2014. https://www.cbsnews.com/
news/90-year-old-man-2-pastors-charged-with-feeding-homeless-in-florida/.

"90-year-old among first charged under Fort Lauderdale's strict rules against
feeding homeless." FOX News. November 4, 2014. http://www.foxnews.com/
politics/2014/11/04/0-year-old-among-first-charged-under-fort-lauderdale-strict-
rules-against.html.

Chasmar, Jessica. "Florida Pastors Face 60 Days in Jail for Feeding Homeless." *The
Washington Times*. November 4, 2014. https://www.washingtontimes.com/
news/2014/nov/4/florida-pastors-face-60-days-in-jail-for-feeding-h/

Conlon, Kevin, and Catherine E. Shoichet."90 Year Old Florida Man Charged With Feeding Homeless." CNN. November 5, 2014.https://www.cnn.com/2014/11/04/ justice/florida-feeding-homeless-charges/index.html.

Grace Guarnieri, G. "Why It's Illegal to Feed the Homeless in Cities Across America." *Newsweek.* January 16, 2018. http://www.newsweek.com/illegal-feed-criminalizing-homeless-america-782861.

"H. R. 2897 – Bringing America Home Act." Congress.gov. 2003–2004.https://www. congress.gov/bill/108th-congress/house-bill/2897.

"HUD Awards Record $2 Billion to Thousands of Local Homeless Assistance Programs Across U.S." US Department of Housing and Urban Development. January 11, 2018. https://www.hud.gov/press/press_releases_media_advisories/ HUD_No_18_001

Linnekin, Baylen. "Bans on Sharing Food with Homeless Persist." reason. April 19, 2014. http://reason.com/archives/2014/04/19/bans-on-sharing-food-with-homeless-persi.

"McKinney-Vento Act: NCH Fact Sheet #18." National Coalition for the Homeless. June 2006. http://www.nationalhomeless.org/publications/facts/McKinney.pdf.

Myrtle Beach, South Carolina, Code of Ord., Sec. 16–31. Current May 27, 2017. https://library.municode.com/sc/north_myrtle_beach/codes/ code_of_ordinances?nodeId=COOR_CH16OFMIPR.

National Coalition for the Homeless. "Criminalization of Homelessness." http://www. nationalhomeless.org/projects/nhcrop.html.

National Coalition for the Homeless. "NCH Public Policy Recommendations, Bringing Home America Act." http://www.nationalhomeless.org/projects/baha.pdf.

National Coalition for the Homeless. *Share No More: The Criminalization of Efforts to Feed People In Need, National Coalition for the Homeless.* October 2014. http:// nationalhomeless.org/wp-content/uploads/2014/10/Food-Sharing2014.pdf.

National Coalition for the Homeless."HomelessBilloRights." http://nationalhomeless. org/campaigns/bill-of-right/National Law Center on Homelessness & Poverty. *HomesNotHandcuffs:TheCriminalizationofHomelessnessinU.S.Cities.*2009. http:// nationalhomeless.org/publications/crimreport/CrimzReport_2009.pdf.

National Law Center on Homelessness & Poverty. *No Safe Place: The Criminalization of Homelessness in U.S. Cities.* 2014. https://www.nlchp.org/documents/No_Safe_ Place.

Newport, Rhode Island, Newport Mun. Code, tit. 9, ch. 9.04, section 9.04.060. https://library.municode.com/ri/newport/codes/code_of_ordinances?nodeId= COOR_TIT9PUPEWE

Orlando, Florida, Code of the City of Orlando, Fla., tit 11, ch. 43, section 43.52. Current December 12, 2017.

"Part B- Education for Homeless Children and Youths." 42 USC Chapter 119, Subchapter VI. http://uscode.house.gov/view.xhtml?path=/prelim@title42/chapter119/subchapter6/partB&edition=prelim

Smith, Jacquelyn, and Natalie Walters. "17 Rich and Famous People Who Were Once Homeless." *Business Insider,* October 27, 2015. http://www.businessinsider.com/rich-and-famous-people-who-were-homeless-2015–10.

US Conference on Mayors. *Hunger and Homelessness.* 2017.

US Department of Education. "Education of Homeless Children and Youth (ECHY) Program." 2018. https://nche.ed.gov/downloads/ehcy_profile.pdf.

US Department of Housing and Urban Development. "The 2017 Annual Homeless Assessment Report (AHAR) to Congress." December 2017. https://www.hudexchange.info/resources/documents/2017-AHAR-Part-1.pdf. https://www.usmayors.org/category/task-forces/hunger-and-homelessness/.

United States Interagency Council on Homelessness. *Opening Doors: Federal Strategic plan to End Homelessness.* Last modified 2015. https://www.usich.gov/resources/uploads/asset_library/USICH_OpeningDoors_Amendment2015_FINAL.pdf

Virginia Beach, Virginia, Virginia Beach City Code, ch.33, art. 1, section 33–10. Current January 8, 2018. https://library.municode.com/va/virginia_beach/codes/code_of_ordinances?nodeId=CO_CH33STSI_ARTIINGE_S33-10SIRELYDOSTSI

Social Service Workers and the Poor: A Broken System

Shannon Woolf Connolly, LCSW

WHEN PEOPLE BEGIN conversations about poverty and why people are poor, they often become heated and emotionally charged. Part of the reason for this is that we imagine ourselves to be captains of our own destinies—if we are successful, we want to be able to point to the things we did individually that led to our success. There are, however, a host of factors that contribute to our success which are beyond our individual control, such as the social class into which we are born. This factor alone has an enormous impact on our quality of life—and it's something over which we have no control. Hard work factors into success, as do things like sacrifice, perseverance, and discipline, but hard work is far from the most important indicator of success.

We often ignore the external factors that contribute to our success and only focus on our efforts. If we really stop to think about it, however, we must admit that there are factors beyond our control that contribute to our success. We then must also acknowledge that the reasons some people are poor are beyond their control as well. This is the point at which the discussion becomes a bit more difficult, and emotional bias can cloud the way we think about the issue. It is also the point at which we start using stereotypes and extraordinary examples to prove our point that poor people are those who brought their problems upon themselves—they made bad choices, they are unwilling to do what is necessary to succeed, they are not trustworthy with the assistance the government provides. Comments such as "People are poor because they are lazy and don't want to get a job"; "People aren't really poor in this country, plenty of other countries have higher poverty rates than the United States"; "Poor people aren't really poor, they just make bad choices with their money"; and "People who grow up on welfare stay on welfare because we make it too easy for them," are often heard in discussions and arguments about poverty and the poor.

In just about any society you can find people who are lazy, who lack a work ethic, or who attempt to game the system and circumvent the rules. But what percentage of all poor people fit into this category? What about the rest of the population, who are trying their best to achieve the American Dream the way our culture suggests they should? Why can't they make it no matter how hard they try?

The reality is that there are a host of factors that impact people who are poor beyond their individual choices—things like changing labor markets and where certain jobs are being eliminated through outsourcing, deindustrialization, corporate mergers, or advances in technology. Another issue relates to the costs of childcare, a critical component to understanding poverty as well as employment. When a family realizes that the costs of childcare are higher than what they would earn in a full-time minimum wage job, one has to wonder if it makes sense to stay home instead.

Still other issues relate to transportation costs, housing costs, the cost of living in a particular city or town, and other factors, including the lack of an adequate safety net if circumstances change. All of these factors influence how and why people are and remain poor. Unfortunately these factors are often not part of the thinking (or arguing) about poverty, but they are critically important in understanding the problem and why so many people remain poor.

THE CYCLE OF POVERTY

One way to understand the difficulties of living in poverty is to grasp the interplay of factors that not only create circumstances that generate poverty, but how those factors can prevent someone from escaping from it. Essentially, the cycle of poverty contends that the impact of poverty can also contribute to its causes. As poor families have limited resources, a lack of education, few connections with people who can provide them with opportunities to succeed (what sociologists often call social capital), and limited access to affordable childcare, the absence of these resources and opportunities traps poor people into a cyclical or circular spiral that makes it nearly impossible to break out of poverty. According to a 2014 article in *The Atlantic* about the cycle of poverty focused on the Mechanicsville community just outside of Atlanta, Georgia, "In Atlanta, a child raised in the bottom-fifth of income levels has only a 4 percent chance of rising to the top-fifth income level" (Semuels 2014).

For example, as the United States shifted from a manufacturing-based to a service-based economy, those people who lost their jobs in the manufacturing sector were not qualified for new high skilled service sector jobs. To put this into context: "As a share of the overall [US] workforce, manufacturing has been dropping steadily ever since the Korean War ended, as other sectors of the U.S. economy have expanded much faster. From nearly a third (32.1%) of the country's total employment in 1953, manufacturing has fallen to 8.5% today." (DeSilver 2017) As a result, there has been a disconnect between available jobs and qualified workers, particularly those in predominantly poor communities. This is an important factor in understanding the cycle of poverty, as chronic unemployment continues to plague many poor communities. It can also be difficult to find unemployment statistics that give an accurate picture of the situation because "the underemployed—part-time workers who would prefer to work full-time—are counted among the employed. And discouraged workers—people who'd like a job but have stopped looking because they don't believe any work is available—aren't counted as part of the labor force at all." (DeSilver 2017)

Similarly, an inadequate education or the lack of a quality education can serve to perpetuate poverty. Many commentators, policymakers, and experts argue that education is the primary path out of poverty. However, there is evidence that low-performing schools, predominantly found in poorer neighborhoods, typically hire the least qualified teachers, often those who grew up in the same neighborhoods. It is often the case that these teachers are the only ones who want to work in that type of environment, thereby ensuring that the schools do not readily improve. It also means that students from those schools do not develop the social capital needed to be successful. Margaret Simms, director of the Low Income Working Families Project at the Urban Institute put it this way:

> We aren't as great an opportunity society as we think we are. The assumption is that anybody can pull themselves up by their bootstraps, but we don't always make it feasible for people to do that. If you live in a poor neighborhood, you're probably going to a school that is not as well stocked, that doesn't have as experienced teachers, and you're going to school with a lot of other poor kids who have the same disadvantages you do (Zeller 2012).

Finally, another structural obstacle that perpetuates the cycle of poverty relates to illness. People who live in poor neighborhoods also suffer disproportionately from high rates of disease and illness, some of which are physically disabling and can exclude them from working in certain occupations or at a high level of productivity. This also can limit one's ability to improve their social and economic standing. In an article released by the University of California San Francisco, Tom Boyce, MD, chief of UCSF's Division of Developmental Medicine within the Department of Pediatrics states that "socioeconomic status is the most powerful predictor of disease, disorder, injury and mortality we have" (Conway 2016) The article goes on to say that "the predictive power of income alone is perhaps most obvious when considering life expectancy. Impoverished adults live seven to eight years less than those who have incomes four or more times the federal poverty level." (Conway 2016)

Thus, the cycle of poverty is worthy of consideration in the discussion of why people are and remain poor, but only to illustrate the structural problems that cannot be overcome with a strong work ethic or a willingness to sacrifice to succeed. Many of the obstacles that prevent the poor from becoming successful are structural in nature and cannot be easily resolved by a particular individual or group. (Zeller 2012)

THE NEAR POOR

There is a great deal of misinformation about the poor, driven by stereotypes and half-truths offered in the media, by politicians, and even policymakers. For instance, one of the most common myths about the poor is that they do not have a solid work ethic. In fact, most poor people are working full-time, some with multiple jobs. It is indeed difficult to argue laziness is a factor when people are already working a full-time job—and some work more than full-time by having part-time jobs in addition to their full-time one (Steenland 2013).

These people are often part of what is called the "near poor," which means that their salaries are above the poverty thresholds that would make them eligible for assistance, but that they still do not earn enough to make ends meet. There isn't a "legislative mandate or policy directive defining near poverty" (Hokayem n.d.); however, the generally accepted definition for statistical purposes is people living at between 100 percent to 125 percent of the official poverty threshold. Using this definition, in 2017 a family of four making between $24,600–$30,750 is classi-fied as near poor. This happens because the jobs that the near poor have are in the lowest paying sectors of the market place. According to the US Department of Labor, the federal minimum wage (unchanged since July 2009) is $7.25 per hour. (United States Department of Labor 2018). Using these numbers as a basis for calculation, a household that includes two full-time (forty hours per week), minimum-wage ($7.25/hour) incomes makes $30,160 a year, which puts them in the 'near poor' category. If there is only one wage-earner in a household of two or more people, working a full-time, minimum-wage job puts them well below the federal poverty line.

WELFARE

Related to the reasons people are poor, there are those who argue that welfare creates a disincentive for people to work or perpetuates a life in poverty. As a matter of policy, we have designated income as the main criteria for determining if someone gets assistance from the government. In 2017, for instance, a family of four that was making $24,600 (Department of Health and Human Services, 2017) or less in the forty-eight contiguous states was eligible for a variety of programs, including food stamps, section 8 (subsidized) housing, Medicaid, and Temporary Assistance for Needy Families, which is the cash component of welfare. Alaska and Hawaii have different income thresholds because of the higher cost of living in those states.

When welfare reform passed in 1996, the criteria for eligibility included purported efforts on the part of welfare recipients to get the help they needed to become more self-sufficient. This means job training, educational achievement, and rehabilitation for a variety of health issues, etc. The notion was that while the person remained on welfare, which was time limited to five years (although individual states could elect to decrease the time limit by up to 20 percent), the person would take the necessary steps to become independent so that by the time they met their lifetime eligibility, they would no longer need help from the government in the form of welfare. Essentially the United States has gone from a single welfare system supervised by the federal government to fifty different programs, as welfare reform has essentially become a block grant program, where each state sets its own criteria for assistance and uses the funds as it sees fit (Weissman 2016).

As many states have added accountability measures, such as work requirements, drug testing, and limits on funding for welfare programs, the result has been the removal of millions of welfare recipients. However, while many former recipients have found work, the jobs they have received are in the lowest paying sectors of the market, often minimum wage jobs. However, this has also resulted in the elimination of their benefits (Weissman 2016). According to a 2013 press release by the National Low Income Housing Coalition:

> Between 1996 and 2011, the period directly after welfare reform ended cash entitlement for poor families for children, the number of families living on $2 or less in cash income (per person, per day) rose from 636,000 to 1.65 million. This represents a growth rate of 159%. In 1996, households in extreme poverty made up just 1.7% of all households. This figure increased to 3% by 2010 and reached 4.3% by mid-2011 (National Low Income Housing Coalition 2013).

One reason it is so difficult to unpack the welfare system relates to how we measure poverty. There are two different measures by which the government determines the federal poverty level: poverty thresholds and poverty guidelines. According to the Institute for Research on Poverty:

Since 1965, there have been two slightly different versions of the federal poverty measure: poverty thresholds, which are more detailed and primarily used for statistical purposes such as the annual poverty report; and poverty guidelines, which are a simplified version of the thresholds, primarily used for administrative purposes such as determining public program eligibility (Institute for Research on Poverty n.d.).

These measures are based on a calculation originally developed in the early 1960s by Mollie Orshansky. The basic formula was based on the assertion that food costs accounted for one-third of the average family budget. The poverty line was then determined by taking the minimum cost to feed a family and multiplying that number by three. Since 1963 this figure is adjusted yearly using the Consumer Price Index (CPI) in an attempt to control for inflation.

In addition to these measures there is the more comprehensive Supplemental Poverty Measure (SPM), yearly tracking for which began in 2010. The SPM takes into account government benefits and necessary expenses (such as taxes, medical expenses, and childcare expenses). Both guidelines and thresholds and the SPM are measures by which to determine the poverty line, but only the SPM takes into account what people spend today on basic needs such as food, clothing, shelter, and utilities. Despite providing a clearer picture, the SPM is not used to determine federal benefits.

Critics of Welfare

Critics of welfare often argue that fraud and abuse of the system is rampant or that the idea of welfare runs counter to the American values of independence and self-sufficiency. Thus, critics of welfare, in various forms and arguments, argue that welfare as both an idea and as a matter of policy is antithetical to the American way and is far too costly to provide to large segments of the population indefinitely (Weissman 2016).

What's missing are those discussions about finding ways to create well-paying jobs and adequate training programs, affordable housing and childcare, and other issues that keep people poor. In reality, most people take advantage of welfare as a short-term, stop-gap measure that helps them to get back on their feet when adversity strikes, as it was intended from the beginning. Such circumstances may include a layoff, the closing of a factory, or an illness of some kind that results in the loss of a job and the consequences that come from these events (such as eviction, the need for job training, medical expenses) (Weissman 2016).

As part of a larger effort to provide assistance to the poor, caseworkers play a critical role in the welfare process and in identifying particular issues for families as well as offering them customized services given the particular challenges a family faces. Why would anyone get involved in such a broken system that not only perpetuates the circumstances of the poor and often prevents them from getting out of such situations, but then seems to stigmatize people for being poor and needing help in the first place?

Caseworkers Who Work with the Poor

While most discussions about poverty center around the structural and cultural problems for families, one area that can easily be overlooked is the workers whose responsibilities are to assist families in need. Because the problems go beyond financial need and include issues related to substance abuse, child neglect and even abuse, the lack of quality education for poor children, and the issues relating to the job market, the case workers that attempt to advocate and provide help to these families carry an enormous burden.

However, not all caseworkers are the same, with staffers ranging from those with no educational background to those with advanced graduate training. Regardless of the type of caseworker, the responsibilities are considerable and the training inadequate, to say nothing of their meager salaries. For instance, according to the US Department of Labor, the average salary for a caseworker is between $20,000–$40,000 per year, depending on their qualifications (Department of Labor 2016).

The typical training curriculum, which varies by state and job classification, usually includes modules that focus on topics such as identifying and reporting child abuse and neglect. Those caseworkers with a child development background enter the profession with a good general knowledge base around typical development and attachment theories. In addition to a baseline knowledge of child development, those with a degree in Social Work also have a working knowledge of the systemic factors relating to poverty. This gives the social worker (as opposed to a caseworker with a different educational background) a greater ability to see the big picture, which is invaluable. People don't exist in a vacuum and it's very important to look at the whole person (which necessarily includes individual needs, family systems, community involvement, and larger societal issues). Given the limited resources, both in terms of training as well as in the programs available to help clients, such a demanding job carries with it long hours, high caseloads, stressful situations involving heartbreaking stories, and the possibility of discouragement, cynicism, and even apathy in the face of a steady dose of human tragedy. Supporting these caseworkers by providing applicable continuing education, emotional support, and the time and financial resources is crucial to creating positive outcomes.

What is life like for these workers, who are on the front lines in helping families overcome the enormous challenges of being poor? What does sociology have to offer in terms of understanding this often-overlooked segment of the helping professions? How do they cope with the stress, the burnout, and the heartbreak of dealing with dysfunctional families? I worked with caseworkers and families on a contract basis through the Department of Family and Children Services (DFCS) and although there's no one-size-fits-all solution to the problem, training caseworkers in the basic tenets of social and emotional development as well as the effects of systemic poverty would be a great place to start.

EDUCATIONAL TRAINING IMPACT

After earning an undergraduate degree in sociology, I went on to study community partnerships and graduated with a Master's degree in Social Work (MSW). An important piece of my MSW study was a field work internship where I worked in a group home for children in foster care. I shadowed the full-time counselor for the facility and worked directly with the children who lived there as well as the staff who were charged with their care.

As a young white woman with an upper middle-class background, the cultural and socioeconomic differences were a huge part of my learning experience. Although I was raised in a socially-conscious environment, there is no substitute for face-to-face interaction. The division of communities along socioeconomic, cultural, and educational attainment lines is inherent in today's culture and to learn about people whose experiences are different from our own requires concerted effort. Our experiences inform our worldview, and the lessons I learned as a result of this field work experience are invaluable.

There was a little girl living in the group home at the time (I will call her Lola here, although this was not her real name) who had multiple behavioral issues. She had a tendency to act in an impulsive and sometimes defiant manner. Particular members of the staff quickly labelled her a problem and as such they interacted with her in ways that ultimately ended up being counterproductive. While these staff members weren't the root cause of Lola's behavioral issues, they were unknowingly inciting the problem behaviors that they found so frustrating. By labeling Lola a troublemaker, she acted accordingly. From her perspective one of the few means by which to garner attention with staff was to act in the way they expected her to: throwing tantrums, being aggressive towards staff and other children in the home, and acting in a generally defiant manner. She was living up to the expectations that had been clearly expressed to her through the actions (and unfortunately, words) of her caregivers.

Taking into account her developmental stage and applying what I'd studied in school about attachment theory, it seemed clear to me that she needed firm boundaries expressed in a kind way, as well as encouragement to reinforce positive behaviors (no matter how small). The counselor under whom I was interning and I worked to develop a system by which to help both the staff and the little girl curb the destructive behaviors and replace them with positive coping skills.

A few months into my internship at this group home, I discovered that a member of the staff had been filling out her daily paperwork during her shift, instead of after it was over, in an effort to go home earlier. Part of this paperwork included behavioral reports about each child in care at the time. As I looked through the behavioral reports she'd written on Lola, it became clear that she was describing behavior that, although plausible, was not an accurate description of Lola's behavior on that particular day. The staff member was ignoring any progress this little girl might have made on a particular day and filling out paperwork according to her expectations of Lola, not her actual behavior. The staff member wanted to go home as soon as possible at the end of her shift, and since the behavioral logs were the last things she was required to do each day, she began filling them out early. I understood her motivations and that she probably intended no harm to Lola, but in doing so she was falsifying records and further cementing Lola's label as troublemaker.

After discovering what was going on, I reported this person to the director of the group home and, as a result of my report, she was suspended without pay (since she was an hourly worker) for a month. This particular staff member had been working in this group home for years (longer than any other direct caregiver on staff), and since it was a small organization, everyone knew that I had reported her. She worked in a low-paying job and losing her income for that month probably put a financial strain on her and her family. She saw my report as the spiteful actions of an overprivileged child. I saw it as a necessary response to the discovery of the unethical treatment of a minor.

In this particular situation, as well as a host of others over subsequent years, I felt strongly that a basic knowledge of typical child development, as well as some specifics about social and emotional development (and the effects of poverty, abuse, and neglect on both), could have made a major positive impact on outcomes. Hiring people with degrees and training in child development, social work, and other related fields would help tremendously in creating and fostering social service environments that affect positive change. Providing training to existing caseworkers and caregivers (particularly those without an applicable educational background) to expand their understanding of how social constructs affect the individuals living within them is another area for improvement.

As a social worker, I am bound by a professional code of ethics laid out by the National Association of Social Workers (NASW). As a part of this code of ethics I agree to "respect the inherent dignity and worth of the person" (NASW). Child Protective Services (CPS) case managers (unless they are also trained as social workers) and, in Lola's case, group home caregivers, are not held to the same ethical standard. They don't necessarily receive the education about child development, social and emotional development, and big-picture societal issues that lead to poverty and inequality and that creates a knowledge gap that is important to note.

Why Choose to Become a Caseworker?

As a newly-minted MSW I took on contract work with the state DFCS, performing comprehensive child and family assessments (CCFAs) and helping families with parenting skills. I was brand new to the field, but the lessons I learned were invaluable. I should also note here that my contract work was required by law to be performed by someone with an MSW, but because there are relatively few MSWs working in the Georgia DFCS system, they have to pay independent contractors to complete the necessary assessments. At the time that I attended Georgia State University's MSW program, DFCS provided a loan-forgiveness program in which the student completed their internships at DFCS (instead of choosing from a list of GSU-approved internship sponsors) and agreed to work for DFCS upon graduation for a certain number of years. Only a few of my classmates opted to avail themselves of this program. I didn't participate because I didn't want to be confined to one area of interest. But I also knew enough about the DFCS system in Georgia to know that I didn't want to be required to work there as a condition of my graduation. I was not alone. The fact that I was in a cohort of students who would have been among the best candidates for work within the DFCS system but that most of us opted to take other avenues is a glaring example of one of the major problems facing the system. MSWs are among the best candidates for social service jobs. But we would have been paid such low wages and expected to work endlessly long hours, while facing heartbreaking situations. Most of us weren't willing to sacrifice our sanity to do so. And that speaks volumes.

My most memorable client was a woman who was a recovering cocaine addict with eight children. When I received the contract and spoke with her DFCS caseworker, I was given basic information about her and her children and was sent into her home under the auspices of providing parenting support. As I look back on it now, I can see how it might have looked from the perspective of this mother (we'll call her Anne for the purposes of this writing). She may have felt it utterly ridiculous that DFCS expected a twenty-six-year-old newlywed with no children of her own to provide parenting advice to a thirty-nine-year-old single mother with eight children.

I vividly remember the day I met Anne and her children. The sun was shining as I got out of my late-model compact car (a graduation/birthday/Christmas gift from my supportive parents) in my carefully chosen outfit (not too formal, but sufficient to engender confidence in my abilities), casefile and notebook in hand. I could feel the eyes of the neighborhood on me. Everyone trying to figure out who the outsider was, likely forming explanations about why I was there and what business I could possibly have with Anne. I had come into their world, I was on their turf, and I stuck out like a sore thumb.

I could feel her sizing me up from the moment I walked into her house. I don't pretend to know how she felt in that moment, but I know that if I were in her position I would have felt a great deal of judgment. She later confided in me that in the beginning she saw me as a requirement she had to fulfill, and she expected nothing more. Her youngest child was in foster care at the time and she hoped that her compliance with my visits would help her to regain custody. She was cautious but compliant, because she had everything to lose.

I visited Anne on a weekly basis for several months. It took her a while to relax around me and to trust that I didn't think worse of her as a mother or a person because of her circumstances. She was raised in poverty by a drug-addicted parent. The family business owned by her father exposed her to alcohol, drugs, and crime at a very early age. By the time I met her she was thirty-nine, had eight children, and was in recovery for cocaine addiction. Her doctors had told her that the cocaine abuse had weakened her heart muscle such that one more hit could kill her. She was grateful to have found Section 8 housing that included a washer-dryer and was within walking distance of the local elementary school (since she didn't have a car).

She was constantly fighting off a roach infestation—a battle that was nearly impossible to win without help from her landlord. She attended regular meetings at the rehab facility where she had most recently detoxed from cocaine addiction and was regularly screened for any drug use. On the surface, our lives couldn't have been more different. What I learned from all those months of being a part of Anne's life and the lives of her children was that although our circumstances were vastly different, we actually had many things in common. We both had a strong desire to do the very best that we could with what we were given. To an onlooker, the effects of this shared desire may have seemed miles apart, but the core was the same shared human desire.

Anne had been written off by her family, by previous DFCS caseworkers, and generally by society. She was in poor health and had very few resources such that even something as simple as getting groceries took days of planning out the logistics of childcare and transportation and yet another full day to complete. She carried the social stigma of poverty with her everywhere she went. By comparison, I had family support, financial stability, and access to education and health care.

I believe that most people who enter into social service as a career do so with good intentions (in order to immerse yourself fully in something so emotionally taxing while being paid such comparatively low wages, there must be motivations that reach far beyond drawing a paycheck). These are people with big hearts who set out to provide a service and do some good for the communities in which they serve. They work long hours, often involving themselves in heartbreaking situations that may appear to have no good solutions. They often give of their own time and resources in an attempt to help their clients. They are on the front lines of the battle of social inequality with very little armor, and I applaud them for their efforts.

A major problem facing a lot of these workers is that they are not afforded access to the education and training necessary have the most positive impact. The reason that's given time and time again for this lack of access is that the funds aren't there to provide the proper training. These workers provide services to the most vulnerable among us: the elderly, the children, and those fighting chronic illness to name just a few. But these workers aren't perfect, either. They have flaws, limitations, and biases just like everyone else. They're human.

There are an almost infinite number of factors that play into why people become caseworkers. The ongoing debate about whether nature (genetic factors) or nurture (learned behaviors) is more likely to determine the type of person into which a person grows has no easy answers. No one really knows for sure which factor will inform a person's choices in any given situation, but understanding that a person is the sum of his or her experiences (including, but not limited to, any social stigma and/or societal labels they may carry) as well as those factors written in their DNA (propensity towards disease, mental health issues, etc.) is an important step towards seeing the whole person.

Without seeing the whole person (or at the very least making a reasonable attempt to do so), it is nearly impossible to develop an informed viewpoint on a situation. When we go into a realm as fraught with issues as the social service system in this country without an informed viewpoint, we are doing ourselves and our clients a huge disservice. When we don't give front line social service workers the training and education they need to make informed decisions, we are doing our society a huge disservice.

THE ART AND SCIENCE OF HELPING

One of the most challenging aspects regarding the training and education of social service workers is that in every good worker there is a balance between making decisions based on quantitative and qualitative factors. Much like teaching, there's an art associated with working effectively with people and communities. The best teachers aren't those who only teach to test—they use the training and education they receive in school (a certain level of which is required by law) to inform their teaching methods, but they also constantly learn and change by working with students in the classroom.

Great teachers have a fluid, adjustable balance between the art and the science, the qualitative and the quantitative. Great social service workers do the same, but they aren't required to have the same level of training and aren't paid as much. We are far from solving the puzzle of providing great public education, and we are just as far from providing great social services to our most vulnerable populations. I don't pretend to have the answers to fixing either of these broken systems, but there are several contributing factors that relate to basic sociological tenets that bear mentioning.

SOCIOLOGICAL THEORY AND POVERTY

What role does sociology have to play in understanding poverty in general, people who are poor in particular, and the case workers that try to help them? As was mentioned, there is an underlying belief in this country that everyone has the ability to pull themselves up by the bootstraps. Americans love a rags-to-riches story and hold tight to the ideal that hard work can save people from poverty. Because of this belief, we tend to oversimplify the societal causes and effects of poverty. To quote Martin Luther King Jr.: "It's all right to tell a man to lift himself by his own bootstraps, but it is cruel jest to say to a bootless man that he ought to lift himself by his own bootstraps" (Page, 2017).

This perception of why people are poor can be explained in part by our puritanical beginnings. German Sociologist Max Weber wrote about this in his work *The Protestant Ethic and the Spirit of Capitalism.* Weber describes the protestant work ethic (sometimes referred to as puritanical work ethic) by saying that, in some cultures, there is real value attached to hard work and in fulfilling one's calling, which, especially in the Calvinist view, were deemed signs of an individual's election or eternal salvation (Weber 1905). In other words, Puritans believed that although everyone was a sinner, working hard and achieving success could be ways to show their God that they were worthy of salvation. If you worked hard and were pious, you would be rewarded by God.

The inverse of this idea is that if you weren't rewarded, it was likely because either you weren't working hard enough or you simply weren't a part of the chosen few. It was your fault for not being good enough, not working hard enough, not living in a pious enough manner. We have certainly evolved as a society since the early Puritans arrived from England, but the idea that people who live in poverty choose to do so by not working hard enough persists.

This distinction between what is more commonly known as the deserving poor and the undeserving poor, has its roots in social policy regarding poverty—in those instances when the public can understand and sympathize with a person's plight that occurred through no fault of their own, that person would be characterized as part of the deserving poor, meaning assistance (and sympathy and compassion) are provided. However, should the situation be explained through a lens of poor choices, laziness, or factors that can be attributed to the individual, the public labels these individuals as those who are not entitled to assistance (Cooke, Rhode, and McNeil 2012). When attributing a person's station in life purely to their actions, it follows that welfare would be limited to only those people who are members of the deserving poor, since their situations warrant society's assistance. Using the narrow lens of personal responsibility without looking at the whole person, the community and society in which they live, and the history that formed the society, does everyone a disservice. Poverty is not a simple, easily categorized issue, and treating it as such only exacerbates the problem.

As it relates to the value and purpose of social work, Americans tend to remain focused on the alleviation of symptoms or quick-fix solutions rather than addressing the causes of chronic problems like poverty. Despite the old Benjamin Franklin adage "an ounce of prevention is worth a pound of cure," we seem far more willing as a nation to help someone who is lying in the street bleeding to death than to address the issues that led up to the situation.

Social work can be that ounce of prevention, but as a culture we can't seem to see it that way. If done correctly, in ways that utilize both the art and the science behind best practices; if carried out by well-trained, caring professionals; if practiced by people who are consistently allowed (and are allotted the resources of time and money by which) to continue educating themselves and challenging their own biases, we could turn that ounce of prevention into a pound of cure. Even from a purely financial standpoint it costs far less to put a bandage on a small wound and show someone how to care for it than it does to pay for an emergency amputation after the wound becomes infected.

At a more micro-level of understanding of the public's stigmatization of the poor is the work of Erving Goffman. In his 1963 book *Stigma: Notes on the Management of Spoiled Identity*, Goffman defined stigma as: "The phenomenon whereby an individual with an attribute which is deeply discredited by his/her society is rejected as a result of the attribute. Stigma is a process by which the reaction of others spoils normal identity" (Goffman 1963, 3).

The social stigma of poverty is an issue with immeasurable impact on American society. It informs how laws are made, how assistance is provided, and how people interact with each other on a daily basis. In an ideal world, everyone would be fully aware of their own biases and would work to challenge those biases regularly. While it is easy to see that this isn't the case, addressing the issue isn't something that's easily accomplished. Social stigma informs much of the way people interact with other people, their communities, and society as a whole. It's hard to move beyond the lines drawn along socioeconomic, cultural, and educational divides to decrease that stigma, but it's an important part of effective social work.

CONCLUSION

As was mentioned, in discussions of poverty, there is a general understanding that a distinction should be made between those who deserve society's help in the form of assistance and those who do not. The deserving poor are those who merit help, while in other cases the public tends to believe that the person is not entitled to long- or short-term assistance. In these latter cases, social mores dictate that the person should pull themselves up by their bootstraps and become productive members of society.

Also embedded in any discussion of poverty are elements of the labeling theory of deviance. This theory posits that once a person is given a deviant label, sometimes known as a stigma, and society responds to that person based on the negative label, the person is socially outcast and generally left to themselves in terms of interacting with others. That is, one dimension of labeling theory focuses on the process of acquiring a label, but once assigned there are a host of negative consequences for that person. As a result of this societal isolation, the person begins to live up to the label given to them and begins to engage in additional and more systematic deviant behavior (Goffman 1963).

As members of a society we all carry labels. We also assign labels to others based on stereotypes. Sometimes these labels are accurate and fair, other times they are inaccurate and punitive. Labeling theory thus posits that once a label is applied (the focus in this case being deviant), the person to whom it is applied internalizes the label and it becomes a self-fulfilling prophecy, where they begin to live up to that negative label. Lola's situation is a good example of how the labeling theory functions—where she was treated as being a problem child initially and ultimately lived up to those expectations. But the behavior by itself is less important than the reasons for it—Lola was responding to her caregiver's assessments and comments and the labeling that took place.

Caseworkers, like the public in general, are susceptible to biases and stereotypical understanding of a person's behavior, and Lola's situation is a good example of what can happen if caregivers fail to recognize the bias for what it is—a product of an interaction between society and the person, with a negative label attached that causes further inappropriate behavior. As many psychologists point out, sometimes negative attention is better than getting none at all.

Some of this tendency to label the poor can be tempered with training; however, many caseworkers fall victim to this labeling process and can begin to treat all poor people from a negative perspective that assumes laziness drives a person's behavior. Many case workers enter the profession with little real understanding of the issues or preconceived notions about why people become and remain poor. It is also very easy for caseworkers to become cynical about the explanations for poverty and to ignore or minimize the structural issues that continue to hamper poor people, even those who are healthy and willing to work. Given the absence of adequate training and the helpless feeling many caseworkers have about being able to remedy the assortment of problems that keeps people poor, it is not surprising that the stigmatization that accompanies poverty can also result in caseworkers buying into those stereotypes and acting accordingly.

Bibliography

Conway, Claire. "Poor Health: When Poverty Becomes Disease." University of California at San Franscisco. January 6, 2016. https://www.ucsf.edu/news/2016/01/401251/poor-health.

Cooke, Kristina, David Rhode, and Ryan McNeil. "The Undeserving Poor." *The Atlantic*. December 20, 2012. https://www.theatlantic.com/buisness/archive/2012/12/the-undeserving-poor/266507/.

DeSilver, Drew. "Employment vs. Unemployment: Different Stories from the Jobs Numbers." Pew Research Center. March 7, 2017. http://www. pewresearch.org/fact-tank/2017/03/07/employment-vs-unemployment-different-stories-from-the-jobs-numbers/.

———. "Most Americans Unaware that as U.S. Manufacturing Jobs have Disappeared, Output has Grown." Pew Research Center. July 25, 2017. http://www.pewresearch.org/fact-tank/2017/07/25/

Goffman, Erving. *Stigma: Notes on the Management of Spoiled Identity*. Englewood Cliffs, NJ: Prentice-Hall, 1963.

Hokayem, Charles, and Misty Heggeness. "Living in Near Poverty in the United States: 1966–2012." UC Davis Center for Poverty Research. May 2014. http://

poverty.ucdavis.edu/sites/main/files/file-attachments/us_census_near_poverty_2012.pdf

Institute for Research on Poverty. "Frequently Asked Questions." https://www.irp.wisc.edu/poverty-faqs/

National Low Income Housing Coalition. "Extreme Poverty Rise in the United States." May 17, 2013. http://nlihc.org/article/extreme-poverty-rise-united-states.

Page, C. "Martin Luther King Jr.'s Legacy, 20 Years On." *Pulitzer.* Available at: http://www.pulitzer.org/article/martin-luther-king-jrs-legacy-20-years

Semuels, Alana. "A Different Approach to Breaking the Cycle of Poverty." *The Atlantic.* December 24 2014. https://www.theatlantic.com/business/archive/2014/12/a-different-approach-to-breaking-the-cycle-of-poverty/384029/

Steenland, Sally. "Working Full-Time and Still Poor." Center for American Progress. February 20, 2013. https://www.americanprogress.org/issues/religion/news/2013/02/20/53929/working-full-time-and-still-poor/.

United States Department of Health and Human Services. "Annual Update of the HHS Poverty Guidelines." 2017.

United States Department of Labor. "Minimum Wage." 2018. https://www.dol.gov/general/topic/wages/minimumwage.

Weber, Max. *The Protestant Ethic and the Spirit of Capitalism.* Boston, MA: Unwin Hyman, 1905.

Weissman, Jordan. "The Failure of Welfare Reform." *Slate.* June 1, 2016. www.slate.com/articles/news_and_politics/moneybox/2016/06/how_welfare_reform_failed.html

Zeller, Tom J. "The American Poverty Rate." *Huffington Post.* March 1, 2012. https://www.huffingtonpost.com/2012/03/01/american-poverty-rate_n_1304269.html

Attachment Theory and the Paradox of the Child Welfare System

Brett A. Loftis, JD

I WAS STILL in college working on my undergraduate degree when I decided that I had to answer my call to be a child advocate. For some people, this might seem like a young age to declare a "life's work," but for me it had been a long time coming. My mother always jokes that she found some papers that I wrote in middle school about what I wanted to be when I grew up, and there it was in black and white, my proclamation that one day I would be an attorney that represents children. Of course I have no conscious memory of writing that in my early adolescence, but it doesn't surprise me. I have always known.

During my sophomore year of college, I had the incredible opportunity to work in Washington, D.C., as an intern for a semester. My dream internship at the Children's Defense Fund was offered to me a few weeks too late, because I had already accepted a role at a lobbying group for public education funding. I was devastated to turn down CDF, a place where I had dreamt of working, but I had already made a commitment that I felt I needed to honor. As life tends to develop, it turned out exactly like it should have. While on The Hill, I learned a lot about how the sausage gets made and how legislation comes to life. I loved it, and it was terrifying all at once. How could such important social problems get addressed through legislation when the people making the decisions were so beholden to conflicted constituencies, and when they were so scarcely informed about the issues? It was sobering for sure, and in spite of my declared major in political science, I could not see a place for me in that world. The soul searching that followed led me to back to a burgeoning passion and a true home in the field of sociology. Quickly I realized that I had already earned too many politcal science credits to dump that major, but if I was meticulous with class scheduling, I could add an additional major of sociology. With this new knowledge, I was off to the races. Now the challenge in front of me was to fashion a career with degrees in political science and sociology, disciplines which I was convinced made me highly informed and completely well-rounded but only educated to wait tables and tend bar!

While still in D.C. I ran across a book, or as my memory recalls, a book chose me. As a poor college student living in substandard intern housing in the nation's capital, I was not in the habit of buying books, especially hardcover books, that were not required for a class. But still, *I Speak For This Child* by Gaye Courtney found its way to me. This book was a compilation of stories from a woman that had spent many years advocating for abused and neglected children in the court system as a volunteer Court Appointed Special Advocate (CASA) or as known in some states, Guardian ad Litem (GAL.) As a trained volunteer advocate, this heroic woman had witnessed the best and the worst of our public child welfare system, and her stories were as compelling as they were heartbreaking.

After finishing the book, I was hooked. This is something I could do, and I could do it now. I was tired of waiting until I was "older" or "more educated" or whatever list of reasons people like to give you for only focusing on yourself and your career aspirations when you are young. I was nineteen. Wasn't that old enough to do something that mattered? That question seems funny now as a middle aged, mid-career person for whom nineteen sounds so very young, but I still believe it was the right question, and I'm glad that the universe led me to ask it and to search out answers.

So, at nineteen, I entered training to become a volunteer Guardian ad Litem in the South Carolina Court System. Shortly after I completed the required twenty hours of training, I took my first case and met my new clients, Eric and his sister Brittany. They had been taken into the custody of social services for a laundry list of reasons that included maternal substance use, inappropriate supervision, questionable parental discipline, housing challenges, and the ever-exacerbating realities of poverty. Little did I know that my first real exposure to the public child welfare system would encompass the most common factors that continue to drive the system today. The same sad, paradoxical truth present then is still true today—to protect a child you often have to remove them from their primary attachment figures.

John Bowlby, the twentieth century British psychologist, eventually became known as the "Father of Attachment Theory." He researched and wrote about a truth that I am convinced that many mothers know in their gut—the foundations of all human connections and relationships are built on the critical early interactions between a mother/caretaker and her child. From the moment a child enters into the world, her brain begins to respond to her mother. Skin to skin contact releases oxytocin and other chemicals to calm the developing nervous system. Eye contact, cooing, and mimicking of facial expressions are more than just adults responding to a cute baby; it is our biological imperative, deep within our brains, to assist the next generation of developing brains on their path of growth and development. The connection with a fully attuned caregiver is an essential process in the development of a healthy brain.

This evolutionary theory of attachment is seen most clearly in the absence of meaningful attachment. Bowlby believed that children who had experienced what he called maternal deprivation, had an increased likelihood of delinquency, aggression, depression, cognitive deficits, and antisocial behavior. There are numerous stories of orphanages in Russia, Bulgaria, Romania, and other countries where children were left in cribs and never held, nurtured, or talked to. This resulted in children who simply stopped crying. When a child's cries do not prompt a loving and nurturing response, their brains learn that asking for help and waiting for connection is futile. In the most severe cases, this pathogenic care before the age of two creates a debilitating psychological response, an attachment disorder, which impairs the child's future ability to connect to other people and can lead to antisocial and even violent behavior (McLeod 2007).

After I graduated from law school and began representing children exclusively, I developed an expertise in representing very young children who were experiencing extreme mental illness and behavior disorders. After representing a few children who had been diagnosed with the controversial Reactive Attachment Disorder (RAD), I quickly began to get referrals from other parents of children with similar problems. The situations were different, but their stories were surprisingly similar. Each family had adopted a child from a poorly run foreign orphanage, or from an extremely neglectful and abusive family, and the child appeared calm and compliant at first, but severe problems began to develop.

These children were displaying uncontrollable anger, destructive fits, lying, stealing, intense manipulation, and often physical violence. The parents all described children who could not seem to bond with them as caregivers, and the children seemed to show no remorse for their maladaptive behaviors. Each family was similarly worn down and emotionally devastated. Tragically, some of them wanted to terminate their own rights and relinquish the children back to "the system." After a series of successful lawsuits, the state began to locate attachment-based treatment centers across the country that were equipped to serve the children and to attempt reunification with the adopted parents. Eventually, the state determined that it was cheaper (an important motivator for government bureaucracies) and ultimately better for children to have treatment that is close to home and can incorporate their attachment figures into treatment. Several attachment-based programs opened and began serving children and families closer to home. Even with expert care, the children with the most severe disruptions in early primary attachment had difficulty developing relationships and fully integrating into society.

This is just one of many examples of how "the system" is often not designed or equipped to meet the needs of children and families. When referring to "the system" there is often confusion about what encompasses a child services system. This graphic provides a visual representation of the child services system as it is currently designed in most states. Each component is a publicly funded group of individual systems that often have their own rules, expectations, language, and restrictions. If a child or family "falls through the cracks," it is most likely a crack inside or between these complicated systems.

FIGURE 6.1 **5 rings**

- Education – preschool through college
- Health – physical health, mental/behavioral health from prevention through acute care
- Juvenile Justice – from prevention to incarceration for anything that would be a crime if the person was an adult and had several status offenses (i.e. truancy, running away, incorrigible or beyond the control of parents.)
- Civil Court – divorce, child custody, visitation, etc.
- Social Services – public benefits "welfare" programs, child protection, foster care, adoption, etc.

We know that when children experience a disrupted attachment, it impairs their brains' ability to develop normally. The good news is that unlike the belief that existed during most of Bowlby's research, which stated that brain development ends about age ten when the physical growth of the brain stops, we now know that our brains continue to develop and change throughout the course of our lives. Brains can heal. Unfortunately, most of our public systems have not incorporated the latest brain science into their development of interventions with children and families. The starkest examples are in the public child welfare system(s).

Imagine this scenario. When Alan was born, his mother was coming out of a domestic violence relationship. During his entire gestational period Alan's mother was plagued with chronic stress and feared for her safety. Now that Alan has been born and his father is gone, his mother is left with unstable housing and no income. Her government-provided food stamps help to keep food in the home, but life is uncertain and chaotic. In order to provide for Alan, his mother leaves him most days with a neighbor while she looks for work. The neighbor is kind, but she has three other small children and the attention she can give Alan is sporadic. Alan's mother finds part-time work, but it is not enough to cover the rent and childcare so she quits to stay home with Alan after his first sickness. Within a few months, Alan's mother is depressed, facing eviction and feeling hopeless.

By the time Alan is six months old his mother is using prescription pain killers to numb her feelings of anxiety and fear. As her depression worsens, her addiction begins to take over. Soon she is doctor shopping to find enough pain killers to help her cope with a life that is spiraling out of control. When she tries to quit using the drugs on her own, the side effects are severe and she becomes ill. One time, she leaves Alan home alone for a few hours while she tries to find someone to give her money for pills. The neighbor that had previously cared for Alan hears his continual crying through the apartment door and calls the police. The police show up and find Alan alone in the messy apartment with a very dirty diaper. There is very little food in the home.

The police wait with Alan until his mother returns, and she is charged with a misdemeanor child endangerment and a referral is made to Child Protective Services. After a brief investigation, a petition for removal is filed with the county court; Alan is removed from his mother's care, and he enters his first foster home. Alan's mother is given a case plan by a social worker and is told that she has one year to get stable housing and a job that pays her bills, and she must get clean and sober. She is also required to attend weekly parenting classes and to follow all the recommendations from her drug treatment provider. When Alan is taken into custody, his mother loses her Medicaid and her food stamps. Alan's mother's depression worsens, and she goes on a drug binge. When she eventually overdoses, she winds up in the emergency room. She has no insurance, no job, a full-blown addiction, and she feels suffocated by the shame and sadness of losing Alan.

Meanwhile, Alan spends his first birthday in foster care. His foster mother is kind and loving. She is a single mother, and she works long hours to care for her two biological children and Alan. Alan attends a day care center in the neighborhood from 8 a.m.–6 p.m. on most days. The day care center is clean and colorful, but they struggle to find consistent staff and there is regular turnover. Alan appears to be quiet and compliant in his foster home, but at day care he begins to show signs of distress. He bites other children and cries for several hours each day. Within a few months, Alan is suspended from his day care for consistent biting. His foster mother takes off work to care for him. Eventually, Alan is kicked out of the day care center and his foster mother cannot take off any more work because of Alan's behavior, and she reluctantly tells the county that they will have to move Alan into a new foster home. By the time Alan is two, he has been in three day cares and two foster homes.

What will happen to Alan and his mother? For those of us that spend our days working with Alan and children like him, we see the impacts of disrupted and insecure attachment. Alan is connected to his mother. She is his primary attachment figure, and they have a real connection, even though the connection is insecure and disjointed. However, Alan's mother struggles with addiction and a life that is complicated by grief, depression, and the exacerbating effects of poverty. The government systems charged with protecting Alan are not designed to foster the connection and heal the bond between Alan and his mother. The child protection laws require a child to be removed if the home environment is not safe.

The federal funding for child welfare is primarily tied to the removal of a child. Most funding goes to the investigation of the abuse and to the small stipend paid to the volunteer foster parent. Decisions about where the child should live are not made on the basis of the child's attachment. For instance, Alan would not be placed with the caring neighbor who he knew and trusted, because she was not a biological relative; but the system would quickly place him with a distant cousin he had never met. Children like Alan are also moved away from a foster parent they are bonded with to be placed with an unfamiliar and often less desirable family member. This is not to discount the importance of keeping biological families together, but rather to point out that most decisions in the child welfare system are made from the prospective of the adult and not from the viewpoint of the child and his attachments.

Child Welfare is also the only public system in the country that is built on the assumption that volunteers can meet the needs of a child. In my experience, most foster parents are wonderful servants who want to help children. The truth is that the majority of foster parents receive twenty to thirty hours of training before a child is placed in their home. There is no education requirement or professional standards that are linked to knowledge of attachment, trauma, or professional parenting. As such, the average child in foster care experiences multiple disrupted placements.

For most children in foster care, their advocate is also a volunteer (CASA or GAL). Remember Eric and Tiffany? I became their advocate when I was nineteen. My job was to investigate the entire circumstances of these children's lives and to make recommendations about where they should live, who they should visit, and what services they needed. I had not been trained about trauma, addiction, implicit bias, structural racism, or a host of numerous other factors that were present in each case. Volunteer CASAs and GALs are heroic folks serving a critical purpose, but they are not professional advocates.

National life outcomes like education, employment, mental health, and incarceration are abysmal for children in the child welfare system. Many social workers bemoan working with successive generations of the same family that are still struggling with similar problems. Child welfare professionals will consistently say that one of the most frustrating parts of their work is that many children who are removed from abusive and neglectful families will return to their families once they turn eighteen. This is primarily true for children who are in foster care in their teen years. If they are not adopted and part of a supportive and connected community, they will likely return to their families of origin. As Bowlby taught us, there is a biological imperative to seek attachment, even if that attachment is damaged or damaging. We want and need attachment to survive.

Why is this important? Maya Angelou said, "When you know better, you must do better." Now, as a field of child development and attachment experts, we know better, so it is time to do better. How do you feel when you read about Alan? Do you picture his sweet face as he sits in day care, sad and confused, crying and biting as his only forms of communicating the pain that is inside him? Do you want to grab his mother by the shirt and beg her to change or yell at her to get her act together? It is vitally important to know how we feel about the people that we serve.

I spent many years of my career feeling anger and resentment towards parents who neglect and abuse their children. If you stay in the work long enough, you have the heartbreaking experience of watching children that you care about become adults who repeat the same patterns that their parents started. I have been faced with seeing the irresponsible decisions of adults through the lens of them as my former child clients.

Now I know better, so I must do better.

Everything about my work and my advocacy for children changed when I became aware of the seminal research done by the Centers for Disease Control and Prevention and the private insurance company, Kaiser Permanente in the late 1990s. What started as a study about the causes of obesity transformed into the largest public health study ever conducted in the United States. The study compared over seventeen thousand participants' answers to a childhood trauma questionnaire with long term health outcomes, and the correlations were astonishing. The Adverse Childhood Experiences study found that childhood abuse, neglect, and chronic stress in the household are positively correlated with a host of negative life outcomes, including addiction, heart disease, cancer, and early death.

Now we have compelling evidence that trauma impacts the brain/body in substantial ways. Children who experience early trauma often struggle with developmental trauma disorders that look like Post Traumatic Stress Disorder (PTSD.) The area of the brain that regulates emotions and protects us from danger becomes chronically over active and hyper aroused. This results in a child that is always seeing danger even when none is present, and even innocuous interactions can trigger a trauma response of fight, flight, or freeze. Children in the foster care system, who already have disrupted and insecure attachments, are further impaired by a brain that may be overactive in sensing danger and experiencing debilitating fear.

Often children will fight (resist connection, argue, or become physically aggressive), flight (run away, avoid connection or intimacy), or freeze (shut down, disassociate, or appear stuck). Thankfully we also know much more about neuroplasticity and the ability for the brain to form new connections and to heal damaged neuropathways. With healthy attachments and appropriate, trauma-informed therapeutic and social/emotional interventions, people are not doomed to be products of their childhood trauma.

How does the Adverse Childhood Experiences research connect to attachment theory? If we return to the Alan's story, we see a boy who has experienced numerous disruptions in his primary attachment during his most critical years of development. As Bowlby and his colleague Mary Ainsworth opined, he would likely suffer from attachment issues that appear as avoidant, anxious, and/or disorganized. Alan needs safe, stable, and secure attachment figures. Ideally, those attachment figures would be trained about attachment problems and the impacts of trauma on the developing brain.

Alan needs the system to move swiftly to determine if he can be reunited with his mother, and he would need to have a permanent home within a year, if not sooner. If Alan's mother cannot make enough progress to give Alan a safe home, then her rights should be terminated within a reasonable time so that Alan can be adopted. Alan needs the foundation of secure attachments so that he can begin to heal from the loss and trauma he has experienced. As Alan progresses through his developmental stages, he will likely need trauma-informed professional therapeutic support.

Even a child as young as Alan could benefit from parent/child therapy and play therapy or other developmentally appropriate interventions. In short, for Alan to have the best chance for success, he needs consistent and supportive permanent caregivers and an array of supportive services for him and his attachment figures. Ideally, Alan's mother would get help from the underlying trauma and loss that is leading her to make dangerous choices.

To truly help Alan, we must be able to look at his mother and ask, "What happened to you?" and in turn, we must resist the temptation to ask, "What is wrong with you?" This critical shift in perspectives is not about absolving people from their behavior, but rather is about opening up the opportunity to see behind to the behavior, so that the root causes can be addressed. To best protect Alan, we must address the trauma of his primary attachment figure. Even if Alan is unable to safely stay with his mother, it is likely that Alan will not be her last child. To stop the intergenerational effects of trauma, we must start with the adults in front of us or the cycle will continue.

After more than two decades as a professional child advocate, 1 am convinced that the most important obstacle to overcome is how we think and feel about children. What we believe about children impacts everything about the system. If we believe that they are the property of their parents, then their rights and needs will always be relegated beneath the rights for adults that have "ownership" or parental rights. If we believe that a roof over their heads and adequate food and clothing will bring about healing, we will continue to prolong their pain and recreate the dysfunctions of their biological families.

Their trauma disrupted attachments will be passed down to future generations, and the cycle will continue. If we believe that adults struggling to parent are fundamentally flawed and unable to heal, then we will continue to build systems that reward jumping through hoops rather than searching out real healing and attachment. In order to change the trajectory of our country's most vulnerable young people, we must build beliefs and responsive systems that acknowledge the critical importance of attachment and utilize the best science to promote healing. When we know better, we must do better.

Race and Ethnic Relations

Does Race Really Shape Social Interaction?

RACE AND ETHNICITY

There is a connection between the topics of race and ethnicity and social inequality and poverty. Part of the reason is due to the fact that racial and ethnic minorities are disproportionately more likely to experience unemployment and/or poverty than other groups. It is also the case that race, like poverty, is an emotionally charged issue—one that evokes strong reactions in people when discussions about racism and discrimination occur. This makes any objective or reasonable dialogue about the problems stemming from race and ethnicity difficult to sustain.

While there are many dimensions to race and ethnicity, some of the more profound ones are seen when social policies designed to address either the historical or current challenges facing minorities create a backlash of disagreement. This is particularly true for programs that generally do little to improve racial harmony, and, likely, increase tension between groups. All of these challenges occur despite the fact that the United States has proclaimed a commitment to diversity and to welcome people from all sorts of backgrounds. However, we may be seeing a shift in that position, as some sections of the population have felt too much consideration has been given to minorities at the expense of others. Evidence of this is seen in President Trump's effort to ban certain groups from entering the country, ostensibly to protect the United States from terrorist activity, along with extraordinary measures to enforce immigration reform. These events are occurring during an extraordinary time when some segments of the general public believe that the police use excessive force against minorities and the entire justice system is biased against minorites. In response, police officers are being attacked in ambushes and assassinations while on duty. Thus, the discussion of race and ethnicity is a central feature of American society, and like the polarizing effect of the discussions of poverty, people's opinions are highly charged and drawn along emotional lines.

The articles in this section offer glimpses of how we might begin to think about race in society and the role it plays in understanding social relationships. Jeannie Haubert, for example, examines the impact of hurricane Katrina on many poor sections of New Orleans. From these accounts, it is much easier to understand the relationship between race and poverty, as residents in parts of New Orleans continue to struggle to cope years after a devastating disaster impacted their communities. Lucy Sanders describes the role of race and ethnicity in labor disputes. As she describes, while many people have experienced problems with employers, there appears to be a pattern involving race and ethnicity in understanding the trends and how disputes are resolved. Finally, Robert McNamara offers insight into the African American experience with the criminal justice system. Given that

African Americans are overrepresented at virtually every stage of the criminal justice process, what are some of the reasons for this trend? Is it due to higher rates of offending, selective enforcement and bias by the police, or is the entire system racist? These and other issues will be explored in this section.

A Color-Blind versus a Color-Conscious Approach to Disaster Recovery

Jeannie Haubert, PhD

I don't see color. I treat everyone the same, no matter what.

THIS IS WHAT we tell ourselves it means to be nonracist, one of the hallmarks of being a good person in this country. This is how most of us try to raise our children, how teachers are supposed to view students, how we say we hire people for jobs, and how many of our state and federal policies are written, because we are taught that paying attention to race means that we are being racist if we are white or being overly sensitive if we are not white. This is something no one wants to be accused of, least of all federal and state policy-makers who are still rebuilding their reputations after centuries of racist policies and practices that have distorted the American dream for racial and ethnic minorities. So, we ignore race. We sweep it under the rug, and pretend it doesn't have a long and consequential history in this country that affects everything from where and how people live, to what opportunities are available to them. And this color-blindness is how we will bring about equality in our country, or so we think.

Building on the research and conclusions of many other racial and ethnic relations scholars, I argue here that this color-blind approach may result in equal, but not equitable, treatment (Wise 2010; Bonilla-Silva 2017). What is the difference? In short, equality means treating everyone the same. For example, in the case of funding following a natural or man-made disaster, it would mean ensuring that all communities were allotted the same amount of resources per resident. On the other hand, advocating for equity would mean recognizing that some neighborhoods—like low-income communities of color—will actually need more resources (evacuation plans, emergency shelters, funding to rebuild) if we expect those communities to recover.

Why do we need more equitable disaster recovery plans? Perhaps an analogy will help. Imagine that four runners are running a race on an oval track like the kind typically found at high schools. If you started the runners all at the same point on

233

the track, the runners on the inside track would have a distinct advantage, because the track is shorter on the inside. Instead, it makes sense to stagger the starting points so that everyone has to run the same distance to successfully complete the race. Note that they still have to run. No one would suggest that some get a free ride around the track while others run, just that staggered starting lines make sense for a fair race. In the same way, some neighborhoods—depending on the starting social position and the relative power of community residents—have an inside track on disaster recovery. And when something bad happens—a hurricane, an earthquake, a flood, a major fire—those residents have a somewhat easier time getting up on their feet to again start running the race.

It is imperative that we urgently design equitable disaster recovery plans for two reasons, which I will flesh out with supporting evidence in the sections that follow. First, natural disasters are increasing in frequency and impact. Second, some populations have higher social vulnerability, which means that these groups predictably have heightened risks during a disaster and a slower pace of recovery afterward. If we want to create resilient communities that can bounce back after disaster strikes, then we have to design disaster preparation and recovery plans with staggered starts. Let's start with the first reason: the idea that natural disasters are increasing in frequency and impact. Then I'll explain social vulnerability and what we can do to promote equity in disaster recovery.

HEIGHTENED VULNERABILITY

We are increasingly more vulnerable to disasters today as compared to the past as a result of population migration to coastal areas and climate change. According to the US Federal Emergency Management Agency, "The challenges posed by climate change, such as more intense storms, frequent heavy precipitation, heat waves, drought, extreme flooding, and higher sea levels are altering the types and magnitudes of hazards faced by communities" (www.FEMA.gov). Take a look for example at FEMA data over the past fifty years. Even if we just look at three types of disasters, fires, severe storms, and hurricanes, we can clearly see the increase in federally declared disasters starting in the late 1990s. Below is a visualization of fire declarations over time (www.FEMA.gov).

Hurricanes and severe storms display a similar pattern as shown in the two charts below from the same FEMA website.

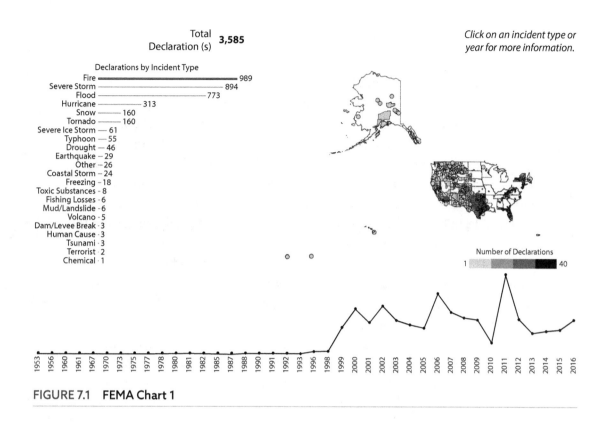

FIGURE 7.1   FEMA Chart 1

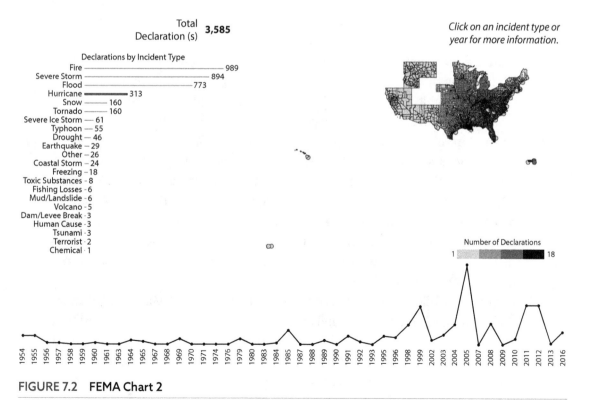

FIGURE 7.2   FEMA Chart 2

What is causing the spike? Well, it could be some alien forces changing the magnetism in our atmosphere, or it could be what the vast majority of scientific data points to, human-caused climate change. As climate change accelerates, "natural disasters" become more frequent. It makes sense to put this term in quotes because simply referring to these trends as "natural" obscures the hand that humans have played in creating them. Humans are not only to blame in terms of neglect or direct manipulation of the environment, which causes sea temperatures to rise and hurricanes and severe storms to become more intense, but humans too are to blame for the neglect of man-made structures designed to control the environment. For example, in New Orleans, the levee system built to control flooding from the river and lake was neglected for decades (Squires and Hartman 2006). Maintenance requests were repeatedly ignored to shore up the system built by the Army Corp of Engineers in the 1970s. As a result, when the category three storm known as Hurricane Katrina hit to the east of New Orleans in August 2005, catastrophic flooding covered more than ninety thousand square miles and 1,300 people died just in that one city (Erikson 2010). That was a man-made disaster, as that levee system was originally built to withstand that level of storm. It was also a man-made disaster because oil drilling off the coast of Louisiana has been contributing to the rapid depletion of the wetlands that have traditionally protected cities more inland from impacts. Hitting the wetlands first, hurricanes would slow down and weaken before moving inland, but with the rapid pace of wetland erosion, inland communities are more vulnerable than ever (Haubert 2015).

Extreme weather events have increased in both frequency and severity worldwide, killing thousands of people every year and displacing thousands more (National Oceanic and Atmospheric Administration). Wildfires, mudslides, floods, earthquakes, hurricanes, and heatwaves can strike with little to no warning, but they are an inevitability. CNBC characterized 2017, as did many other news organizations, as "a year of disasters" in which millions were affected worldwide by catastrophic floods, earthquakes, fires, and hurricanes (CNBC 2017). The 2017 disasters came with a $306 billion price tag, a record total and a 68 percent increase over 2016. Let's consider for a minute just the extreme weather events in the United States for 2017. California had the wettest winter on record and the most destructive and largest wildfire season ever. Oklahoma, Missouri, and Arkansas reported record flooding. Arizona and South Carolina had the warmest year on record. Three major hurricanes, Irma, Harvey, and Maria, killed thousands and were listed as the second and third costliest hurricanes on record (Vox 2018). Moreover, if we look at global climate trends, there is reason to believe that the intensity and frequency of these disasters will continue to rise. The chart below is from the National Oceanic and Atmospheric Administration, which predicts temperatures will rise another 2–4 degrees Celsius (2.5–6.5 fahrenheit) in the twenty-first century. Warmer oceans mean more hurricanes, and warmer temperatures mean more wildfires, droughts, and flooding from melting snow. We saw increasingly intense and frequent weather events in the 2000s with just an increase of 0.5 degrees Celsius, so imagine the disasters that a 2–4 degree increase will bring in the next ninety years.

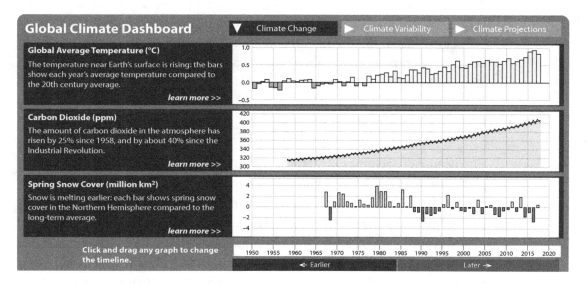

FIGURE 7.3   Global Climate Dashboard

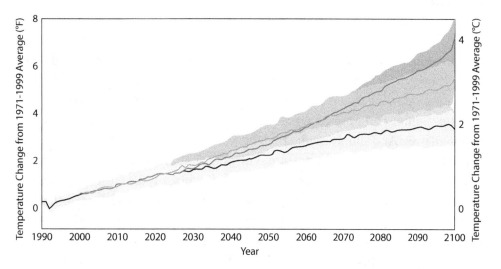

FIGURE 7.4   **Projected global warming over the 21st century using three SRES greenhouse gas emissions scenarios. Data from CMIP3 (2007)**

Source: nooa.gov

Certainly, ecological responsibility is imperative to try to ensure that the temperatures increase as little as possible; but, as illustrated above, in even the most conservative projection, where we make the most ecologically responsible choices in every country around the globe, there is still a significant global temperature increase and therefore a heightened risk of impact from disasters. To be prepared, we must build more resilient communities that better protect those most at risk. This does not just mean geographically vulnerable populations, but also includes various subgroups that may have greater difficulty recovering from disaster.

But aren't hurricanes, floods, and fires equal opportunity destroyers?, one might ask. The question becomes a sociological one at this point—what social factors affect disaster impact and recovery?

SOCIAL VULNERABILITY

The beauty of sociology is that it is a science that enables us to test commonplace assumptions about everyday life using real-world data. Using a sociological perspective, one can analyze the causes and contributing factors of prior events, such as weather-related disasters, and make predictions regarding the impact of future events on populations. An examination of the historical patterns shows that race and ethnicity matter quite a bit in understanding who is most heavily impacted during a disaster and who has the most difficulty recovering. In short, one's place in the social hierarchy matters in predicting disaster vulnerability and recovery.

Wait a minute... are you arguing that we only need to protect some racial and ethnic groups from these inevitable and catastrophic disasters? Of course not. However, just as some might argue that "all lives matter," and we should be concerned about every innocent citizen who dies at the hands of a police officer with a gun, there is another side that argues that highlighting the fact that black folks disproportionately suffer from police aggression does not mean that one does not care about all lives. And simply saying that "all lives matter" dilutes and obscures this social fact. Yes, all lives matter—that is obvious; but it is just as important for us to understand, and it is perhaps less obvious, that black folks are dying from this at much higher rates than other groups, and this social problem needs its own race-conscious spotlight to reveal it. In the same vein, all lives matter in terms of natural and man-made disasters, and scholars are just as concerned about elderly and poor white folks in Florida who died following Hurricane Irma as we are about the thousands of black and brown folks who died following Hurricanes Irma, Harvey, and Maria. BUT, black and brown folks are more likely to live in substandard housing that leaves them in a more vulnerable position. They are more likely to live in neighborhoods with crumbling infrastructure that leaves them in a more vulnerable position. They are more likely to live in communities that suffer from poverty and geographic isolation from good-paying jobs, leaving their bank accounts in the red and little money for evacuation or recovery. Because race overlaps with class and geography in this country, the impact of disasters is typically worse for nonwhite communities. Of course, it is not only race that matters—class, age, and disability also matter in survival and recovery rates—but race is impolite to talk about and often gets pushed aside during these conversations, so it is being highlighted here.

How do race and ethnicity matter in disaster vulnerability? Let's take this step by step and look first at pre-disaster living conditions, next at the ability to get out of harm's way during a disaster, and lastly the ability to pick up the pieces post-disaster.

Pre-disaster, racial and ethnic minorities are more likely to live in substandard housing and geographically vulnerable areas. This is connected with our country's long history of racialized housing practices and policies. Over many decades and into the present, government, banking, and real estate institutions have systematically excluded groups from certain communities and channeled them into different areas using a variety of means, such as racially restrictive covenants in neighborhoods, blockbusting, redlining, steering, restrictive zoning and land use policies, and discriminatory lending and rental practices. This means that in many cities throughout the United States, when whites left inner cities for homeownership in the suburbs, racial and ethnic minorities could not follow them. They were either left out of the homeownership market altogether, or relegated to rentals or public housing in inner cities.

Many white families were able to ascend into the middle class thanks to new loan terms that required only a small percentage down backed by the federal government. Between 1934 and 1962, the Federal Housing Administration and Veterans Administration financed more than $120 billion worth of new housing; yet only 2 percent of this real estate was available to nonwhite families (PBS 2003). When whites left, businesses often followed, leaving inner cities with few job opportunities or amenities such as grocery and retail stores. This disinvestment caused housing values in many urban areas to decline, locking families of color out of opportunities for wealth accumulation. Eventually racially restrictive covenants were outlawed, as were discriminatory housing practices, but the wheels had already been set in motion and "white spaces" had already become associated with a neighborhood's desirability.

Thus, when families of color were finally able to follow white families into the suburbs, white families perceived this as problematic and were told so by realtors seeking to make a profit from the sale—a practice known as blockbusting. White families then moved further out into outer suburban rings, again bringing their resources and businesses with them and further isolating inner city residents of color. Thus, Jim Crow segregation came to be replaced by geographic segregation, and white spaces became areas that were seen as good investments, leaving neighborhoods with nonwhite majorities to deteriorate.

Families living in these neighborhoods are not able to accumulate wealth at the same rate as their white counterparts, because for most families in the United States, their wealth is tied to the value of their home. Because homes in minority neighborhoods have less demand than homes in white neighborhoods, property values are lower and homes do not appreciate at the same rate as they would in all-white areas. This deprives families living in minority neighborhoods of key opportunities to accumulate wealth.

As a result, the average white family in the United States has about ten times the wealth of the average black family and about eight times the wealth of the average Latino/a family. While some might argue that it's class, not race, that matters, even among low-income households, whites still have four times as much wealth as black families and three times as much wealth as Hispanic families. Much of this has to do with homeownership rates, as noted here by the Pew Research Center (Kochher and Cillufo 2017).

In 2016, lower-income white households had a net worth of $22,900, compared with only $5,000 for black households and $7,900 for Hispanic households in this income tier. To some degree, this reflects differences in homeownership rates among families—49 percent for lower-income whites, versus 31 percent for lower-income blacks and 30 percent for lower-income Hispanics. It is also important to note that only 25 percent of white households are in the lower-income tier, compared with about 50 percent each of black and Hispanic households. Thus, low levels of wealth are much more prevalent among black and Hispanic households than among white households (Kochher and Cillufo 2017).

All of this is to say that brown and black families are more likely to live in rental housing, more likely to live in dilapidated housing, more likely to live in concentrated poverty, more likely to live in geographically isolated inner cities, and more likely to live in environmentally hazardous areas, including low-lying areas of town, as compared to whites. In New Orleans, for example, as the city grew, swamps were drained and houses put in those former swamps (Colton 2005).

That land was of course less valuable than the higher ground that had traditionally been settled along the crescent-shaped city. The lower lying lands were where families of color (primarily African Americans and later Vietnamese immigrants) could afford to live, and when hurricane Katrina hit in 2005, it was those lower lying areas where the most people drowned. Thus, race, class, and geography in this country are deeply intertwined, which leads to heightened vulnerability even before a disaster hits. According to FEMA:

> Families living in housing units that are well maintained and consistent with current building standards are typically more resilient to hazards than families living in poor housing conditions. Substandard housing may be more susceptible to the impacts of hazards, resulting in property damage, injury, or death during an event and extensive repair costs in both time and money after an event. These costs are especially challenging for the typically lower-income families that occupy housing units with severe problems... Households not overburdened by housing costs are able to invest in property enhancements, have financial flexibility for post-disaster uncertainties, and generally have more capacity to absorb and bounce back from unanticipated events. (US Department of Homeland Security 2016)

Also as a result of geographic segregation and class disparities by race, racial and ethnic minorities are more likely to live in inner cities and therefore rely on public transportation. They are less likely to have their own means of transportation to be able to evacuate when disasters are announced. Nationwide, whereas only 5.4 percent of white households don't have a car, 24 percent of black households and 12 percent of Latino households do not have a car (Stephen and Stoll 2001). Therefore, evacuation plans must include public transportation out of the affected area and must be resumed quickly to access medical and social services as well as their places of employment. When public transportation is not included in disaster planning, racial and ethnic minorities are disproportionately impacted.

Even for the 76 percent of black families and 88 percent of Latino families that do have a car, one also needs to have a place to go and funds for evacuation expenses (gas, lodging, restaurants, etc). This points to the importance of social networks and income levels as factors affecting the likelihood of evacuation. Both are tied up with race in this country. African Americans who are poor are more likely than poor whites to live in close proximity to other poor people. This is even truer in the United States in the years since the great recession. In the years 2010–2014, "poor Hispanics were more than three times as likely as poor whites, and poor blacks were almost five times as likely as poor whites, to live in an extremely poor neighborhood" (Kneebone and Holmes 2016).

Therefore, high levels of neighborhood distress remain a much more prominent feature in the lives of poor African Americans and Hispanics than similarly situated whites. Not only is neighborhood condition affected, but the strength of social networks is too. When poverty is concentrated, not only are you poor, but most of the people you know are poor. In other words, African Americans and Hispanics who are struggling are typically surrounded by other families in the same predicament and are less likely to have social networks outside the affected area that might be able to provide emergency housing should an evacuation become necessary. While they avoid mentioning race, the importance of income, unemployment rates, and social connectedness in disaster recovery is highlighted by FEMA reports on resiliency—the ability to bounce back after a disaster (US Department of Homeland Security 2016).

Across sociodemographic groups, income builds adaptive capacity and allows individuals to prepare for, respond to, and recover from disasters. Individuals with low incomes are less likely to have access to high-quality housing units, social support networks, or other resources to limit their exposure to hazards. They are also less able to recover and rebuild their quality of life when disaster results in the destruction of their property or adverse impacts to their health. They may be unable to afford housing in a new location, or pay for repairs and disaster-related medical bills. Conversely, higher income individuals tend to live in higher quality, more resilient housing and have the financial capacity to prepare for, respond to, and recover from disaster. A community's general economic vitality and employment levels, among several other factors, are related. High employment rates indicate community stability and a general economic ability to absorb disaster impacts and recover quickly. Communities with high unemployment, on the other hand, tend to have more residents who are disproportionately affected by disasters. Social connectedness is a critically important element of community resilience capacity. Socially isolated individuals are less resilient than socially connected individuals are, because they have less access to shared resources and are vulnerable to mental health challenges. At the community level, concentrated levels of isolation are a major factor of community vulnerability.

While FEMA asserts that more economically developed communities are more resilient, one might counter that some poverty in a capitalistic society is an inevitability. *Couldn't local governments simply put plans in place before disasters to provide transportation for evacuation or adequate emergency shelters for those living in substandard housing?* Yes, but often people of color are underrepresented on planning boards, disaster management teams, and in local governments, so issues such as linguistic or cultural barriers that might present themselves during a disaster can easily get overlooked. For example, the particular needs of immigrants are often overlooked as their voices are often not at the planning table. Immigrants may have particular trouble accessing emergency housing, as shelters sometimes turn away non-English speakers, may have diets that are incompatible with emergency food rations, or may have immigration status concerns that interfere with their ability to trust authorities or reach out for assistance.

Following a disaster, residents typically have to scramble to find new housing, fight insurance companies—if they were lucky enough to have insurance to begin with—and sometimes find new jobs as places of business are destroyed alongside the housing stock. Moreover, the rebuilding of public infrastructure (education, public housing) often is a process dominated by color-blind elites that leaves out racial and ethnic minorities.

For example, as of the one-year anniversary of the 2015 Canadian wildfire in Fort McMurray, known as "the beast," only 1 percent of the destroyed structures had been rebuilt and building permits had only been issued for about half of the damaged structures (New York Times 2017). The residents who returned tended to be working age (Hauber 2015), white, middle or upper-class (homeowners). This is the common demographic trend on who comes back first following a disaster. Why? Well, in the housing market, the process goes something like this. Real estate prices are suppressed initially in the damaged area, but that brings investment opportunity for those with capital. These investment opportunists often swoop in to acquire low-cost properties to buy and flip or buy and rent. Once the recovery period nears completion, housing prices are often much higher than pre-disaster, as are taxes and insurance costs (Haubert 2015).

Grant opportunities and federal and state-level investments mean that the surrounding area, including businesses and public infrastructure, often gets a face lift. Low-income residents do not have the economic cushion to absorb the initial slump in home values, the increased tax burdens to reinstate public services, or the spike in rents that follows a constriction in housing supply (BBC 2017). This can cause displacement of low-income residents who are priced out of the recovery zone. This is both a race and a class issue. When race and class intertwine, disaster recovery experiences differ. For example, in the case of Hurricane Katrina, researchers have found that African American and Vietnamese American groups experienced substantial differences in not only evacuation experiences, but also in the stresses associated with returning (Wei et. al 2010).

Additionally, racial and ethnic minorities are at increased risk of housing discrimination when the livable housing stock is limited by a disaster. This fact was recognized by local officials drafting Fort McMurry's recovery plans when they decided to, "implement a diversity plan to mitigate potential increases in discrimination post-disaster and to foster acceptance and inclusion of diverse peoples." This was an insightful addition to the early planning document; however, the 184-page "lessons learned" document released by the local government just post-disaster made no mention of diversity or discrimination in this context. Instead, racial and ethnic minorities had to depend on each other for services as indigenous populations were left out of the initial disaster management planning (Regional Municipality of Wood Buffalo 2017).

Why might an antidiscrimination plan be needed? Simply put, following a disaster, discrimination is more likely, less detectable, and less regulated than before (Haubert 2015). It is more likely because major disasters, whether fires, floods, hurricanes, or otherwise cause a severe constriction in the livable housing stock. When demand for housing is high but supply is low, the landlord is in a particularly powerful position to be able to choose his or her ideal renters, and because of negative stereotypes surrounding people of color in this country, landlords and rental agents are more likely to be white and more likely to view other whites as ideal renters. Housing discrimination is less detectable and less regulated because those who study or regulate housing discrimination are also temporarily disabled from doing their jobs following a disaster. Fair housing agencies may be recovering themselves.

Even if they are not, the conditions in the housing market change to such a degree that housing audits, typically the methodology used to uncover discrimination, are rendered useless (Haubert 2015). In essence, the rental housing market, largely controlled by whites, is unregulated following a disaster and rental agents have their pick from hundreds of families for any one vacancy. Often racial and ethnic minorities lose out in the competition for scarce resources. In much the same way that there is a housing scramble after a disaster, there is also a jobs scramble. And for many of the same reasons that housing discrimination is more likely following a disaster, employment discrimination may follow suit, making recovery all the more difficult for families of color.

Lastly, racial and ethnic minorities are less likely to have their losses insured (Miller and Mills 2016) and are less likely to be able to make up the difference for uninsured losses by relying on family members for help. As noted earlier, African American and Latino households have lower rates of homeownership than white households. While homeowners are required to have insurance to get a mortgage, renters are not. Therefore, renters whose houses or apartments are flooded or burned or blown to bits by severe storms are likely to lose everything without the infusion of funds to replace it. They may not be able to rely on family members for help either because of the wealth gap and concentration of poverty discussed earlier.

AN EXAMPLE OF COLOR-BLIND DISASTER RECOVERY POLICY

Race and class-neutral policies in the allocation of recovery funds ignore the glaring reality that racial and ethnic minorities are less likely to have funds—insurance, expendable income, or savings—to recuperate losses following a disaster. To illustrate one of these color-blind disaster allocations, let's take the examples of Hurricanes Irma, Harvey, and Maria that all hit the United States in August 2017. Hurricane Harvey hit Texas in late August 2017 and quickly ascended to the rank of second costliest hurricane to hit the United States, at an estimated $125 billion in insured and uninsured costs. Irma hit Puerto Rico, the US Virgin Islands, and Florida in early September, doing significant damage along the way but not nearly as much as her sister, Maria, who hit Puerto Rico and the US Virgin Islands less than two weeks later. Maria was ranked the third costliest hurricane in US history, just behind Harvey, at $90 billion in estimated damage. For both hurricanes Irma and Maria combined, FEMA distributed $1,025,971,337 (as of Dec 26, 2017) in individual and household assistance, plus another $559,062,972 in public assistance grants (www.FEMA.gov).

While Florida and the US Virgin Islands were both impacted by the one-two punch of Maria and Irma, a comparison between Texas and Puerto Rico is particularly illustrative in understanding race/class-neutral disaster recovery policies because of the differential starting points of each of these two areas. Although there are large proportions of racial and ethnic minorities in Texas, many of whom were heavily impacted, Texas residents as compared to Puerto Rican residents were less likely to be living in poverty and were more likely to own their own homes and hold homeowners and flood insurance (Palm and Hodgson 1993).

To be fair, a great many residents in Texas did not hold flood insurance, but more so than in Puerto Rico. Texans also had more options for fleeing the disaster than waterlocked Puerto Ricans, and Texans, unlike Puerto Ricans, had neighboring areas that were unaffected that could provide recovery resources—shelter, volunteers, schools, hospitals and the like. Texas, as a state, was prosperous. Puerto Rico, as a territory, was suffering from crushing debt, and infrastructure was already strained. Buildings in Texas generally were constructed under different codes and were in better condition to withstand winds—though admittedly flooding is what did the most damage in that area. Harvey was disastrous for the people of Texas and there is no intent to minimize that here, but I argue simply that Texans were in a better position to prepare for, withstand, and recover from the hurricane than was Puerto Rico.

Early analyses may very well reveal that black and brown households in Texas suffered disproportionately in terms of deaths and costs, so race may very well be a predictor of outcomes there too, but I argue that Puerto Rico, an entire island of black and brown folks, was already in a marginalized position prior to their hurricanes and that marginalized position will no doubt make recovery more difficult. It is too early to tell the pace at which each will recover, but we can at least note their differential starting points in trying to gauge how much help each will need in the coming years.

We can also gauge how much help each has gotten from the Federal Emergency Management Administration thus far. According to FEMA's website, Texas garnered $1,554,932,049 in individual and household programs and another $625,355,355 in public assistance grants during the same time period. Texas had 370,454 individual assistance applications approved. Puerto Rico, in contrast, had 430,551 individual assistance applications approved in the same time period. That means that roughly 50,000 more households applied for assistance in Puerto Rico, but there were less funds to go around for those households ($4,170 per application were available for Texas residents, $2,383 per application were available for Puerto Rican residents). All total including public assistance grants and individual funds, Texas got $2.18 billion for its $125 billion hurricane; Puerto Rico got $1.59 billion from the federal government for its $90 billion hurricane. On the surface, this seems very fair, because it means that the federal government helped with about the same percentage of the total damage costs—around 17 percent—for each of these storms; however, this ignores the fact that Puerto Ricans had many more housing assistance applications and that residents were much less likely to have insurance that could supplement rebuilding costs.

In other words, the federal government appears to have taken a very class- and race-neutral approach to disaster recovery funding even though Puerto Ricans had lower quality housing stock pre-disaster, had more requests for assistance following the disaster, and had fewer ways to make up the shortfall, such as lower levels of savings and homeowners insurance. Thus, race and class-neutral policies are problematic when we know that race and class affects residents' ability to recover on their own.

To be clear, race is not the only factor nor is it even the most important factor affecting social vulnerability, but it is one factor that is very often ignored. We also ignore the way that race is tangled up with class due to a long history of marginalization and racial oppression in this country. This chapter then is designed to make some of the invisible visible again by showing how race is tied up with class, homeownership rates, housing quality, the quality of public infrastructure, transportation access, and the strength of social networks, all of which affect disaster experiences and the pace of recovery.

WHAT EQUITY IN DISASTER RECOVERY LOOKS LIKE

It is rare that South Carolina gets praise for its socially progressive policies, but in their handling of the 2015 floods that ravaged the eastern part of the state, that state provided a model for others to follow, one that centers social vulnerability measures in its approach to recovery. The case below illustrates how social science data can be used not only for describing or explaining past events, but also in predicting future outcomes and making informed planning and recovery decisions.

In October 2015, South Carolina experienced unprecedented and historic rainfall and flooding resulting from over twenty inches of heavy rainfall in just five days. The floods caused the deaths of nineteen South Carolinians and extensive damage to many dams, bridges, roads, businesses, and homes estimated at nearly $1.5 billion (Murphy 2016). Families, including many urban residents of low-to-moderate income, had to abandon their homes only to return weeks later to extensive damage. According to the South Carolina Disaster Recovery Office (SCDRCO), more than 33,100 homes in the state were impacted by at least a foot of water, and standing water created dangerous toxic mold and necessitated expensive remediation before these homes could be occupied (South Carolina Department of Commerce 2016).

Flood insurance was of limited help. It is only mandated on homes in flood plains that have a mortgage. As a result, only 4 percent of the state had flood insurance in 2016. Although FEMA provided individual household assistance, their mission is just to bring the housing up to a safe/sanitary level, not necessarily to address all of the damage or meet all of the needs. Fortunately, the state government also was allocated funds ($97 million) by HUD to assist with "unmet needs" in the recovery which, due to the low rates of flood insurance, was substantial. The state then had to determine where to spend this money in order to maximize impact. In other words, all affected households got FEMA money but it was not much, and all insured households should have gotten insurance money, but few houses were insured against floods. The question was then, how should South Carolina use its funds for "unmet needs" to maximize impact? How should they decide where the additional funds were most needed? An innovative use of social science data informed this process.

South Carolina has taken a cutting-edge approach to its disaster recovery process by assessing social vulnerability as part of its recovery strategy. The State partnered with the University of South Carolina's Hazard and Vulnerability Research Institute to identify those areas most impacted and most vulnerable across the state. They created an index that delineated the most socially vulnerable census tracts within each county and overlaid that data with FEMA damage assessments to inform the allocation of funds. They considered county-level factors, such as average level of education, percent with a disability, percent African American, percent over age sixty-five, percent in poverty, and percent without health insurance.

In doing so, they recognized the uneven capacity for preparedness and disaster recovery and where resources might be used most effectively. Informing the state recovery plan, if a county had more than one-third of its homes damaged and had high social vulnerability, that county became a priority in the allocation of funds. These "hot spots" were areas that were both heavily impacted and had a lower capacity to absorb such losses. Using social science data in this way turns historical disaster impact measures into actionable information for emergency managers, recovery planners, and decision makers as a whole.

I don't see color. I treat everyone the same. Perhaps at the individual level, this makes sense as an interpersonal relationship strategy, but in a society that still stratifies by race, we must take account of it in our societal level decision-making. And not just race needs to be considered, but also wealth, age, and disability and other factors that put some populations at higher risk and make recovery more challenging. When we ignore social vulnerability the outcome is predictable: whiter and wealthier communities bounce back whereas other areas come back at a much slower pace if at all.

Equity in disaster recovery then means allocating resources to those areas with high concentrations of residents who were both heavily impacted and have fewer outside recovery resources that could help, such as savings, personal transportation, and dispersed and economically varied social networks. Or we could treat everyone and every community the same in allocating assistance and resources. On the surface the latter appears fair, but since people live in very unequal conditions to start with, such an approach leads to very uneven recovery. Some people are already running on the inside track and don't need to run as far to cross the finish line. Let's make a fairer race for those starting on the outside track.

Bibliography

Bonilla-Silva, Eduardo. *Racism without Racists*, 5th ed. Boston, MA: Rowman and
    Littlefield, 2017.

Brown, Michael, Elliott Currie, David Oppenheimer, and David Wellman. *Whitewashing
    Race: The Myth of a Colorblind Society*, 2nd ed. University of California Press, 2005.

Colten. C. E. *An Unnatural Metropolis: Wresting New Orleans from Nature.* Baton
    Rouge: Louisiana State University Press, 2005.

Erikson, Kai. "Forward." In *The Sociology of Katrina*, 2nd ed, edited by David Brunsma,
    David Overfelt, and J.Steven Picou. Boston: Rowman and Littlefield Publishers, 2010.

Haubert, Jeannie. "Introduction." In *Rethinking Disaster Recovery: Lessons Learned from Hurricane Katrina*, edited by Jeannie Haubert. Lexington Books, 2015.

———. "Housing Market Mayhem: Studying Discrimination Post-Disaster." In *Rethinking Disaster Recovery: A Hurricane Katrina Retrospective*, edited by Jeannie Haubert. Lexington Books, 2015.

Irfan, Umair, and Brian Resnick. "Megadisasters Devastated America in 2017 and They're Only Going to Get Worse." Vox. January 8, 2018. https://www.vox.com/energy-and-environment/2017/12/28/16795490/natural-disasters-2017-hurricanes-wildfires-heat-climate-change-cost-deaths.

Jeffrey, Adam. "2017–A Year of Disaster." CNBC. Dec 26, 2017. https://www.cnbc.com/2017/12/26/2017--a-year-of-disaster.html.

Kneebone, Elizabeth, and Natalie Holmes. "U.S. Concentrated Poverty in the Wake of the Great Recession." Brookings Institute. March 31, 2016. https://www.brookings.edu/research/u-s-concentrated-poverty-in-the-wake-of-the-great-recession/

Kochhar, Rakesh, and Anthony Cilluf. "How Wealth Inequality has Changed in the US Since the Great Recession." Pew Research Center. November 1, 2017. http://www.pewresearch.org/fact-tank/2017/11/01/how-wealth-inequality-has-changed-in-the-u-s-since-the-great-recession-by-race-ethnicity-and-income/.

"Lessons Learned from the 2016 Horse River Wildfire." Regional Municipality of Wood Buffalo. July 27. https://www.rmwb.ca/News-Room/RMWB-Wildfire-Information/Lessons-Learned-and-Recommendations-from-the-2016-Horse-River-Wildfire.htm.

Li, Wei, Christopher Airriess, Angelea Chia-Chen Chen, Karen Leong, Keith Verna. "Katrina and Migration: Evacuation and Return by African Americans and Vietnamese Americans in an Eastern New Orleans Suburb." *The Professional Geographer* 62, no. 1 (2010). https://www.tandfonline.com/doi/full/10.1080/00330120903404934.

Miller, DeMond Shondell and John Thomas Mills. "Challenging Race-Based Environmental Conflicts" *Peace Review: A Journal of Social Justice*, 28(4):420–426, 2016.

Murphy, John D. "The Historic South Carolina Floods of October 1–5, 2015." National Oceanic and Atmospheric Agency (NOAA), US Department of Commerce. July 2016. https://www.weather.gov/media/publications/assessments/SCFlooding_072216_Signed_Final.pdf

National Oceanic and Atmospheric Administration (NOAA). https://www.climate.gov/news-features/category/extreme-events.

"One year later, 15,000 residents still had not returned to Fort McMurray." BBC. May 2, 2017.

Palm, R., and M.E. Hodgson. "Natural Hazards in Puerto Rico" *Geographical Review* 83: i3, (1993).

"Race: The Power of an Illusion." PBS. 2003. http://www.pbs.org/race/000_About/002_04-about-03-01.htm.

Sarmiento, Camilo, and Ted E. Miller. "Inequities in Flood Management Protection Outcomes." American Agricultural Economic Association Meetings, Long Beach, CA. May 2006. https://ageconsearch.umn.edu/bitstream/21042/1/sp06sa08.pdf.

Squires, Gregory,. and Chester Hartman. *There is No Such Thing as a Natural Disaster: Race, Class, and Hurricane Katrina*. London: Routledge, 2006.

State of South Carolina, Department of Commerce. "State of South Carolina Action Plan for Disaster Recovery." July 19, 2016. https://www.sccommerce.com/sites/default/files/hud_submittal_action_plan_160719.pdf

Stephen, R. and Stoll, M. "Can Boosting Minority Car-Ownership Rates Narrow Inter-Racial Employment Gaps?" Brookings-Wharton Papers on Urban Affairs. 2001.

US Department of Homeland Security. "Draft Interagency Concept for Community Resilience Indicators and National-Level Measures." FEMA. June 2016. https://www.fema.gov/media-library-data/1466085676217-a14e229a461adfa574a-5d03041a6297c/FEMA-CRI-Draft-Concept-Paper-508_Jun_2016.pdf

Wise, Tim. *Colorblind: The Rise of Post-Racial Politics and the Retreat from Racial Equity*. New York: City Lights Publishers, 2010.

"Worry in Scorched Fort McMurray: How Many Will Walk Away?" *New York Times*. May 5, 2017. www.newyorktimes.com

Figure credits

Figure 7.1: Source: https://www.fema.gov/data-visualization-summary-disaster-declarations-and-grants.

Figure 7.2: Source: https://www.fema.gov/data-visualization-summary-disaster-declarations-and-grants.

Figure 7.3: Source: https://cpo.noaa.gov/sites/cpo/Images/EduAndOutreach/Dashboard_600p.jpg.

Figure 7.4: Source: https://commons.wikimedia.org/wiki/File:Projected_global_warming_over_the_21st_century_using_three_SRES_greenhouse_gas_emissions_scenarios._Data_from_CMIP3_(2007).png.

The Relationship Between African Americans and the Criminal Justice System: A Review of the Literature

Robert McNamara, PhD

IT IS DIFFICULT to watch the news or listen to media accounts about crime in American society without race becoming a central part of the discussion. Advocates promote a perspective that suggests police officers and the entire criminal justice system is racist and discriminates against minorities, particularly African Americans. Others point out that the reason for the disproportionate numbers of African Americans in the system is due to the fact that members of this group commit more crimes and the data simply reflects those trends. Few disagree with the data that demonstrate that African Americans are more likely to be found in the system and are more likely to be stopped, searched, arrested, charged, convicted, and sentenced, compared to whites, but the disagreement occurs as to the reasons for this trend. So what does the data actually tell us?

AFRICAN AMERICANS AND THE CRIMINAL JUSTICE SYSTEM

Perhaps the most controversial interaction that African Americans have with the criminal justice system relates to the police. Much has been said and written about police-minority relations, the use of force by police officers against African Americans, and racial profiling. There are a number of sensational cases in which the police have mistreated members of minority groups. Examples include the famous cases in Ferguson, Missouri; the Freddie Gray case in Baltimore, MD; the shooting of Laquan McDonald in Chicago, who was shot sixteen times by a police officer; or the famous Eric Garner (I can't breathe) case in Staten Island, New York. In addition, there have been several instances where police officers were ambushed and murdered by suspects who professed an allegiance to the Black Lives Matter movement or a hatred of the police. Some minority leaders, as well as others, have asserted that the police, and to some extent the entire criminal justice system, are prejudiced and racist. These individuals argue that situations like the ones described above are indicators that the police target minorities and treat them differently. Is there any truth to these assertions? Are the police racist? Do they treat minorities differently? How does the public perceive the police?

Public Opinion and the Police

According to a 2013 Justice Department report, an estimated sixty-three million people in the United States have some form of contact with the police every year. This contact was initiated by residents and the police and includes interactions such as traffic stops or stopping persons in public places. Approximately 93 percent of those who asked for help from the police, about 90 percent of people who experienced a traffic stop, and about 70 percent of those who were questioned by the police on the street, felt the actions of officers were appropriate (Langton and Durose 2013).

The report also showed that, among those stopped by the police during a traffic stop, Blacks were slightly more likely than whites and Hispanics (13 percent vs. 10 percent each) to be pulled over by police in a traffic stop; however, blacks, whites, and Hispanics were about equally as likely to be stopped by officers on the street. This is quite different from data in the early 1990s that reflected a tendency to "stop and frisk" minorities more often than whites. Further, about 80 percent of drivers in traffic stops and 60 percent of those involved in street stops believed they were stopped for a legitimate reason (Langton and Durose 2005).

While this latest study from the Department of Justice shows some promising trends, it is important to note that these findings have been consistent since 2005 (Langton and Durose 2013). These figures indicate that a large percentage of the population think the police are doing a good job. However, minorities generally have lower opinions about the quality of police service they receive and are generally less trustful of officers. Another important factor is the characteristic of the neighborhood. One study found that people living in high-crime neighborhoods and low-income communities tend to have more contact with the police and report less overall satisfaction. Furthermore, because minorities tend to live in these types of neighborhoods, it is not surprising that their confidence in the police is lower than that of whites (Smith and Visher 1991).

A 2003 study in four neighborhoods in Los Angeles found that residents who lived in high-crime areas were less likely to approve of the police. Conversely, those residents who lived in lower crime neighborhoods and had a variety of contacts with officers tended to rate them higher on their assessment of performance (Ashcroft, Daniels, and Hart 2003).

Other studies showed that while race and ethnicity had been identified as important factors in approval ratings, the level of social and physical disorder in the community was even more important in assessing the overall satisfaction with the police. Where race and ethnicity did matter concerns the perception of how the police treated minorities. For example, African Americans were more likely to say that officers acted unprofessionally towards them than towards whites. This study also found that the media had little influence on public opinion of the police. While limited in its ability to make an overall assessment of the public's opinion of the police, this study nevertheless raised a number of questions about how to change the public's perception of police officers (Maxon, Hennigan, and Sloan 2003).

Why do police officers have more contact with low-income and minority neighborhoods? Part of the answer is that this group makes greater use of police services than other groups. Police departments assign more patrol officers to these neighborhoods because of greater calls for service and because minority groups in these areas have higher crime rates. Another reason is that minorities and low-income people are more likely to call the police to solve a variety of noncriminal matters. Compared to middle-class Americans, for instance, people in the low-income category are more likely to call the police for assistance with medical emergencies and family problems. This means that the police are more actively and intrusively involved in the daily lives of people from these areas. Greater contact also means that the decisions made by officers may not be what the members of these neighborhoods prefer, resulting in lower levels of satisfaction. In sum, evidence suggests differential treatment of minorities by police on a variety of indicators, including violent crime, deadly force, arrests, and other minor forms of abuse (Murdock 2015; McKenzie 2014; Palazzolo 2013; Walker, Spohn, and Delone 2004).

Violent Crime

Perhaps due to the distortion of crime and criminals in the media, as well as their own experiences with crime, many people, including the police, believe that African Americans and other minorities are more involved in violent crime than whites. Moreover, this perception affects how officers respond to violent crimes. For instance, using data from the *National Crime Victimization Survey*, one study examined the relationship between the victim and the offender's race with regard to robbery and aggravated assault. The variables considered were the response time to the scene, the amount of effort made by officers to investigate these crimes at the scene, and the likelihood of arrest (Bachman 1996).

The study found that officers tended to respond more quickly and showed a greater investment of effort in the investigation (e.g., searches) when the incident consisted of African American offenders and white victims. This was true even when things like poverty, the victim's gender, and whether or not the victim was injured were taken into account. With regard to aggravated assault, particularly those involving strangers, officers were more likely to be more thorough in the investigation if it involved a white victim and an African American offender.

Officers were also more likely, all other things being equal, to respond more quickly and to put forth a more determined effort if there was an injury to the white victim, particularly by an African American offender. None of these findings applied when the victim was an African American and the offender was white. Thus, evidence suggests that the race of the victim and the offender plays a role in how the police respond to violent crime. If the crime involves a white victim and African American offender, officers seem to respond more quickly to the scene of the crime and investigate it more thoroughly, and arrests are more likely to occur (Bachman 1996).

Arrests

Is race a factor in the arrest of a suspect? The answer appears clear as minorities are arrested out of proportion to their representation in the population. According to the *Uniform Crime Reports*, in 2014, African Americans represented about 14 percent of the population but approximately 28 percent of all arrests and 39 percent of arrests for violent crime. In 2014 approximately 70 percent of all individuals arrested were white, with the remaining 2 percent from other races. White individuals accounted for approximately 60 percent of all violent crimes. Of adults arrested for murder, about 51 percent were black and 47 percent were white, with other races making up the remaining percentage. As it relates to juveniles, blacks comprised nearly 53 percent of all juveniles arrested for violent crime while white juveniles accounted for nearly 60 percent of all juveniles arrested for property crimes (US Department of Justice 2015). However, there is a great deal of controversy surrounding this issue. What are the reasons for this apparent differential treatment? Do police officers arrest African Americans more frequently due to racial bias or because blacks commit more crimes? What variables are considered in the decision to arrest?

Donald Black (1971) in his famous article "The Social Organization of Arrest," found that, in general, the decision to arrest was predicated on a number of factors, including the strength of the evidence, the seriousness of the crime, whether or not the complainant or victim wanted the suspect arrested, and whether the suspect was disrespectful toward the officer. The decision to arrest was also based on the relationship between the victim and the offender. If the suspect was a stranger to the victim, the officers were more likely to arrest him or her.

Interestingly, Black found that race was not a factor in the decision to arrest. He did find that African Americans were arrested more often than whites, but this was mainly due to the fact that whites were more likely to show deference to the officer. As he describes, this creates a vicious cycle, where the African American men who are arrested more often have negative feelings towards the police. When these feelings are demonstrated, they are more likely to be arrested, which increases the hostility felt by African Americans.

Much research following Black's earlier work found that race does matter. In the 1980s, for instance, race was considered in terms of the decision to arrest. One study found that in those instances where the suspect was African American and the victim was white, officers were more likely to make an arrest. Similar to Black's findings, in these situations, officers were also more likely to arrest the suspect upon the victim's request to do so (Smith and Visher 1991).

Another study found that African Americans and Hispanics were more likely to be arrested on less evidence than whites. The study also found that blacks and Hispanics were more likely to be released without the case going to the prosecutor. While at first glance this may appear to be advantageous, arrest still represents a form of punishment even though formal charges may not be filed (Petersilia 2005). The evidence seems to suggest then, that the race of the victim and of the offender play an important role in the decision to arrest (Son, Davis, and Rome 1998).

Use of Force

The Rodney King example is perhaps the most visible and memorable reminder of excessive use of force by police officers. King, who was driving while intoxicated, led the police on a high-speed car chase in 1991. After he eventually stopped, four officers were videotaped beating King, while several other officers observed the beating. The video, one of the first of its kind, was sent to the media and resulted in the arrest of four officers who were charged with assault with a deadly weapon and excessive use of force. Three officers were eventually acquitted of all charges and the fourth officer was acquitted of the assault charge, but the jury deadlocked eight to four in favor of acquittal on the excessive use of force. These decisions were said to be the reason for the subsequent riots that occurred in Los Angeles that led to millions of dollars in property damage and other crimes. After the state trial, federal charges were brought against the officers for violating King's civil rights. The result was that two of the officers were acquitted again and two officers were found guilty (PBS 2015).

However, prior to the King incident in 1991, there was considerable academic interest in the use of force topic. In his classic study of the police, Albert J. Reiss (1971) found that race per se was not a determining factor in the use of excessive force. Instead, "Class rather than race determines police misconduct." The typical victim of excessive force is a lower class male, regardless of race. Others, however, disagree and see excessive use of force as particularly prevalent against African American men. According to a 1999 Bureau of Justice Statistics report on police-citizen contacts, there were substantial racial and ethnic disparities in police use of force. African Americans are three times as likely to experience force or threatened force than whites. Hispanics were more likely than whites but less likely than African Americans to experience police use of force (Adams 1995).

The implications of this trend are particularly significant for African Americans. Even if the overall rate of the use of force comprises one percent of all police/citizen encounters, if those incidents are concentrated in low-income neighborhoods and consist of lower class men, who are likely to be African American, the effects of these incidents accumulate over time to create a perception that the police routinely harass African Americans (Walker, Spohn, Delone 2004). The symbolic significance of the excessive use of force should not be overlooked. As representatives of the larger system, police officers who engage in excessive use of force serve as a reminder of the larger problems of discrimination and exploitation felt by African Americans. More recently, according to a US Department of Justice report, law-enforcement agencies received approximately twenty-six thousand complaints from citizens about the excessive use of force by officers. This number translates into a rate of about 6.6 complaints per 100 full-time sworn officers. About 8 percent of these complaints contained enough evidence to discipline officers for their actions; about one-third of the cases were unsubstantiated allegations, and about a quarter were unsupported by the facts (or the incident did not occur); and 23 percent ended in exonerations because the officers acted properly (Hickman 2006).

Deadly Force

Despite the notoriety when such events occur, there has been a general decline in the incidence of deadly force by the police (Hickman 2006). However, a great deal of attention has been given to the frequency with which police officers use deadly force against minorities (Shoop 1998; Fyfe 1998; Dunham and Alpert 1992; Westley 1970). When compared with their numbers in the population, African Americans are disproportionately killed by the police. However, these findings also suggest that when compared with rates of police/citizen contacts, arrest rates and resistance to or attacks upon the police, there is no apparent racial disparity in the use of deadly force by the police (Fyfe 1988; Gellar and Scott 1993).

One study found that from 1970–1984, the police use of deadly force declined substantially, particularly against African Americans (Cohen and Sherman 1986). More recently, the data indicate that the racial disparity in the number of people shot and killed by the police has decreased from about seven African Americans for every white to about three to one (Walker, Spohn, and Delone 2004).

Another situation in which deadly force is justified occurs when the officer prevents the escape of a person who is extremely dangerous (Roberg and Kuykendall 1993). In *Tennessee vs. Garner* (471 U.S. 1. 1985), two officers used deadly force against an African American juvenile who was fleeing the scene of a burglary. At that time, the officers were justified in using deadly physical force against a fleeing felon. However, the Court ruled that this was no longer acceptable. As a result, many departments were required to modify their policies concerning use of force against fleeing felons. Thus, while there was a time when officers were given wide latitude in using deadly force, since 1980 departments all over the country have changed their policies regarding the use of force and the number of incidents have declined considerably.

In 2011 the US Department of Justice released a report on arrest-related deaths, which noted that between 2003 and 2009, 4,813 persons died during or shortly after law-enforcement personnel attempted to arrest or restrain them, and almost two-thirds of these incidents were classified as homicides.

Of those who died during the process of arrest, almost all (95 percent) were male, and nearly half (about 42 percent) were white. In comparison, about a third were black and about twenty percent were Hispanic or Latino. More than half (55 percent) were between the ages of twenty-five and forty-four. Of those who committed suicide during the process of arrest, 60 percent were white, 15 percent were black, and 20 percent Hispanic or Latino (Burch 2011).

Racial Profiling

In the mid-1990s, the New Jersey State Police were investigated for ordering officers to concentrate on stopping Black drivers. Three state troopers stated they were instructed by their superior to identify African Americans for traffic stops. Additionally, a 1992 study of traffic stops in Florida found that while 5 percent of the drivers on the road were African American or Hispanic, 70 percent of those stopped and 80 percent of those searched were African American or Hispanic (Cole 1999).

About ten years later, another controversy was created when, in April 2005, a report on racial profiling was scheduled to be released by the Department of Justice's Bureau of Justice Statistics. The study found that about 9 percent of all drivers were stopped by the police that year. However, once drivers were stopped, Hispanics were searched by the police about 12 percent of the time, while blacks were searched about 10 percent of the time. In comparison, white drivers were only searched about 4 percent of the time. The study found that officers were more likely to threaten or use force against blacks and Hispanics and officers were more likely to issue tickets to Hispanics than whites. The inflammatory nature of these findings allegedly led the Justice Department to try to suppress some of the information or to change the findings.

While strenuously arguing that the results should not be altered for political purposes, the director of the Bureau of Justice Statistics was demoted (Lichtblau 2005). What should also be considered in reviewing the trends cited in the earlier studies is the more recent data highlighted at the beginning of this chapter. While it may be reasonable to assume that some form of profiling may exist at an individual officer level, the fact that the trends are far different from what was discovered during the 1990s indicates that changes were made in police practices as it relates to police-citizen interactions.

What seems to be missing from the discussion of the perspective that white officers are racist and disproportionately kill blacks, a sentiment that created the Black Lives Matter movement, is the data about the extent of this trend. As one article points out, in New York City, which has a Civilian Review Board that was created in the 1990s to address police abuse of authority and excessive force, the data for 2014 indicates the number of complaints filed against the police have decreased 10 percent and the number of excessive force claims have decreased by 11 percent. Additionally, profanity accusations dropped by 20 percent. Further, according to the NYPD's 2013 Annual Firearms Discharge Report, NYPD officers killed eight people in 2013, and five of these cases involved a suspect with a handgun, one of whom fired six times at two officers on a subway, one of whom was armed with a knife. In comparison, in New York City in 2013, 335 citizens were murdered, and in 63 percent of those cases the suspect was black. According to the Uniform Crime Reports for 2013, 90 percent of black murder victims nationally are killed by black assailants (Murdoch 2015).

So while questions about police misconduct are worthy of an in-depth discussion and require specific action by departments and other agencies, it is not completely clear the extent to which the police are responsible for the number of blacks killed each year. Some data show, for instances, that while blacks are more than six times likelier than whites to have been a murder victim in 2011, blacks were also almost eight times likelier than whites to have committed murder (Murdock 2015). Thus, care must be taken to ensure that all of the data has been presented and interpreted in a fair and unbiased way. To do otherwise is to create a climate of mistrust and fear and an unwillingness to work collaboratively to solve the larger problems in the black community.

The Courts and African Americans

Not only is there some evidence to suggest that blacks are more likely than whites to be stopped, searched, arrested, and killed by police officers, they are also more likely to receive harsher treatment once they arrive in court. In fact, there are many who contend that the War on Drugs is really a war on African Americans (Tarver, Walker, and Wallace 2002). An analysis of sentences by the US Sentencing Commission found that prison sentences of black men were almost 20 percent longer than those of white men for similar crimes (Palazzolo 2013). The Sentencing Commission report recommended that federal judges give the guidelines more significance. The latest study by the US Sentencing Commission, which focused on the period between 2007 and 2011, found that black males were serving about 20 percent longer sentences than whites for similar crimes and that black males were 25 percent less likely than whites to receive a sentence below the guidelines' range. While this study does not, by itself, prove that judicial discretion caused greater black-white federal sentencing disparity, it nevertheless is an improvement in the understanding of what happens to similar types of offenders in terms of the outcome of their cases (Palazzolo 2013).

A related conclusion appears in murder cases. Researchers found that when the level of seriousness is controlled for, such as the degree of severity and the number of persons killed, prosecutors and juries are more likely to demand the death penalty if the victim is white and the offender is black than in any of the other possible racial combinations (e.g., white victim/black offender; white offender/black victim; black offender/black victim; white offender/white victim (Ekland-Olson 1988).

A number of studies demonstrate racial bias in sentencing. A study in thirty-nine states found that blacks typically serve longer sentences than whites for robbery, rape, and murder (Hacker 1989). A growing body of research indicates that in many cases the key factor is the race of the victim. Preliminary evidence suggests that when the victim of rape or robbery is white, the sentence is likely to be more severe (LaFree 1980). More recently, a metaanalysis of eighty-five research studies revealed that, after taking into account the defendant's criminal history and the seriousness of the offense, blacks and Latinos were generally sentenced more harshly than whites. However, the research available on sentencing patterns of whites compared to those of Asians or Native Americans does not reveal significant differences between these groups. In general, there appears to be some evidence to suggest that disparities in sentencing still occur, even involving sentencing guidelines (Mitchell and Mackenzie 2014).

The conclusions from such findings, naturally, explain varying racial perceptions of crime and criminals, and foster the basis of understanding why blacks and Latinos, while accounting for 30 percent of the general population, account for nearly 60 percent of the prison population. These perceptions also drive the belief by some groups that the criminal justice system is biased against blacks.

Such a belief is underscored by the results of the survey, which showed that over two-thirds of African Americans saw the system as biased compared to only 25 percent of whites (Mitchell and Mackenzie 2014).

Corrections and African American

There is a long history of disproportionality in the criminal justice system with regard to race, and this is clearly reflected in statistics regarding incarceration. In 2014, according to the US Department of Justice, there were an estimated 1,561,500 prisoners in state and federal correctional facilities, a decrease of one percent from 2013. By any measure, African Americans are disproportionately incarcerated. According to the report:

> while they represented approximately 14 percent of the overall population in this country in 2014, African Americans represented 36 percent of those incarcerated in state and federal prisons. Whites represented about 75 percent of the population yet they only constituted 34 percent of the inmate population. Hispanics represented about 17 percent of the population, but about 22 percent of those incarcerated in 2014. (Carson 2015)

According to the Bureau of Justice Statistics, at the beginning of 2014, among those inmates with a sentence of more than one year, black males comprised 516,900 inmates, white males made up 453,500, and Hispanic males consisted of 308,700. This translates into more than 36 percent of all sentenced males were black, about 32 percent were white, and about 22 percent were Hispanic. Female prisoners reflected a slightly different distribution, with whites comprising the largest percentage of female inmates at 53,100, followed by African Americans with 22,600 inmates, and Hispanics with 17,800 prisoners. This means that of all sentenced females, 50 percent were white, 22 percent were black, and 17 percent were Hispanic (Carson 2015).

According to the Bureau of Justice Statistics, which bases its projections on the last day of a given year, on December 31, 2014, the rates for black males were up to eleven times greater than white males and up to three times greater than rates for Hispanic males. Among female prisoners, black females were up to four times more likely to be imprisoned than white females (Carson 2015).

Type of offenses also varied by race and ethnicity, although compared to violent and property offenders in state prisons, those serving time for drug offenses had very little racial disparity. Overall, about 48 percent of white male prisoners, 57 percent of black, and 59 percent of Hispanic male inmates were convicted of violent offenses. However, white offenders were more likely serving time for a property offense (25 percent) compared to blacks (16 percent) and Hispanics (14 percent). As was mentioned, drug offenders were about evenly distributed, with blacks representing the largest percentage of offenders (16 percent) followed equally by whites and Hispanics (14.5 percent each) (Carson 2015).

CONCLUSION

How does one explain these alarming trends? As MacDonald (2015) notes, one possible explanation is that African Americans are overrepresented in the crime statistics because they are more likely to become involved in criminal activity and more likely to get caught. Such a theory is a popular one offered by political conservatives, as it focuses the blame squarely on the people who are adversely affected. Thus, according to this position, the data is not discriminatory against African Americans, rather it is an accurate reflection of what actually occurs (MacDonald 2015).

Another theory offers the explanation that the disproportionality is based on inherent biases within the criminal justice system. At the heart of this explanation is that African Americans are mistreated based on the public's fears of that group. Motivated by the perception that African Americans represent a greater threat than white offenders, police, judges, and other court officials treat African Americans more harshly (Wilbanks 1987).

In his book, *The Myth of a Racist Criminal Justice System,* Wilbanks (1987) argues that the explanation is not found in a racist system that systematically singles out blacks for special treatment. Rather, there are other factors at play, which contribute to the involvement of blacks in the justice system, namely poverty, negligence, and previous involvement in crime.

In short, Wilbanks offers the idea that the disparity in the legal system has more to do with poverty levels than race. The argument suggests that crimes like assault, drugs, burglary, and robbery are a function of the adversity families and individuals are facing as a result of being poor. Empirical support for this position was offered in the 1990s when researchers noted that a decrease in poverty levels was related to reductions in crime rates, particularly in the early part of the twentieth century. To be fair, some studies suggested a link between poverty and crime, but other evidence began to emerge that suggested race was playing a role in the justice process. Thus, while Wilbanks's approach garnered some credibility for a time, and perhaps today with conservative thinkers, the weight of the evidence suggests that something is amiss with regard to the relationship between race and the justice process.

A third position is offered by Walkher, Spohn, and DeLone (2004). After an extensive review of the literature, they suggested a more moderate theory that contends the system is neither completely free of racial bias nor does it contain the type of systematic bias that other experts assert. Walker, Spohn, and DeLone agree that racial and ethnic groups are in fact treated more harshly at some (or many) stages of the system but at other points they are not singled out compared to whites who are going through the justice process.

Bibliography

Abrahams, Roger D. *Singing the Master: The Emergence of African American Culture in the Plantation South*. New York Pantheon, 1992.

Adams, K. "Measuring the Prevalence of Police Abuse of Force." In *And Justice for All*, edited by William Geller and Hans Toch. Washington, D.C.: The Police Executive Research Forum, 1995.

Anderson, Elijah. *Streetwise*. Chicago: University of Chicago Press, 1990.

Allen, E. "Religious Heterdoxy and Nationalist Tradition: The Continuing Evolution of the Nation of Islam." *Black Scholar* 26, no. ¾ (1996): 2–34.

Ashcroft, J., Daniels, D. J., & Hart, S. V. (2003). *Youth victimization: Prevalence and implications.* Washington, DC: U.S. Department of Justice.

Bachman, R. "Victims' Perceptions of Initial Police Responses to Robbery and Aggravated Assault: Does Race Matter?" *Journal of Quantitative Criminology* 12, no. 4 (1996): 363–90.

Baker, Al. "Beyond the Chokehold: The Path to Eric Garner's Death. *New York Times*. June 13, 2015. http://www.nytimes.com/2015/06/14/nyregion/eric-garner-police-chokehold-staten- island.html.

Baldus, David, George Woodworth, and Charles A. Pulaski. *Equal Justice and the Death Penalty: A Legal and Empirical Analysis*. Boston: Northeastern University Press, 1990.

Bennett, L. *The White Problem in America*. Chicago: Johnson, 1966.

Besharov, D. J. "The Economic Stagnation of the Black Middle Class." Testimony before the US Commission on Civil Rights. July 2005.

Black, D. "The Social Organization of Arrest" *Stanford Law Review* 23, (1971):1087–111.

Black Lives Matter. http://blacklivesmatter.com.

Bowers, W. J., and G. Pierce. "Deterrence or Brutalization: What is the Effect of Executions?" *Crime and Delinquency* 26, (1980): 453–84.

Brown, Emily. "Timelines: Michael Brown Shooting in Ferguson, MO." USA Today. August 10, 2015. http://www.usatoday.com/story/news/nation/2014/08/14/michael-brown-ferguson-missouri-timeline/14051827/.

Browning, S. L., F. T. Cullen, L. Cao, R. Kopache, and T. J. Stevenson. "Race and Getting Hassled By the Police: A Research Note." *Police Studies* 17, no. 1 (1994): 1–11.

Burch, A. "Arrest-Related Deaths 2003–2009." US Department of Justice, Bureau of Justice Statistics. 2011. http://www.bjs.gov.

Butler, J. S. "The Return of Open Debate." *Society* 39, (1996): 11–18.

Carson, E. A. "Prisoners in 2014." U.S. Department of Justice, Bureau of Justice Statistics. 2015. http://www.bjs.gov/content/pub/pdf/p14.pdf.

Cleaver, K. "How TV Wrecked the Black Panthers." *Channels*, (1982): 98–9.

Cohen H., and L. Sherman. "Exploiting Police Authority." *Criminal Justice Ethics* (Summer/Fall 1986): 23–31.

Cole, David. *No Equal Justice: Race and Class in the American Criminal Justice System.* New York: The Free Press, 1999.

Crank, John P. *Understanding Police Culture.* Cincinnati, OH: Anderson, 1998.

Crawford, C., T. Chiricos, and G. Kleck. "Race, Racial Threat and Sentencing of Habitual Offenders," *Criminology* 36, no. 3 (1998): 481–511.

Dubois, W. E. B. *The Negro American Family.* Cambridge, MA: MIT Press, 1970.

Dunham, Roger, and Geoffrey Alpert. *Critical Issues in Law Enforcement.* Cincinnati, OH: Waveland, 1992.

Durose, Matthew R., Erica L. Smith, and Patrick A. Langan. "Contacts Between Police and the Public, 2005." US Department of Justice, Bureau of Justice Statistics. April 2007. https://www.bjs.gov/content/pub/pdf/cpp05.pdf.

Ekland-Olson, S. "Structured Discretion, Racial Bias, and the Death Penalty: The First Debate after Furman in Texas." *Social Science Quarterly* 69 (December 1988): 853–73.

Fausset, R.; Perez-Pena, R. and Robertson, C. 2016. "Alton Sterling Shooting in Baton Rouge Prompts Justice Department Investigation." *New York Times*, July 6th, available at: http://movile.nytimes.com/2016/07/06/alton-sterling-baton-rouge-shooting.html?

Ford, M. 2014. "Racism and the Execution Chamber." *The Atlantic*, June 23rd. Available at: http://www.theatlantic.com/politics/archive/2014/06/race-and-the-death-penalty/373081/

Franklin, John Hope, and Alfred A. Moss. *From Slavery to Freedom: A History of African Americans*, 8th ed. New York: McGraw-Hill, 2000.

Frazier, Franklin. *The Negro Church in America.* New York: Schocken, 1964.

Free, Marvin D. *African Americans and the Criminal Justice System.* New York: Garland, 1996.

Friedrich, R. J. "Police Use of Force: Individuals, Situations, and Organizations." *Annals of the American Academy of Political and Social Science* 452, (1980): 82–97.;

Fyfe, J. J. "Police Use of Deadly Force: Research and Reform." *Justice Quarterly* 5, (1988): 165–205.

Geller, W. A. and M. Scott. *Deadly Force: What We Know.* Washington, DC: Police Executive Research Forum, 1993.

Gray, J. "Panel Says Courts are Infested with Racism." *New York Times.* June 5, 1991: B1.

Hacker, A. "Affirmative Action: The New Look." *New York Review of Books* 36 (October 12, 1989): 63–8.

Harris, Frederick C. "The Next Civil Rights Movement?" *Dissent Magazine*. Summer 2015. https://www.dissentmagazine.org/article/black-lives-matter-new-civil-rights-movement-fredrick-harris.

Harris, J. *Fathers Behind Bars and On the Street*. St. Louis, MO: Family and Corrections Network, 2002.

Hickman, M. "Citizen Complaints About Police Use of Force." US Department of Justice, Bureau of Justice Statistics. 2006. http:/bjs.ojp.usdoj.gov/index.cfm?tv=pbdetailiid=553.

"I Don't Move to the Back of the Bus?" https://www.thehenryford.org

Jansen, Bart. "Three Police Officers Fatally Shot in Baton Rouge; Dead Suspect Identified." USA Today. July 17, 2016. http://www.usatoday.com/story/news/2016/07/17/reports-baton-rouge-police-officers-shot/87218884/.

Johnson, Alex. "Michael Slager, S.C. Cop Who Killed Unarmed Motorist Walter Scott, Released on $500,000 Bond." NBC News. January 4, 2016. http://www.nbcnews.com/storyline/walter-scott-shooting/michael-slager-s-c-cop-who-killed-unarmed-motorist-walter-n490066.

Killian, Lewis M. *The Impossible Revolution, Phase 2: Black Power and the American Dream*. New York: Random House, 1975.

Kluger, Richard. *Simple Justice*. New York: Random House, 1998.

Knapp, Andrew. "Feds Seek to Charge North Charleston Police Officer in Walter Scott Shooting." *Post and Courier*. December 3, 2015. http://www.postandcourier.com/article/20151204/PC16/151209762.

———. "Federal Civil Rights Trial for Michael Slager Anticipated This Spring." *Post and Courier*. December 14, 2016. http://www.postandcourier.com/news/federal-civil-rights-trial-for-michael-slager-anticipated-this-spring/article_c7f64bd2-c183-11e6-b628-373f8053c64c.html.

Lacy, Dan. *The White Use of Blacks in America*. New York: McGraw-Hill, 1972.

LaFree, G. "The Effect of Sexual Stratification by Race on Official Reactions to Rape." *American Sociological Review* 45, (October 1980): 842–54.

Langton, Lynn, and Matthew Durose. "Police Behavior During Traffic and Street Stops." US Department of Justice, Bureau of Justice Statistics. September 2013. http://www.bjs.gov/content/pub/pdf/pbtss11.pdf.

Lewinson, Paul. *Race, Class, and Party: A History of Negro Suffrage and White Politics in the South*. New York: Universal Library, 1965.

Lichtblau, E. "Profiling Report Leads to Demotion." *New York Times*. August 24, 2005: B1.

Liebow, Elliot. *Tell Them Who I Am*. Chicago, IL: University of Chicago Press, 1999.

Lopez, German, Jennifer Williams, Libby and Nelson. "Dallas Shooting Kills Multiple Police Officers: What We Know." Vox. July 9, 2016. http://www.vox.com/2016/7/7/12125740/dallas-shooting-police-protests.html.

MacDonald, Heather. "Officer Beaten Unconscious Due to Fear of Racism Charge." *The National Review*. August 16, 2015. http://www.nationalreview.com/article/422605/Birmingham-cop-beaten-unconscious-feared-racism-charge.

Maxon, C., K. Hennigan, and D. Sloane. *Factors that Influence Public Opinion of the Police*. Washington, D.C.: National Institute of Justice, 2003.

McKenzie, K. "Is Black on Black Crime a Blast from the Past?" *USA Today*, April 17, 2016. Available at: https://www.commercialappeal.com/story/news/local/2017/04/17/black--black-crime-blast-past/100307478/

"Medical Examiner Rules Eric Garner's Death a Homicide, Says He Was Killed by Chokehold."

NBC New York. August 21, 2014. http://www.nbcnewyork.com/news/local/Eric-Garner-Chokehold-Police-Custody-Cause-of-Death-Staten-Island-Medical-Examiner-269396151.html.

Mitchell, O., and D. L. MacKenzie. *The Relationship Between Race, Ethnicity, and Sentencing Outcomes: A Meta-Analysis of Sentencing Research*. Washington, DC:

National Institute of Justice, 2014. https://www.ncjrs.gov/pdffiles1/nij/grants/208129.pdf.

Murdock, D. "If There is a War on Black America, the Warriors are Not Copies but Blacks Murdering Blacks." *National Review*. January 8, 2015. http://www.national-review.com/article/395919/assassination-truth-deroy-murdock.html.

Oaks, J. "Slavery." In *Encyclopedia of American Social History*, edited by M. K. Clayton, E. J. Gorn, and P. W. Williams, 1407–14419. New York: Scribners, 1993.

Oberschall, A. "The Los Angeles Riot of August 1965." *Social Problems* 15, (1968): 322–41.

Palazzolo, Joe. "Racial Gap in Men's Sentencing." *Wall Street Journal*. February 14, 2013. http://www.wsj.com/articles/SB10001424127887324432004578304463789858002.

Paternoster, R. "Prosecutorial Discretion in Requesting the Death Penalty: A Case of Victim-Based Racial Discrimination." *Law and Society Review* 18, (1984): 437–78.

Petersilia, Joan. *Racial Disparities in the Criminal Justice System*. Santa Monica, CA: RAND, 1983.

Potter, K. and Forliti, A. "AP News Guide: More Unrest as Police Shooting Probe Goes On." *Los Angeles Times*. July 28, 2016. www.latimes.com.

Rawick, George P. *From Sundown to Sunup: The Making of the Black Community*: Westport, CT: Greenwood Press, 1972.

Roberg, Roy R., and J. Kuykendall. *Police and Society*. Belmont, CA: Wadsworth, 1993.

Shaefer, R. T. *Racial and Ethnic Groups*, 9th ed. Upper Saddle River, NJ: Prentice-Hall, 2004.

Shoichet, Catherine E. "Walter Scott Shooting Case: Court Documents Reveal New Details. CNN. September 15, 2015. http://www.cnn.com/2015/09/08/us/south-carolina-walter-scott-shooting michael-slager./

Shoop, J. G. "National Survey Suggests Racial Disparity in Police Use of Force." *Trial* 34, no. 1 (1998): 97.

Smith, D. A., and C. Visher. "Street Level Justice: Situational Determinants of Police Arrest Decisions." *Social Problems* 29, (1991): 167–77.

Son, I. S., M. Davis, and D. M. Rome. "Race and its Effect on Police Officers' Perceptions Of Misconduct." *Journal of Criminal Justice* 26, no. 1 (1998): 21–8.

Stammp, Kenneth. *The Peculiar Institution: Slavery in the Ante-Bellum South*. New York, 1956.

Swaney, Anne. "Chicago Police Officer Jason Van Dyke Charges With 1st Degree Murder in Laquan McDonald Shooting." ABC News 7. November 24, 2015. http://abc7chicago.com/news/cop-charged-with-1st-degree-murder-in-laquan-mcdonald-shooting/1097312/.

Sweeney, Annie, and Jason Meisner. "A Moment-by-Moment Account of What the Laquan McDonald Video Shows." *Chicago Tribune*. November 25, 2015. http://www.chicagotribune.com/news/ct-chicago-cop-shooting-video-release-laquan-mcdonald-20151124-story.html.

Tarver, Marsha, Douglas Walker, and Harvey Wallace. *Multicultural Issues in the Criminal Justice System*. Boston, MA: Allyn and Bacon, 2002.

"The Legacy of Rodney King." Frontline, PBS. 2015. http://pbs.org/wgbh/pages/frontline/shows/lapd/race/king.html.

The Sentencing Project. *Race and Punishment: Racial Perceptions of Crime and Support for Punitive Policies*. 2014. http://sentencingproject.org/doc/publications/rd_Race_and_Punishment.pdf.

US Department of Justice, Federal Bureau of Investigation. "Crime in the United States. Table 43." FBI. 2015. https://www.fbi.gov/about-us/cjis/ucr/crime-in-the-u.s/2014/crime-in-the-u.s.-2014/tables/table-43.

Walker, S., C. Spohn, and M. Delone. (1996) (2000) 2004. *The Color of Justice: Race, Ethnicity and Crime in America*. Belmont, CA: Wadsworth.

Hermann, Peter, and John Woodrow Cox. "A Freddie Gray Primer: Who Was He, How Did He Die, Why is There So much Anger?" *Washington Post*. April 28, 2015. https://www.washingtonpost.com/news/local/wp/2015/04/28/a-freddie-gray-primer-who-was-he-how-did-he-why-is-there-so-much-anger/.

Rector, Kevin. "The 45-Minute Mystery of Freddie Gray's Death." *The Baltimore Sun*. April 25, 2015. http://www.baltimoresun.com/news/maryland/freddie-gray/bs-md-gray-ticker-20150425-story.html.

Watnabe, T. "Righting Islam's Image in America." *Los Angeles Times*. May18, 1999: B2.

Weitzer, R., and S. A. Tuch. "Race, class and perceptions of discrimination by the police." *Crime and Delinquency* 45, no. 4 (1999): 494–507.

Westley, William. *Violence and the Police: A Sociological Study of Law, Custom, and Morality.* Cambridge, MA: MIT Press, 1970.

White, M. F., T. C. Cox, and J. Basehart. "Theoretical Considerations of Officer Profanity and Obscenity in Formal Contacts with Citizens." In *Police Deviance*, 2nd ed., edited by T. Barker and D. L. Carter, 275–97. Cincinnati, OH: Anderson, 1991.

Wilbanks, W. *The Myth of a Racist Criminal Justice System.* Belmont, CA: Waveland Press, 1987.

Wilson, William J. *The Declining Significance of Race.* Chicago: University of Chicago Press, 1978.

———. *The Truly Disadvantaged.* Chicago: University of Chicago Press, 1987.

Race Discrimination in Employment: Acknowledging that Bias Still Exists

Lucy C. Sanders, JD

TWO FEDERAL LAWS, Title VII of the Civil Rights Act of 1964 and 42 U.S.C. Section 1981, prohibit employers from taking an adverse employment action against an individual because of his or her race (Civil Rights Act of 1964). Despite the laws written in the books, race discrimination in employment certainly still occurs in our country. Discrimination based on race is more pervasive in certain industries and regions than others, but even in recent years, claims of employment discrimination based on race continue to be filed in all fifty states of the country (FY 2009–2017 EEOC Charge Receipts by State). This article examines the legal framework of race discrimination claims, theories which offer insight into racially motivated employment decisions, and examples of possible progress in our society's willingness to at least acknowledge that race discrimination still exists in employment decisions.

Reactions to race discrimination claims are mixed and are likely dependent on a person's background and experiences. For example, individuals who work for companies which employ a diverse workforce and are committed to achieving racial equality might quickly dismiss court filings as speculative claims filed by disgruntled employees. However, recent race discrimination court filings and workplace surveys suggest that companies, even fifty years after the passage of Title VII, are still making employment decisions based on race. Further, several recent cases have resulted in significant jury verdicts. While a jury verdict in favor of a plaintiff does not prove with certainty that the allegations of a race discrimination claim are true, it stands as evidence that a group of impartial jurors believed the plaintiff's allegations and determined that the employer violated antidiscrimination laws. In addition to court filings and workplace surveys, developments in technology have made it easier for plaintiffs to present evidence of race discrimination in some cases. In these circumstances, it becomes nearly impossible for juries to ignore the reality of racially motivated employment actions. Employees now have the ability to easily record conversations with a smartphone and use the recording as proof of racial bias or animus, whereas, in the past, many plaintiffs had to attempt to prove racial bias and animus with their own testimony about what they heard a supervisor communicate to them, often without any witnesses present.

THE LEGAL FRAMEWORK OF A RACE DISCRIMINATION CLAIM IN THE EMPLOYMENT SETTING

With the more frequent use of audio recordings and our country's possible increased awareness that racial bias still exists, plaintiffs in employment discrimination lawsuits may see a shift in their ability to win cases. However, despite this shift, prevailing in a case will continue to be an uphill battle. A plaintiff in a Title VII or Section 1981 case is faced with navigating a maze of legal elements and trying to prove bias, which is often hidden or difficult to uncover. Even if evidence exists and elements are met, a plaintiff still faces the difficulty of convincing jurors to believe her claims. In order to fully understand the challenges affecting plaintiffs, it is important to first review the legal framework of a discrimination claim.

Title VII and Section 1981 clearly prohibit employers from demoting, firing, or refusing to hire an employee because of race. Nor can employers create a working environment that is hostile to an employee because of that employee's race (Civil Rights Act of 1964). Bringing claims pursuant to these statutes is difficult and proving claims can be nearly impossible unless an employee has a significant amount of evidence. Violations can be proven by direct evidence, such as a business owner telling a hiring manager to only hire white employees, or can be proven through indirect and circumstantial evidence. After the plaintiff has offered direct or indirect proof of racial discrimination, the employer has the opportunity to offer evidence that the employment decision was made based on a "legitimate non-discriminatory reason" (*McDonnell Douglas Corp. v. Green*, 411 U.S. 792, 802–804 (1973).

For example, an employer may offer evidence that the plaintiff was terminated from employment because he had been tardy to work for five days in the past month, which was a violation of the company's attendance policy. In response, the plaintiff can offer proof that, even if the employer's stated reason for termination is based on true facts, the reason is pretext for race discrimination. To prove pretext, a plaintiff can show that he was treated differently than a nonminority employee who engaged in similar conduct. For example, if a nonminority employee was also tardy for five days, but not terminated, the Court will consider this evidence as support for the plaintiff's race discrimination claim, as it is proof that the employer's reason for termination may have been legitimate, but not "non-discriminatory."

A plaintiff can also show pretext by offering proof that the employer changed its stated reason for terminating the plaintiff (which suggests a lack of honesty or credibility), failed to document the alleged poor performance or violation of policy at the time it took place, or undertook a substandard investigation (or no investigation at all) related to the plaintiff's alleged misconduct. A jury would then decide whether the employer's decision was actually based on race discrimination or based on the employer's proffered reason (or any other reason aside from race discrimination) and, what, if any, damages the plaintiff has suffered as a result of the employer's actions.

SOCIOLOGICAL THEORIES AFFECTING RACE DISCRIMINATION IN EMPLOYMENT

To understand race discrimination in employment, it is helpful to review sociological theories and terminology that help define and explain discrimination. At its core, discrimination is caused by stereotypes. Most individuals accept that stereotypes are pervasive in our communities. A stereotype is an oversimplified idea about a group of people. We might have stereotypes about people with blonde hair, graduates of certain colleges, or fans of particular sports teams, but many of us also have stereotypes about people of certain races Believing a stereotype does not violate an employment law or any other law, but it affects our perceptions and can cloud our ability to be impartial employers or impartial jurors.

A stereotype can evolve into prejudice, which is defined as thoughts and feelings about the groups for which you have a stereotype. We might think that all people who support a certain politician are narrow-minded, which is an example of a stereotype. However, to then harbor feelings of distrust or anger against those individuals is to have prejudice. Discrimination exists when we move past thoughts and feelings and take actions against people in the groups for which the stereotype and prejudice apply. Believing that all people with blonde hair are unintelligent is a stereotype. Thinking that I cannot trust a person with blonde hair to complete a job adequately is prejudice. Refusing to hire the person with blonde hair because of the stereotype and prejudice is discrimination.

Racism is a type of prejudice and is unique in that it has a historical background in our country, as it was once an accepted prejudice and a legal form of discrimination. Even though employment discrimination based on race is now prohibited by federal law, racism continues to be perpetuated by our society, often in unintentional or unconscious ways. For example, racial steering exists when real estate agents guide homeowners away from certain neighborhoods based on the racial makeup of the neighborhood or stereotypes about the neighborhood's residents (Pager and Shepherd 2008). The same likely occurs in education and employment. Teachers and guidance counselors guide students away from certain careers and colleges based on stereotypes about race. Staffing companies guide applicants away from certain businesses based on stereotypes about race. However, discrimination exists when employers actually fail to hire or promote an employee based on stereotypes and prejudice about race. Because these decisions are often motivated by unconscious prejudice and very rarely take place with overt comments about race, a racial discrimination case can be extremely difficult to prove and win.

Race discrimination in employment can also be understood by examining Max Weber's theory of social closure (Smith 2002; Weber 1968). Social closure explains discriminatory employment decisions through the idea that "social elites preserve power and privileges by limiting opportunities for mobility to themselves or similar others." Thus, as applied to race discrimination in employment, white supervisors, managers, and owners inherently believe that their power will be preserved if they exclude minorities from opportunities to advance and share (or take) their power (Tomaskovic-Devey 1993). The theory is not limited in application to race discrimination, but applies to gender discrimination, as well (Reskin 1993).

Rosabeth Moss Kanter's idea of homosocial reproduction also offers some explanation for race discrimination in employment (Reskin, McBrier, and Kmec 1999). Kanter's theory suggests that managers face inherent uncertainty when promoting subordinates to higher job positions and, as a reaction to the uncertainty, tend to develop management groups of individuals "who share a common set of social and demographic characteristics" (Smith 2002). The theory has been used to explain why male supervisors promote male subordinates but can also offer some explanation for racial differences in promotion rates (Baldi and McBrier 1997).

Two different hypotheses exist in regards to the effect of an increased proportion of women and minorities in an organization. Kanter's homosocial reproduction theory, as well as the "strength in numbers" hypothesis, (Jacobs 1992) suggests that as diversity in an organization increases, mentors, role models, and allies of the minority race or gender increase as well, which, in turn, increases the likelihood of promotions and leadership opportunities for minorities. However, a 1967 study of racial segregation (Blaylock 1967) demonstrated that a higher number of blacks moving into white neighborhoods actually created heightened resistance from whites. Applied to employment and organizations in general, this hypothesis suggests that a higher proportion of minorities in an organization could lead to increased white, male resistance and, thus, would not create an environment in which minorities had increased opportunities for promotion (Pfeffer and Davis-Blake 1987).

VERDICTS, SURVEYS, AND RECORDINGS: EVIDENCE OF CONTINUED BIAS

Recent race discrimination verdicts, workplace surveys, and overt, direct evidence of racial bias are a few indicators that our country still struggles with accepting racial equality. Two notable workplace surveys demonstrate that race discrimination still exists in employment decisions (Pager and Shepherd 2008). The first survey utilized undergraduate psychology students who participated in a simulated hiring experiment by evaluating job applications and recommending applicants for hiring. No evidence of discrimination based on race existed when the applicants were highly qualified or poorly qualified for a position. However, when job applicants had "acceptable" qualifications, the students were almost 70 percent more likely to recommend the white applicant than the black applicant (Dovidio and Gaertner 2000).

Several years later, in a separate survey, researchers mailed resumes to employers in Boston and Chicago to determine whether racial prejudice affected hiring decisions. The researchers used resumes that were equivalent in all respects except for the names of the applicants. The resumes did not specifically indicate the race of the applicant but used what the researchers considered to be racially identifiable names. Names like Jamal and Lakisha were intended to signal African American applicants and names like Brad and Emily were intended to convey that the applicant was white. The callback rate was 50 percent higher for white names than equally qualified applicants with traditional African American names. Even more troubling, the difference in callbacks increased as the qualifications increased, suggesting that the employers in this survey held a stereotype that blacks were suited for lower qualification jobs, but not jobs requiring advanced qualifications (Bertrand and Mullainathan 2004).

In addition to workplace studies, court filings and recent verdicts demonstrate that racial discrimination still exists in employment. A case filed in the United States District Court for the District of Colorado in 2012 alleged that Matheson Trucking and Matheson Flight Extenders, Inc., separated black and white employees on opposite sides of the warehouse during working hours and allowed white employees to use racial epithets and refer to blacks as "lazy, stupid Africans" (Mitchell 2015). The company only gave holiday shifts to white employees despite the fact that black and white employees requested these shifts in order to earn the double pay, which was linked to holiday shifts, and despite the fact that some black employees had more seniority than their white counterparts (and thus should have received preference in scheduling).

Ultimately, a white employee at the facility stood up for the black workers, contacted management to report the harassment and discrimination, and was shortly thereafter terminated from his job. The black employees who had been harassed and discriminated against were subsequently fired as well, and many were replaced with white temporary employees. Evidence of harassment, discrimination, and bias was not only provided through witness testimony, but also through internal company memos which indicated the company was intentionally targeting black employees for termination and attempting to portray the firings as downsizing.

In another case, a company's first and only African American manager alleged other employees in the facility repeatedly used racially derogatory terms when referring to him, specifically that coworkers, supervisors, and high-ranking managers often used the "n" word behind his back. Managers and human resources were aware of the conduct but did not take any action to remedy it or keep it from continuing to occur. The plaintiff was eventually terminated from employment due to "not getting along" with his coworkers, which was alleged to be pretext for racial discrimination and retaliation (Los Angeles Superior Court 2017).

Both cases survived legal challenges from the defense and resulted in significant verdicts, which suggests that judges and juries may be more willing to acknowledge the reality of racial discrimination in the workplace. The verdicts are especially significant in light of a study from Wendy Parker. In her article, "Lessons in Losing: Race Discrimination in Employment," she found that while courts likely believe that racial discrimination in the workplace is wrong, the judiciary appears to often believe that the particular facts in a case fail to demonstrate discrimination, because the plaintiff's claims lack legal merit and the defendant can prove its defense as a matter of law, without regard to the determination of factual disputes. Thus, the author suggests that "the unconscious discrimination infecting American society infects its judiciary as well" (Parker 2006). In the race discrimination cases studied by the author (which admittedly did not include cases that settled and only included cases for which the court resolved on the merits), plaintiffs won only 6 of the 421 cases. Further, plaintiffs who won trials were reversed on appeal about 42 percent of the time, while defendants who won trials were reversed on appeal only about 7 percent of the time (Clermont, Eisenberg, and Schwab 2003). As explained by Michael Selmi, "[C]ourts often analyze race cases from an anti-affirmative action mindset, one that views both the persistence of discrimination and the merits of the underlying claims with deep skepticism" (Selmi 2001). Perhaps the recent verdicts are at least a small step in the right direction and provide some encouragement that judges are beginning to view race discrimination cases with an increased willingness to believe the claims of plaintiffs and let juries sort out factual disputes. Regardless, the factual accounts provided by the plaintiffs, witnesses, and corroborating documents in the two lawsuits described above serve as a disappointing reminder that racial discrimination in employment certainly still occurs in our country.

In addition to proof of discrimination from workplace surveys and court filings, recordings serve as direct evidence that racial discrimination and harassment still exist in the workplace. In a 2009 case in Greenville, South Carolina in which I was involved, an African American employee alleged that his supervisor used racially derogatory terms when speaking to him and referring to him. The employee did not file the case in hopes that a jury would believe his personal testimony regarding the harassment or that a coworker would come forward and testify about hearing the derogatory terms. Instead, the plaintiff moved forward in court armed with saved voicemails in which his supervisor yelled at him and blatantly used racially derogatory terms in addressing him.

This case is not the only one of its kind. More and more employees are beginning to record conversations with supervisors or harassers. In many states, unannounced audio recordings are legal and can be used as evidence in court either to prove harassment or discrimination. While the ability to record a conversation has existed for decades, advances in technology have made it increasingly easy to make a high-quality recording through the use of a smartphone or similar device.

CONTINUED CHALLENGES

The large majority of race discrimination cases still rely on indirect evidence, even though some plaintiffs are able to present direct evidence through recordings or documents. In most cases, a plaintiff faces an uphill battle, not only because of a lack of direct evidence but also because there are individuals in our society who may not believe a company would fire an employee because of his or her race. Still others may believe a supervisor had racial prejudice but didn't actually act upon it and instead fired the employee for some justifiable reason. Unfortunately, some individuals may believe an employee was fired because of his or her race but may also think that an employer should have the freedom to make a decision based on race or what the employer believes is in the best interest of the company. A plaintiff in a race discrimination case must trust that the majority of the jurors assigned to the case are both willing to believe that racial discrimination still exists and willing to take action to identify it and speak out against it through a verdict.

A risk of a verdict in favor of an employer is that a plaintiff may believe that he has "let down" his community and created more skepticism of others who summon the courage to complain of race discrimination. Community members may be less likely to believe that racism still exists and have any motivation to eradicate it if their only experience with employment discrimination based on race is a case in which the plaintiff ultimately couldn't prove race discrimination or offered only indirect, weak evidence of race discrimination. Such a case can send the message that racism doesn't still exist, yet some individuals are still trying to take advantage of the system and historical racial inequalities.

Choosing to bring a case of race discrimination requires courage and perseverance. A plaintiff must be willing to subject himself to a full review of his employment history and performance, because employers will defend against the case by arguing that an employment decision was justified. A plaintiff must also be willing to allege that members of his community (often powerful companies or long-standing institutions) harbor racial bias. But perhaps the greatest risk for plaintiffs exists in the psychological harm that can be created through a jury's verdict in favor of an employer. A jury's verdict in favor of an employer not only signals defeat, but, in many instances, can create a situation in which an already fragile individual faces depression and loses trust in his community.

A jury's verdict may communicate that the employee's performance was subpar and justified his termination, but, even worse, may suggest that a jury of peers simply doesn't believe the plaintiff's claim of race discrimination or doesn't care, which can be devastating. As an attorney and advocate, a plaintiff's potential reaction to losing a case is a factor in determining whether a case should be settled or proceed to trial. While the decision is ultimately left to the client, advocates must be careful not to sugarcoat the chances of prevailing at trial and the emotional toll of losing. Determining how a jury will react is difficult but can be aided by studying a community's perception of and reaction to current events.

For example, in Charleston, South Carolina, EEOC claims of race discrimination increased in the two years after nine African American individuals were murdered by a self-avowed white supremacist (FY 2009–2017 EEOC Charge Receipts for South Carolina). The increase in claims was likely not due to an increase in racial discrimination, hostility, and harassment after the massacre. Instead, the increase in claims likely resulted from the community's willingness to acknowledge that racial issues still existed, which encouraged potential plaintiffs to proceed with a claim in hopes that the community would actually believe their stories, instead of turning a blind eye or insisting that racism didn't still exist and certainly didn't motivate employment decisions. As individuals see and hear blatant, painful, open racism, they cannot continue to operate as if racism has long been eradicated.

While a case carries certain risks, there is certainly the chance for great reward as well. Obviously, a verdict in a plaintiff's favor creates a monetary reward for the plaintiff, but often an employment discrimination plaintiff does not find fulfillment in a monetary reward. More than anything, most employment discrimination plaintiffs simply want their former employers to be held accountable and want to know that their communities value them regardless of their race and have heard and believed their stories. Thus, while a jury's primary function is to analyze the facts of a case and apply the law to determine whether a violation has occurred, the jury also serves as the conscience of the community. This function as a conscience is present in many cases but is perhaps uniquely important in cases related to race. Yet, jury members are human. Jury members do not enter a courtroom as blank slates. Each jury member brings his or her own bias, background, and experiences to a case.

A jury member's perception of a plaintiff's credibility is influenced by his or her own experiences and thus, each member's decision is also largely dependent on his or her background and experiences. If a jury member has witnessed race discrimination in the workplace or otherwise, he or she is more likely to believe that it exists. A jury member who has been sheltered from race discrimination (either through naivety or through exposure to ideal workplaces where diversity is celebrated and honored) may be less likely to believe a plaintiff's story of workplace harassment or discrimination.

Our legal system serves a useful and necessary function in abolishing race discrimination but cannot be the only avenue for change. Its role is important but admittedly limited. True progress must come from an individual recognition of bias and a willingness to embrace equality and find effective solutions to remedy past inequalities. As our country struggles to process recent race-related tragedies such as the murders at Charleston's Mother Emmanuel church and the numerous race-related police brutality cases, we can hope that these tragedies, as well as the facts of recent race discrimination cases, serve as a catalyst to acknowledge our country's need to seek and obtain true equality.

Bibliography

Baldi, S., and D. B. McBrier. "Do the Determinants of Promotion Differ for Blacks and Whites?" *Work and Occupations* 24, (1997): 478–97.

Bertrand M., and S. Mullainathan. "Are Emily and Greg More Employable Than Lakisha and Jamal? A Field Experiment on Labor Market Discrimination." *American Economic Review* 94, (2004): 991–1013.

Blalock, Hubert M. *Toward a Theory of Minority Group Relations*. New York: Wiley, 1967.

Civil Rights Act of 1964 § 7, 42 U.S.C. § 2000e et seq (1964); 42 U.S. Code § 1981.

Clermont, K., T. Eisenberg, and S. Schwab. "How Employment Discrimination Plaintiffs Fare in the Federal Court of Appeals." *Employee Rights & Employer Policy Journal* 7, (2003): 547.

Dovidio, J. F., and S. L. Gaertner. "Aversive Racism and Selection Decisions." *Psychology and Science* 11, no. 4 (2000): 315–19.

"FY 2009 – 2017 EEOC Charge Receipts by State." US Equal Employment Opportunity Commission. Last accessed January 30, 2018. https://www1.eeoc.gov/eeoc/statistics/enforcement/charges_by_state.cfm.

"FY 2009 – 2017 EEOC Charge Receipts for South Carolina." US Equal Employment Opportunity Commission. Last accessed January 30, 2018. https://www1.eeoc.gov/eeoc/statistics/enforcement/charges_by_state.cfm#centercol.

Jacobs, J. "Women's Entry into Management: Trends in Earnings, Authority, and Values Among Salaried Managers." *Administrative Science Quarterly* 37, (1992): 282–301.

"Los Angeles Superior Court Upholds Largest Racial Discrimination Verdict in California." Yahoo Finance. September 28, 2017. Last AccessedFebruary 5, 2018. https://finance.yahoo.com.

Mitchell, K. "Denver Jury Awards Nearly 15 Million in Racial Discrimination Case." *The Denver Post*. February 11, 2015. https://www.denverpost.com.

Pager, D., and H. Shepherd. "The Sociology of Discrimination: Racial Discrimination in Employment, Housing, Credit, and Consumer Markets." *The Annual Review of Sociology* 34, (2008): 181–209.

Parker, W. "Lessons in Losing: Race Discrimination in Employment." *Notre Dame Law Review* 81, no. 3 (2006): 889–954.

Pfeffer, J., and A. Davis-Blake. "The Effect of Proportion of Women on Salaries: The Case of College Administrators. *Administrative Science Quarterly* 32, (1987): 1–24.

Reskin, B. "Sex Segregation in the Workplace." *The Annual Review of Sociology* 19, (1993): 241–70.

Reskin, B., D. B. McBrier, and J. A. Kmec. "The Determinants and Consequences of Workplace Sex and Race Composition." *The Annual Review of Sociology* 25, (1999): 335–61.

Selmi, M. "Why Are Employment Discrimination Cases So Hard To Win?" *Louisiana Law Review* 61, (2001): 555–62.

Smith, R. "Race, Gender, and Authority in the Workplace: Theory and Research." *The Annual Review of Sociology* 28, (2002): 509–42.

Tomaskovic-Devey, Donald. "Labor Process Inequality and the Gender and Race Composition of Jobs." *Research on Social Stratification and Mobility* 12, (1993): 215–47.

———. *Gender and Race Inequality at Work: The Sources and Consequences of Job Segregation*. ILR Press, 1993.

Weber, Max. *Economy and Society,* edited by Guenther Roth. New York: Bedminster, 1968.

Education

Does Social Class Matter?

EDUCATION AND SOCIETY

The previous discussions about race and ethnicity, along with those about social inequality and poverty, are relevant to the one about public education in the United States. In fact, there is a close link between all of these variables, thereby providing an opportunity to extend the previous discussions to include how and in what ways we might consider changes to policy and public opinion about all of these issues. Historically there has been a social class bias in education, where affluent children were the ones who attended school while less wealthy children were needed to work on the farms and in the fields. These social class distinctions have remained in education, even in public schools, where there should theoretically be a more level playing field. This is particularly true after laws were passed and Supreme Court cases were decided that called attention to the inequality in public schools in the United States.

The challenges related to this inequality and greater accountability for school districts have come in part as a result of parents becoming increasingly dissatisfied with the product offered by public schools. In many instances, those parents that can afford to do so are turning to private education or charter schools as a solution. This can have a potentially devastating effect on public education as a brain drain of the best and brightest students leave public schools, leaving needy students with less funding and fewer positive role models to emulate.

An important part of the problem in public education has been attributed to its bureaucratic nature, particularly an emphasis on No Child Left Behind laws. The rewards and sanctions of these laws have generally led many school districts to "teach the test" to improve student test scores, instead of teaching the knowledge that the test is supposed to demonstrate. There are other issues as well, such as the enforcement of zero tolerance policies that suspend and expel students for minor infractions. Because such policies and their enforcement impact minority students, the opportunities for poor and minority students to receive a quality education are further eroded.

The articles in this section offer insight into the problems in the education system in this country. For example, Tracey Nance Pendley describes some of the challenges of school choice and the gaps in students' educational achievements. That these gaps quickly become cumulative means that whatever obstacles or issues that exist become more pronounced as the child progresses through the system, often resulting in high dropout rates. While some might think that the answer to public education problems is charter schools, there are issues found in the operation and management of those institutions as well.

Krista Green Hayes compares the differences between public and private education, a longstanding issue in the field, using foreign language as a backdrop to highlight the problems. Finally, Robert McNamara offers insight into the challenges of school absenteeism and truancy. While missing school may not seem like a big deal to many people, there are a host of issues that have far-reaching implications.

School Choice and Gentrification in Atlanta

Tracey Nance Pendley

THE RISE OF school choice politics and the increase in the number of charter schools in America's cities has coincided neatly with a surge in urban gentrification. While gentrification's community revitalization efforts are often seen as positively impacting low-income neighborhoods, the confluence of school choice and gentrification in many areas has only served to reinforce socioeconomic and racial inequality. Proponents of charter schools, the fastest growing type of school choice, argue that every parent should be allowed to choose their child's school, with many advocating for a school voucher system in which individual pupil funding follows students to their public and private institutions. To be sure, every parent wants and deserves what is best for his or her child.

This concept is nothing new. More privileged families have been using their wallets to exercise school choice for hundreds of years through private school and neighborhood choice, but what happens when this choice is extended to public schools, and how is its impact different in gentrifying communities? Market theory purports that charter schools will improve traditional public schools through increased market competition for students and services (Chubb and Moe 1990; Friedman 1962). The lived experiences of many students and schools in urban America, however, tell a different story.

While one might think that gentrification would lead to integrated and stronger traditional public schools, quite the opposite is occurring in major US cities. Despite gains in civil rights, extensive community development, and the emergence of school choice, there remains a troubling gap in the equity of education students receive. This is especially evident in Atlanta, Georgia, a city that has seen a huge uptick in gentrification and charter school growth in recent years. In order to better understand the impact of school choice on students in gentrifying urban communities, this paper seeks to use a sociological lens and analysis of how school choice is exercised in one corner of Atlanta Public Schools to explore the questions, "Who benefits from school choice?" and "How does school choice in gentrifying communities impact traditional public schools and their students?"

Examining school choice research, relevant theory in the sociology of education, and the historical and socioeconomic context of public schools in Atlanta's most rapidly gentrifying neighborhoods allows for several important conclusions. First, the confluence of school choice, gentrification, and racial inequality in Atlanta has led to segregated charter and public schools, unaffordable housing, and contrary to what the application of market theory purports, competition that has harmed public schools and the educational outcomes of their low-income students.

Qualitative and quantitative studies and interviews specific to the focal neighborhoods demonstrate that school choice fuels gentrification and reproduces inequality when left to market forces and individual choices alone. This article argues that, regardless of individuals' political allegiances, the dominant social class finds new ways of replicating its dominance, whether intentionally or not, and that private school choice decisions have important consequences for public school students and their families. While both school choice and gentrification have the potential to positively impact disadvantaged communities, understanding and planning for their collective shortcomings is necessary to ensure educational equity.

CHARTER SCHOOLS AND MARKET THEORY

The term *school choice* refers to publicly funded choices parents have for their child's schooling, including charter schools, magnet programs, specialty schools, and open-enrollment policies within districts. Charter schools are public schools funded by the government, but they are managed differently than traditional public schools. Established under a charter run by parents, educators, community groups, universities, or private organizations, charter schools have more autonomy and are encouraged to be innovative (Berends 2015). For example, charter schools exercise more control in shaping the length of their school day, hiring, spending, and pursuing special curriculum initiatives. A lottery system is typically used when a charter school has more applicants than spots available. While a portion of charters are digital State Charter Schools, this paper is concerned with charter schools that are governed by parents, community board members, and private organizations in gentrifying urban areas.

Though charter schools have been in existence for over twenty years, the charter school movement has experienced its most significant growth during the last decade. Between 2007 and 2017, national charter school enrollment almost tripled, growing from serving 1.2 million to 3.1 million students in more than 6,900 charter schools (National Alliance for Public Charter Schools 2017). The Bush Administration's signature law, No Child Left Behind (NCLB), encouraged the growth of the charter sector by suggesting these schools would remedy failing public schools. Later, President Obama encouraged charter school reform as a way for states to gain a competitive edge in his Race to the Top program (Berends 2015). According to popular education author Diane Ravitch (2013), both of these federal interventions put significant pressure on schools to achieve the right test scores and created a multitude of entrepreneurial opportunities.

There is a lot of money to be made when public education hits the free market, igniting new markets for consultants, test materials, after-school programming, data analysis, and even further urban development in some instances (Patrick 2015). In that charter schools are championed as providing innovative education opportunities, promoting big business, and offering families access to a more "private" public education, it is no wonder school choice has received bipartisan support.

School choice itself is a neoliberal principal based on the idea of market theory. Neoliberalism, a political movement that became popular in the 1970s, sees the creation of markets as necessary for individual liberty, and seeks to create markets within all public institutions (Connell 2013). Within this framework, sometimes referred to as liberation theory, people are not really free unless their public institutions resemble markets and offer a range of consumer options. This view assumes that supply, demand, and competition govern school and student outcomes, and will therefore diminish racial and socioeconomic stratification as all students are able to compete for enrollment (Friedman 1962; Betts 2005).

It was economist Milton Friedman (1955, 1962) who first used market theory to argue that parents should be given government funded vouchers allowing them to choose the schools their children attend, whether public or private. Secretary of Education Betsy Devos and President Donald Trump have both supported moving towards a voucher system. Some states are already moving toward this extreme. Called Education Savings Accounts (ESAs), five states allow students to withdraw from public school and use their per pupil funding for private school, home schooling, or online schooling, including Arizona, Florida, Mississippi, North Carolina, and Tennesee (EdChoice 2018).

Proponents of choice use market theory to argue that privatization allows charter schools to positively impact student achievement through instructional innovation and new organizational strategies (Fusarelli 2002). Examining whether or not charter schools increase student achievement, the research is extremely inconsistent. Simply put, some charters show results in student achievement (Hoxby and Rockoff, 2004; Foster 2014) and some do not (Tock 2010; Buddin and Zimmer 2003; Ravitch 2013).

An extensive review of the literature by Bluestone, Sjoquist, and Warner (2016) demonstrated that positive gains were mostly limited to urban schools serving predominantly disadvantaged students, known as "No Excuses" schools because of their emphasis on strict discipline, longer school days, and traditional reading and math. Successful "No Excuses" charter schools include schools such as Harlem Children's Zone schools and KIPP schools (Almond 2012). The charter schools in the KIPP network are among Atlanta's most successful charter schools; KIPP operates seven of Atlanta Public Schools' sixteen charter schools and currently serves a 100 percent African American student population at each location (Georgia DOE 2017).

More broadly speaking, however, most studies have found that charter schools' achievement gains are either comparable or worse than those found in traditional public schools (Berends 2015; Buddin and Zimmer 2003). Despite these achievement conclusions, parental satisfaction data provides that parents find value in other aspects of charter schooling as well. Though there is no data to support that charter schools do a better job of promoting discipline, engaging parents in their children's education, or offering safe environments, survey data suggests that parents strongly believe their new voucher and charter schools are outperforming their previous public schools in terms of nonacademic outcomes (Gill, Timpane, Ross, and Brewer 2001).

In addition to increasing student achievement, market theorists and school choice advocates believe that charter schools will improve neighboring traditional public schools through increased market competition for students and services, driving educators to be more inventive in the classroom and more appealing to parents (Chubb and Moe 1990, Friedman 1962). Do charter schools actually improve traditional public schools? Are these schools more innovative? Again, no consensus has been reached.

In an extensive study examining the competitive effects of charter schools on student achievement, Zimmer et al. (2005), found that across seven large cities, only Texas suggested any positive impact on achievement at the local traditional public school, the estimated impact of which was small. Analyzing charter schools' impact on public schools in Florida, Sass (2006) concluded that the presence of one or more charter schools within a 2.5-mile radius was correlated with an increase in traditional public school math gains, but this finding has not been replicated (Zimmer and Buddin 2005).

Instead, some studies have concluded that charter school proximity actually has a negative impact on students in traditional public schools. Contrary to what competition theory suggests, Buddin and Zimmer (2005) found that reading scores at the elementary and high school level were higher when charter schools were located further away. One possible reason for this is that charter schools may compete for students by drawing higher performing students from neighboring public schools, decreasing public schools' enrollment and test scores, and therefore their funding too. Journalist and former charter schoolteacher, Allie Gross, argues that this is exactly what occurred in Detroit's public schools when venture philanthropists, including Betsy Devos, ushered school choice into Michigan over twenty years ago (2016).

An increasing number of charter schools gutted Detroit's public schools of students and resources, prompting dozens of school closures and ironically, removing school choice for lower income families desiring a neighborhood school. Market-based approaches to educational reform have fallen flat in other areas as well. According to Professor of Education and researcher, Jessica Shiller, merit-based pay for teachers and creating theme-based schools has not enhanced innovation in the classroom, particularly in urban areas (2012). Examining more than three hundred small schools in New York that were funded by the Gates Foundation and tasked with creating "innovative programs and theme-based schools." Shiller found that rather than innovate, these schools narrowed their curriculum in order to prepare for standardized testing.

Why is the literature so inconclusive on the effects of school choice on student achievement and traditional public schools? What's missing is an understanding of each location's socioeconomic and historical context. Market theory and school choice politics ignore the fact that market forces do not exist in a true meritocracy, free of outside influences and systemic barriers to entry. Friedman's (1955) essay on school choice and market theory itself was not written in a context free of social, economic, and political biases. Rather, Friedman's essay closely followed *Brown v. Board of Education* (1954) in which the Supreme Court struck down the lawfulness of racially segregated public schools. At the time, his work on school choice was seen as an alternative to "involuntary segregation" or "involuntary desegregation," both of which he opposed. This neoliberal trust in the existence of a completely free market, both then and now, ignores the ways in which racial discrimination and socioeconomic privilege impact access to employment, housing, schools, and other public accommodations.

In order to understand the impact of charter schools on student achievement and neighboring traditional public schools, a sociological lens is necessary to examine the geographic, historical, and socioeconomic context of school choice's successes and shortcomings. In Atlanta, as in many urban neighborhoods today, the confluence of gentrification and systemic racism is changing the way school choice is utilized by different groups of people.

SOCIOLOGICAL THEORY

Sociology of education is defined as the study of how public institutions and individual experiences shape the educational outcomes of groups and individuals (Marshall and Scott 1998). Other disciplines and strands of sociology are deeply intertwined with sociology of education because of the way these phenomena and societal institutions impact students' life chances and educational outcomes. For example, according to Eve Ewing, a sociologist of race and education at the University of Chicago, "The notion of [school] choice suggests that all options are on the table for all parents, but when resources like transportation, childcare, and information access are unequally distributed, the choices on the table are in fact very constrained" (Joseph 2017, 7). Sociology helps us to see the people, places, and distribution of power around us, and as such, can help us answer the questions: Who has access to school choice?; Why does location matter?; and how has the charter movement impacted neighboring public schools in Atlanta?

Frequently acknowledged as the father of sociology of education, Emile Durkheim (1956) saw the key function of the education system to be socializing and integrating individuals into larger society. At school, students obtain knowledge, skills, and a moral education, the latter of which is the basis of social solidarity for Durkheim. A dominant sociological perspective until the 1960s, structural functionalism follows this line of reasoning, ascertaining that societal groups are like a body in that the various parts all serve different but equally important roles. Structural functionalism acknowledges that there is inequality in educational outcomes and opportunities, but sees the differences a result of ability, family orientations, and individual motivations or interests (Parsons 1959).

For structural functionalists, schools are institutions that pave the way to equal opportunity, allowing upward social mobility to those who do well in school (Sever 2012). This view of the school as a neutral place that is organized to provide students with necessary skills acknowledges the importance of student achievement as a determinant of social mobility, but similarly ignores the impact of inequality on families' access to school choice.

While market theory says that schools look different, there is actually more support for sociology's institutional theory, which recognizes that successful charter schools are not all that different from successful public schools in how they actually operate (Berends 2015). Institutional theorists such as Meyer and Rowan (1977) see school systems as bureaucratic, rational networks that have resulted in a system of categories and rules that guide schools, teachers, and students. These rules are called ritual classifications, accepted norms of what constitutes legitimate school and schooling activities, and actually make schools look more alike than different.

This phenomenon and its diffusion is referred to as isomorphism (Bidwell & Dreeben 2006). Downey, Hippel, and Hughes' (2008) research support this notion, taking it a step further by comparing schools of various achievement levels both in and out of urban districts. They found that when schools are evaluated for student growth (rather than achievement scores), socioeconomic differences shrink or disappear altogether. The question that follows then, is if schools are more alike than they are different, and public and charter performance is comparable, what drives choice of charter schools over neighborhood public schools?

As it did in the 1950s, research shows that race and socioeconomic class have a whole lot to do with it. White families avoid schools with higher percentages of nonwhite students, and wealthier families avoid schools with higher poverty rates (Saporito 2003; Renzulli and Evans 2005). When the word *class* is used to refer to how people in a society are stratified, they are most often referring to Karl Marx's definition of class, an idea central to his conflict theory, whereby power comes directly from one's economic class position, with groups of various means vying for social rewards.

For Marx, education stratifies into two classes naturally by the sheer existence of educator and student. Conflict theorists believe that social reproduction occurs because the entire education system is overlain with the ideology of the dominant class (Berends 2015). Inequalities are reproduced because the dominant class controls the means of production. Weber (1944) improves upon Marx's economic framework by complicating the term to include socioeconomic class because it takes into account the social status attached to certain professions and educational attainment and to sociocultural aspects of one's life that one is socialized into by one's family.

Social class itself refers to the social networks and types of support individuals have, which is another reason sociologists of education are interested in stratification. Social network theory stresses the importance of your connections and what narratives get repeated to various individuals, which is critical when considering the stratified networking done by gentrifying families in newly integrated communities (Jennings and Lauen 2016). One's social class is closely connected to one's level of cultural capital, the cultural knowledge, mannerisms, and status held and reproduced by the dominant class (Bourdieu 1974; Connell 2013).

As the dominant class dictates what knowledge and experiences are rewarded in US society, the reproduction of cultural and social capital explains why the dominant class is able to reaffirm its status. One note of caution is needed here, however. When comparing the cultural capital of different socioeconomic classes, it is important that we not view the minority class' cultural capital as somehow lacking solely because it is not of the majority.

Class is important because the fact that it exists illuminates unequal access to rights, resources, and power in society. As such, it has a significant effect on educational attainment and quality of education, economic advantages gained through social networks, civic participation and power, and even health and life expectancy. What science tells us is that the choices that families make—and are able to make—most often have implications for how society is stratified and segregated by social class and race/ethnicity (Lareau and Goyette 2014; Patillo et al. 2014,; Roda and Wells 2013; Sattin-Bajaj 2014).

Taking into account this reality, education researchers Gloria Ladson-Billings and William Tate (1995) use race as a theoretical lens for examining social inequality in education. Originally posited by Derrick Bell, Critical Race Theory (CRT) shifts away from perspectives that suggest black communities are culturally deficient (Yosso 2005) and acknowledges that education policies are frequently barriers to opportunity for people of color (Ransaw 2017). Ladson-Billings and Tate examine student outcomes and race as they intersect with inequality and property rights. They argue that civil rights law addresses human rights but fails to address the impact of disadvantaged groups' lack of access to property in the United States.

Rejecting the notion of a free market, the authors state,

> As critical race theory scholars we unabashedly reject a paradigm that attempts to be everything to everyone and consequently becomes nothing for anyone, allowing the status quo to prevail. Instead, we align our scholarship and activism with the philosophy of Marcus Garvey, who believed that the black man was universally oppressed on racial grounds, and that any program of emancipation would have to be built around the question of race first. (Ladson-Billings and Tate, 62)

RACE AND EDUCATION IN ATLANTA

Race and inequity in education has been a long-standing topic of interest in American education. Issued as a result of the Civil Rights Act of 1964, the now infamous Coleman Report made some very bold claims at a time of great social unrest. Coleman and his team used data from over six hundred thousand students and teachers across the country, and found that student achievement was less related to school quality or funding, and more related to the school's social composition, the students' sense of control of their environment, and the student's family socioeconomic status (Coleman 1966). The most salient takeaway for most at the time was that the report suggested low-income

African American students would do better were they in mixed-race and mixed-income schools.

There have been a number of federal attempts to respond to the inequalities highlighted by the Coleman Report, including Head Start Pre-K programming and No Child Left Behind (2001) legislation, which tied high-stakes testing results to federal funding (Ravitch 2013). The first response was busing, proposed by Coleman himself, in which thousands of students were driven to other neighborhoods as a means of forced desegregation of public schools. In a later report, Coleman (1975) stated that busing had not worked as planned.

What was the primary reason? Federal desegregation of schools had sparked massive white flight to the suburbs across the nation's cities, and desegregation moved at a snail's pace through the courts in southern cities like Atlanta. Hornsby (1991) describes Atlanta's "Freedom of Choice" program, a school choice program that allowed families to move their children to the public school they desired. At the beginning of desegregation, there were approximately one hundred thousand children attending Atlanta Public Schools, 56 percent of whom were white and 40 percent of whom were black. Almost two decades after *Brown v. Board of Education*, the percentage of black students in Atlanta Public Schools had shifted to almost 80 percent black and 20 percent white (Hornsby 1991).

The rapid departure of middle-class whites impacted schools, businesses, and housing in several ways. While a strong black middle class continued to emerge in Atlanta, schools still did not have equitable resources and many middle-class jobs left with the dominant class. The Better Schools-Atlanta issued a major report in 1968, which concluded that students in Atlanta's black elementary schools attended larger classes, had fewer textbooks, had fewer speech therapy programs, poor equipment and furniture, and less physical space. Sixty-five percent of schools were totally segregated, and 92.3 percent of black elementary students were in enrolled in all-black schools.

Today, Atlanta Public Schools has an active enrollment of 51,662 students, 73.7 percent of whom are black, 15.6 percent white, and less than 4 percent Asian/Pacific Islander, Hispanic, or American Indian (Georgia DOE 2018). Schools are still largely segregated by race, but APS has seen a slight increase in the number of white students enrolling in its gentrifying communities on the east side. As an influx of white middle-class families move into the city, gentrification could help alleviate school segregation if new families attend their zoned public schools, but the reality is that these new families often seek private and charter school options first (Jordan and Gallagher 2015).

GENTRIFICATION IN ATLANTA

School choice has serious potential to impact neighborhoods and cities, particularly in communities undergoing gentrification. Gentrification occurs when young (usually), white, middle-class families move into a low-income area, revitalizing older buildings, replacing old homes, and attracting middle-class businesses. Chicago sociologists Robert Park and Ernest Burgess (1925) created an urban map using concentric circles, explaining that the tendency was for each ring to invade the next, displacing one group to the next outer ring. Indeed, this made sense as whites fled to the suburbs in the 1960s and 70s, leaving the urban core largely segregated by race and income. With gentrification the displacement continues, except now from the outer ring directly back to the center, in the form of young, white, middle-to-upper class families and progressives, and their trendy lofts, multi-use complexes, organic grocery stores, and pricey breweries.

While Atlanta has experienced gentrification since the 1970s, the 1996 summer Olympics and Atlanta's Beltline Project (2005) sparked rapid growth, and revitalization efforts across the city turned to attracting middle- and upper-class families. The CEO of Atlanta Midtown's Ponce City Market shared how important gentrification is, noting that that it leads to an increased tax base and aspects of city life that everyone craves such as arts, education, and parks (Kahn 2017).

Young urban professionals enjoy the perks of this life, but gentrification is not victimless. A sure sign of a neighborhood in transition is one with "We Buy Homes, Any Condition" signs peppering its advertisement space. Between 2000 and 2010, the US Census reports that the white population in Atlanta grew by over 22,800 people, while during the same time frame, the African American population dropped by more than 30,300 (Sledge 2017). The sweeping changes that gentrification brings displace minorities at an alarming rate. We speak of neighborhoods as transitioning when being gentrified because there seems to be no halfway point of integration and mixed-income living. It is most frequently a full makeover.

A possible benefit of gentrification is the value added from development and the creation of diverse communities with integrated public schools. Gentrification is largely associated with neighborhood improvement, but research is just emerging on whether or not these improvements extend to the neighborhood public schools. Examining whether changes in the composition of the student body account for any changes in achievement, University of Chicago sociologists, Keels, Burdick-Will, and Keene (2013) found that neighborhood public schools experience no academic benefit from the effects of gentrification. This is most likely because gentrifiers with children tend to pay for private school or exercise school choice when it is available, resulting in little change to other schools (Jordan and Gallagher 2015; Keels, Burdick-Will, and Keene 2013).

One early response to the return of middle- and upper-income whites to urban areas was indeed the championing of charter schools. Educational reform around school choice drives gentrification because it removes choice of residence as a primary determinant of school, and therefore may indirectly prompt gentrifying parents to consider neighborhoods or areas they may have otherwise regarded undesirable (Jordan and Gallagher 2015).

 Researchers Francis Pearman and Walker Swain (2017) examined whether expanded school choice options drive gentrification in racially segregated urban communities. Not surprisingly, they found that college-educated white households are far more likely to gentrify communities of color when charter school options exist, even increasing the likelihood of gentrification by up to 22 percent in the most racially segregated neighborhoods.

What is the impact of school choice in the racially stratified and gentrified context that I have described? How does it impact minority students and the neighborhood's traditional public schools? There's always been tension between the social and political constructions "public" and "private," but it is important to note that charter schools themselves are not the problem. Though charter schools have received mixed reviews in terms of student achievement, some have surely been important educational allies to children in low-income neighborhoods. Rather, school choice reinforces inequality when white gentrifiers, who want to live in the city but not attend its public schools, highjack charter schools as a means to a more private education. More advantaged groups continue to create new constructs for discrimination, whether intentionally or not (Ball, Bowe, and Gewirtz 1995). Rather than improve educational outcomes and raise the performance of neighboring traditional public schools, the confluence of school choice, social inequality, and gentrification creates segregated schools, unaffordable housing, and competition that is harmful to public schools.

THE IMPACT OF SCHOOL CHOICE ON PUBLIC SCHOOLS IN EAST ATLANTA

Several East Atlanta neighborhoods undergoing gentrification have been impacted by others' school choice decisions, including Kirkwood, Edgewood, Old Fourth Ward, Grant Park, and East Atlanta Village (Sledge 2017). There are multiple charter schools with which neighboring traditional public schools must compete, and new charters are being added every year. Though Atlanta Public Schools has been historically resistant to charter schools, frequently denying charter applications and creating legal obstacles to charter school contracts, they have added several in the last few years (Holley, Egalite, & Lueken, 2013). Under pressure from community stakeholders and government oversight in the wake of the very public 2009 cheating scandal, Atlanta Public Schools leaders began taking steps to consolidate its lowest performing schools in addition to granting a number of charter applications.

Atlanta Public Schools currently has seventeen charters schools that operate within its charter system. Approximately 60% of Georgia's charter schools are in the metro Atlanta area. The Atlanta Public Schools district received *charter system* status during the 2016–17 school year, meaning that it has greater flexibility in how it allocates school budgets and chooses its charter operators. Seven of APS's charters belong to the KIPP network, Kindezi operates two, one is a conversion school (meaning it was an elementary school that converted to a charter school), and six are start-up charter schools backed by parents, venture philanthropists, developers, and community stakeholders. The greatest concentration of charter schools, by far, is in East and Southeast Atlanta – the city's current gentrification hotbed. We will next examine the public and charter schools in the Grant Park, Kirkwood, East Atlanta Village, and Old Fourth Ward neighborhoods of East Atlanta in order to highlight the specific challenges of school choice as it relates to both and racism and gentrification.

Segregation

The first major impact of providing more school choice in Atlanta's gentrifying communities is continued school segregation. Despite what we know about the benefits of integration (Clotfelter 2004; Coleman 1966; Kirp 2012) and despite gentrification's promise to integrate communities across race and income, the growing presence of charter schools and their white enrollment in the Grant Park, Kirkwood, Old Fourth Ward, and East Lake neighborhoods are significantly out-pacing the rate of white enrollment in the same neighborhoods' traditional public schools (Downey 2017). While these charter schools have become more integrated, gentrifiers' school choices essentially prevent the traditional public schools from benefiting from the same racial and income integration. On the question of who benefits from school choice, the research is clear –nonwhite low-income families are far less likely to exercise school choice than white middle-income families, with the majority of white families using school choice to avoid neighborhood schools composed of nonwhite children (Saporito 2003; Keels, Burdick-Will, and Keene, 2013; Schneider and Buckley, 2002; Moredechay & Ayscue 2017).

Interestingly, the large majority of white gentrifiers are politically progressive, but interviews and research in the focal neighborhoods suggest that progressives' ideals do not align with their actions. DeSena (2009) uses the phrase "parallel play" to describe neighborhoods that are integrated yet racially stratified by school attendance. In an interview with The Atlantic, journalist and activist Nikole Hannah-Jones stated, "Whether you have integrated communities or segregated communities, we have school segregation. In communities that are gentrifying, the gentrification stops at the schoolhouse door" (Douglas 2017, 7). Hannah-Jones describes how inner-city whites do not want all-white schools because they are liberals, but they also do not want "too many minority kids." She calls this *curated diversity* claiming that the word *diversity* itself is a word that makes white people feel good. "If you could just get white liberals to live their values, you could have a significant amount of integration" (Douglas 2017, 5).

At the beginning of Atlanta's charter school relationship, new charters seemed to serve largely disadvantaged communities. Opened by real estate investors and a community board, the first charter school in Atlanta Public Schools was Drew Charter Elementary School in 2000 in the East Atlanta community. Drew brought with it a mixed-income housing development and the goal of improving student outcomes by integrating the school by income (Garland 2012). It was followed by a parent charter start-up in nearby Grant Park in 2001, Atlanta Neighborhood Charter Elementary School. Drew went from a 12% white student population in 2001 to 24% white in 2017, while ANCS changed from 40% white to more than 80% white during the same time. Meanwhile, the traditional neighborhood public schools in these communities remained more than 90% African American until just recently.

Interviewing and collecting data from gentrifying families in Grant Park and East Atlanta, Childers-Roberts (2012) found that parent-gentrifiers often champion racial and economic diversity, but when given other options, make choices that contradict those ideals. Roberts and Lakes (2014) similarly found that while middle-class mothers in East Atlanta expressed an equity agenda honoring educational diversity, they levied social capital and networking to share valuable information about the charter school selection process and readily accepted when offered the opportunity to attend the neighborhood charter.

Gentrification has the potential to improve the community and its public schools, but this can't happen if students continue to school separately. Indeed, Saporito's (2003) primary claim that private choices have public consequences is true for East Atlanta. Even when controlling for the desire to avoid non-performing schools, this desire does not account for the race-based choice patterns of white families. This is problematic for school choice advocates who argue that giving vouchers to low-income students will solve the problem. Saporito's (2003) conclusion is very much in line with Critical Race Theory's insistence that any civil rights law must also consider race. He states, "Targeting low-income students may not be enough to limit the influence of race-based avoidance patterns displayed by white families" (199). Saporito argues that these findings urge policy makers to reconsider "laissez faire school choice policies" that allow unfettered movement of children in and out of schools and that may harm the educational conditions for low-income students left behind in the neighborhood public school (Saporito 2003, 195).

Unaffordable Housing

As housing values and neighborhood taxes increase, the second major impact of added school choice in East Atlanta's gentrifying communities is increased rates of displacement for low-income families (Sledge, 2017). While gentrifiers tend to select charter schools with other gentrifying families, not only do they not improve the neighborhood public schools, they also make it difficult for longtime residents to stay due to the rising costs of housing (Burgess et al, 2004). Teachers at Kirkwood and Edgewood's public elementary schools have said goodbye to scores of students as their apartment complexes were torn down and replaced with $700,000+ condos. A Georgia State University study recently found that charter schools in East Atlanta actually accelerate rising property values in their priority attendance zones, making it even more difficult for low-income families to get by (Patrick 2015). As families compete to move inside Priority Zone 1, they purchase older, rundown homes at high prices and replace them with brand new multi-story homes. Albright (2017) found that prices in neighborhoods bordering the south side of the Atlanta Beltline Project increased by 40% from 2011–2015, while prices further away increased by 18%. Exercising school choice in this way is prohibitive for most low-income families.

Strain on Traditional Public Schools

Consistent with the research of school choice in gentrifying communities (Rosenblat & Howard, 2015), East Atlanta's traditional public schools have paid the price of gentrifiers' private choices. Following the opening of additional charters in the area, low enrollment resulted in the need for 3 traditional public school closures in East Atlanta, resulting in 4 different mergers and a great deal of upheaval in the last five years. As enrollment shifts from the traditional public schools to the charters, so does the schools' per-pupil funding. Unable to compete with the resources and state of the art school building that nearby Drew Charter offers, the teachers at Kirkwood's public elementary school refer to it as "The Little School that Never Could." Despite attempts to attract the neighborhoods' newest families with additional languages such as Mandarin, robust PTA offerings, and new International Baccalaureate programming initiatives, these schools take a back seat to the shiny charters that enjoy additional financial assistance from prominent supporters. For example, Drew is supported by the East Lake Foundation, founded by developer Tom Cousins. A campaign completed in 2014 raised $75.6 million for Drew's breathtaking high school expansion. Even for the neighborhood elementary schools that perform at high levels and attract more gentrifying families than others such as East Atlanta Village's Burgess-Peterson Academy, there is a palpable fear amongst parents that their children will have to next attend the cluster's predominately low-income and African-American middle school, Martin Luther King Jr. Middle. This fear causes middle-income families to begin their quest for charter admission long before their children become of preschool age (Downey 2017).

The strain on public schools caused by gentrifying families' charter school preference is not solely financial or race related. Public schools are further impacted by charter competition in terms of lost human and social capital, as research shows that parents in charter schools tend to be more involved (Ball, Bowe, & Gewirtz, 1995; Garland 2012; Renzulli & Evans 2005). Why have East Atlanta's traditional public schools not seen a surge of interest and a rise in performance with the arrival of gentrifiers and a baby boom? Atlanta Education Journalist Maureen Downey states that it is "a complicated question that touches on the role of charters in drawing away more capable students and committed parents and leaving behind the hardest-to-educate children and least-able-to-advocate families" (2017, 3). With the exception of Atlanta Neighborhood Charter Middle School, all Atlanta area charter schools serve a much lower percentage of Special Education Learners than the APS average of 10% (GaDOE, 2017).

NEXT STEPS

Realizing the impact of East Atlanta's seven charter schools on the neighboring public schools, the district and its stakeholders have begun to take proactive measures that have proven successful in other cities, as well as a few innovative approaches that hold great promise. Denver Public Schools became less segregated as a result of several strategies enlisted by the school system, including redrawing school boundary lines, providing weighted priorities for socio-economic status, improving transportation, and opening "enclave schools" that attract students of various socio-economic statuses (Eschbacher 2017). Planning for and taking action towards solving the problems that gentrification and school choice creates now will only serve to assist future students of all colors to be balanced and educated children.

An important measure thus far has been a new law allowing the use of weighted lotteries that give better numerical odds to low-income students. Having received attention for the way its student demographics shifted from low-income to 81% white and 91% middle-income, Atlanta Neighborhood Charter School helped advocate for The Utopian Academy Act, which went into effect in Georgia last year. That increased the percentage of kindergartners coming from poverty from 9% to 20%. With Drew Charter School following suit in 2018, we can be hopeful that other East Atlanta charter schools will take similar steps towards preventing segregation and easing the strain on neighborhood public schools. Additionally, charters and school districts must work on increasing the knowledge of charter school process since we know that low-income nonwhites are less likely to take advantage of school choice options.

One of the more innovative steps APS Superintendent Dr. Mería Carstarphen has taken is the creation of Partner School Charter Relationships. This plan embraces both neighborhood public schools and high performing charter schools by pairing Charter Schools such as Drew with low performing public schools and charter groups with established patterns of high performance such as Purpose Built Schools. The first Partner School, Thomasville Heights, has seen immense success in the last three years, increasing its overall performance index by over 30 points. This increase is not due to better leadership or a different student population, as the school has been operated by the same principal as the afore-mentioned Kirkwood "Little School that Never Could." On the topic of Partner Schools and charters' critics, Dr. Carstarphen states, "This is a chance for them to prove that charter schools' successes are due to how they teach — not the students who choose their schools" (Bloom 2016, 5). Three new Partner Schools will open in the upcoming school year.

A grant-funded teacher training initiative envisioned by Program Director Elizabeth Hearn at Atlanta Neighborhood Charter School is also making a big splash in East and South Atlanta's charter and public schools. CREATE (Collaboration and Reflection to Enhance Atlanta Teacher Effectiveness) began in 2015, with just 5 school sites. The program accepts approximately 20 Georgia State University Education majors into an intensive training program tailored to turning out reflective, well-connected, and highly supported new teachers into the East and South Atlanta's schools. Teacher mentors and Cooperating Teachers from both the community's charter and traditional public schools train resident teachers in the target schools. The program further builds community, expertise, and cultural competence across schools by offering Cognitive Based Compassion Training (CBCT), Critical Friends Training, and other professional development opportunities to all resident teachers and staff members at participating schools. This year, CREATE will train residents at ten public and charter schools.

Finally, understanding that gentrification is likely an inevitable force for the beltline area, especially as it continues to expand, the Anne E. Casey Foundation (2018) and other community organizations are working to ensure that neighborhoods in the Southeast do not experience the same level of community displacement as in the eastern parts of Atlanta. This will mean efforts such as acquiring vacant homes to revitalize them, moving in stable working-class citizens, enforcing restrictions on future sale prices, tax stabilization, and education on property values to avoid homeowners selling to flippers.

CONCLUSION

At a recent community gathering in APS's Therrell cluster where the latest gentrification trend in Atlanta is beginning, black parents and community members opposed the proposed opening of the cluster's first charter school. Their loudest question was, "Why?" As one parent put it, "If our schools already have all of the same programs your school has, why do we need your school?"

We have found that when left to individual choices and market forces alone, middle class families will take full advantage of "the market" to maintain or reaffirm their class advantages (Ball, Bowe, & Gewirtz, 1995). To be sure, the decline of education outcomes for African Americans is the result of racism, discriminatory school policies, and housing displacement (Ransaw, 2017). The truth is that schools with higher percentages of low-income students face a range of challenges that wealthier schools do not (Steward et al. 2017). Moredechay & Ayscue (2017) argue that "successful management of the gentrification process is essential to ensuring that it creates inclusive communities rather than displacing low-income residents and residents of color" (p. 24). It is of upmost importance that researchers, policy writers, and all citizenry examine the impact of school choice as it relates to the particular socio-economic and historical contexts within which it operates. We must make a plan for affordable inner-city housing, transportation, and above all else, educational equity for the sake of our next generation.

Bibliography

Albright, Cliff. "Gentrification is Sweeping Through America. Here are the People Fighting Back."

The Guardian. November 10, 2017. https://www.theguardian.com/us-news/2017/nov/10/atlanta-super-gentrification-eminent-domain

Alexander, K. "Is It Family of School? Getting the Question Right." *RSF: The Russell Sage Foundation Journal of the Social Sciences* 2, no. 5 (2016): 18–33.

Almond, M. "The Black Charter School Effect: Black Students in American Charter Schools." *The Journal of Negro Education* 81, no. 4 (2012): 354–65.

Ball, S., R. Bowe, and S. Gewirtz. "Circuits of Schooling: A Sociological Exploration of Parental Choice of School in Social Class Contexts." *The Sociological Review* 43, no. 1 (1995): 52–78.

Berends, M. "Sociology and School Choice: What We Know After Two Decades of Charter Schools." *Annual Review of Scoiology 41*, (2015): 159–80.

Betts, Julian, and Tom Loveless, eds. *Getting Choice Right: Ensuring Equity and Efficiency in Education Policy*. Washington, D.C.: Brookings Institution Press, 2005. http://www.jstor.org/stable/10.7864/j.ctt12879sq

Bidwell, C. E., and Dreeben, R. "Public and private education: conceptualizing the distinction." *In School Sector and Student Outcomes*, ed. MT Hallinan, Notre Dame, IN: Univ. Notre Dame Press, (2006), 9–37.

Bifulco, R., and H. Ladd. "Institutional Change and Coproduction of Public Services: The Effect of Charter Schools on Parental Involvement." *Journal of Public Administration Research and Theory: J-PART* 16, no. 4 (2006): 553–76.

Bluestone, P., D. Sjoquist, and N. Warner. "Review of Charter Schools' Effects on Student Achievement and Life Outcomes." *The Center for State and Local Finance*. Georgia State University. Septermber 29, 2016.

Bourdieu, Pierre. "The School as a Conservative Force: Scholastic and Cultural Inequalities." In *Contemporary Research in the Sociology of Education*, edited by John Eggleston, 32–46. Methuen, London: Routledge, 1974.

Bowles, S., and H. Gintis. "Schooling in Capitalist America Revisited." *Sociology of Education* 75, no. 1 (2002): 1–18.

Buddin, Richard, and Ron Zimmer. "Academic Outcomes." In *Charter School Operations and Performance*, 37–62. RAND Corporation, 2003.

Buddin, R. and Zimmer, R. "Student achievement in charter schools: A complex picture." J. Pol. Anal. Management, 24 (2005): 351–371.

Burns, Rebecca. "Charter School Snapshot." *Atlanta Magazine*. January 6, 2015. http://www.atlantamagazine.com/great-reads/charter-school-snapshot/.

Chub, J. E., and Moe, T.M. *Politics, Markets, and America's Schools*. Brookings Institution Press, June 1, 1990.

Clotfelter, Charles T. "Private Schools, Segregation, and the Southern States." *Peabody Journal of Education*, vol. 79, no. 2, 2004, pp. 74–97.

Coleman, J. S. "Equality of Educational Opportunity." US Department of Health, Education, & Welfare. 1966. https://files.eric.ed.gov/fulltext/ED012275.pdf

Connell, R. "The Neoliberal Cascade and Education: An Essay on the Market Agenda and Its Consequences." *Critical Studies in Education* 54, no. 2 (2013): 99–112.

Davis, T., and D. Oakley. "Linking Charter School Emergence to Urban Revitalization and Gentrification: A Socio-spatial Analysis of Three Cities." *Journal of Urban Affairs* 35, (2013): 81–102.

Douglas, Dianna. "Are Private Schools Immoral?" *The Atlantic.* December 14, 2017. https://www.theatlantic.com/education/archive/2017/12/progressives-are-undermining-public-schools/548084/

Downey, M. "Poor Schools, Rich Schools: Never the Twain Shall Meet in Atlanta." *Atlanta Journal Constitution.* January 26, 2017.http://getschooled.blog.myajc.com/2017/01/26/poor-schools-rich-schools-never-the-twin-shall-meet-in-atlanta/

Downey, D., P. Von Hippel, and M. Hughes. "Are 'Failing' Schools Really Failing? Using Seasonal Comparison to Evaluate School Effectiveness." *Sociology of Education* 81, no. 3 (2008): 242–72.

Durkheim, E. *Education and Sociology.* New York: Free Press, 1956.

Eschbacher, Brian. "Integrating Schools in a Gentrifying City Through Choice." Brookings. September 19, 2017. https://www.brookings.edu/blog/brown-center-chalkboard/2017/09/19/integrating-schools-in-a-gentrifying-city-through-choice/.

"Estimated Charter Public School Enrollment 2016–2017." National Alliance for Public Charter Schools. 2017. www.publiccharters.org.

"Fast Facts on School Choice." EdChoice. April 24, 2018. http://www.edchoice.org/our-resources/fast-facts.

Foster, A. "Time for Détente Between Charter and Traditional Public schools." *The Phi Delta Kappan* 95, no. 5 (2014): 18–22.

Friedman, M. *The Role of Government in Education.* Collected Works of Milton Friedman Project records. Hoover Institution Archives, Stanford, Ca., 1955.

Friedman, M. *Capitalism and freedom.* Chicago: University of Chicago Press, 1962.

French, R. "Many Georgia Parents Seeking School Choice Don't Get It." *Atlanta Journal Constitution.* August 9, 2015. http://www.myajc.com/news.local-education.many-georgia-parents-seeking-school-choice-don-get/MPYVBTksNpcurUBw7ePLHl/

Fusarelli, L. "Charter School: Implications for Teachers and Administrators." *The Clearing House* 76, no. 1 (2002): 20–4.

Gajendragadkar, S. "The Constitutionality of Racial Balancing in Charter Schools." *Columbia Law Review* 106, no. 1 (2006): 144–81.

Garland, Sarah. "Rich Kid, Poor Kid: How Mixed Neighborhoods Could Save America's Schools." *The Atlantic.* July 25, 2012. https://www.theatlantic.com/national/archive/2012/07/rich-kid-poor-kid-how-mixed-neighborhoods-could-save-americas-schools/260308/

Georgia Department of Education. "The Georgia Department of Education's District Flexibility and Charter Schools Division 2017 Annual Report submitted on behalf of the State Board of Education." 2017. http://www.gadoe.org/External-Affairs-and-Policy/Charter-Schools/Committee%20Members/2017%20Charter%20Systems%20Annual%20Report%20-%202018-01-30.pdf.

Gill, Brian P., P. Mike Timpane, Karen E. Ross, and Dominic J. Brewer. "Choice." In *Rhetoric V. Reality*, 115–36. RAND Corporation, 2001.

Green, Josh. "How Gentrification Really Changes a Neighborhood." *Atlanta Magazine*. March 2016. http://www.atlantamagazine.com/homeandgarden/the-gentrifier/.

———. "Atlanta's 'Runaway Gentrification' Chronicled by National, International Media." *Atlanta Curbed*. November 15, 2017. https://atlanta.curbed.com/2017/11/14/16640524/atlanta-gentrification-article-citylab-guardian.

Gross, Allie. "Out of Options." *Vice News*. December 19, 2016. https://news.vice.com/en_us/article/a3j5va/school-choice-detroit-betsy-devos

Gupta, Arun. "How education reform drives gentrification." Al Jazeera America, March 7, 2014. http://america.aljazeera.com/opinions/2014/3/education-reform-portlandpublicschoolsgentrification.html.

Holley, M. J., A. J. Egalite., and M. F. Luken. "Competition with Charters Motivates Districts." *Education Next*. (Fall 2013): 29–35.

Hornsby Jr., A. "Black Public Education in Atlanta, Georgia, 1954–1973: From Segregation to Segregation." *The Journal of Negro History* 76, no. ¼ (1991): 21–47.

Hoxby, C., and Rockoff, J. E. The Impact of Charter Schools on Student Achievement. *Rand.org*, November, 2004.

Jennings, J., and Lauen, D. L. "Accountability, Inequality, and Achievement: The Effects of the No Child Left Behind Act on Multiple Measures of Student Learning." *RSF: The Russell Sage Foundation Journal of the Social Sciences* 2, no. 5 (2016): 220–41.

Jordan, R., and M. Gallagher. "Does School Choice Affect Gentrification?." *Urban Institute,* (2015): 1–14.

Joseph, G. "What Betsy Devos Didn't Say About School Choice." *Citylab,* January, 2017. https://ww w.citylab.com/equity/2017/01/what-betsy-devos-didnt-say-about-school-choice/513269/.

Kahn, Michael. "Developer: 'Gentrification' Necessary for Atlanta's Future Growth, Education, Arts Scene." *Atlanta Curbed*. June 27, 2017. https://atlanta.curbed.com/2017/6/27/15878514/gentrification-necessary-good-atlanta-education-arts-jamestown-bronfman

Keels, M., J. Burdick-Will, and S. Keene. "The Effects of Gentrification on Neighborhood Public Schools." *City and Community* 12, no. 3, (2013): 238–59.

Kirp, David. "Making Schools Work." *The New York Times*. May 19, 2012. http://www.nytimes.com/2012/05/20/opinion/sunday/integration-worked-why-have-we-rejected-it.html?_r=0

Ladson-Billings, G., and W. Tate. "Towards a Critical Race Theory of Education." *Teachers College Record* 97, no. 1 (1995): 47–68.

Lareau, A., and Goyette, K. *Choosing Homes, Choosing Schools: Residential Segregation and the Search for a Good School.* New York: Russell Sage Foundation, 2014. Project Muse.

Marshall, G., and Scott, J. *A Dictionary of Sociology: Third Revised Edition.* Oxford University Press, 2015.

Meyer, J., and Rowan, B. "Institutionalized Organizations: Formal Structure as Myth and Ceremony." *American Journal of Sociology,* 83:2 (1977):340–363.

Mordechay K., and J. Ayscue. "White Growth, Persistent Segregation: Could Gentrification Become Integration?" *The Civil Rights Project,* (2017): 2–33.

Nathan, J. "Heat and Light in the Charter School Movement." *The Phi Delta Kappan* 79, no. 7 (1998): 499–505.

Park, Robert E., and Ernest W. Burgess. *The City.* Chicago: The University of Chicago Press, 1925.

Parsons, T. "The School Class as a Social System: Some of its functions in American society." *Harvard Education Review* 29, (1959): 297–318.

Patillo M, O'Connor L. D., and Butts F. "High stakes choosing." See Lareau & Goyette 2014: 237–67.

Patrick, Carlianne. "Willing to Pay: Charter Schools' Impact on Georgia Property Values." *Georgia State University Andrew Young School Fiscal Research Center,* (2015):1–20.

Pearman, F., and W. Swain. "School Choice, Gentrification, and the Variable Significance of Racial Stratification in Urban Neighborhoods." *Sociology of Education* 90, no. 3 (2017): 213–35.

Perry, Theresa, Claude Steele, and Asa Hilliard III. *Young, Gifted, and Black: Promoting High Achievement Among African-American Students.* Boston: Beacon Press, 2003.

Powers, Benjamin. "Putting the Brakes on Runaway Gentrification in Atlanta." *Citylab.* November 10, 2017. http://www.citylab.com/equity/2017/11/putting-the-brakes-on-runaway-gentrification-in-atlanta/545555/.

Ransaw, Theodore. "Understanding the Classroom Matrix of Race, Class, Gender, and Cultural Competency in Analyzing Same-Race Students and Teacher Arguments." In *Emerging Issues and Trends in Education,* edited by T. Ransaw and R. Majors, 85–115. Michigan: Michigan State University Press, 2017.

Ravitch, Diane. *Reign of Error The Hoax of the Privatization Movement and the Danger to America's Public Schools.* New York: Vintage Books, 2013.

Renzulli, L., and L. Evans. "School Choice, Charter Schools, and White Flight." *Social Problems* 52, no. 3 (2005): 398–418.

Roberts, A., and R. Lakes. "Middle-Class Mothers on Urban School Selection in Gentrifying Areas." *Education and Urban Society* 48, no. 3 (2014): 203–20.

Roberts, Amy Childers. "Gentrification and School Choice: Where Goes the Neighborhood?" Dissertation: Gerogia State University, 2012. https://scholarworks.gsu.edu/eps_diss/88

Rosenblat, J., and T. Howard. "How Gentrification is Leaving Public Schools Behind." *US News.* February 20, 2015. www.usnews.com.

Roda A., Wells A. S. "School choice policies and racial segregation: where white parents' good intentions, anxiety, and privilege collide." Am. J. Educ., 2013. 119(2): 261–93.

Saporito, S. "Private Choices, Public Consequences: Magnet School Choice and Segregation by Race and Poverty." *Social Problems* 50, no. 02 (2003): 181–203.

Sass, Tim R. "Charter Schools and student achievement in Florida." Education Finance andPolicy 1, no. 1 (Winter 2006):91–122.

Sattin-Bajaj C. "Unaccompanied Minors: Immigrant Youth, School Choice, and the Pursuit of Equity." Boston, MA: Harvard Educ. Press, 2014.

"School Vouchers: An Educational Conundrum for Black America." *The Journal of Blacks in Higher Education* 35, (2002): 79–80.

Scott, J., and A. Villavicencio. "School Context and Charter School Achievement: A Framework for Understanding the Performance 'Black Box'." *Peabody Journal of Education* 84, no. 2 (2009): 277–243.

Sen, A. "Whose Opportunity?." *Center for Popular Democracy*, (2016): 1–25.

Sever, M. "A Critical Look at the Theories of Sociology of Education. *International Journal of Human Sciences* 9, no 1 (2012):650–671.

Shiller, J. "Venture Philanthropy's Market Strategies Fail Urban Kids." *The Phi Delta Kappan* 93, no. 8 (2012): 12–16.

Sledge, V. "How Gentrification is Reshaping Housing and Displacing Residents in Atlanta." *Georgia State Signal.* November 10, 2017. http://georgiastatesignal.com.

Stewart, Evan, and Neeraj Rajasekar. "School Choice and Social Inequality." *The Society Pages.* February 16, 2017. https://thesocietypages.org/trot/2017/02/16/school-choice-and-social-inequality/.

The Annie Casey Foundation. (2018 March 10). Residents, Partners, Casey Foundation Celebrate Groundbreaking for Atlanta's Pittsburgh Yard. *The Annie Casey Foundation Blog.* Retrieved from http://www.aecf.org/blog/residents-partners-casey-foundation-celebrate-groundbreaking-for-atlantas/.

Toch, T. "Reflections on the Charter School Movement." *The Phi Delta Kappan* 91, no. 8 (2010): 70–1.

Weber, Max. "Class, Status, Party." trans. by Gerth HH and Mills CW, *Politics* 1, no. 9 (1944): 271–8.

Wilson, William Julius. *The Truly Disadvantaged*. Chicago: The University of Chicago Press, 1987.

Yosso, T. J. "Whose Culture Has Capital? A Critical Race Theory Discussion of Community Cultural Wealth." *Race, Ethnicity, and Education, 2005. 8(1): 69–91.*

Zimmer, R., and R. Buddin. "Is Charter School Competition in California Improving the Performance of Traditional Public Schools?." *Public Administration Review* 69, no. 5: (2009): 831–45.

Zimmer, Ryan, Brian Gill, Kevin Booker, Stephane Lavertu, Tim Sass, and John Witte. "Competitive Effects of Charter School on Student Achievement in Traditional Public Schools." In *Charter Schools in Eight States*, 77–82. RAND Corporation, 2009.

World Languages in the Twenty-First Century Classroom

Krista Green Hayes

A COMMON SENTIMENT spoken when reflecting on the present state of the world is that the globe is shrinking; connecting with people from around the world is easy, quick, and accessible; and ultimately, the ability to engage with anyone anywhere can happen instantaneously. While such statements are true, how much interacting is done naturally via multiple languages? While technology allows us to engage easily, it also provides tools to help with language translations. However, isn't communication much richer when not interrupted by a translator or translation device? Considering such preferences and observations, how are American students learning to communicate in other languages and in which languages are they learning to do so?

Is our educational system adequately preparing students to work, relate and/ or live in a multicultural and multilingual environment? Or are we hindering students from developing adequate skills necessary to contribute to a global society by not federally mandating world language graduation requirements? Do students in private schools have an advantage for gaining proficiency in a world language over public school students or vice versa, and will this impact future employability? What is working well in world language education to support what the country demands in terms of raising competent world citizens?

My twelve years of teaching Spanish in both private and public schools, teaching at a summer immersion academy for two years, and teaching as an adjunct instructor have allowed me to observe much that is evolving and improving in world language education while, unfortunately, recognizing a list of factors that prevent students from gaining notable levels of proficiency in the target language. Ultimately, in a country that claims to embrace diversity, our limited ability to communicate with individuals whose first language is not English is restrictive. We claim to educate students to become productive members of a global society, but we fail to make that an obtainable linguistic opportunity for most of them. As a national survey discovered, "there is a huge mismatch between what is happening in our schools and what the country is demanding; that is, an education system that prepares all children to be competent world citizens, who can communicate in more than one language" (Pufahl and Rhodes 2011, 272). To improve upon the disparity that exists between what we say we do as an educational system and what actually occurs, more schools and districts must commit to world language learning in the elementary years, preferably with an immersion program.

INTERNATIONAL COMPARISONS

Explaining the discrepancy between what the American educational system demands in relation to world languages with what takes place in local schools, begins by considering world language learning in other developed countries. The European Union, for example, requires students to study "the mother tongue plus two world languages in school," whereas schools in the United States lack "early-start, long-sequence world language and immersion programs" (Davin and Heineke 2017). In fact, instead of amplifying our language programs and demanding world language education that better compares with international programs, the United States lacks federal policy; the decisions are left to state or local governments. Consequently, "42 of the 50 states have no world language graduation requirement at all. In the seven states and the District of Columbia where there are world language graduation requirements, the maximum obligation is two years of coursework beginning in high school" (Davin and Heineke 2017; O'Rourke, Zhou, and Rottman 2016). As O'Rourke and colleagues (2016) go on to say, "The lack of recognition by state policy makers of the basic parameters for successful language learning underlines the lack of prioritization for world language education, even in states that have requirements" (797).

An additional comparison can be made when looking at examples from a friend of mine who moved to Dubai with her young family in 2016. When asking her about the language programs in her daughter's elementary school, she said they are learning three different languages. They are required to learn Arabic and then can make elective choices for the other two, such as Chinese, French, or Spanish. Their Arabic classes are one hour per day. Even her son in preschool is addressed by teachers in Arabic, French, and English. When reporting on the benefits of such multilingualism, Kroll and Dussias (2017) report that, "[a]lthough most of the world is multilingual [like Dubai], the use of two or more languages in the United States has historically been marked as a complicating factor rather than a benefit" (Introduction). Consequently, the United States is a country with insufficient graduation requirements for world languages and blatantly lacks federal commitment (regulations/financial support) towards world language education. Nonetheless, through the help of advocates, stakeholders, policymakers, administrators and educators, world language education continues to evolve.

WORLD LANGUAGE PROGRAMS IN THE ELEMENTARY SCHOOLS

With each passing decade, language offerings and the levels at which they are taught fluctuate. Fortunately, schools and districts have begun to embrace the fact that younger brains truly are better equipped for language learning. While teenagers and adults alike can learn a second or third language, "experts say children are especially wired to learn language in the most natural ways, through play and exploration" (Chandler 2014). Allowing students to apply this truth through immersion schools assists in an improved rate of bilingualism and/or multilingualism in the United States. What begins in the immersion programs leads to a considerable number of students who "succeed in reaching the ACTFL [American Council on the Teaching of Foreign Languages] Intermediate levels of proficiency by the end of high school" (*What Proficiency Level*). This suggests that students, on average, are graduating with the "ability to create with the language when talking about familiar topics related to their daily life" (*ACTFL* 2012). While some may read that statement and think intermediate proficiency is inadequate, for students who only are immersed for a limited part of their day, summers and other breaks not included, it really is an accomplishment. Additionally, "[l]ike children who grow up in multilingual settings, monolingual children will also benefit from bilingual immersion programs because they too will experience the cognitive and linguistic advantages that are associated with growing up bilingual" (Kroll and Dussias 2017).

School districts and/or individual schools that commit to the immersion programs recognize the importance of teaching young students to value other cultures, of embracing diversity, and of improving proficiency so that with time, students will be better equipped to contribute to the global community. After all, beyond the academics of schooling, throughout each school day students are learning a lot about their society and their place in it. They are also learning how to interact with their peers. When a classroom is integrated with a diverse population of students and with a generally unfamiliar language, the students naturally learn to accept those conditions as the norm. This acceptance and ability to interact with people unlike themselves is a lesson that stays with them indefinitely. Such attitudes and opinions are important to instill in order to counter the harsh reality that many people living in the United States who have not come from such culturally diverse experiences are rather ethnocentric, meaning that they believe "in the inherent superiority of [their] own ethnic group or culture" (dictionary.com). Although we claim to value diversity, it seems to be embraced to a limited degree. The current political climate of 2017 and 2018 seems to have also heightened xenophobia throughout our country as political leaders invoke fear in relation to immigrants. To deter such fears and behaviors and to truly aim to raise more globally prepared citizens, the educational system in the United States must work towards educating and preparing more accepting and culturally aware young people.

As previously stated, statistics suggest that immersion programs are the most adequate for allowing students to grow in levels of proficiency throughout their educational years. As students learn to communicate in another language (or two), it is natural that an improved acceptance of that studied culture grows. However, only 6 percent of public elementary schools with language programs offered immersion learning (Pufahl and Rhodes 2011). Most likely that percentage has increased in the past few years, but overall, if immersion is such a successful model, why do only a limited number of schools offer it? What does it take to convince stakeholders, decision makers, and school administrators to value language learning and to implement more immersion programs? Governmental decisions can often have the greatest impact. Consider Utah: "In 2008, the Utah Senate passed the International Initiatives (Senate Bill 41), creating funding for Utah schools to begin Dual Language Immersion programs in Chinese, French, and Spanish" (*Why Immersion* n.d.). Utah made these decisions hoping to "address the needs for language skills in business, government, and education." Utah schools experienced such success with their immersion implementations that target dates for completion were accelerated and Portuguese was also added to the language choices. With such accomplishments, other school districts, presumably from across the country, have aimed to model what Utah has done. Still others, however, may know what is best but are still working through programming issues or are hesitant to fully embrace the immersion model.

Funding is often stated as a factor for avoiding world language implementation in schools, as implementation requires more staff. This can, of course, be a legitimate concern. However, As Friedman (2015) points out:

> advocates say dual-language programs are cost-effective because they typically don't require extra materials for the language instruction; a science textbook, for example, would simply be published in the target language. That means districts buy the same number of materials as they would without the language element. The same goes for the number of teachers needed—though those teachers need to be bilingual as well.

Instead of having to hire additional staff to teach isolated language courses, "foreign language teachers also teach the core academic classes, and so they are built into the school district's standard funding formula" (Chandler 2014).

A bridge between no elementary language offerings and full immersion exists at schools and in districts where either a FLES (Foreign Language in Elementary Schools) or FLEX (Foreign Language Exploratory) program exists. In such programs, the students may only have the language class once every three to four days during a special period, for example. Or the language instruction may change each semester or quarter. For example, I have a nephew in Kentucky who has Spanish once every six days during his special period. This special time lasts forty-five minutes but is shared with recess, which means he learns Spanish for twenty to twenty-five minutes every sixth school day.

Across the county, a friend's daughter who is the same age as my nephew is learning Japanese. She has the class for thirty minutes multiple times per week. Yet at other elementary schools in the district, language is not offered at all (FCPS). The details of FLES/FLEX programs are open-ended and often unique to each school, based on teachers, schedules, funding, etc. While such programs are to be applauded for at least trying to introduce the students to other cultures and languages (something is better than nothing, right?), are these programs adequate? While the students' language abilities are not greatly improved through such models, is it possible that the schools with FLES/FLEX programs are indeed thinking of better socialization of the children? While they might not be fully applying the facts about language acquisition at a younger age, it appears that they are supporting the idea that the exposure to other cultures will foster more tolerant attitudes and acceptance by students, therefore preparing them to better interact with the diverse world.

MIDDLE SCHOOL WORLD LANGUAGE PROGRAMS

A variety of programming and instruction exists in the middle schools, too. Some schools, public or private, choose to introduce Spanish as an academic course in sixth, seventh, or eighth grade. Doing so allows students to earn Spanish 1 credit in middle school, and then students can enroll in Spanish 2 in high school. Such opportunities are usually given to more academically advanced students who are excelling in their Language Arts courses. For example, in North Carolina, I taught high school students who attended a private Catholic school for the middle grades where they earned Spanish 1 credit. Public school students were not afforded this opportunity. Therefore, when these two populations of students intermingled in public high school, only the students who came from the Catholic school, along with native speakers, were able to continue through Spanish 5 prior to graduation (in other schools, they could have continued through Advanced Placement Spanish instead of Spanish 5, but our school did not offer the AP course).

Other middle schools choose to offer languages as exploratory classes like what many elementary schools do. Some may offer exposure to a different language and culture every nine weeks for one academic year. Others may offer only one language course in which students can enroll for one semester as an elective course. I taught at a public middle school in South Carolina that offered Spanish to students as an exploratory elective course. While I know I was able to ignite an interest in the Spanish language and culture for many students, I was often frustrated by the limited opportunity to help students develop in their language ability. I had the autonomy to design the course as I desired, and looking back, it should have been more about cultural exploration than language development.

HIGH SCHOOL WORLD LANGUAGE PROGRAMS

My mother taught high school Spanish more than four decades ago. She tells of how she seldom actually spoke Spanish in class, especially not in a conversational manner. Her instruction was mainly grammatical, teaching students the written language. We recognize the stark differences in our teaching practices. If shifting from primarily written instruction like my mother used to more communicative-based instruction that occurs nowadays was the only needed improvement in the language classroom, we would probably have more bilingual or multilingual students graduating from high school. Instead, we still have students who are graduating with either a very low level of proficiency in their language of study, or for some, graduating without ever stepping into a language classroom. In fact, "only one out of every five [K-12] students" is studying a world language (Mitchell 2017).

If you are reading this article, you most likely graduated high school with at least two credits in a world language, or, if you were a student passionate about the language or who simply thrived in it and wanted to study further, or you were hoping to boost your grade point average, at most you graduated with Advanced Placement or International Baccalaureate credit for the language. The minimum requirement for admission to most colleges and universities is two years of world language study. However, only "a total of 11 states have foreign language graduation requirements; 16 states do not have foreign language graduation requirements; and 24 states have graduation requirements that may be fulfilled by a number of subjects—one of which is foreign languages" (National K-12 Foreign Language 2017, 6). While I cannot speak with personal experience for schools and districts making decisions about graduation requirements, the evidence is clear—there is a lack of commitment in our country to teaching and learning world languages, despite what we claim to value. Some universities show greater appreciation for language study by requiring at least three years of coursework for admission. But is this truly reflecting a value of world languages or a preference for students who commit to more academically challenging courses and the development of their cognitive skills?

Aside from graduation requirements, what is occurring within the high school classrooms? If this is our country's norm for developing language proficiency in our students, what challenges exist? Why can't two or three years of language instruction be enough to allow students to develop more than novice level proficiency? And why after even three to four years of language study are students only graduating with a high-novice or low-intermediate level of proficiency (*What Proficiency Level* 2010)?

SCHEDULING

First, one must consider scheduling. Most high schools are set up on either a traditional six to eight periods per day class schedule or the block schedule where the classes change at the semester mark or last for the entire year but meet every other day. With a period-style schedule, students typically are exposed to the language for forty-five to fifty-five minutes per day, assuming the teacher begins the class promptly, uses the language solely throughout the class, and teaches until the final bell rings. On a block schedule, students have longer exposure to the language per day, usually about ninety minutes, but the course usually ends at the semester mark or students' schedules alternate daily so that they only engage with the language every other day until the end of the year. In an ideal situation, students can arrange their schedule so that they have their language courses in consecutive semesters, but unfortunately, some students are often forced to skip semesters without the language due to other scheduling conflicts. Consequently, they enter the next level of the language basically having to relearn what is most likely forgotten during the scheduling gap. Of course there are plenty of students who overcome these challenges. They thrive with learning the language, are eager to learn more and work to fluency, and prioritize the language courses in their schedules.

CLASS SIZE

Class size is another challenge for many public schools. Private schools often recruit students and new families based on the advantage of a much lower student-teacher ratio. On the other hand, public high schools and middle schools that are teaching beginning level courses and are restricted by budget, funding, or their own scheduling issues, often permit an excessive number of students in a world language classroom. While many teachers, especially experienced ones, can handle a larger class size, other challenges exist when given a large number of students.

In my most recent teaching position in North Carolina, classroom management was not greatly impacted by the quantity of students. Teaching thirty-six students at once, however, did restrict the amount of time each student was given to communicate in the target language. The challenge was providing enough useful minutes for the students to use the target language daily. I, like many teachers, utilize cooperative learning groups or partner work to provide more input/output opportunities and natural speaking scenarios. However, classroom spacing can even become a restrictive factor. Maneuvering the desks of thirty-six students in a small classroom so that students could interact in groups or pairs was a physical challenge. This may seem like a minor issue, but it is reflective of how the instructional and applicable minutes of language learning are reduced due to class size.

When teaching in a private school, however, the most students I ever had in one class was eighteen, and that was rare! Twelve or thirteen was a more common number, and such ratios allowed me to engage with students on multiple accounts during a class period. Granted, as students in both private or public schools advance to higher levels, the natural progression leads to fewer students in a classroom and those wanting to truly advance in the language are more capable of doing so in smaller classes.

CLASSROOM MANAGEMENT

Class size naturally relates to classroom management. Again, this issue is situational based on teacher effectiveness and quality, but even the best teachers must deal with behavior issues, which in turn, affect instructional time and the overall opportunities students are given to engage with the language. Teachers of any subject must monitor classroom management and address disruptive students; however, arguments can be made that beginning language instruction in lower divisions of school could impact and change the ways in which teachers can address discipline with students in world language classes.

NATIVE STUDENTS & SOCIOLINGUISTICS IN THE WORLD LANGUAGE CLASS

Ideally, having a mix of native and non-native students in the same classroom would provide the best scenario for learning. (By native, also known as heritage students, I refer to students whose first language is Spanish, or the world language being taught.) Native Spanish-speakers offer models of authentic pronunciation, alternative expressions, and cultural experiences that a non-native teacher such as myself may not provide. In my experiences, however, teaching native and second language learners together in the same high school classroom, especially beginning level (Spanish 1 and 2) can be rather conflictive. Moreover, in some of my experiences, the intermingling of cultures and language has, unfortunately, allowed social hierarchies and cultural segregation to be amplified.

To clarify this point, we must consider the motivations that exist for students to enroll in foreign language classes. Many students truly want to learn a second language; however, some lose that motivation quickly when they realize the difficulty or the effort that may be required in the class (a cyclical argument for why beginning language learning in the elementary schools is imperative). Others are simply college-bound; they know what colleges expect to see on their transcripts, and they arrange their schedules accordingly. Some students, especially in smaller schools with fewer course options, end up in a world language class by default when their first choices are full. And lastly, native speakers may choose to take the course for an "easy A," for the opportunity to have a class that is less demanding, and/or for the sake of honing their language skills, especially if they know they are weak in reading and writing. Consequently, in a beginner level language course and sometimes in upper level courses (primarily level 3 courses where many students are, in fact, just aiming for the stronger transcript/college acceptance), the motivation of students is quite varied.

I did not have any native Spanish-speaking students until I began teaching in the public school. This is not to say that private schools across the country do not have Spanish-speaking students, but there is a general lack of diversity—despite efforts by school leadership to change this trend. Therefore, despite having six years of teaching experience under my belt when I transitioned to the public system, there was a learning curve with regard to teaching native students.

In fact, while reflecting on these scenarios, I realized my inability to resolve the conflictive issues between natives and non-natives in my classroom, and my failure to foster a more respectful and accepting classroom culture was due to a focus on teaching the language above the culture. Separating the two, of course, is a poor teaching practice. Truthfully, however, my own educational experiences were not that diverse, and it has taken being out of the classroom and reflecting on this topic to make me realize areas that need significant improvement—for myself and more importantly, for my students.

As we again reflect on the idea of ethnocentrism is the United States, the superiority of non-Hispanic students in my Spanish classes was apparent. Cultural segregation happened frequently, as well. As an educator, I expected the non-native students to be in awe of the native Spanish-speakers and their abilities. And many truly were! However, maybe out of frustration at their own lack of bilingualism, as a defense mechanism, or even as a reflection of our country's real ethnocentric problems, the native speakers were often shunned, dismissed, or even ridiculed for their ability. In the same day, however, these students would be approached for assistance in written assignments both in and out of the class. Again, somewhat of a reflection of the social rank that many non-Hispanic (mostly white) students have over Hispanics in their schools and reflective of the pressure students have for "making the grade."

Collaboration of native speakers and second language learners within my classes was also very challenging. When I would assign groups or partners, the pairings/groupings were more diverse. The results of this could vary dramatically, mainly dependent on the individual. In some pairings of natives with non-natives, the native speakers would help instruct the partner and assist in pronunciation or vocabulary, for example. Other groupings, however, could result in the native workers doing all the work, sometimes by choice (the "let's just get it done" attitude) and sometimes by social pressure. Conversely, when I allowed students to choose their own partners and groups, most often the diversity was lacking. Native speakers worked together, and non-natives worked together. Occasionally, a few non-native students may be good friends with Hispanics and aim to work together frequently, but this was a rarity across the board. This situation illustrates a bigger picture of our society—we say we want to be diverse, celebrate other cultures, integrate, be color-blind, etc., yet when given the choice, even at younger ages, we naturally segregate. What's the explanation?

Before expounding on this, it is important to note that native speakers are an asset in the dual-immersion programs (also a possible solution for reducing ethnocentric attitudes). As in Utah, the "Dual Language Immersion Program uses a fifty-fifty model, in which students spend half of their school day in the target language and the other half-day in English." Furthermore, "[t]his program serves English speakers and L2 [second language] speakers. A 1:1 ratio is the ideal ratio to be maintained for these two language groups, but a minimum requirement is a 2:1 ratio, or at least one-third of students [being] native speakers of the L2" (*Why Immersion n.d.*). At an early age, students have not been fully conditioned to recognize or emphasize cultural biases. With the dual-immersion program, it appears that all students are on an even playing field—native English speakers have the linguistic advantage for 50 percent of the day and then the native speakers have the advantage for the other 50 percent of the day. There is no time for social (or at least cultural or linguistic) hierarchies to develop.

CONTENT

When looking at the layers of challenges that exist socially for students in a world language classroom (or many other classrooms, too), the basic level of the introductory content can prove to be an additional challenge. As with young children who are learning to speak their primary language, beginning vocabulary in a first level language course is basic. To introduce students to the common sounds of the language, teachers and textbooks alike begin with common greetings, pleasantries, and move towards other vocabulary such as hobbies, colors, numbers, foods, etc. For many high school students, this content is rather childish and potentially boring, therefore at times making it difficult for the teacher to truly "hook" the student with the language.

Conversely, I have taught many energetic and extroverted students who enjoy participating in class, regardless of the content, and expressing the color of a classmate's eyes, for example, is the most exciting comment of the day! This issue is broad, though, especially for the teachers. We know that speaking the target language during class for 100 percent of the time is the goal; yet we also know we want students to be engaged and active participants in their learning. Balancing all of that can be conflictive when the beginning level content does not support what students want to communicate. Consequently, the language is even more restricted to the classroom as students aren't leaving eager to talk repeatedly about the color of their cat. Granted, with each higher level of the language, the content becomes more applicable and interesting, but when students do not feel capable of fully expressing themselves in the target language, conversations are limited. Beginning language learning in the elementary schools would provide a more natural and continual language growth, again contributing to the development of more globally competent students who can graduate with a vocabulary that is more applicable and beneficial in the global market. Integrating grade-level curriculum into the world language classes also "helps to reinforce what students are learning and to build up their academic vocabularies in a second language so they are not just talking about colors and numbers and songs" (Chandler 2014).

STANDARDIZED TESTING

Finally, when evaluating world language programs at the high school level one must address standardized testing. To the best of my knowledge, standardized state assessments for world languages only exist in a few states. When I was teaching in North Carolina, the state was attempting to create an evaluative tool using a portfolio system. Oddly enough, this portfolio would only be submitted for evaluation by a few randomly selected students per teacher, and then used as a representation of teacher effectiveness.

Some states have incorporated other portfolio assessments or use the ACTFL Oral Proficiency guidelines for assessment. The lack of standardized testing can be applauded by many educators. Personally, I enjoyed not having to face the pressure of testing. I was given sole responsibility for passing or failing students, assessing their abilities with the language, and recommending them for further language study. While there are many flaws in such freedom, I was a teacher who thrived in the autonomy to create my classes in the way that I felt best equipped and prepared my students. Of course, to convince administrators, stakeholders, board members, or other decision makers of the effectiveness of a program, more objective and reliable assessments can be influential.

MULTI-LEVEL CHALLENGES

Teachers Wanted

While immersion or dual-immersion programs socialize students to be less egocentric and advance students in their bilingual proficiencies, they are not free from their own struggles and issues—predominantly, hiring and keeping highly qualified and certified teachers. While there may be many individuals who are eager to teach and share their native language, earning the credentials is challenging: the time and financial sacrifice to earn the credentials can be a deterrent. And as the commitment to immersion programs grows, the quantity of teachers (native or non-native) does not keep up.

While non-native teachers are quite capable of teaching an immersion class, the numbers still do not balance. As a result, programs sometimes must end—or fail to even begin—due to a lack of staffing. This dilemma only perpetuates the problem as more students cannot work towards fluency and therefore cannot create a new generation of language teachers. As one analyst noted, "You can't expand the language education if you don't have the pool of teachers to teach it [...] And, if the students aren't learning the language and becoming proficient, they won't become teachers" (Friedman 2015). It's an unending cycle.

Beyond finding bilingual or multilingual teachers, the issue of teacher quality and efficacy come into play. Unlike most content areas, world language teachers earn a certification that qualifies them to teach kindergarteners through seniors in high school. Since I started teaching in a private school, I did not have any teacher certifications; my bachelor degrees were in sociology and Spanish. At that time, I questioned my ability to teach middle schoolers.

Fortunately, good mentors and a strong work ethic allowed me to gain confidence early in my career. However, I am still certain that I should not teach elementary students. I do not have any experience with them, and there is a lot more involved to teaching students beyond the content, especially the younger ones. Nonetheless, every state where I have taught disagrees with my self-evaluation and by means of my K-12 certification says, "Yes, you can!" to teaching a very needy age group. While I appreciate the encouragement and support, the reality is a troublesome reflection of the state of our world language efficacy. It's as if decades ago the educational system in the United States began digging a vast hole by not enabling students to work towards bilingualism or multilingualism. Now, the figurative hole is so deep that there are not enough qualified, or perhaps willing, teachers to work towards creating a new generation of bilingual graduates.

PUBLIC VS. PRIVATE SCHOOLS

My first six years teaching middle school Spanish were in a private school in Kentucky. Following that, I taught two years of middle school Spanish at a public school in South Carolina, then one year in a public high school in South Carolina. The last three years of teaching, before taking a leave to stay home with my sons, were in a public high school in North Carolina. I believe my range of experience in various schools has provided me with insight to significant factors of the private and public world language programs.

In relation to teacher preparedness and hiring constraints, private schools have an advantage over public schools in that many do not require teacher certification. Administrators and heads of school are often more impressed by the credentialed candidate, but they also have the flexibility to hire engaging teachers whose experience in the work force or elsewhere provide richer opportunities for the students than any university teacher candidate program. Now, it is important to recognize that public schools may approve emergency or temporary certification, but that can be a risky albeit necessary move. As for me, my lack of certification is what drew me to teaching in a private school in the first place. It was my only option, and fortunately, my experiences and interviews convinced the administrators to give me a chance.

Private schools have greater flexibility in other areas, as well. While some private schools belong to certain associations or have licenses that demand specific curricula, most give teachers or departments the autonomy to map their learning as they see fit for the students. Along the same lines, the general lack of state standardized testing for private schools allows the administration more flexibility in their scheduling.

Public schools that receive state funding based on student performance on standardized tests tend to cut elective classes, such as world languages, to focus more on the success in reading and math. Class credit can also be offered differently for courses in a private school. The school directors can decide what qualifies for credit. My private school students were in Spanish for three years (grades six to eight) and earned a Spanish 1 high school credit for those three years. Beyond earning the credit, they entered the high school with more exposure to the language than what typical freshmen earn in a Spanish 1 class that lasts one academic year.

The flexibility and individuality of programming may be strong factors impacting the decision to keep world languages in the private schools. Families who enroll students in private education also tend to favor the holistic experience. This might be why "[i]n public high schools with foreign language programs, 48% of all students were enrolled in language classes, compared with 73% of students in private schools" (Pufahl and Rhodes 2011, 263). Interestingly, Pufahl and Rhodes go on to report that "public schools offered more immersion programs than private schools" (264–5). If a private school were to begin an immersion program in the lower grades, then overall, the school would be known for that focus. Private schools, driven by budgets and funding as much as public schools, may choose not to make such a commitment to languages out of fear that it might adversely affect enrollments. Unfortunately, such a decision may do a disservice to students and their bilingual development in the long run.

Economic Impact

As I reiterate the importance of socializing and educating students to be more competent world citizens using world languages, I have yet to mention the economic impact. According to Kroll and Dussias (2017), "[m]ultilingualism is a significant economic asset for individuals, and a bilingual and biliterate workforce is a national asset." Surveys of businesses in California "found that 66% preferred bilingual employees, [...and] 41% of respondents gave preference to multilingual candidates during recruitment" (Davin and Heineke 2017).

With such truths, we must continue to ask why our educational system is ill-equipping students by not prioritizing language learning? The benefits of being bilingual or multilingual extend beyond employment and communicating. Research further suggests that, "being bilingual or multilingual also changes the mind and the brain in ways that create resilience under conditions of stress and that counter some of the deleterious effects of poverty and disease" (Kroll and Dussias 2017). Ultimately, one simply cannot deny that monolingualism is an unacceptable condition of students graduating high school in the twenty-first century.

CONCLUSION

The United States, as diverse as we are with regard to race, ethnicity, and language, is also equally diverse in educational offerings. There are many benefits that come from keeping decisions about schooling on the state and local levels. However, localized governance allows for inconsistencies across the country, especially regarding world language offerings, potentially putting students at a disadvantage simply based on where they live. Why, for example, are 51.18 percent of students in New Jersey enrolled in world language classes while only 8.5 percent of students are in New Mexico (*National K-12 Foreign Language* 2015)? Such a discrepancy across states is evidence of a greater disparity between what our country claims to value in education with how we educate our young people.

The issue is complex, and exists on a large scale: neither one teacher, one school, one district, nor one state can improve the situation for all students. However, improvements must continue to be made, and for now, that seems most plausible on a small scale. After assessing world language education for three decades, "[o]ne of the most important lessons learned was that a foreign language program must be viewed by all stakeholders as a central component of the overall curriculum in order to successfully reach its language proficiency and cultural goals" (Rhodes 2014, 118). I'd argue that for our country to meet our educational goal of creating competent world citizens, we all must see language learning as a central part of education that begins as soon as students enter into our educational system.

Bibliography

ACTFL Proficiency Guidelines 2012. Alexandria, VA: ACTFL, INC, 2012. https://www.actfl.org/sites/default/files/pdfs/public/ACTFLProficiencyGuidelines2012_FINAL.pdf

Boyson, B. A., M. Semmer, L. E. Thompson, and M. H, Rosenbusch. "Does Beginning Foreign Language in Kindergarten Make a Difference? Results of One Districts Study." *Foreign Language Annals* 46, no. 2 (2013): 246–63.

Chandler, Michael A. "From Spanglish to Bilingual: Parents Seek Early Foreign Language Courses, But Most Schools Start Late." *Washington Post*. October 31, 2014. Last accessed January 04, 2018. https://www.washingtonpost.com/lifestyle/magazine/parents-want-elementary-pupils-to-learn-foreign-languages----but-where/2014/10/30/2b2f0864-4d7e-11e4-aa5e-7153e466a02d_story.html?utm_term=.89ec2cb84816

Damari, R. R., W. P. Rivers, R. D. Brecht, P. Gardner, C. Pulupa, and J. Robinson. "The Demand for Multilingual Human Capital in the U.S. Labor Market." *Foreign Language Annals* 50, no. 1 (2017): 13–37.

Davin, K. J., and A. J. Heineke. "The Seal of Biliteracy: Variations in Policy and Outcomes." *Foreign Language Annals* 50, no. 3 (2017): 486–99.

"FCPS World Language Programs 2017–2018." Fayette County Public Schools. Last accessed January 06, 2018. https://www.fcps.net/cms/lib/KY01807169/Centricity/Domain/2324/languages.pdf.

"Foreign Language Enrollments In K-12 Public Schools: Are Students Prepared for a Global Society?" (Rep.). Committee for Economic Development. Last accessed January 14, 2018. https://www.ced.org/pdf/actfl-k12-foreign-language-for-global-society.pdf

Friedman, Amelia. "America's Lacking Language Skills." *The Atlantic*. May 10, 2015. Last accessed November 18, 2017. https://www.theatlantic.com/education/archive/2015/05/filling-americas-language-education-potholes/392876/.

Kroll, J. F., and P. E. Dussias. "The Benefits of Multilingualism to the Personal and Professional Development of Residents of the US." *Foreign Language Annals* 50, no. 2 (2017): 248–59.

Mitchell, Corey. "How Much Foreign Language Is Being Taught in U.S. Schools?" *Education Week*. June 2, 2017. Last accessed December 10, 2017. https://blogs.edweek.org/edweek/learning-the-language/2017/06/striking_knowledge_gap_about_foreign_language_education.html

Moreno-López, I., A. Ramos-Sellman, C. Miranda-Aldaco, and M. T. Quinto. "Transforming Ways of Enhancing Foreign Language Acquisition in the Spanish Classroom: Experiential Learning Approaches." *Foreign Language Annals* 50, no. 2 (2017): 398–409.

"National K-12 Foreign Language Enrollment Survey Report." Last accessed January 18, 2018. https://www.scribd.com/document/350069842/National-K-12-Foreign-Language-Enrollment-Survey-Report#from_embed

O'Rourke, P., Q. Zhou, and I. Rottman. "Prioritization of K-12 World Language Education in the United States: State Requirements for High School Graduation." *Foreign Language Annals* 49, no. 4 (2016): 789–800.

Pufahl, I., and N. C. Rhodes. "Foreign Language Instruction in U.S. Schools: Results of a National Survey of Elementary and Secondary Schools." *Foreign Language Annals* 44, no. 2 (2011): 258–88.

Rhodes, N. C. "Elementary School Foreign Language Teaching: Lessons Learned Over Three Decades (1980–2010)." *Foreign Language Annals* 47, no. 1 (2014): 115–33.

Shin, N. L., M. H. Henderson. "A Sociolinguistic Approach to Teaching Spanish Grammatical Structures." *Foreign Language Annals* 50, no. 1 (2017): 195–213.

Sparks, R. L., J. Luebbers, and M. E. Castañeda. "How Well Do U.S. High School Students Achieve in Spanish When Compared to Native Spanish Speakers? [Abstract]." *Foreign Language Annals* 50, no. 2 (2017): 339–66.

"Teaching and Learning: Welcome to Dual Language Immersion." Utah State Board of Education. Last accessed November 12, 2017. https://schools.utah.gov/curr/dualimmersion.

Thompson, G. L., and K. Harrison. "Language Use in the Foreign Language Classroom." *Foreign Language Annals* 47, no. 2 (2014): 321–37.

"What Proficiency Level Do High School Students Achieve?" Center for Applied Second Language Studies, University of Oregon. Last modified April 23, 2010. Last accessed January 19, 2018. https://casls.uoregon.edu/wp-content/uploads/pdfs/tenquestions/TBQProficiencyResults.pdf

"Why Immersion?" Utah Dual Language Immersion. Last accessed January 26, 2018. http://www.utahdli.org/whyimmersion.html.

Wolfram, Walt. "Sociolinguistics." Linguistic Society of America. Last accessed December 15, 2017. https://www.linguisticsociety.org/resource/sociolinguistics.

Xu, X., A. M. Padilla, and D. M. Silva. "Learner Performance in Mandarin Immersion and High School World Language Programs: A Comparison." *Foreign Language Annals* 48, no. 1 (2015): 26–38.

The Challenges of Chronic Absenteeism and Truancy

Robert McNamara, PhD

WHEN MOST PEOPLE think of skipping classes or school for the day, they typically do not think of it as a national problem with a host of social, economic, and political implications. Recent estimates show that more than seven million students are chronically absent each year (Amhad and Miller 2015). Chronically absent means students are missing more than 10 percent of school days regardless of the reason or whether the absence is excused. This is different from being truant, which is defined as a certain number of unexcused absences (AttendanceWorks.org). Regardless of the reasons, not attending school can present a host of challenges. For example, being chronically absent can result in preschool, kindergarten, and first grade students being much less likely to read at grade level by the third grade. Why is that significant? Students who do not read at grade level by the end of third grade are four times more likely than adequate readers to drop out of high school (US Department of Education 2016).

In fact, attendance can be a better predictor of whether students drop out before graduation than test scores. In fact, some evidence shows that even a single episode of chronic absenteeism in one year between eight and twelfth grade led to a dropout rate seven times higher than that of proficient readers (US Department of Education 2016). So it doesn't take consistently missing school to have an effect—even one year of that experience can have disastrous effects. Why does dropping out matter so much? Because it translates into the lack of opportunities that have lifelong consequences. The US Department of Education estimates that dropping out of high school is associated with poverty, poor health, criminal activity, unemployment, and a host of other challenges.

What is even more disturbing is that while this is a national trend, different constituencies of students experience and are affected by chronic absenteeism more than others. Compared to whites, American Indian and Pacific Islander students are over 65 percent more likely to miss three weeks of school or more and African American students are 36 percent more likely, with Hispanics about 11 percent more likely to be chronically absent. Further, students with disabilities are 1.5 times more likely to be chronically absent compared to students without disabilities. Interestingly, gender does not seem to influence chronic absenteeism—males and females are about equally as likely to be chronically absent (AttendanceWorks.org).

High school students have the highest rates of absenteeism, at 20 percent, or nearly two million students per year, while middle school students hover at about 12 percent. Elementary school students have the lowest rates of chronic absenteeism. But there is a noticeable social class difference with regard to chronic absenteeism. According to AttendanceWorks.com, children living in poverty are two to three times more likely to be chronically absent, and these absences are likely to be related to health or mental health problems. Other barriers include the lack of access to a nearby school bus, a safe route to school, or food insecurity, which make it difficult to go to school each day.

TRUANCY INSTEAD OF CHRONIC ABSENTEEISM

Thus, while chronic absenteeism is a challenge since it covers any type of absence, excused or unexcused, and while there may be chronic and structural reasons for children missing school on a regular basis, with the consequences of missing school being well known for many years, much of the attention about missing school has centered on unexcused absences or truancy.

Although national data on truancy rates are unavailable, partly due to the fact that no uniform definition exists, many cities wrestle with the problem of truancy (Amhad and Miller 2015; Baker, Sigmon, and Nugent 2001). In New York City alone, it has been estimated that 150,000 of its one million public school students are absent on a typical day (Garry 1996). In fact, so significant is the problem of truancy that a national review of discipline issues in public schools found that principals identified student absenteeism, class cutting, and tardiness as the top discipline problems on their campuses (Heaviside, Rowand, Williams, and Farris 1998).

The implications for truancy extend far beyond simply the educational deficiencies for those students who miss school. Truancy has been identified as one of the most important gateway activities for additional problem behaviors. In fact, the US Department of Education has gone on record, stating that truancy is the most powerful predictor of juvenile delinquent behavior (2016). Many studies have connected truancy to dropping out of school, teen pregnancy, substance abuse, gang involvement, and serious forms of delinquency (Amhad and Miller 2015; Puzzanchera et al. 2003; Bell, Rosen, and Dynlacht 1994; Huzinga, Loeber, and Thornberry 1995; Rohrman 1993). There is also a link between truancy and adult problem behaviors, such as violence, marital problems, welfare dependency, chronic unemployment, adult crime, and incarceration (Amhad and Miller 2015;

Dryfoos 1990; Snyder and Sickmund 1995; Catalano et al. 1998). With regard to social class, race, and sex, commonly cited demographic variables, a few trends are noteworthy. For instance, the relationship between race and truancy is not well established. Some data suggests that whites are underrepresented in petitioned cases (Bell, Rosen, and Dynlacht 1994; Puzzanchera et al. 2003). Other studies have found that African Americans and Latinos consistently have the highest drop out rates of all categories of students (Amhad and Miller 2015; Kaufman, Alt, and Chapman 2001). Additionally, while the relationship between income and truancy is not well known, it is generally believed that students from lower income families have higher rates of truancy (AttendanceWorks.org; Bell, Rosen, and Dynlacht 1994). Finally, there is some evidence that boys and girls are about evenly divided in the truancy statistics, with the peak age for truancy cases being fifteen years old (Puzzanchera et al. 2003). However, while girls tend to demonstrate a slightly higher rate of absenteeism in high school than boys, the latter are more likely to become chronically truant, especially in the later grades (Allen-Meares, Washington, and Welsh 2000).

With regard to juvenile crime, in several jurisdictions, law-enforcement officials have linked high rates of truancy to daytime burglary and vandalism. In Tacoma, WA, the police department reported that one-third of burglaries and one-fifth of aggravated assaults occurring between 8 p.m. and 1 p.m. on weekdays were committed by juveniles. In Contra Costa County, CA police reported that 60 percent of juvenile crime occurred between 8 a.m. and 3 p.m. on weekdays. Recent studies also indicate that truancy may be a precursor to serious violent offenses, particularly by males (Baker, Sigmon, and Nugent 2001).

According to the Office of Juvenile Justice and Delinquency Prevention (OJJDP), adults that were truant at an early age were much more likely (than those who were not truant) to have poorer physical and mental health statuses, lower paying jobs, a higher likelihood of living in poverty, more reliance on welfare support, and to have children who exhibit problem behaviors. While these figures are central to understanding the impact of truancy, they should not overshadow the impact of the loss of federal and state education funding (US Department of Education 2016; Baker, Sigmon, and Nugent 2001).

A related phenomenon worth mentioning consists of students who simply refuse to attend school despite any efforts made by parents, schools, or the courts. *School refusal* is defined as a psychological condition in which the child is reluctant (and often outright refuses) to go to school. Children suffering from school refusal tend to seek the comfort of home and to remain in close proximity to parental figures during school hours. They also tend to display visible and emotional outbursts at the prospect of attending school, yet do not seem to have any other problems of controlling their behavior or aggressiveness for other matters. In addition to violent outbursts, some students also identify physical ailments at the thought of going to school, such as headaches, diarrhea, and stomach aches. While this disorder is more of an emotional reaction to leaving home than it is related to school per se, nevertheless, it has an impact on truancy (US Department of Education 2016; Berg 1997).

Finally, another dimension of truancy consists of students who are referred to as push-outs. Many states are phasing in a series of challenging end of course tests that are required for graduation. This is part of a larger effort to improve public education. However, as more and more schools are being held accountable for educating today's youth, one strategy to ensure higher overall scores has been to convince poorly performing students that they should leave school. Critics of high-stakes testing policies have charged that do-or-die exams prompt struggling students to drop out of school, either because they are discouraged by their failure to pass exams or because schools do not want their ratings decreased by lower scoring students (Amhad and Miller 2015; Rubin 2004). In other words, high stakes accountability testing has led some school districts to push students out of school illegally because of low test scores, low grades, chronic truancy, or other issues.

CAUSES OF TRUANCY

According to the National School Safety Center, in 2003 about 5 percent of students in grades nine to twelve skipped school because they felt unsafe at school or on their way to or from school. Others miss school because of family health issues and financial demands, substance abuse, or mental health problems. Research shows that some of the most important factors contributing to truancy stem from four areas: school configuration, personal and developmental issues, the student's family situation, and community characteristics (Baker, Sigmon, and Nugent 2001).

SCHOOL CONFIGURATION

According to the National Center for Education Statistics, large school systems in low-income, inner-city urban school districts have higher rates of absenteeism and truancy compared to suburban and rural school systems. Research consistently reports high absenteeism rates for urban schools, with approximately 8 percent of these students labeled chronically truant (US Department of Education 2016; Epstein and Sheldon 2002).

Truancy is also more likely to occur in those schools that have not made it a priority in terms of policy, in those settings where there is little or no constructive interaction between teachers and parents, in those schools with a high percentage of uncertified teachers, and where homework assignments are lacking in academic rigor (US Department of Education,2016; Dougherty 1999; Epstein and Sheldon 2002). Truancy is also related to low teacher expectations, high teacher absenteeism, and inconsistency in school discipline (US Department of Education 2016; Baker, Sigmon, and Nugent 2001; Strickland 1998).

PERSONAL AND DEVELOPMENTAL ISSUES

Typically, the problems of absenteeism and truancy stem from the experience the child has while in the classroom. There is a wealth of research that suggests poor performance causes students to lose interest in school, which results in them falling behind and beginning to avoid class, then stop going to school all. The response by the school to the lack of attendance is usually punitive, which further alienates the student from the institution (Allen-Meares, Washington, and Welsh 2000). The onset of this problem is particularly apparent in middle school.

FAMILY ISSUES

There is evidence to indicate that the relationship of parental involvement and truancy is inversely related. When parents participate in their child's education, whether it be monitoring homework, helping to improve their reading ability, or attending PTA meetings, the probability of truancy decreases (Epstein and Sheldon 2002). Parental involvement is also related to social class. Research shows that parents with high socioeconomic status (SES) tend to be more involved with teachers and schools as well as being more involved with their child's educational and learning development. Part of the reason for this is that affluent parents tend to have more resources, time to spend with their children, and they place a high value on education.

Youths from single-parent homes tend to have higher rates of absenteeism and truancy than youths from two-parent households; single-parent homes also tend to be lower income families (US Department of Education 2016; Oman et al. 2002; Klein 1994). One study found that youths who lived in one-parent households had a greater likelihood of skipping school, fighting, using alcohol or tobacco, and participating in sexual intercourse (Rohrman 1993). Other studies show that where parenting styles are weak or nonexistent, meaning children are given too much autonomy in decision making and less corrective direction, truancy increases (US Department of Education 2016; Oman et al. 2002; Rohrman 1993).

NEIGHBORHOOD AND COMMUNITY FACTORS

As was mentioned, social class is an important variable in understanding truancy. Children living in low-income and/or inner-city neighborhoods are more likely than suburban youth to experience acts of violence, maltreatment, neglect and abuse, and receive below average educations. This, in turn, affects student motivation about education in general and attending school in particular.

Related to social class, of course, are the physical conditions of the neighborhoods in which children live. The research demonstrates a substantial link between neighborhood context and truancy (Epstein and Sheldon 2002; Teevan and Dryburgh 2000). Exposure to mental and physical health stressors (e.g., abuse, neglect, domestic violence, family strife) and other signs of disorder (e.g., abandoned buildings and cars, condemned housing, illegal drug markets) are all related to truancy (Wandersman and Nation 1998).

THE COSTS OF TRUANCY

Regardless of race or gender category, high school dropouts claim more in government-funded social services expenditures than high school graduates. For men in particular, dropouts incur more in criminal justice costs. The average dropout costs society more than $800,000 over the course of his or her lifetime. Discounted for the current value of money, that amount is approximately $200,000. A study of the costs and benefits of three truancy reduction programs and three truancy courts operating in Colorado discovered that since one high school dropout costs $200,000 in current dollars, the truancy programs operating in Adams County and the City of Denver, each of which cost about $50,000 a year, can each operate for four years for the same cost. These programs serve about eighty-five students a year (National Center for School Engagement 2005). Therefore, even if those programs only encourage one out of three hundred program participants to graduate from high school, they will yield a positive return on their investment.

The cost/benefits of truancy programs in general are readily self-evident: while cost assessment studies are limited, given their low cost of operation, and the high cost of dropping out, it is highly likely that all the truancy reduction programs and the courts pay for themselves many times over.

STRATEGIES THAT WORK TO REDUCE TRUANCY

While every state has its own set of laws regarding truancy, and national trends do not always reflect local policy, it is important to note that there is no single cause for truancy. This means there is no single model for each state to follow.

However, there is substantial evidence to suggest that the most effective programs are those that can demonstrate an alliance between parents and teachers, systematic monitoring and recording of absenteeism and truancy, a consistent imposition of penalties for repeat offenders, support for intervention programs, and patience with regard to implementing new programs (AttendanceWorks.org; Teasley 2004).

The evidence also shows that those highly punitive programs that place the problem of truancy on the individual have not curbed truancy rates. Zero tolerance polices have done more to alienate students from school than to improve teaching and learning (Civil Rights Project 2000). The best programs seem to be those that have a "carrot and stick" approach, whereby parents are involved, students are held accountable by both the school district and the courts, who are working collaboratively rather than trying to shift their burden of responsibility, a court system that can impose sanctions beyond school suspension on both the parent and the child, and some sort of positive reinforcement to the child (Amhad and Miller 2015).

While the hard-line approach to truancy would be that attending school is something students should simply do and not be rewarded for it, the realities of the lives of many students is that they need something to say "yes" to rather than being told about the potential negative consequences of their actions. This is not coddling kids; this is realizing that simply expecting children to do what they are supposed to do "or else" is an ineffective way of addressing truancy.

Granted, there are some children for whom help is limited in effectiveness; however, the more proactive approach is designed to alleviate the problem before it becomes a chronic one. Positive reinforcement, even for small things like completing a life skills program, which is part of some anti-truancy prevention programs, can have a significant impact on a young person who is deciding which behavioral path to take.

INNOVATIVE WAYS TO COMBAT TRUANCY

In an effort to address truancy in schools, many states have offered a variety of programs: suspension for missing a certain number of classes, fining the parents for each day the child misses school, and other punitive measures. However, a punishment such as school suspension, particularly for a habitual or chronic truant, actually rewards the problem behavior. Punishing a child who does not want to come to school with removal from the classroom is an illogical and counterproductive approach.

Similarly, fining a parent for the behavior of the child, while clearly providing an incentive to motivate the parent to elicit the cooperation of the child, holds very little in the way of real accountability for the one who is failing to show up for school. The data clearly demonstrate that these programs have had very little impact on the problem of truancy. Consequently, many states are beginning to recognize that the best way to get school attendance to improve begins with making the problem of missing school painful to the student (Amhad and Miller 2015). They accomplish this by asking the obvious question: What do kids want?

From the time they become teenagers, most youth count down the days to when they can obtain their learner's permit and, ultimately, their official driver's license. Obtaining a driver's license is a teenager's symbolic sign of maturity, freedom, and a passport to adulthood. Given its social and practical importance for teens, many states have begun using it to improve school attendance. A number of states, including New Jersey, Minnesota, and South Carolina, have implemented programs that stipulate that if a student has more than an allotted number of unexcused absences in a year, the student's right to obtain a driver's license is delayed for a fixed period of time, usually six months. In those cases where students miss school but already have their license, it is revoked/suspended for the same period of time. Additionally, some states are currently developing added punishments for repeat offenders (Jones 2005).

Critics contend that states do not possess the authority to revoke a driver's license for a school-related behavior. However, a strong argument could be made that a driver's license is not a right but a privilege extended to those who demonstrate sufficient maturity, responsibility, and trust. A student who does not attend school demonstrates a lack of all three of those ideals. That there exists legal precedent only reinforces the logic of the argument that a license is not guaranteed. For instance, many states, such as New Jersey, provide for the suspension of a driver's license if a parent is delinquent in paying their child support awards. A license suspension also occurs when a person fails to appear at a child support hearing or when an arrest warrant is issued for nonpayment of support (Jones 2005).

Another way to decrease truancy is to link welfare assistance to satisfactory school attendance. Beginning in the late 1980s a number of states began implementing such a program that is similar to those of welfare-to-work initiatives. Linking welfare benefits to school attendance was said by proponents to reinforce the idea supporting the parameters and spirit of the Welfare Reform Act of 1999 (Wright 2005). As Wright discovered in her evaluation of seven different programs, case-management services provided by welfare agencies are critical to the success of the programs in general and of school attendance in particular.

However, it should be noted that there is a wealth of evidence that suggests truancy is not the primary issue of school absenteeism among welfare recipients:

health issues are the major cause of the problem (Fein, Wang, Lee, and Schofield 1999). Thus, students on welfare are not avoiding school for conventional reasons (e.g., poor performance, laziness). Rather, health conditions or related problems within the family explain why they miss school. Thus, the strategies to address truancy for this group should take into account the somewhat unique circumstances for this segment of the truant population.

Other communities, such as Houston, Texas, have implemented volunteer programs, where school officials and community residents descended on more than six hundred homes to persuade older truants and dropouts to return to school. Many students who had dropped out cited day care and employment responsibilities as the reason they left school. Many, however, said they simply got into the habit of not showing up for school, particularly if their parents worked during the day (Stover 2005).

CONCLUSION

The problems associated with truancy are significant and their implications have many far-reaching consequences. There is substantial evidence that truancy is a gateway activity to an assortment of problems, ranging from chronic delinquency, substance abuse, adult crime, teen pregnancy, unemployment, gang behavior, poverty, and dropping out of school. While there are a host of programs designed to reduce and prevent truancy, the most salient features of successful programs are those that involve parents, collaborate and coordinate with the local school district, court intervention for difficult cases, and provide positive reinforcement for participants along the way.

Bibliography

Ahmad, Farah Z., and Tiffany D. Miller. "The High Costs of Truancy." Center for American Progress. August 25, 2015. https://www.americanprogress.org/issues/race/reports/2015 /08/25/109863/the-high-costs-of-truancy/

Allen-Meares, P., R. O. Washington, and B. L. Welsh. *Social Work Services in Schools.* Boston: Allyn and Bacon, 2000.

Baker, M. L., J. N. Sigmon, and M. E. Nugent. *Truancy Reduction: Keeping Students in School.* Washington, D.C.: U.S. Department of Justice, Office of Juvenile Justice Programs, Office of Juvenile Justice and Delinquency Prevention, 2001.

Bell, A. J., L. A. Rosen. and D. Dynlacht. "Truancy Intervention." *The Journal of Research and Development in Education* 27, (1994): 203–11.

Berg, I. "School Refusal and Truancy." *Archives of Disease in Childhood* 76, no. 2 (1997):90–2.

Capps, W. R. "The New Face of Truancy," *School Administrator* 60, no. 4 (2003):34.

Catalano, F. R., M. W. Arthur, J. D. Hawkins, L. Berglund, and J. J. Olson. "Comprehensive Community and School-Based Interventions to Prevent Antisocial Behavior." In *Serious and Violent Juvenile Offenders: Risk Factors and Successful Interventions*, edited by David Farrington and Rolf Loeber. Thousand Oaks, CA: Sage Publications, 1998.

Civil Rights Project Harvard University Conference. "Opportunities Suspended: The Devastating Consequences of Zero Tolerance and School Discipline Policies." 2000.

Dougherty, J. W. "Attending to Attendance." *Phi Delta Kappa Fastbacks* 450, (1999):7–49.

Dryfoos, Joy G. *Adolescents at Risk: Prevalence and Prevention*. New York: Oxford University Press, 1990.

Epstein, J. L., and S. B. Sheldon. "Present and Accounted For: Improving Student Attendance Through Family and Community Involvement." *Journal of* Educational Research 95, (2002):308–18.

Fein, D. J., Lee S. Wang, and E. S. Schofield. *Do Welfare Recipients' Children Have a School Attendance Problem?* Report prepared for the Delaware Health and Social Services Department, Cambridge, MA: Abt Associates, 1999.

Garry, E. M. "Truancy: First Step to a Lifetime of Problems." Washington, D.C.: U.S. Department of Justice, Office of Juvenile Justice and Delinquency Prevention, 1996.

Heaviside, S., C. Rowand, C. Williams, and E. Farris. "Violence and Discipline Problems in U. S. Public Schools: 1996–1997." Washington, D.C.: U. S. Department of Education, Office of Educational Research and Improvement, National Center for Education Statistics, 1998.

Huzinga, D., R. Loeber, and T. Thornberry. "Urban delinquency and Substance Abuse: Initial Findings." Washington, D.C.: U.S. Department of Justice, Office of Juvenile Justice and Delinquency Prevention, 1995.

Jones, L. R. "Ending School Truancy in One Step," *New Jersey Law Journal*. March 7, 2005.

Kaufman, P., M. N. Alt, and C. D. Chapman. "Dropout Rates in the United States 2000." Washington, D. C.: U. S. Department of Education. National Center for Education Statistics, 2001.

Kleine, P. A. "Chronic Absenteeism: A Community Issue." East Lansing, MI: National Center for Research on Teacher Learning, 1994.

Mogulescu, S., and H. J, Segal. "Approaches to Truancy Prevention." New York: Vera Institute of Justice, Youth Justice Program, 2002.

"No Show, No License." *Scholastic Scope* 53, no. 11:21.

Oman, R. F., K. R. McLeroy, S. Versely, C. B. Aspy, D. W. Smith, and D. A. Penn. "An Adolescent Age Group Approach to Examining Youth Risk Behaviors," *American Journal of Health Promotion* 16, (2002): 167–76.

Puzzanchera, C., A. L. Stahl, T. A. Finnegan, N. Tierney, and H. N. Snyder. "Juvenile Court Statistics 1998." Washington, D.C.: U.S. Department of Justice, Office of Juvenile Justice and Delinquency Prevention, 2003.

Rohrman, D. "Combating Truancy in Our Schools-A Community Effort." *NASSP Bulletin,* 76, no. 549 (1993): 40–51.

Rubin, H. G. "NYC Settles Lawsuit Alleging Students Were "Pushed Out" Education Daily 37, no. 6 (2004): 1–2.

Snyder, H. N., and M. Sickmund. "Juvenile Offenders and Victims: A National Report."

Washington, D.C.: U.S. Department of Justice, Office of Juvenile Justice and Delinquency Prevention, 1995.

Stover, D. "New Ways, More Reasons to Fight Truancy." *The Education Digest* 70, no. 5 (2005):4 8–52.

Strickland, V. P. *Attendance and Grade Point Average: A Study.* East Lansing, Ml: National Center for Research on Teacher Learning, 1998.

Teasley, M. L. "Absenteeism and Truancy: Risk, Protection, and Best Practice Implications for School Social Workers," *Children and Schools* 26, no. 2 (2004): 117–29.

Teevan, J. J., and H. B. Dryburgh. "First Person Accounts and Sociological Explanations of Delinquency." *Canadian Review of Sociology and Anthropology* 37, no. 1 (2000): 77–93.

US Department of Education. "Truancy Fact Sheet." 2016. https://www.education.com/reference/article/truancey-fact-sheet/

———. *Conditions of Education: 1993.* Washington, D. C.: US Department of Education, 1993.

Wandersman, A., and M. Nation. "Urban Neighborhoods and Mental Health: Psychological Contributions to Understanding Toxicity, Resilience, and Interventions." *American Psychologist* 53, (1998): 647–56.

Wright, J. "Rethinking Welfare School Attendance Policies." *Social Service Review* 79, no. 1 (2005): 2–27

Religion

How Do Beliefs Shape Behavior?

RELIGION

What role do a person's religious beliefs play in understanding their attitudes, values, beliefs, and behaviors? How does a person's socialization and family structure influence their religious beliefs? Is the United States a religious society or have technology and advancements in science caused a change in people's understanding of the world around them and their place in it? These are all questions posed by sociologists who study the role of religion in society.

Religion is a matter of faith, which can be defined as belief based on personal conviction rather than on scientific evidence. Some people with strong faiths may be disturbed by the thought of sociologists turning a scientific eye on what they hold sacred. However, a sociological study of religion is no threat to anyone's faith. Sociologists study religion just as we study the family or any other dimension of society. In this instance, it is to understand religious experiences around the world and how religion is tied to other social institutions. Sociologists make no judgments that a specific religion is right or wrong in terms of ultimate truth. Rather, they take a more holistic approach, asking why religions take a particular form in one society or another and how religious activity affects society as a whole.

Other topics in the sociology of religion include issues such as how religious Americans compare to citizens of other countries, which religions have the greatest popularity in the United States, what it means to be devoutly religious, and whether there is an actual trend towards secularization in this country.

The articles in this section explore a number of fascinating aspects of the role of religion in society. Paige Rawson examines how some religions address the issue of homosexuality in their churches. This is particularly true of Christian religions. As is noted in media accounts, this is a salient issue for some churches, as their ideology is often at odds with the notion of homosexuality. Brian Krawczyk examines the impact of the church in the transformation of a community. In his analysis he explores what types of influence a church can have in reshaping a culture and the sense of optimism about a community's future. Finally, I offer insight into one of the most fascinating developments in religion: the rise of the mega church. Why have they become so popular and garnered so much media attention? These and other questions will be addressed.

Inside Out/Side, In (side): Gender, Sexuality, Desire, and the Church

A. Paige Rawson, PhD

AT THE AGE of eleven, I cornered my mother for the second time with a question that would make any Southern Baptist parent shudder; at eight, it was Santa, three years later it was my sexuality, and in both cases her reassurance was ruined by my reality. Even as I was unconvinced by stories of some old white guy who yearly spans the globe in a twenty-four-hour period, I was equally confounded by my gender and sexuality in light of the Church's teaching. This was not the first time I'd had queries about gender or sex and God, it was simply the first time I'd found the courage to ask about my sexuality. I've always been curious. Since I can remember, I have wondered: Why is God "He"? Why was Adam created first? Why did the serpent approach Eve and why did she take the first bite of the "apple"? Why does God favor men? Why were there only male disciples? And, of course, why can't women be pastors, preachers, or priests?

While I will not be able to address all these questions, in this article, I will address the central issue I have struggled with since my youth, which is in some way related to all the questions: Can one be a Christian and LGBTQ? Since this is a sociology textbook, we will consider the Church's historical stance on same-sex love and LGBTQ people as it relates to social norms, the construction of gender, sexuality, and desire, and the constitution and policing of certain behaviors, practices, and identities in order to create what is considered "normal" and what is considered "deviant."

The United States of America may overtly claim separation of church and state, but due to the historical collusion of the Church and Western European empires, it is necessary to consciously consider the influence of the Church upon societies, then and now. So after I share a bit more of my story, I will unpack this important entanglement en route to some important conclusions about Christianity and the LGBTQ community in the twenty-first century.

Everything changed the day I uttered the words, "Mom, am I gay?" My unsuspecting mother quickly assured me I was not. However, inside, I knew what she could not see from the outside. Unfortunately, it would take me another fifteen years before I was ready to come out. In that decade and a half, I kicked it into overdrive; there is very little I do without passion or zeal and my faith was no exception. I memorized the Bible as my "life manual" and hid any and all feelings and romantic relationships I had with women. I wore a giant cross and dated jocks who were equally as on fire for Christ; but it was all a façade.

Outside I had it all together; inside I was riddled with doubt and plagued by fear and shame. After college, I moved to Singapore to work in a church; I was "answering God's call," and hoping I would evade greater temptation. As they say, however, "wherever you go, there you are," so rather than making things easier, the change of location left me feeling even more isolated and afraid. I played it straight until I was compelled (what I understood to be conviction from the Holy Spirit) to confess to the pastor of the church I was serving. At that point, everything changed, and not for the better. My secret was out, and it felt as though everyone knew and was disgusted by me. I was told repeatedly that I was "oppressed" or "possessed by a demon of homosexuality and a demon of unbelief," and I spent the next five years in ex-gay ministries and undergoing exorcisms, Christian counseling, and reparative therapy. I became convinced that if homosexuality was a sin and a sickness—as I'd been told time and again—and one could be delivered or healed, it was going to be me!

Stories such as mine are not uncommon. You may have heard or read or may even know someone who has experienced something similar, and it is tragically possible that this person did not survive. Ironically, while the Church's teachings on LGBTQ issues almost drove me to end my life, other teachings also deterred me from it—growing up hearing that "people who commit suicide go to Hell" prevented me from even entertaining the idea. Now, while many people who have walked in my shoes were placed on the path by their parent(s) or another concerned adult before they were old enough to make the decision for themselves, I had just turned twenty-two when I sought reparative therapy, and I did so willingly.

While I was inarguably influenced by my faith community and my family, I was coerced but never forced. I was simply acting, by faith, on what I had heard all my life and come to believe as *the* truth. Namely, that woman was created to be the feminine counterpart to man, and man alone was created in the image of God (who was unquestionably male and masculine); woman, then, was and is to willingly submit to man as his helpmate—a virtuous wife who will become a homemaker, bear children, and honor her husband above all else. Accordingly, God's perfect design is heterosexuality, and anyone who believes or practices otherwise is disordered and under the influence of the Devil.

I currently teach the Bible, religion, and philosophy at a liberal arts university in North Carolina, and I work with students who hold the above to be true, just as I did at their age. I often wonder, in fact, had my life not changed so drastically at twenty-six, might I still hold those beliefs? I moved back to the United States after living in Singapore for three years, and two years after my return I was hospitalized; a month later I was diagnosed with Crohn's Disease. The diagnosis forced me to face my own mortality, not to mention the tremendous traumatic and psychosomatic effects of the teachings I had once held so dear. What I had been taught as truth by well-meaning, loving, genuine Christians, had betrayed me. In that time, I came to see that *their* truth was for me a lie, which led to pain, separation, and death rather than healing, connection, and life. I am absolutely convinced that had I not come to embrace myself and my story, the silence, self-rejection, fear, and the very lies that masqueraded as truth would have killed me.

Once I awoke from the nightmare that had become my life, I quit my job at the church and moved to the one place I was sure was safe for LGBTQ people like me: San Francisco. I got a job at a coffee shop, enrolled in graduate school, and began studying sexuality, religion, and the Bible from the other side. I created community with other outsiders who found a way to remain inside the Church; people who believed the Church was originally founded by "deviants" just like us. After spending a quarter of a century learning how much God hated me for my gender nonconformity and my sexual deviance, I began to embrace myself. After all, maybe God could actually love me "Just As I Am."

In this article, I utilize my experience as an ostensible outsider on the inside to think about not only the Church's historical stance on gender, sexuality, and desire, but the way in which the Church's teaching has dictated what is and is not socially acceptable. In the first section, I define the frameworks I employ and interrogate the terms around which this chapter centers: gender, sexuality, and desire, on the one hand, the Church, the Bible, and the politics of interpretation, on the other. In the second section, I broadly map the development of the Church, its (ironic) rise to power, its foundational doctrines, and its intimate relationship to politics and economies of thought and commerce, highlighting the ways in which the Church has historically represented, reinforced, and even reified social norms—particularly those within countries and cultures affected by Western European (neo)colonialism.

Next, I evaluate the Church's traditional teachings on gender, sexuality, and desire, which have established a gendered and racialized hierarchy wherein primarily white males are attributed the sole authority as divinely authorized intermediaries between God and humanity. Of course, the Church's teaching has been established on biblical doctrine. Therefore, in the third section, I address the biblical texts upon which this teaching is ostensibly based—the so-called "Clobber Passages"—arguing that rather than universal mandates from God, these texts were written in particular sociohistorical contexts and should be read accordingly. In the final section, I offer an analysis of the politics and ideologies that have legitimated and propagated this structure of intelligibility and conclude with some reflections on the way forward.

GENDER, SEXUALITY, AND DESIRE: THE CHURCH, THE BIBLE, AND THE POLITICS OF INTERPRETATION

In sociology, there are three primary theoretical frameworks through which to think about society and social interactions (structural-functional, social conflict, and symbolic interactionism). In a more general sense, frameworks are structures that support any sort of system, object, or text, and they directly influence how and what we perceive. In fact, law professor and sociologist, *Kimberlé Crenshaw*, pointed out that we may hear or read information but will discard it unless we have the proper mental framework to hold it. One of the frameworks, which is deconstructed in the work of gender theorists and LGBTQ scholars is what we could call *binary hierarchy*. In such a dualistic structure of intelligibility, rather than perceiving two elements in an egalitarian relationship, these entities or ideas are set in contrast and the primary term is privileged and prioritized over the other.

In other words, the first concept is "on top" and, accordingly, holds power within this structure while the second is "on bottom" and does not. Some examples are public/private, good/bad, man/woman, masculine/feminine, white/black, self/other, straight/gay, and us/them. Because they *appear* to order reality, binary hierarchies such as these appear natural. However, such frameworks are constructed rather than essential. That is to say, though binary hierarchies may give the impression of inherency, they only *seem* to be natural because we live in a society that conditions, or socializes, us to identify phenomena as such, since these binary oppositions define the framework (or structure of intelligibility) through which reality is constructed and, therefore, interpreted. Those born into Western European influenced societies were raised to see the world in this way; as a result, critically analyzing this structure requires us to step back and to think like a sociologist. Before we dive into our critical sociological analysis, however, there are two sets of concepts, which should be explained directly. The first group includes gender, sex, and sexuality and the second, the Church, the Bible, and interpretation.

GENDER, SEX, AND SEXUALITY

One of the strengths and benefits of sociology is that it is interdisciplinary. In sociological research, one is not limited to a single set of scholarly discourses or resources, but may incorporate various theories, sciences, and perspectives across disciplines. In this way, the everyday sociologist is able to approach complex notions such as gender, sex, and sexuality from various angles and multiple layers. Gender is typically conceptualized as a set of traits, characteristics, or behaviors associated with a certain biological sex. In Western European societies gender has historically been confined to "masculine and feminine," has viewed variance as deviant, and has limited bodies to one or the other "corresponding" gender. While this paradigm is daily being challenged by research across the arts and sciences, it is still the most prevalent framework.

Since the inception of modern (Western) medicine, the doctor delivering the baby was also tasked with identifying and/or attributing the child's sex and, therefore, "her" or "his" gender. Sex, then, has been conceived of as biological and is most often determined according to the perceived primary sex characteristics, which are those directly associated with reproduction. Bodies with ambiguous genitalia, or intersex bodies, have been and are most often still subjected to a scale and then assigned the sex and gender. Sexuality has been presumed, particularly in Western European societies, to operate according to the gender binary and to coincide or agree with a person's gender and sex; this alignment is traditionally viewed as an expression of one's gender where a normative male should be masculine and sexually aroused by females and vice versa. Sexuality refers to a person's sexual or erotic attraction and is often denoted by the term *orientation*. Interestingly, the term *homosexual* did not even appear in the English vernacular until the late nineteenth century—the same time as the term *heterosexual*, because they were used over and against one another to identify two oppositional identities.

THE CHURCH

With an estimated 2.22 billion followers, Christianity is the largest religious group in the world. Christianity and "the Church" are used interchangeably to identify this global collective that is not so much a *what* as a *who*. The Old English word *church* is a derivation of the Greek word *kyrios*, which means "master" or "lord." So the roots of *church* are explicitly linked to what biblical scholar Elisabeth Schüssler Fiorenza has deemed kyriarchy, which "is best theorized as a complex pyramidal system of intersecting multiplicative social structures of superordination and subordination, of ruling and oppression" (Fiorenza 2010). As an improper noun, the word signifies an edifice and also a specific church, denomination, or sect. When capitalized, the term *Church* represents a sociocultural religious body made up of persons who understand themselves to have a unified collective identity according to a few general characteristics. All people who are members of the

Church (1) identify with Jesus Christ as his followers and, though they often distinguish between their group, type, variety, or denominational affiliation, consider themselves "Christians;" (2) worship the God represented in the Bible as the divine parent (or "Father") of Jesus and supreme authority in the world; and (3) affirm the Bible as the authoritative Word of God (though what this means is subject to interpretation).

Beyond this universal definition, each specific church and/or denomination has its own particularity, which is often identified through the church body's unique by-laws or doctrinal statements. Interestingly, in the first century, the movement was quite diverse. In the early fourth century, the Roman Emperor Constantine unified Rome under the one Roman Catholic Church—still the largest Christian church—and over the past century and a half other churches and denominations have diversified, emerging as people disagreed over issues related to politics, interpretation, doctrine, traditions, practices, and the like. Churches and denominations are defined by their theologies, teachings, and traditions.

Each group also has its own set of expectations and involves particular requirements; in order to be an active and legitimate member of the community (or "in-group"), one must follow certain rules. These laws or norms may be enforced by the governing body, but they might also be latent and prescribed implicitly. Because participation is primarily voluntary, as in other such social organizations, there are many more implicit norms than explicit; and one of the implicit requirements of most churches is heterosexuality. Accordingly, adherents are expected to *only* experience attraction toward and pursue intimate relationships with members of the perceived opposite gender/sex *and* to perform and, therefore, conform to the gender/sex they were assigned at birth. While some Protestant denominations have voted to include LGBTQ people and even to officiate same-sex marriages, the majority of Christian churches have not.

THE BIBLE

Literary theorist Stanley Fish coined the term *interpretive communities* in reference to churches and/or groups of people who read and interpret the Bible collectively (Fish 1982). Each church, then, is a distinct interpretive community and those communities are subdivided (and at times organized) into various smaller groups (i.e., committees, Bible studies, Sunday School classes, cell groups, family units, or other forms of social clustering). The Bible is the primary sacred text of Christianity and it can be found in the pews of every Church, the homes of most Christians, and the bedside table of just about any hotel room south of Pennsylvania. The Bible is a collection of texts written across the Mediterranean region and over hundreds, if not thousands, of years. Through councils, conflicts, and finally consensus, a group of men with great ecclesial influence settled on the "canon"—those writings deemed authoritative. While churches may differ on the exact arrangement and inclusion, each divides the Bible into the "Old" and "New" Testaments. The Old Testament was inherited from Judaism while the New Testament is unique to Christianity.

THE BIBLE VS. CHURCH TRADITION—THE POLITICS OF INTERPRETATION

I often talk with students about the way in which interpretation is an active part of our everyday life, but most of the time it is happening unconsciously. We are constantly receiving information through our senses and those stimuli must be interpreted in order for us to make meaning in our world. Two of the most common explanations I hear when I ask undergraduate students why they believe a certain thing about the Bible are: "I don't know, I just do" and "I believe it because that's what it says." Having spent eight years as a pastor before becoming a professor, I am aware that this is a prevalent perspective preached from the pulpit and, therefore, promoted in many churches, so I am not surprised by this response. In fact, when I was in college, I responded much the same way. Twenty years later, however, I am concerned that it is still so difficult, even threatening, for many of my students to take a critical step back in order to question the assumptions of their upbringing. Nothing exists in a vacuum. Even sacred texts are contingent upon context.

In order to think of the Bible more complexly, then, scholars consider the Bible in terms of three worlds that exist simultaneously behind, inside, and in front of the text. The Bible is undoubtedly a sacred text and, like any other book, it was written at a certain place, in a certain time, and for a particular purpose. Of course, because it is composed of so many different texts, and is a composite, it would be more accurate to say it was written in many places, at different times, for a number of purposes; not to mention the fact that it was copied and edited innumerable times over hundreds of years.

What this means is that different versions of the Bible actually contain different translations and sometimes very different information, not intended to be applied centuries after these texts were written. The world "behind" the text is what scholars understand to be the social context or contexts in which the Bible was written and, therefore, they employ historical critical methods in their analyses. The Bible is literature, and scholars apply literary critical tools in order to analyze what they consider to be the world "inside" the Bible. In this way, they think about things such as a story's characters and its plot, as well as its tensions. The final and arguably the most important influence upon the interpretive process is what scholars have deemed the world "in front" of the text. When one considers this world, she, he, or they, are looking at the context of the person or community interpreting the Bible and are attentive to the ways in which the reader's individual experience and communal context influence her, his, or their interpretation of the text.

One final point to be emphasized about the Bible and its interpretation, in light of the three worlds of the text, is that one may never simply read the Bible at face value. Just as it was not written in a vacuum, we cannot read the Bible (or any text) independent of our culture, biases, and preconceptions—we are always reading, as we are living, under their influence. To say the Bible is a complex, layered, and theologically robust text, is an understatement. Even as there is no way to fully understand another human being (or ourselves), due to the processes of socialization and the subconscious, the words that exist on the pages of the Bible will never be identical to those read or heard.

There are too many variables involved to ever establish an absolutely accurate and viable interpretation of biblical texts. Another major variance regards ancient (oral and figurative) versus modern (literal and literary) frameworks; this major difference demands that the contemporary reader set aside her, his, or their post-Enlightenment predisposition toward rationalism and empiricism. Since this task is nearly impossible, the responsible reader must at least remember that the authors of the biblical text wrote almost two thousand years ago with no intention of being read in the twenty-first century (much less guiding millennials)—most of Jesus's followers at the time believed the world would end before their lives did. In this way, then, the Bible must be taken seriously without having to be interpreted literally. In considering how we might take the Bible seriously, without necessarily taking it literally, we must also consider the way in which ideology influences the interpretation of the Bible, as well as the translation and transmission of one particular perspective over another—this, of course, is largely a matter of politics and power.

THE AUTHORITY OF THE CHURCH: PATRIARCHY, POWER, AND PERFORMATIVITY

While Jesus Christ is recognized as the founder and figurehead of Christianity, the religion finds its roots in an Ancient Near Eastern cult that would evolve into

Judaism. Interestingly, much like heterosexuality was only identified and named in relation to homosexuality, historians have argued that while Judaism predates Christianity by hundreds of years, it was cultural and did not gain its status as a religion until Christianity came to define itself over and against its parent tradition, establishing itself as a movement entirely independent of Judaism—a process that happened around the fourth century, when Constantine ruled the Roman Empire. One might say Judaism began with a small nomadic tribe living around contemporary Israel-Palestine, who called themselves "Israel," worshipped the god YHWH and the goddess ASHRH, and shared various oral traditions that would eventually be collected and recorded after their temple was destroyed and a significant number of their community was enslaved in Babylon. The Hebrew Bible (which Christians renamed the Old Testament) is a collection of the folktales, traditions, poems, proverbs, and apocalypses orally transmitted by these people who have also been called "Hebrews."

This community, which was itself a composite, would eventually rebuild their temple only to see it destroyed again by the Roman Empire in 70 CE. It was not long before this traumatic event that the Galilean Rabbi, known as Jesus of Nazareth, was performing miraculous feats and teaching about the Kingdom of God as a way of life. While Jesus taught the law given by God to Moses (whose name means "Messiah" in Hebrew), it is written that he believed "the greatest commandment" is to love God and others "as you love yourself" (Mark 12:28–34; Luke 10:27; Matthew 22:37), which was his interpretation of an ancient Hebrew commandment (cf. Deuteronomy 6:5).

The life, teachings, and miracles of Jesus are recounted in four books of the New Testament, which are collectively called Gospels, from the Greek work *euangelion* ("good news"). Each individual account offers a slightly different perspective on Jesus, but all seem to agree on a few central ideas: in particular, that the Rabbi's teachings were so unconventional that he was persecuted by the Roman Empire as well as teachers and practitioners of his own (Jewish) culture. In fact, his teachings and practices are what led him to death by crucifixion. Much of what churches now practice and teach comes not from the teachings of Jesus, but the writings of Paul—a Jewish Jesus follower and apostle—who believed Jesus was the Christ (which means "Messiah" in Greek) and the so-called Church Fathers—the men who held authority in the early Church. Paul has had such a profound impact upon Christianity that one might even say Christianity would not be Christianity without Paul—on account of his divine calling to preach the good news (*euangelion*) of Jesus Christ to non-Jewish Gentiles, which led to numerous missionary journeys and epistles.

All of Jesus's teachings and miracles, and his life and his death, have been filtered through Paul. Of course, the Paul we read in the New Testament is not unfiltered either. While we have access to the letters he wrote various churches, these writings have been heavily edited. The Bible's scribes determined what would and would not be included in these texts and in the fifth century CE the canon was determined by some of the later Church Fathers. Prior to this decision, numerous councils had been held wherein the heads of the Catholic Church—who were all men and many of whom were deemed the Church's Fathers—gathered to determine the creeds, conventions, and theologies of Christianity.

The choices made by these powerful men have defined Christian orthodoxy, or right belief. Rather than a Church leader, however, the first council (at Nicaea) was convoked by the Roman Emperor Constantine. In fact, once he instituted the Christianization and, therefore, greater unification of the Roman Empire in the early fourth century, these ecumenical councils made all the Church's most important decisions. Constantine's rule undeniably established and secured the relationship between the Roman Empire and the Church; the authority of Rome and the authority of the Catholic Church henceforth became synonymous. Ironically, a movement begun in the first century by a Galilean peasant, which was anti-Rome and arguably anti-imperial, was—by the early fourth century—the very tool through which the Roman Empire colonized lands and people.

Now, while the term *colonization*, like the term *homosexuality*, postdates the Bible, the process is as old as empire itself, and one could argue Rome was one of its most effective implementers. (In fact, its reinterpretation and redeployment of the message of Jesus may be one of the most convincing arguments for this case.) Colonization is, at its most basic, the process of establishing a colony, and it historically entails a more powerful entity acquiring territory from a weaker entity, typically by force. This process not only entails the appropriation of land but the extrication of goods and services, as well as the acquiescence and often absolute annihilation of the cultural practices and traditions of the people previously occupying this land (if not the people themselves).

One of the most insidious results of colonization, and particularly of colonization by Western European empires, is the loss of many of the rich and diverse traditions, practices, and relics from societies and cultures around the world. Due to the collusion of Christianity and various empires since Rome, an especially unfortunate and all-too-ironic legacy of the life of Jesus of Nazareth, and his message of loving others in spite of difference, is its appropriation by a patriarchal hegemony that has historically operated with the intent to level difference and derogate diversity in favor of deference to its traditions, values, beliefs, and practices, as well as its primary framework: hierarchical binaries. The predominant hierarchical binaries that characterize the collusion of Christianity and Western European empires define the social norms in all its colonized territories and place Western European powers on the side of God (as man) and, therefore, the good, towering over other religions, cultures, practices, and peoples, who are equated with evil and other weak and/or negative qualities, ideas, or entities.

Colonization, then, mandates that one perform according to this binary system. The nefarious repercussion of this relationship is the way in which this particular framework has kept almost all the explicit authority in the Church in the hands of cisgender, heterosexual males, which has thus relegated women to second class status and shamed and shunned LGBTQ people.

CHURCH HIERARCHY AND THE BINARY GENDER SYSTEM

It has become a bit of a truism to say that those in power do not surrender that power easily, if at all. If we take this to be accurate, it is no wonder that women do not hold great official authority in the Catholic Church or many of the largest Protestant denominations worldwide. The Church Fathers did not desire to share their authority with women and, as a result, Church tradition has dictated the leadership and, therefore, trajectory of the Church across time and place. Interestingly, however, when one looks to the precedent set by Jesus in the Bible and in other noncanonical gospels (those deemed heretical by the Church Fathers and so not included in the canon), there were undeniably women who held leadership positions in the early Church. In fact, we read in the New Testament that Jesus himself appeared to and entrusted the message of his resurrection to women before men. (See Matthew 28; Mark 16; Luke 24; and John 20.) In the Church, dominated by cisgender males, it would appear that Jesus's practices, and even the egalitarian approach taken by his earliest followers, have been dismissed and almost entirely disregarded to maintain a very particular—patriarchal and heterosexist—type of order in the Church. I believe this bias has not only been detrimental for the Church but has led to its demise and has the capacity to destroy it, unless it is radically disrupted. In order to do so effectively, we must identify and critically analyze the ways in which hierarchical binaries, and specifically the binary gender system, have led to the misinterpretation of the Bible, the misrepresentation of God, the disfiguration of the body of Christ, and the inexcusable shaming and shunning of LGBTQ people.

THE AUTHORITY OF THE BIBLE; THE AUTHORITY OF (LGBTQ) EXPERIENCE

The Bible and Humans: The Clobber Passages, Queries, and Queer Interventions

As I shared, after I came out, I moved to California—searching for LGBTQ friendly communities, not to mention more tolerant congregations with more inclusive theologies. Prior to my exodus, however, I began to read the work of pastors, prophets, and poststructuralists, who had already been interrogating the oppression and dehumanization of LGBTQ folks, both inside and outside the Church.

Since the early 1990s, theorizing of gender as performance has exploded. Judith Butler's *Gender Trouble* is typically recognized as the text that incited this trend. Butler (herself influenced by Foucault's use of Nietzsche) argued that gender is "the discursive/cultural means by which 'sexed nature' or 'a natural sex' is produced and established as 'prediscursive,' prior to culture, a politically neutral surface on which culture acts" (Butler 1990). In so doing, she exposed the way in which gender—as with sexuality and desire—is composed of culturally scripted acts, not biological facts. That is to say, there is no stable gender or sexual identity, there are only sociocultural scripts that, when performed over and again across time, feign stability. The means by which a human being is either "properly" male *or* female—masculine or feminine respectively—as well as whom one should desire, has become so deeply entrenched in Western European society that these roles in fact *appear* to be static, substantive, and natural—as if they had existed as such since the origin of time itself or since creation.

It is the idea of origins and that gender, sex, sexuality, and desire were clearly delineated "in the beginning," which leads me to the Bible, Creation, and those biblical passages affectionately deemed "the clobber passages." Churches often claim they hold anti-LGBTQ views and prohibit same-sex sexual relations due to the Bible's teaching and God's creative design and desire for humanity. However, personal, cultural, and ideological biases undeniably precondition biblical interpretation.

There are seven passages traditionally considered to be homophobic and anti-LGBTQ; they are Genesis 1:27, Genesis 19 (cf. 18:20), Leviticus 18:22 (20:13), Deuteronomy 23:17–18, Romans 1:26–27, 1 Corinthians 6:9, and 1 Timothy 1:10. Contrary to conservative Christian interpretations of these passages, over the past few decades, LGBTQ biblical scholars, theologians, and ministers, such as Marcella Althaus-Reid, Ellen Armour, Patrick Chen, Bob Goss, Deryn Guest, Teresa Hornsby, Virginia Ramey Molenkott, Ken Stone, Justin Tanis, and Mona West, as well as their allies in Christian ministry, have sought to dispel this misinformed view, to identify the way in which the cultural context of all biblical texts is entirely contingent upon their historical framework, and to provide alternative readings to the misinterpretations and misrepresentations of these passages, which are LGBTQ affirming rather than shaming or condemning.

The Bible was written around the Mediterranean over the course of almost a thousand years, the Bible's authors and editors were men (because women were generally uneducated), and their primary concerns were (1) constructing their communal identity as the people of God over and against other pagan cultures and (2) maintaining order within their own social group. In the time the Bible was recorded, one's identity and value were determined according to his or her cultural status, where elite men were at the top of the hierarchy and female slaves were at the very bottom. People did not conceptualize identity in terms of sexuality or sexual orientation because who one had sexual relations with was not a marker of identity—it was a behavior. The idea of homosexuality as an identity, therefore, was entirely foreign to the biblical world.

Since we do not have the time to deconstruct each of the seven passages, I will address the larger issue LGBTQ Christians emphasize. Rather than interpreting the clobber passages as condemning homosexuality specifically and more generally excluding LGBTQ people from Christian fellowship unless they repent and change their behavior, LGBTQ Christians and their allies highlight the overall message of the Bible and the Good News of Jesus, which is one of love and acceptance. Each of these texts, like all texts in the Bible, represent the particular biases of their author and his community, and in the case of all the biblical texts that appear to be about homosexuality, the actual issues at hand were either the maintenance (or establishment) of social order or procreation (the means to growth as a community). Laws or stories about those who have transgressed (or sinned) operate not only to perpetuate the established sociocultural structures but are often instituted to create them. Just like the existence of LGBTQ people shines a light on lived reality in distinction from ideology, so the laws instituted in the Bible reflect a culture in which those in power wanted to create order through the prohibition and enforcement of particular cultural practices.

Why would you institute a law to ensure a particular practice if people were already naturally performing that behavior? Or why prohibit an activity unless it was in some way threatening official power or its maintenance of order? Unfortunately, due to the pervasion of patriarchy in Judeo-Christian tradition and Church polity, men and women have been restricted to very specific gender roles, which are often located in the second creation story of Genesis—Adam and Eve in the Garden of Eden—where man appears to have been created in God's image and woman led to the "fall" of humankind. If we are not cognizant of the three worlds of the text (behind, inside, and in front), we might interpret this literally, rather than realizing the story was written by a community trying to answer existential questions and create a narrative to support their (hierarchical) social order, where man rules over woman and woman's desire is for man (see Genesis 3:16).

The portrayals of gender and sexuality pervasive in popular culture continue to be inflected by restrictive gender binaries and normative modes and models of intelligibility, which can indubitably be found in the Bible. However, while the Church (and its biases) may have had tremendous influence upon culture and views regarding gender, sexuality, and desire over the past two thousand years, with the exponential influx of information and capacity to communicate with various peoples and cultures around the world, social perspectives and practices are shifting, and the Church is losing its foothold. In fact, this is one of the reasons Bishop Jack Spong wrote a book entitled, *Why Christianity Must Change or Die*, which was published a decade after *Living in Sin? A Bishop Rethinks Homosexuality*.

In the former, Spong (1990), a Bishop in the Episcopal Church, argues that as culture is shifting, the Church must reevaluate and revise some of its most deeply entrenched, misinformed, and condemning ideologies and traditions. In the latter, he describes his own path toward embracing gay and lesbian people and ultimately encourages the entire Church to do likewise. Spong is not the only Christian minister who has written books in support of full LGBTQ inclusion within the Church; another is Jack Rogers. Rogers, a Presbyterian minister, shares his own personal journey and interpretation of the clobber passages in *Jesus, the Bible, and Homosexuality*. His argument, like Spong's, is based not only on the radical love of Jesus—who never once spoke directly about sexuality or gender—but on his understanding of the Bible reflecting cultural norms regarding social status rather than God's views on someone's gender identity or sexual preference.

While official Church authority may appear to institute and maintain the established social order, LGBTQ theologians, biblical scholars, ministers, and their allies, for the most part, understand Jesus's ministry, teaching, cohort, and performance of the miraculous to have been a politically charged disruption of social norms and the reason why he was crucified. Through often provocative means, LGBTQ theologians and biblical scholars draw our attention to what the Church has traditionally denied or swept under the rug; namely, the queer origins of Christianity. Utilizing the work of queer theorists, like Judith Butler, they expose the constructedness of the very idea of origin, essence, or fixed (gendered, racialized, classed, etc.) identity. In all his inordinance and indeterminacy, Jesus performed a countercultural existence, which was resurrected in the lives of his followers. Accordingly, LGBTQ scholars claim the disruption of norms, not their maintenance, to be the legacy of Christianity and, therefore, challenge the Church to embrace, not exile, queer Christians.

CONCLUDING REMARKS

I cannot help but wonder, if Jesus stepped into 2018 and saw the sort of judgment and intolerance the Church has shown to LGBTQ people, WWJD? (What Would Jesus Do?) Admittedly, life is messy, and it seems to be a messy sort of solidarity to which Jesus called others. In fact, when considered through the experience and interpretations of the LGBTQ community, the Church is both the issue and its antidote. If Jesus was interpreting and embodying the ancient Hebrew teaching that love is the highest law, the early Church would have undoubtedly been a queer space filled with deviants and society's outcasts.

Jesus himself, as represented in the gospels, was a deviant and a sociopolitical revolutionary, and the Church, despite claims to the contrary, has always been composed of the very bodies it has officially identified as deviant and threatening. What LGBTQ biblical scholars, theologians, ministers, and allies highlight—that queer bodies are important precisely because of their capacity to disrupt cultural convention—is that those whom the Church has rejected might be the very ones who will save it.

LGBTQ people are a legitimate and necessary part of the body of Christ particularly because they fail official systems and expose their constructedness, thereby challenging us to question: if the system is capable of breaking down, is anyone truly capable of perfectly performing the standard? When we interpret LGBTQ lives through the teaching of Jesus, queer obstinacy and provocations might instead be interpreted as a refusal of oppressive rules and roles that delimit divine creation and creativity. And this refusal of the hegemony of homogeny is precisely, I would argue, what LGBTQ folks offer a Church so desperately in need of diversity.

By highlighting the ways in which the lines that institute intelligibility are constructed and perpetually disrupted, LGBTQ people offer all humans the opportunity to live beyond the restrictive binaries that threaten to divide and destroy us. The Church is undoubtedly a complex institution, one which has oppressed *and* liberated, and represented various interpretations of the same text, reflecting the way in which no single identity, ideology, or ethic can be absolute or universal; *life is*, and everywhere life is, it is in all ways always diverse, dissident, and downright dirty.

Since we have no access to the original ancient texts found in the Bible—only copies of copies—and we don't inhabit the same temporal or cultural space as the authors, how might we better understand our reactions and respond more ethically? At the very least, thinking with and through LGBTQ experience and LGBTQ affirming biblical interpretation might just help the Church and all of us to be a little more aware of and tender toward the messiness of life and the ways in which, as hard as we may try, none of us conforms absolutely to the prescribed rules or (gender) roles, regardless of our culture, race, or place.

I'd like to conclude with a quote from Judith Butler (2009), who writes,

> If we accept the insight that our very survival depends not on the policing of a boundary—the strategy of a certain sovereign in relation to its territory—but on recognizing how we are bound up with others, then this leads us to reconsider the way in which we conceptualize the body.

Ultimately, the Church, as the Bible, exists as an enigma; for even as it has historically represented the perpetuation of the binary gender system, homophobia, transphobia, misogyny, and even racism, it ensures their impossibility. After all, the Church understands itself as a body and claims to be the Body of Christ in the world (1 Corinthians 12:27) and the Bible contains one of the most egalitarian statements of any ancient sacred text: "In Christ there is neither Jew nor Greek, slave nor free, male and female" (Galatians 3:28).

As LGBTQ Christian advocates and allies have asserted for years, the Church is a champion of love and liberation as it blurs lines and betrays rigid binaries, emphasizing community, interdependence, and incarnation. (The very idea of Jesus as God-Man blurs the definitive boundary between human and divine, power and vulnerability!) Therefore, if the Church wants to survive and thrive in the twenty-first century, I believe it is called now more than ever to embody the radical challenge of Jesus Christ and to live in love and harmony as responsible citizens of this, our shared, world, working to understand *what* got us here and *how* we all might intentionally live together toward a better tomorrow.

Bibliography

Butler, Judith. *Gender Trouble: Feminism and the Subversion of Identity*. New York: Routledge, 1990.

Fiorenza, Elisabeth Schussler. *In Memory of Her: A Feminist Theological Reconstruction of Christian Origins*. London: Crossroad/Herder and Herder, 2010.

Foucault, Michel. *The History of Sexuality. Volume I*. New York: Vintage Books, 1978.

Goss, Robert E., and Mona West. *Take Back the Word: A Queer Reading of the Bible*. Cleveland: The Pilgrim Press, 2000.

Rogers, Jack. *Jesus, the Bible, and Homosexuality: Explode the Myths, Heal the Church.* Louisville: Westminster John Knox, 2009.

Spong, John Shelby. *Living in Sin? A Bishop Rethinks Homosexuality.* New York: HarperCollins, 1990.

Fish, Stanley. *Is there a Text in This Class? The Authority of Interpretive Communities.* Boston, MA: Harvard University Press, 1982.

Grace for Monroe

Brian Krawczyk

Never again will you be called "The Forsaken [Abandoned] City" or "The Desolate Land." Your new name will be "The City of God's Delight" and "The Bride of God," for the LORD delights in you and will claim you as his bride.

— Isaiah 62:4

CAN SOMEONE TRULY MAKE A DIFFERENCE WHERE THEY LIVE?

This was the question burning in our hearts in 2012 when my wife, Sadie, and I decided to move our family of five (with one more on the way) to a small town in Walton County, Georgia, an area far enough outside the borders of Metro Atlanta to still be considered rural, but not quite far enough away to escape the ever-expanding tentacles of suburban sprawl. To be completely honest, Monroe was not a place we had ever imagined investing our lives, resources, and energy. In fact, we had just been through a long process of exploring the very real possibility of moving our family across the globe to London.

We had contemplated living in places like Los Angeles, New York, or even downtown Atlanta, but never Monroe! The logical thought was if we wanted to maximize the influence and impact of our lives, we needed to plant ourselves in a fast-paced, population-dense, cultural center. Armed with a sociology degree from Furman University and a theology degree from Fuller Theological Seminary, we knew what we wanted to do with our lives, we just didn't know where. Nor did we have any clue when we agreed to help a small struggling church plant for the summer that we would end up discovering the perfect environment to live out our dreams and passions—to see people transformed in a way that transforms a place.

Monroe itself is a city with a rich, yet tragic, history. On one hand, it is known as the "City of Governors" because of the number of Georgia governors who have claimed Monroe as home. On the other hand, it was also the location of the last mass-lynching in America, a crime that deeply divided the community in 1946, and still remains an open wound because no one has ever been brought to justice.[1] One of the governors born in Monroe, Henry McDaniel, helped found the Georgia Institute of Technology, while another governor who resided in Monroe, Wilson Lumpkin, launched the Trail of Tears. And yet it was Lumpkin's daughter, Martha, born in Monroe, who was the namesake of Marthasville, the original name of the city that would eventually be called Atlanta, "the city too busy to hate."

Monroe, as we found it, was a town filled with kind and warm-hearted people, gifted entrepreneurs and creative artists, and amazing potential for beauty and growth. At the same time, we quickly discovered deeply enmeshed generational poverty, painful and often unspoken divisions along socioeconomic and racial lines, as well as long-simmering and even destructive negative perceptions of the town and its people. In fact, when we first started exploring the possibility of moving to Monroe, the majority of what we heard was, "Why in the world would you want to move there?!" In general, the common perception of Monroe was a lot of poverty, a lot of crime, struggling schools, and, apart from a cute downtown, not much happening. While there were some we met who loved their town, and especially the nostalgic glory days of the past, it seemed to us at the time that Monroe was the place everyone was moving *away* from, not into!

Eventually we got so tired of hearing all the negatives about the place we felt like God was leading us that we made the decision to only speak blessings, not curses. We discovered that in the same way a person can take on an identity, a sense of who they are and their significance and role in the world, so can a place. This is definitely not unique to Monroe. Like the people who dwell there, every city on earth is a glorious mess, an intertwined mix of beauty and brokenness. Some choose to ignore one and focus on the other, either idealizing or vilifying a place. The third, and I believe better, way is to take a brutally honest look at the inevitable brokenness while at the same time identifying the positive attributes and gifting inherent in that location, and then envision the kind of place it could be if the brokenness was made whole and the positives were fully actualized.

Sure, there are sad and dark parts of Monroe's history. Acknowledge it all, but don't just dig up dirt—look for the gold. And do this for the individuals who live there as well. In a small town everyone seems to know each other's stories, and we all have sordid chapters in our past. But we are called to honor all people—be honest about the bad as well as the good, forgive, extend grace,

---

1   For more info see Laura Wexler's *Fire in a Canebrake: The Last Mass Lynching in America*, (Scribner, 2003).

and envision and speak a positive identity and future. That is what it means to bless. *But how could we go from just declaring the positive potential of a place to helping make it a reality?*

At the time of our move to Monroe, I was serving on the pastoral team of Grace Fellowship Church, a suburban megachurch in Metro Atlanta. Grace was planted by Buddy and Jody Hoffman in Tucker, Georgia in 1983, meeting on Sunday mornings in an old day care center. With Bibles in hand and the smell of dirty diapers in their noses, a handful of faithful men and women began to meet, worship, and serve together in the community. As the fledgling congregation grew they eventually moved into a permanent facility a few miles away in the blossoming Parkview school district of Gwinnett County, one of the fastest growing counties in the United States. The driving vision of the church was to reach the next generation, and so the church focused on developing healthy youth and children's ministries, intentionally engaging in the community, and seeking out ways to serve and encourage the local schools.

This strategy worked so well that in 2000, when a plot of land came available a quarter mile from another nearby high school, the church decided to move and build a bigger facility to reach more students and families. Brookwood High School was not only one of the largest schools in the state, it was also at the center of six other massive high schools (including Parkview), spread across southern Gwinnett County. I was hired by Grace that same year as a "local missionary" to the high schools as a church partner with Young Life, a parachurch ministry focused on building mentoring friendships with middle- and high-school students. Buddy was so committed to this idea of empowering leaders to invest in the next generation that he and Jody invited me and my best friend, Tyler, to move into their basement. Tyler had just been hired by Buddy as the senior high youth pastor at Grace. We worked closely together, but while he focused on "church kids," my role took me into the schools to reach out to students who wouldn't otherwise darken the doors of a church. The job description Buddy gave me was simply to, "eat, sleep, and breath Parkview High School."

Hidden in that simple job description was a strategy that, in addition to intentionally investing in the next generation, would become a second key to unlocking the future—to be a part of genuine transformation, move in to the neighborhood. In his book *Charity Detox*, Bob Lupton writes, "Programs don't fix communities, they can't. They may genuinely help some individuals (often by enabling those individuals to escape the neighborhood), but they don't bring about fundamental community change. Only neighbors can do that. Neighbors, after all, are the building blocks of every neighborhood" (Lupton 2015, 134). He calls this intentional process "re-neighboring." Lupton continues, "If transformation is to take place, genuine relationships have to be forged...Sharing life is what transforms a community" (138).

We discovered the power of showing up, moving in, and sharing life in a suburban high school context, not realizing those same lessons would profoundly impact our life and ministry down the road. One of the first kids I met, at a cold and rainy high school football game, was a young sophomore punk named Matt Reynolds. He was a natural leader, but unfortunately at the time was leading a lot of other high school students in a not-so-good direction. I still clearly remember thinking when I met him: *If that kid doesn't end up in prison, he's going to change the world!* Towards the end of his senior year, Matt would make the fateful decision to begin a relationship with Jesus, shifting his focus from selling drugs to serving others. He even went so far as to forego the traditional senior spring break trip to Cancun, Mexico, to go on a church mission trip to Lima, Peru. This decision would not only have massive implications for his own life, but for the future of Grace, as well.

In the four years after their move to Snellville, Grace grew from approximately eight hundred regular attenders (children through adults) to almost three thousand coming on a weekly basis. In the resulting blessed chaos, with every square foot of the new facility already at max capacity, the leadership of the church began to ask, "What next?" After investigating and wrestling through multiple options for growth, from expanding the existing facility on the current property to buying a shopping center, a different opportunity presented itself.

In 2005 a small, struggling church in Midtown Atlanta came to Buddy with an invitation to take over their facility. And so Grace-Midtown was planted with that same driving vision to reach the next generation of college students living and studying in Atlanta. But with this church plant, the leadership also aimed to engage the diverse and growing international community in Midtown. This meant establishing a church culture that maintained the core mission and values of Grace Fellowship, while being shaped in its expression by the indigenous culture in which it found itself, not just replicating a cookie-cutter copy of the original Snellville campus. This decision further developed our understanding of what it meant to "move into the neighborhood." In other words, there is a big difference between moving in and blindly imposing an outside set of norms and values on a place as compared to moving in and seeking to understand and respect the norms and values of that place. It's the difference between walking in to a room with the attitude of, "Here I am!" versus, "There you are!"

While Buddy was still pastoring the congregation in Snellville, he would drive into the city on Sunday evenings to launch the new church service in the old building. He would then ride his bike all over Midtown on Monday morning seeking to know and understand the cultural context—the people and the place—in which the church was being planted. Over the next several years, as that congregation grew, Buddy began to take along another young leader to help him preach and pastor the church. Matt Reynolds had graduated from college by that time and, under Buddy's mentorship, eventually became the lead pastor of Grace-Midtown. Like Buddy had modeled, Matt moved in to the neighborhood, focused on the next generation, sought to understand the cultural context, and in turn began to see the church rapidly expand and grow.

All the while, Grace in Snellville continued to experience growing-pains, wrestling with the question of capacity and healthy growth. In late 2009 a young couple attending Grace-Snellville approached Buddy and Jody with a proposal. They loved the DNA of Grace, and its focus on reaching the "Neighborhoods, Nations, and Next Generation," but didn't enjoy driving forty minutes out of their neighborhood in Monroe, Georgia to get there. With a deep desire to help revitalize the small town where they lived, Paul and Jessica had recently purchased the abandoned cotton mill that generations before had been the economic engine and center of communal life for the city, and offered to help plant a Grace church there. At that time, the once-thriving Monroe Cotton Mills were a painful reminder of the economic reality of the town as it sat vandalized and decrepit, surrounded by chain link fences and barbed wire.

That winter, with a vision for restoration and redemption stirring in the hearts of the Grace staff and elders, the church gathered to pray in that vacant, vandalized, broken—yet beautiful—building. Even our children knelt on the scarred wooden floors of the old mill and asked God for his heart for Monroe. And so, in the summer of 2010, Grace Monroe was planted with the common Grace DNA of reaching the next generation and moving into the neighborhood, but with a unique vision to embody the heart of God by taking that which was old and making something new, that which was broken and crafting something beautiful, that which was dead and bringing forth life, and that which was abandoned and creating a place of belonging—a new vision for revitalizing a city.

To be honest, the first few years didn't go as planned. In fact, after a couple of years Grace Monroe was still struggling to get off the ground, despite the faithful effort of those pioneer families. The leadership of Grace began to ask hard questions about the viability of a next-generation focused church like Grace in a small town like Monroe. Should we continue to invest energy and resources in a place where the soil seemed hard and the fruit insignificant? There were many reasons proposed why Grace-Monroe was struggling to grow and why it wouldn't work: the town was too small, too old, too divided, too traditional. There weren't enough kids. There was too much poverty. The church location was too hidden. The religious traditions in the community were too entrenched. People were trying to get out of Monroe—not come to it.

In 2010, when Grace-Monroe was being launched, I had just stepped off Young Life staff to take a role overseeing the adult discipleship ministry at Grace-Snellville. Two years later, as the church in Monroe struggled, Sadie and I were sent to help for the summer, to assess the health and viability of Grace in Monroe, and to navigate the possible closing of the fledgling church plant. From the Grace elder's perspective, the goal was to eventually close the church doors in the old cotton mill, ironically abandoning the town in much the same way as the Mill had years before.

However, it wasn't long before God gave us a deep love and passion for the town and its families, and a renewed vision for ministry in that place—to equip and empower a community of people to discover their God-given identity and walk out their Kingdom calling in a way that literally transforms the place they live, and flows out to impact the rest of the world. At that point, my family and I made a critical Grace-esque decision that would propel God's purpose for Grace-Monroe forward—we moved into the neighborhood. In 2013 we began our own renovation project, acquiring a dilapidated and abandoned historic home in the heart of downtown on the "wrong side of the tracks," strategically located less than a half-mile from one of the most impoverished and highest crime blocks in the city and less than a half-mile the other direction from multimillion dollar homes, and only a quarter mile from the Mill.

With that decision, it seemed like God opened the flood gates of people who began to get connected to Grace-Monroe and pursue their own dreams and visions—opening businesses, gyms and restaurants, engaging in and even starting schools, launching and expanding ministries, restoring blighted properties, rebuilding and repairing parks and green spaces, creating art projects downtown, and finding all kinds of creative, tangible, practical ways to serve the city and its citizens. It seemed like every facet of culture—from education to government to business to health care—was being engaged with a Kingdom vision of redemption and transformation.

I realized quickly as a pastor in a town like Monroe that it is inadequate to try and meet people's spiritual needs (love, acceptance, belonging, identity) without also addressing the physical needs of a place (healthy living environments, educational opportunities, economic development). It is a mistake to focus solely on the individual without recognizing the impact of a community on a person. The environments we find ourselves in shape who we are, while at the same time we are (consciously or unconsciously) shaping the environments that we are in.

Therefore, to talk about working towards a whole and healthy city is to talk about working towards whole and healthy people.

Grace-Monroe has attracted lots of young people and families—young in age, young in marriage, and young in faith. In addition, people of all ages have been drawn to Grace's commitment to intentionally "move in" and engage in the health and revitalization of Monroe and Walton County, discovering and walking out their God-given identity and destiny. Two of the first people we met when we moved to Monroe were Kyle and Paige, a married couple who were drawn to the idea of a church intentionally engaged in city transformation. Intrigued by our story of renovating a dilapidated house and moving into a more troubled area of town, they ended up selling their beautiful home in a gated community on the outskirts of Monroe and buying an abandoned historic home next to one of Monroe's largest housing authority complexes. The dilapidated house had once been beautiful, but through years of neglect had fallen into significant disrepair due primarily to its location in an "undesirable" neighborhood.

On the first day Kyle and Paige began to renovate their new home, they were approached by a man who had just been released from prison. Darrell had recommitted his life to God while serving his six-year sentence and was committed to getting his life back on track upon his release. He was accepted into a transitional housing program at a local apartment complex, but was required to quickly find a job that could be financially sustainable. On the morning Darrell met Kyle he had on a pair of shorts, a shirt, and flip flops he had just bought with the fifteen-dollar voucher he had been given to a local ministry thrift store, and he a place to sleep that night, but otherwise very little else to his name. His simple request for any kind of work that Kyle could give him would set them on a path that would change both of their lives for the better.

Darrell and Kyle soon became close friends, working together on multiple projects. Darrell served as a constant source of encouragement and strength for Kyle, while Kyle was able to relationally connect Darrell with job opportunities and resources for getting his life back on track, even helping Darrell reconnect with his children whom he hadn't seen since he had left for prison. One common mindset when it comes to poverty alleviation is the idea that there are "haves" and "have-nots," and that it is the role of the "haves" in the world to meet the needs of the "have-nots." The reality is that everyone on the planet is simultaneously a have and a have-not. We all have something we need and we all have something to give. For a more in-depth discussion on the powerful principle of Asset Based Community Development (ABCD), which helped shape the way we view ministry in Monroe, read *When Helping Hurts* by Steve Corbett and Brian Fikkert (2009). They write, "By showing low-income people through our words, our actions, and most importantly our ears that they are people with unique gifts and abilities, we can be part of helping them to recover their sense of dignity, even as we recover from our sense of pride." (64). They continue:

> ABCD is consistent with the perspective that God has blessed every individual and community with a host of gifts...Indeed, the very nature of the question—What gifts do you have?—affirms people's dignity and contributes to the process of overcoming their poverty of being. And as they tell us of their gifts and abilities, we can start to see them as God does, helping us to overcome our sense of superiority; that is, our own poverty of being. (120)

Through the course of their friendship, both Darrell and Kyle grew to understand their own God-given identity more fully, and were emboldened to pursue their dreams and passions. Kyle discovered a love for renovation as well as a passion for walking alongside people in the restoration of their lives. Darrell discovered a powerful gift of encouragement and a love for teaching, specifically investing in the next generation and helping guide kids from a similar background as his down a different path than the one he took.

Another example was a handful of families who had a heart for engaging the community and a passion for health and fitness. They made the decision to take one of the empty warehouse bays next to the church and turn it into a CrossFit gym. However, they wanted to create a gym focused not only on the physical health of its members but also on encouraging the spiritual, emotional, and relational health of all those involved. In a way they saw themselves as a center for mission, reaching out to people who wouldn't necessarily join a church but who were looking for a loving, safe community.

Another couple had a dream of owning a restaurant. However, they viewed their efforts as more than simply cooking great food or creating a cool atmosphere; they saw the restaurant as an opportunity to create space for healthy relationships to develop and flourish. Through both of these endeavors, we began redefining the church not simply as the beautiful building you enter, or the worship service you attend, but a community of people leveraging their God-given dreams, abilities, and resources to be a blessing to others.

All of these individuals and families were independently operating out of a desire to make a positive impact in their own unique way. Each one was making a significant mark on Monroe, yet it was the collective value of a common vision that held it all together. No one person can revitalize a town, but every person has a role to play. In his book *To Change The World*, James Davison Hunter (2010) argues for the power of networks when it comes to making a tangible difference.

He writes, "I would argue (along with many others) that the key actor in history is not individual genius but rather the network and the new institutions that are created out of those networks. And the more "dense" the network—that is, the more active and interactive the network—the more influential it could be" (38).

Thus we return to the beginning—how can a person make a difference where they live? In sum, they can't by themselves. However, in community, as we identify and empower the dreams within one another, move into the neighborhood seeking to understand, value, and bless that unique cultural context, while intentionally investing in the next generation, we can be a part of creating a healthy, flourishing town. In fact, as we surprisingly discovered, it is precisely within the context of a small town, where the relational fabric is thicker, and the impact of intentional effort more easily seen, that true cultural transformation can take place. And even though Monroe is not London, or even Atlanta, what if we began to view London and Atlanta as simply hundreds of Monroe's all smashed together? And what if what we discovered in Monroe is actually the key to flourishing cities, no matter what size they are? The question is, what difference will you make wherever you are?

Bibliography

Corbett, S. and Fikkert, B. *When Helping Hurts*. New York: Moody, 2009.

Hunter, James Davison. *To Change the World: The Irony, Tragedy, and Possibility of Christianity in the Late Modern World*. New York: Oxford University Press, 2010.

Lupton, Robert. *Charity Detox*. New York: HarperOne, 2015.

The Growing Popularity of Megachurches in the United States

Robert McNamara, PhD

SOCIOLOGY CAN BE described as a discipline that attempts to predict people's behavior on the basis of the groups to which they belong and the interactions that take place within those groups. In other words, how we affiliate with one another and form relationships is a key component to understanding why people act the way they do. If this is true, where does something like religion factor into the discussion? Clearly people gather together around their religious beliefs and those ideologies play an important role in understanding how people act. In the sociological study of religion, an interesting question centers around how and why people attend church in the first place. Sociologists might ask questions such as: Why do people go to church? What makes them choose one particular church over another? Are there any patterns about church attendance that tell us anything about society, culture, and people's attitudes, values, and beliefs?

This is not to say that sociology attempts to place a particular value on religion; rather sociologists study religion to understand people's religious experiences and how religion is tied to other social institutions. This article explores the growth and popularity of megachurches. This is an interesting phenomenon, because it comes at a time when church attendance in this country appears to be decreasing and the relevance of religion in people's lives has arguably become less important.

CHURCH ATTENDANCE IN THE UNITED STATES

I have a friend, Vinnie, who is a pastor at a church in Connecticut. He has been a pastor there for a number of years and when asked about the state of affairs in his church and others like it, he offers this commentary:

> I have seen dramatic drop offs in church attendance and even in church membership in recent years. Many of my parishioners are older and some have died, and some become unable to attend church regularly for health reasons. But the big problem is that there isn't a younger segment to the church population to take their place. It

used to be I'd have over two hundred people in church on a Sunday, now I'm lucky if I have fifty, sometimes as few as twenty. And I talk to other pastors and they say the same thing—people just aren't showing up to church on Sundays anymore.

What Pastor Vinnie describes is not unique to his congregation, his region, or church membership in his particular state. Many public opinion polls estimate that only about 40 percent of people attend church regularly, defined as at least three Sundays a month. However, new evidence suggests that number is actually about half that figure (Shattuck 2017), and those numbers continue to decline. In fact, estimates suggest that by 2050, church attendance may be as low as 11 percent. What is perhaps more revealing is that church attendance continues to decline despite significant population growth in this country. By most estimates, since 1990 the population in the United States has increased by about 20 percent, or forty-eight million people. Yet, church attendance during this period has steadily declined (Shattuck 2017).

The problem is not just attendance, it is the lack of growth in members as well. According to the Hartford Institute for Religious Research, between 2010 and 2012 more than half of all churches in the United states did not add a single new member and each year, three million people become disaffiliated with any particular church. This lack of attendance ultimately translates into churches closing their doors. The Hartford Institute of Religious Research estimates that between four thousand and ten thousand churches close every year (Thumma and Bird 2015).

REASONS FOR LACK OF ATTENDANCE: IS IT ISOLATIONISM?

Why is church attendance so low? There are many reasons for this shift, including a population shift, where there are more retirees every year, a lack of attention to Millenials and their needs when it comes to their church experience, along with what has been described as a leadership crisis in the church as a whole, where scandals and unethical behavior by church officials drive people away from religion and church all together (McSwain 2013; Rainor 2015). Adding to the problem are those churches who have attempted to revive their congregations by attempting to attract younger members. Some churches have attempted to upgrade the experience by hiring professional musicians, offering contemporary services and sermons, and rebranding their church through marketing campaigns. While this may work for some churches, for many with a long tradition of a particular ideology or denominational affiliation, the results can backfire. When a church attempts to be something it is not, the effort feels forced and likely fails.

This is particularly true if the church only repackages itself and does not engage in an ideological transformation. In other words, if the church tends not to embrace religious pluralism but tries to convey a message that it does, it will not likely attract new members and could antagonize existing ones (McSwain 2013). Another reason for the lack of attendance and membership in church relates to more macrolevel changes occurring in society as a whole. Some experts note that there has been a tendency for the church experience to lack relevance in people's lives. As a result, dissatisfaction with the messages offered by churches and the lack of relevancy of religion in general has led people to increasingly turn away from churches.

SOCIAL ISOLATIONISM AND LONELINESS

Sociologically, one could argue that the lack of church attendance and/or membership is symptomatic of a larger trend in society, where there is an increasing sense of isolationism created as a part of modernity and a trend away from public social interaction (Slade 2012; Fischer 2009; Fischer and Mattson 2009). For example, in the book *Bowling Alone,* Putnam (2000) argues that society increasingly focuses on individual activities over community-oriented ones. That is, as a feature of modern society, people tend to withdraw from wide social networks and their families and intimate friends become the focal point for social life. Putnam (2000) points out, for example, that while the popularity of bowling remains high, the number of bowling leagues, where people gather together around the activity, have dramatically decreased. This perspective, sometimes referred to as the lost community hypothesis, suggests that loneliness is a chronic feature of modern society (Wellman 1979). As people become more inclined toward spending time at home or engaged in individualistic activities, fewer opportunities exist to physically interact in public spaces with others. For example, people are increasingly watching movies at home instead of going to the movie theater or playing video games online instead of going to arcades. As a result, people can begin to prefer these activities out of the conveniences they offer.

Another example would be where conversations about religion and spirituality occur online or through a blog rather than going to church or joining a life group. Thus, Putnam (2000) and others (McPherson, Smith-Lovin, and Brashear 2009) who espouse this view, believe that modern life results in a less holistic social person, because people are more likely to become isolated from others.

In contrast, another school of thought argues that there is a significant difference between being alone or isolated and feeling lonely. Feeling lonely is often a function of the number of connections a person has and the type of support they offer (Akerland and Harguist 1992; Ciaioppino and Hawkley 2009; Simmel 1905). In this vein, scholars argue that access to social media outlets actually enhances people's feelings of connectedness since people are able to reach others all over the world at a moment's notice while still being able to interact with family and friends locally. Thus, while it may be true that modern society results in fewer actual instances of face-to-face contact, the idea that this form of isolationism translates into loneliness is questionable. In fact, some experts even argue that society often creates roles that require a certain degree of isolation from others (Phillips 2011; Simmel 1951; Fischer 2009). Finally, a third school of thought contends that perhaps what is occurring is a combination of factors, where technology provides an increasing level of opportunities to spend time at home with family, while creating an expanded network of what might be called electronic friends and relationships. This network could cause people to feel more alone since those relationships are much more fleeting and superficial, and require a significant amount of energy to sustain. That is, these relationships require the person to engage in a great deal more impression management (Goffman 1969) and can serve as a reminder that their social networks, while larger, have significantly less meaning (Parigi and Henson 2014).

How does this relate to church attendance? Some sociologists and other experts use this framework of understanding to explain the decrease in church attendance, where people are finding ways to worship that do not involve others (e.g., the electronic church) or simply reframing their understanding of religion and spirituality to focus more on a personal and individualistic emphasis. As one expert noted, "I think church attendance is a close cousin to the other kinds of activities Putnam says Americans are doing alone—indicating that Americans have become increasingly disconnected from family and friends" (Kaleem 2011).

THE MEGACHURCH

Of those people who do attend church, what is the benefit for them? Durkheim (1897), for example, found that religion serves to build a sense of social cohesion among members of a particular religion, and it also serves to encourage acting in a particular way—what we might call social control. In other words, people generally have a need to feel a part of something larger than themselves and religion, and the churches in which it is practiced, provide a sense of community and solidarity that people seek.

Most churches are made up of small congregations: one estimate showed that the vast majority (90 percent) of churches have less than 350 members attending on a weekly basis and half of all churches in the United States have less than 100 members (RaiPer 2015; Bell 2009). Recall Pastor Vinnie's comments—churches tend to be shrinking. Part of the explanation for the advantage of a small church, of course, is the sense of intimacy that is created, where members can get to know the church leadership as well as to live together in some meaningful way.

While most churches are shrinking in size or are consistently losing members, some churches are seeing significant growth (Shattuck 2017). As was mentioned, the reasons for the small church experience makes some sense: people want the intimacy of a small congregation and are able to develop deep and long lasting relationships with other members. But what of the megachurch? Why are so many people flocking to them? And as the trends toward secularization catches up to even the megachurches, how are megachurches responding?

If we can imagine a church like a business, say, a restaurant, how would you address the problem of a decreasing flow of customers? As a restaurant owner you can be reasonably certain that people want to eat out at times and you can also be reasonably certain that those customers are increasingly choosing some other restaurant besides yours. So what do you do? You might realize that something in the business has to change—either the menu, the service, the ambiance, the price, or the hours of operation. Customers are clearly sending you a message by going somewhere else (perhaps even saving the money and not eating out as often).

Maybe the problem is in the messaging or branding of the restaurant—are you appealing to the wrong clientele? If you are an upscale restaurant, you may have to accept fewer customers but the ones you have typically spend a lot more on a dining experience. Or perhaps you are more of a family-oriented restaurant, but the atmosphere is chaotic and the facility is not conducive to family time. In other words, maybe the message is a negative one for your customers. Or perhaps it is too difficult to get to your restaurant and challenges like parking make it hard for customers to patronize your place even if the food is good and affordable. So people don't come.

Now imagine that same type of situation, only you are a pastor at a church. Perhaps the reason for the loss of members or lack of attendance is in the content of the messages offered on Sunday; perhaps it is the delivery; perhaps your church is competing with a host of other activities for families and the added value of church is not readily seen by parishioners. Like the restaurant example, parishioners are sending messages about going to church with their actions: the church either is not relevant, is too "gloom and doom" in its message, the church makes it difficult to fulfill a commitment or is heavy handed in its leveraging of member participation, or is yet another thing that is added on to an already full plate of activities in people's lives. And because going to church leaves people feeling like something is missing anyway, they are empty and unfulfilled. So people don't come.

While traditionalists might scoff at the need to market religion, others have taken the approach that the church experience needs to change. To address the issue of relevance, some pastors have come to believe that there need to be multiple reasons to go to church or travel to the campus. There must be a sense of purpose and community created, meaning the people at the church need to be welcoming, friendly, and inviting. There also needs to be a relaxed atmosphere— where dress codes and a traditional sermon that speaks to the issue of fire and brimstone are things of the past. The sermons also have to be user-friendly and relevant to a person's everyday life, and there needs to be more of an emphasis on one's heart than on their clothing or social standing.

There also needs to be an ambassador of the church—a charismatic leader whose message is easily identified, who is likeable and personable, and whose approach runs counter to traditional church leaders and the standard messaging often found in today's churches. And people want to attend a church that is hip, progressive, unbound by denominational doctrine and ritual, and where they feel they fit in. What you need, then, is a megachurch.

Characteristics of Megachurches

Megachurches, which, by definition include churches that have two thousand or more in attendance each week, are becoming more popular. Why? At first glance one might think that a megachurch would be the last place someone might want to attend. There are so many people, how does one feel connected to the larger community? Why would someone fight traffic to attend service when there are more convenient options available to them in their community?

Megachurches have some unique characteristics from traditionally small churches. Clearly size is one of those features, but that is not all megachurches have to offer their members. Moreover, there appear to be two or three archetypical models to characterize megachurches. These are based on the types of members as well as the type of message the church wishes to convey. Interestingly, the notion of a megachurch is a relatively new phenomenon in religion, developing and expanding on a larger scale only in the last several decades, and there are only a small number of megachurches around the country, perhaps less than fifty (Thumma and Bird 2015).

As was mentioned, by definition, a megachurch is characterized by having two thousand or more members on a weekly basis (Thumma and Travis 2007; Kelly 2012). This is interesting all by itself—how does one come up with such a figure? Is it the actual number of people who show up or the number of seats in the building that can accommodate them? Is it based on a single service or multiple services—just on Sunday or throughout the week? These are interesting questions, and the answer is that the figure should be used as an estimate since the number is often based on the number of people a particular sanctuary can hold and the figure is based on multiple services offered during the week (Thumma and Travis 2007).

However it is determined, size matters since large numbers of people attending a service tend to attract others who are curious as to what that particular church has to offer. Megachurches, by virtue of their large congregations, also have a great deal of flexibility and resources that allow initial growth to be sustained. They are also flexible in terms of their doctrine—whereas some churches struggle with fitting the church experience into the rituals and practices demanded of a particular denomination, megachurches, which are typically nondenominational, are able to adapt their practices and operations to the needs and desires of their members (Thumma and Bird 2015).

More importantly, what brings people to megachurches is often the pastor and the message, not the denominational affiliation. In fact, some experts contend that almost half of the megachurches in the United States are independent or nondenominational. Even if a particular megachurch affiliates with a particular ideology, often the church downplays that connection, including removing identifying markers from literature or branding. Instead the church promotes the pastor or the message they want conveyed about the church, which usually asserts that the church is different from mainstream churches and is welcoming to all types of worshippers (Thumma and Bird 2015; Kelly 2012). Most megachurches offer a more conservative ideology that could be characterized as being either Evangelical, Charismatic, or Fundamentalist in approach. The messaging from megachurches also depends to some degree on the type of audience it seems to attract (Kelly 2012; Thumma and Travis 2007).

In this way, megachurches attempt to target particular groups with their particular messaging and brand. One group might be called "seekers," or those who are unaffiliated with a particular church or who are open to spiritual issues and the notion of religion, but have not found a place to call their church home. This is perhaps the most common type of megachurch audience and it attempts to show people that the megachurch experience is quite different in content and delivery than what seekers may have experienced in church in the past (Thumma and Bird 2015; Kelly 2012).

By making new traditions, dispensing with old ones, and by creating an informal and casual atmosphere, megachurches attempt to appeal to the *idea* of religion rather than the rituals of it. The buildings are differently designed from traditional churches and often contain minimal religious artifacts, but have large and welcoming lobbies, in which members can congregate, food courts, and large sanctuaries with comfortable seating. The music is contemporary and often performed by professional musicians. The sermons are carefully composed, polished, and delivered in a casual but professional manner, usually by a very charismatic pastor who is the driving force behind the creation of the megachurch. The underlying message in the sermons, and in most of the communication from the megachurch, is that religion is not something you only practice on Sunday; religion is a part of everyday life, and the sermons provide illustrations and examples of how best to accomplish that (Thumma and Travis 2007).

A second type of megachurch can be characterized as a significant expansion of the format of a traditional church, but on a larger scale and with greater refinement. Like the seeker megachurch, the choirs are first rate, the preaching is of high quality, and the facilities, particularly the church school, attract members in large numbers. Ministry opportunities abound in these churches, including social activities such as support groups for various types of issues, health and wellness programs, along with advocacy groups of various types. These churches are denominationally affiliated and essentially offer a version of a megachurch that is vastly improving on the traditional model (Thumma and Travis 2007).

A third type of megachurch is more of a blend of the previous two types. In these types of churches, the exterior of the facilities may resemble traditional churches, but on the inside the differences are noteworthy. It is here that the aforementioned contemporary seating and facilities as well as traditional church rituals, such as singing of hymns and liturgical readings from the bible, may be integrated with contemporary Christian music and even contain charismatic healing sessions. These types of churches tend to be less common than the previous two types, largely because it is difficult to successfully integrate the different platforms into a successful model (Thumma and Travis 2007).

The Social Organization of a Megachurch

Regardless of which model is used, there are some common elements to all megachurches that result in their success. First, with regard to demographic characteristics of its members, megachurches tend to draw from similar segments of the population. Most of the research on megachurches suggests that members of megachurches tend to be Caucasians in their early forties, who are married with children and highly educated. They are often highly mobile professionals who live in suburban areas and give generously to their home church (Kelly 2012; Thumma and Bird 2015).

In terms of why members seek out megachurches: first and foremost is that the worship and the sermon are the main attractions for members. As the church grows, the number and style of services adapts to the interests of members, with the church typically offering several services on Sundays, some with different formats, thereby providing something for everyone in terms of what they need in a church experience (Thumma and Bird 2015).

Moreover, as it grows, the level of activity in the church expands as well, with services and events commonly occurring seven days a week and a multitude of groups and activities for members to become more integrated into the church community. As the church services take on a larger audience and a more formalized delivery, the number of people needed to carry out the delivery of a seven-day-a-week church expands as well. Hundreds of volunteers are needed for a wide assortment of activities from children's services, parking, multimedia, communion services, and a host of other activities that must be coordinated for thousands of members and multiple services (Thumma and Bird 2015). This does not include the expansion of the paid staff and clergy, who must also be able to meet the needs of members depending on the issues involved. Thus, one distinguishing feature of a megachurch is the number of actively involved members in the operation of the church.

Charismatic Leaders

The genesis and continued success of a megachurch is almost always based on a visionary and charismatic leader, who provides the mission and vision of the church and is the face of the proverbial franchise. These individuals likely started the church and are the main attractions for members—people come to hear him talk about how to live a Christian life in a biblically practical, nonthreatening way, without the dogma found in many other sermons. The sermons are inspirational, encouraging, practical, and relevant. Interestingly, many pastors of megachurches do not have formal seminary training (Thumma and Travis 2007; Kelly 2012). Olson (1988) reports that one-third of megachurch ministers have had no seminary education.

Integration of Members

A third feature of megachurches are the numerous groups and ministry opportunities that exist there. As was mentioned, the range of activities include job fairs, support and recovery groups, individual counseling services, employment support opportunities, musical lessons, worship services, day care centers, schools, youth groups, weight rooms, racquetball courts, pools, and the like. Thus, the goal here is to immerse the member into church life in as many ways as possible, thereby making the church a veritable one-stop shop for all of a member's social activities (Kelly 2012; Thumma and Travis 2007).

CHALLENGES FOR MEGACHURCHES

The growth and popularity of megachurches has been seen for some time; however, there remain challenges in both the operation of a megachurch and in sustaining its membership. While megachurches are typically found in suburban areas, where large plots of land can be acquired that accommodate the space needed for a megachurch, particularly in terms of parking, not everyone is enamored with megachurches in their communities. As congestion and traffic problems create issues for residents, particularly as the church expands and hosts activities all week long, many communities have attempted to limit this growth through the passage of zoning laws. For example, in Seattle, efforts are underway to limit the size and location of a megachurch and its construction, citing congestion and traffic issues (Grossman 2015).

Other experts express concern that while megachurches are currently very popular, like many fads in American culture, the novelty that attracts people to megachurches will wear off and their popularity will eventually subside. At the heart of megachurches lies the notion of connecting people with the church community, and, just like any good restaurant, keeping customers happy with a solid core of offerings while also recognizing that members can be fickle and may want something new and improved.

Megachurches have experienced such changes, and evidence of their evolution may already be occurring. Increasingly, megachurches have started to offer smaller satellite campuses instead of the massive main campus. While that may remain a fixture for the foreseeable future, an increasing focus on customizing the worship experience based on smaller congregation preferences suggests that people still want that smaller, intimate church experience even if they are affiliated with the larger institution (Grossman 2015).

Additionally, megachurches also appear to be embarking on efforts to further distinguish themselves from other churches (even other megachurches) by focusing on international or global missions work. In short, megachurches will continue to face challenges despite their growth. As people continue to withdraw from church attendance and membership and prefer a more individualized spiritual experience, all churches, including popular megachurches, will be hard pressed to keep members engaged, committed, and connected to the larger community (Grossman 2015).

Bibliography

Åkerlind, I., and J. O. Hörnquist. "Loneliness and Alcohol Abuse: A Review of Evidences of an Interplay." *Social Science & Medicine* 34, no. 4 (1992): 405–14.

Bell, Michael. "What is an Average Size Church?" Internet Monk Jul 13, 2009. http://www.internetmonk.com/archive/michael-bell-what-is-an-average-church.

Brashears, M. E. "Anomia and the Sacred Canopy: Testing a Network Theory." *Social Networks* 32, no. 3 (2010): 187–96.

Burt R. S. "A Note on Strangers, Friends and Happiness." *Social Networks* 9, no. 4 (1987): 311–31.

Cacioppo, J. T., J. H. Fowler, and N. A, Christakis. "Alone in the Crowd: The Structure and Spread of Loneliness in a Large Social Network." *Journal of Personality and Social Psychology* 97, no. 6 (2009): 977–91.

Cacioppo, J. T., and L. C. Hawkley. "Perceived Social Isolation and Cognition." *Trends in* Cognitive Sciences 13, no. 10 (2009): 447–54.

Durkheim, E. *The Elementary Forms of Religious Life.* New York: Basic Books, 1905.

Fischer, C. S. "The 2004 GSS Finding of Shrunken Social Networks: An Artifact?" *American Sociological Review* 74, no. 4 (2009): 657–69.

Fischer, C. S., and G. Mattson. "Is America fragmenting?" *Annual Review of Sociology.* 35, no. 1 (2009): 435–55.

Goffman, E. *The Presentation of Self in Everyday Life.* New York: Basic Books, 1969.

Grossman, C. L. "The Megachurch Rolls On, But Big Concerns are Rising Too." *Religious News Service.* December 2, 2015. https://religionnews.com/2015/12/02/megachurch-evangelical-christians/.

Kaleem, Jaweed. "Americans Have Lost Faith in Religious Leaders and Church Attendance, New Book Says." *Huffington Post.* August 21, 2011. https://www.huffingtonpost.com/2011/08/21/religion-trends-clergy-church-attendance_n_929963.html

Kelly, Peter. "God as a Drug: The Rise of the American Megachurch." University of Washington News. August 20, 2012. https://www.washington.edu/news/2012/08/20/god-as-a-drug-the-rise-of-american-megachurches/

McPherson M., L. Smith-Lovin, and M. E. Brashears. "Social Isolation in America: Changes in Core Discussion Networks Over Two Decades." *American Sociological Review* 71, no. 3 (2006): 353–75.

McSwain, Steve. "Why Nobody Wants to Go to Church Anymore." *Huffington Post.* October 14, 2013. https://www.huffingtonpost.com/steve-mcswain/why-nobody-wants-to-go-to_b_4086016.html.

Olson, R. *The Largest Congregations in the United States: An Empirical Study of Church Growth and Decline.* Dissertation, Ann Arbor, Michigan: Northwestern University, 1988.

Parigi, P., and W. Henson. "Social Isolationism in America." *Annual Review of Sociology* 40, no. 1 (2014): 153–71.

Phillips, D. J. "Structural Disconnectedness and the Emergence of a Jazz Canon." *American Journal of Sociology* 117, no. 2 (2011): 420–83.

Putnam, R. *Bowling Alone*. New York: Harper Collins, 2000.

Rainer, Tom. "One Reason Most Churches Do Not Exceed 350 in Average Attendance." tomrainer.com. March 25, 2015. http://thomrainer.com/2015/03/one-key-reason-churches-exceed-350-average-attendance/.

Shattuck, K. "7 Startling Facts: An Up Close Look at Church Attendance in America." Church Leaders. December 14, 2017. https://churchleaders.com/pastors/pastor-articles/139575-7-startling-facts-an-up-close-look-at-church-attendance-in-america.html/5.

Simmel, Georg. "The Stranger." In *On Individuality and Social Forms*, edited by Georg Simmel, 143–49. New York: Basic Books, 1905.

Slade, Giles. *Big Disconnect: The Story of Technology and Loneliness*. Prometheus Books, 2012.

Thumma, Scott, and Dave Travis. *Beyond MegaChurch Myths*. San Francisco, CA: Jossey-Bass, 2007.

Thumma, Scott, and Warren Bird. "Recent Shifts in America's Largest Protestant Churches: Megachurches 2015 Report." Hartford, CT: Hartford Institute on Religious Research, 2015.

Wellman, B. "The Community Question: The Intimate Networks of East Yorkers." *American Journal of Sociology* 84, no. 5 (1979): 1201–31.

Wirth, L. "Urbanism as a Way of Life." *American Journal of Sociology* 44, (1938): 3–24

Health Care

HEALTH CARE

Some of the most pressing issues in American society relate to health care. Not only is the population aging, meaning more people will need to use the health care system than in the past, the costs of health care continue to climb at an alarming pace. The health care debate is a thorny political issue as well. With the election of Donald Trump as president, the controversies surrounding the Affordable Care Act continued to be played out along political lines. Trump promised to repeal Obamacare and the proposed GOP plan that was presented in Congress as an alternative resulted in a lot of infighting, but ultimately the Republican-controlled Congress was unable to secure a new plan.

The problems relating to health care are not limited to health insurance, however. Americans are beginning to see that the future of health care in this country contains, among other things, a greater out-of-pocket cost to them than in previous eras. Similarly, there remain questions about the ability of the government to sustain Medicare and Medicaid, two critically important programs for the poor and the elderly.

A key issue in any discussion of health care in this country is the role of patients in their health. As dissatisfaction with traditional medicine has prompted many Americans to begin taking greater responsibility for their health and the prevention of illnesses and diseases, there has been a greater understanding of the scope of the problems that relate to lifestyle issues.

The articles in this section explore some of the more common problems for people relating to their health. For example, using the treatment of heart disease as an illustration, Carey Connor McNamara offers insight into how medical providers make decisions about treating patients. While one might think the data, or the best interests of the patient, should guide providers, there are many factors that are considered in such decisions. Valerie Borum Smith offers important insight into the nature of childhood obesity, which is a source of growing concern for many pediatricians and policy makers. As Americans adopt a more sedentary lifestyle, coupled with poor nutrition and dietary habits, along with a lack of regular exercise, it should not be surprising that problems like obesity, in adults and children alike, and the health consequences from such decisions, are becoming quite serious concerns for the medical community. Finally, as most Americans complain of back problems, which are some of the most common reasons for seeking relief, I offer insight into a recent study of the chiropractic profession. As I discovered, despite increases in its popularity as a form of treatment, there remain some concerns about chiropractic medicine by the general public and by many physicians.

Addressing Social Determinants to Improve Health Outcomes

Valerie Borum Smith, MD

IN 2006 I began my career as a pediatrician at St. Paul Children's Clinic in Tyler, Texas. The clinic is part of St. Paul Children's Foundation, which was founded in 1996 with help of local Methodist churches to serve families in need in the northern portion of Tyler. Members of the churches began an after-school program for neighborhood children several years prior, and as they developed relationships with families living in or near poverty, many of whom were first and second-generation immigrants, they quickly discovered these families had a host of other needs. The foundation started with a food pantry and clothes closet and quickly added pediatric medical and dental clinics.

My intention when entering medical school had been to work with an underserved population, and after four years of medical school at the University of Texas Southwestern Medical School and three years of residency at Arkansas Children's Hospital, I was eager to put my knowledge into action serving families in north Tyler. My medical training prepared me well for the disease processes I would encounter—asthma, infectious diseases, developmental delays, attention deficit hyperactivity disorder, and the like. I knew what medications, procedures, or therapies my patients needed in order to be healthy. What I was not prepared to address were the tremendous obstacles their families faced that often prevented them from obtaining the care they needed.

What good did it do if I identified a speech delay in a child, but their family had no transportation to get them to speech therapy? Prescribing preventive medication for asthma management did little to keep a child out of the emergency room with an asthma attack if their parents couldn't afford to buy the medication. How were parents supposed to follow the nutritional recommendations I provided for their obese child when they couldn't afford fresh fruits and vegetables? It was unrealistic to expect a mother working two jobs and relying on a neighbor to provide after school care for her children to implement a behavior management system that requires consistency for her child with behavior problems.

Not only were socioeconomic factors barriers to care for many of my families, but in many instances, they were actually the cause. The child with speech delay was growing up in a home with a mother who couldn't read. A patient's asthma exacerbation was triggered by an insect infestation in their rental home, but her parents were behind on the rent, so they feared eviction if they complained to the landlord. The family of the child with obesity relied on what they received from the local food pantry, which often included high calorie snacks and baked goods but little produce. And the little boy with behavior problems had a list of adverse childhood events a mile long, including abandonment by his father, witnessing the domestic abuse of his mother, and housing instability.

These examples drove home the impact of social determinants of health—a concept taught in public health and sociology curriculum at the time but rarely addressed in traditional medical education. In fact, even after eleven years at St. Paul, I frequently joke that my undergraduate degree in sociology taught me more about my job than my medical degree. The exciting thing is that medical education is evolving to train new physicians to recognize and address social determinants of health, and there are new models to empower health care providers and organizations to engage their communities to address health inequities and community conditions that impact health.

SOCIAL DETERMINANTS OF HEALTH

Health is influenced by genetics, environment, behavior, and access to medical care. Of these factors, only genetics is not impacted by social determinants of health (Longest 2016). Social determinants of health can generally be thought of as "nonmedical factors influencing health" (Braveman, Egerter, and Williams 2011). According to the World Health Organization, social determinants of health are created by the unequal distribution of "power, income, goods, and services" (WHO 2008). The first articles addressing social determinants of health appeared in the early 1990s, and by 2010 more than forty articles appeared each year in US medical and public health publications. Most social determinants of health research focuses on the impact of factors such as living conditions, education, and income on health, strengthening the correlation between social factors and health (Braveman, Egerter, and Williams 2011). While the base of literature supporting the importance of social determinants on health has grown, the amount of spending focused on addressing these determinants has decreased in recent years. Currently, the United States spends more per capita on health care than any other developed country and yet our life expectancy and health ratings are among the lowest. Meanwhile, we spend less per capita on social support programs than other countries with better health outcomes (Longest 2016). The paradox of health and social support spending and the resulting health outcomes in the United States further emphasizes the power of social determinants of health.

Social determinants of health include education, neighborhood conditions, wealth and income, working conditions, and race. Education impacts health by increasing an individual's health literacy, enhancing health supporting social networks, and increasing employment opportunities. Adult health status directly correlates with the number of years of educational attainment. The individual who has not graduated from high school not only has difficulty obtaining employment that provides an income to pay for healthy foods, he also struggles to navigate complex medical regimens used to manage chronic diseases, and frequently has few family or friends with health knowledge to support him during a health crisis.

Neighborhood conditions also have a significant impact on health. Physical characteristics of neighborhoods such as pedestrian safety, air and water quality, housing, and safe recreation spaces can promote or hinder healthy decisions. In addition, the quality of local services such schools, public transportation, and clinics and hospitals, and the availability of healthy foods can directly impact health. Finally, the social networks that form in local communities play a role in the health of the members of the community. The old real estate adage "location, location, location" accurately conveys the reality that the neighborhood you grow up in impacts opportunities such as education and future income ultimately affecting health.

Wealth, income, and employment are directly related to health outcomes. Individuals living in poverty have increased incidence of illness and premature death (WHO 2008). Increased financial resources allow for access to medical care but also create opportunities for recreational activities and diets that can promote health. Working conditions impact health through physical safety and earnings, but higher income jobs also support health through social networks and the provision of benefits such as sick leave, parental leave, and health insurance.

Finally, race is correlated with health status in the United States, with Latinos and blacks suffering from poorer health outcomes. Systemic racism has resulted in persistent segregation in schools and neighborhoods that deepens the health disparities of these minorities. In addition, being exposed to racism throughout one's life increases chronic stress, which has negative health impacts. (Braveman, Egerter, and Williams 2011)

The World Health Organization has developed three recommendations to improve social determinants of health and reduce health inequalities. First, they advocate for the improvement of daily living conditions, particularly for those living in poverty. Next, policies must be enacted that change the unequal distribution of financial resources and power. And finally, more research and education are needed to understand social determinants of health, accurately evaluate interventions, and disseminate best practices (WHO 2008).

CHANGING METHODS OF MEDICAL EDUCATION

In recognition of the role social determinants of health play in overall health, many medical schools are changing the way they educate new physicians. Traditional medical education is based on the biomedical model, which focuses on physiology, pathology, and pharmacology (Duggan and Street 2015). In essence it is a disease-first perspective, where students learn how the human body is intended to function by studying anatomy, genetics, and physiology; disease processes are taught in pathology and microbiology; and finally, diagnostics and treatment of diseases are learned in pharmacology and clinical rotations. Prevention of disease and addressing the context in which disease develops, such as how support structures and community conditions impact health, were rarely addressed in traditional medical education.

The Institute of Medicine (IOM) released the 2004 report "Improving Medical Education: Enhancing the Social and Behavioral Science Content of Medical School Curricula," which outlined six domains critical to medical education that should incorporate social and behavioral sciences: patient behavior, mind-body interactions in health and disease, physician role and behavior, physician-patient interactions, health policy and economics, and social and cultural issues in health care (IOM 2004). The National Institute of Health (NIH) followed by granting nine medical schools across the country five-year grants to integrate behavioral and social sciences into medical training (Association of American Medical Colleges 2011).

Because a complete medical education must include the perspectives and findings from the behavioral and social sciences, the Association of American Medical Colleges (AAMC) released "Behavioral and Social Science Foundations for Future Physicians," an expert panel report to guide medical schools in integrating sociology and other social and behavioral sciences into their curricula (AAMC 2011). The report builds upon the work of the IOM and NIH by specifying how different physician roles can apply the behavioral and social science knowledge domains. The goal is to "shift the stance of the scientist from an outsider/objective view toward an engaged/responsive perspective" (AAMC 2011, 10).

Dell Medical School at the University of Texas at Austin admitted its first class of medical students in 2016 and is striving to integrate social sciences and social determinants of health into their core curriculum. The school is not only charged with the traditional medical school roles of research and physician education, but also with enhancing "the health and well-being of residents of ... central Texas with emphasis on vulnerable persons and those suffering from health inequities" (Tierney 2016). To accomplish this, the school condenses the classic, basic sciences typically taught over two years into one year, allowing for extended time during the third year of medical school for a project based in the community. Students also participate in community and preventive medicine clerkships during their second and third years and can obtain dual degrees, including master's in public health or educational psychology. The goal is to train physicians to provide high-quality clinical care who "care about social, behavioral, and structural determinants of health." (Tierney 2016)

Postgraduate medical training is also evolving to integrate social determinants of health. In my specialty of pediatrics, several institutions, including Boston Children's Hospital, the University of California at San Francisco, Children's National in Washington, D.C., and Baylor College of Medicine in Houston, Texas, have created community-focused pediatric training programs to equip the next generation of pediatricians to better address social determinants of health and health inequalities. According to Dr. Lanessa Bass, co-program director of the Baylor College of Medicine Lead and Acquire Primary Care (LEAP) residency, their program is designed to integrate advocacy, public policy, and health disparities throughout the residency experience. The LEAP track includes clinical experiences in community settings, long-term community collaborations, and integrating community-based care into specialty rotations. As Dr. Bass states, to address the complex medical needs of our communities, "we need more sociologist in pediatrics than biologist."

Community-Centered Health Homes

For decades community health centers across the United States have worked to provide quality health care to those most in need, but this care has not been able to close the gaps in health equity due to social determinants of health. In 2011 the Prevention Institute proposed a new model for community health centers to merge "efficient, accessible, and culturally appropriate care with comprehensive efforts to prevent illness and injury...by improving community conditions" called the community-centered health home (CCHH) (Prevention Institute 2011). The CCHH model builds upon patient-centered medical home concepts by challenging clinics to "not only *acknowledge* that factors outside the healthcare system affect patient health outcomes, but also *actively participate in* improving them" (Prevention Institute 2011).

Focusing on community conditions and population health has typically been the domain of public health, but the CCHH model challenges those providing direct patient care to be actively engaged in the community and advocate for change. The model calls for community health clinics to expand prevention beyond individual patient education and screening and focus on community prevention by changing social norms and promoting policies that support health.

Medical providers are asked to consider "two steps to prevention" when evaluating patients' health problems; rather than simply assessing which patient behaviors and choices are contributing to health problems, the physician examines the social norms, community conditions, health inequalities, and policies that are influencing those behaviors (Prevention Institute 2011). To assist community health clinics with this transition, Prevention Institute provides the Tool for Health and Resilience in Vulnerable Environments (THRIVE), which facilitates identification of community factors that influence health, including housing, transportation, arts and culture, education, racial justice, social networks and trust, and social norms (Prevention Institute 2011).

Clinics adopting the CCHH model use a three-part process to broaden their focus from individual patient care to community conditions: inquiry, analysis, and action (Prevention Institute 2011). Inquiry includes reflection on patient encounters and community experiences to recognize the social, economic, and community conditions impacting patient health, the collection of additional patient data if necessary, and the review of available community-level data. Analysis examines the connection between the data and health problems prevalent in the community and helps to identify underlying factors that can influence health outcomes. This step requires working with community partners to determine priorities and strategies to effect community change. Finally, the CCHH coordinates with partners to take action to reduce health inequities, including mobilizing patients, advocating for community health, and adopting model organizational practices (Prevention Institute 2011).

Since the introduction of the CCHH model, the Prevention Institute has worked with three distinct cohorts to help community health centers across the southern United States transform into agents for community change: the Louisiana Public Health Institute provided funding, training, and technical assistance for five clinics along the gulf coast, the Blue Cross Blue Shield of North Carolina Foundation is focusing on three communities across the state, and the Episcopal Health Foundation is training and equipping thirteen clinics in east Texas to implement the CCHH model. The organization I work for, St. Paul Children's Foundation, is a part of the Episcopal Health Foundation cohort.

And so, I find myself, twenty years after graduating with a BA in sociology, part of a group of physicians and health care professionals across Texas who recognize that "it is unreasonable to expect people to change their behaviors when so many forces in the social, cultural, and physical environment conspire against such change" (IOM 2001).

We are examining our communities for strategic points of action to improve social determinants of health with the ultimate goal of preventing disease and improving the health of the community. At. St. Paul, we are focusing of food insecurity—mapping our emergency food systems, local agricultural assets, and local policies and forming a food security council to take actions that focus on collaboration, organizational practices, and policies. By focusing upstream on policies and practices, we hope to improve conditions not just for our patients but for the entire community and to reduce health disparities. It is by far the most challenging and rewarding undertaking of my career—transforming myself, the organization I work for, and hopefully the community in the process.

As we address social determinants of health in our communities, fewer children will have language delays because parents will have higher education and literacy levels, and they will have access to early childhood education. The city's housing codes will require landlords provide housing for families that is safe and without known exposures, resulting in fewer children with asthma having exacerbations requiring emergency room visits. Childhood obesity rates will drop, because children will have access to affordable healthy foods in their neighborhoods, safe places to play, and school meals that promote health. And the behavior problems associated with adverse childhood events and trauma will occur less often, because families will have more employment and educational opportunities, and support networks will be in place to assist families before they enter a crisis.

Bibliography

Association of American Medical Colleges. "Behavioral and Social Science Foundations for Future Physicians. 2011.

Braveman, P., S. Egerter, and D.R. Williams. "The Social Determinants of Health: Coming of Age." Annual Review of Public Health 32, no. 1 (2011): 381–98.

Cantor J., L. Cohen, L. Mikkelsen, R. Pañares, J. Srikantharajah, E. Valdovinos E., and B. Tierney. "Population health: A New Focus in Academic Medicine." Lecture presented at Episcopal Health Foundation Fall CCHH convening, Houston, TX. September 15, 2016.

Duggan, A., and R. L. Street, Jr. "Interpersonal Communication in Health and Illness." In Health Behavior: Theory, Research, and Practice, edited by K. Glanz, B. K. Rimer, & K. Viswanath. San Francisco, CA: Jossey-Bass, 2015.

Longest, B. B. "Health and Health Policy." In Health policymaking in the United States, 1–47. Chicago, IL: Health Administration Press, 2016.

Institute of Medicine. Improving Medical Education: Enhancing the Social and Behavioral Science Content of Medical School Curricula. National Academy Press, 2004.

———. Promoting Health: Intervention Strategies From Social and Behavioral Research, edited by Smedley, B.D.and L.S. Syme. Washington, DC: National Academic Press, 2001.

Prevention Institute. The Community-Centered Health Home Model: Updates and Learnings. Oakland, CA, 2016.

———. Community Centered Health Homes: Bridging the Gap Between Health Services and Community Prevention. Oakland, CA, 2011.

World Health Organization. Closing The Gap In A Generation: Health Equity Through Action on the Social Determinants of Health: Commission On Social Determinants of Health Final Report. Geneva, Switzerland: World Health Organization, Commission on Social Determinants of Health, 2008

Decision Making by Medical Providers in Treating Heart Disease

Carey Connor McNamara, PAC

HAVE YOU EVER been to a medical provider and wondered if they were ordering the right tests, or prescribing you the best treatment? We have all heard stories of people dying when their condition could have been treated or prevented, or stories about patients who go from doctor to doctor searching for answers and sometimes take years to find a solution. So how can we know if our medical providers are educated on the best tests and treatments available and are implementing them in our medical care? What factors affect the treatment decisions of our medical providers?

There are many ways to practice medicine. Some providers follow the current medical guidelines rigorously and would not consider straying outside these recommendations. They standardize their treatments based on outcome data from large medical studies, practicing what is called population medicine. Yet there are other medical providers who take a more flexible approach, working individually with patients to tailor a treatment plan that best addresses the belief system and lifestyle of the patient. They may take into consideration factors like family history or genetics, or may base some of their decisions on anecdotal experience. Instead of focusing on the conclusions of the latest studies, or just implementing the tried and true methods, these providers can be more open to new tests and treatments, and thus are referred to as early adopters.

Some of these less rigid providers may even focus on natural ways of treating and preventing disease, perhaps even suggesting forms of alternative medicine to address a patient's symptoms. So who is right? Which provider is delivering the best medical care? Is it ultimately good or bad when a medical provider strays from the current standard of care?

The answer to these questions would certainly vary based on personal opinion or circumstances, so it may be better to examine the underlying factors that shape a medical provider's decisions. As one example, we will take a look at heart disease.

HEART DISEASE IN THE UNITED STATES

In the United States, heart disease is the number one killer among both men and women, claiming more lives than all forms of cancer combined (Mozaffarian et al. 2015). For more than half of these patients, they have no warning signs of their illness—sudden cardiac death is actually their first sign of heart disease. And since half of the patients who experience a heart attack have normal LDL cholesterol, the question becomes: can we even beat this disease? (Sachdeva et al. 2009)

Evidenced-based medicine is undeniably a superior foundation for the practice of medicine than mere opinion or selective experience. Since randomized clinical trials have been shown to provide the best evidence, this data drives the formation of our nation's health care guidelines (Sniderman et al. 2013). Yet heart disease remains our number one killer, so what are we missing with this approach?

Some medical providers argue that we currently have the tools available to identify heart disease early as well as the treatments needed to beat this disease, but they are not being implemented in many medical offices. Using these resources in a way that would identify and aggressively treat the problem in the early stages (to effectively prevent a cardiovascular event) would require medical providers to go beyond the current standard of care, and in my experience, I have found that many providers feel uncomfortable deviating from the medical norms. Some providers may simply be unaware of these alternative tests and treatment models, but others are just not convinced there is a better way than following the guidelines. However, going above the current standard of care is not the same thing as going against it.

There are medical providers like Brad Bale, MD and Amy Doneen, DNP, ARNP, who have explored the current possibilities in medicine regarding preventing and reversing cardiovascular disease (CVD), and chosen to implement a more comprehensive approach with their patients. Bale and Doneen combine the use of advanced labs and imaging tests to directly check each patient for hidden risks of arterial disease, and their methods have been shown to halt or reverse CVD in peer-reviewed studies (Cheng et al. 2016). They even wrote a book to help educate others on all they have learned, *Beat the Heart Attack Gene: The Revolutionary Plan to Prevent Heart Disease, Stroke, and Diabetes* (Bale and Doneen 2014). Bale and Doneen stand by their methods, even offering a money-back guarantee to their patients. Their website states,

> Since 2008, we have offered all patients treated at our clinics—the
> Heart Attack & Stroke Prevention Center in Spokane, Washington
> and the Heart Attack, Stroke and Diabetes Center at the Grace Clinic

in Lubbock, Texas—a written guarantee stating that if they suffer a heart attack or stroke while under our care, we will refund 100% of the fees paid during the year. To date, we've only had to give one refund. (BaleandDoneen.com)

Bale and Doneen's (2014) methods for practicing medicine are discordant with current health care guidelines, and not chiefly directed by outcome data from large studies, yet they seem to be working. What do they know that other providers do not, or to which others choose not to subscribe?

When considering how to best answer this question, we need to look at the science behind heart disease. Heart disease begins with atherosclerosis, the process of plaque building up in the arteries, and it takes decades to develop before it leads to an actual event (heart attack, stroke, or death). Over time, plaque can grow in the arteries and eventually obstruct blood flow and oxygen to the heart—this is called obstructive coronary artery disease (AHA, *Heart and Stroke Encyclopedia*). This is the type of heart disease that can be identified by a traditional stress test, but only in the advanced stages of the disease process, usually when 70 percent or more of the artery is blocked (Harvard Medical School 2016). Standard medical practice suggests that a symptomatic patient with this degree of blockage would warrant a surgical intervention (a stent or cardiac bypass surgery), so by the time a cardiac stress test becomes abnormal, we are long past prevention.

However, patients with mild to moderate degrees of plaque growth can be in danger too, because if the plaque is soft and vulnerable, it can rupture and lead to the sudden development of a blood clot (Falk 1992; Harvard Medical School 2015). That clot can then obstruct an artery and cause a heart attack or stroke, even in a patient who has recently passed a stress test with a cardiologist. In fact, the majority of heart attacks occur from ruptured plaques, so traditional testing with a cardiologist would not detect these patients at risk (Texas Heart Institute). This is what happened with NBC journalist Tim Russert. His cholesterol and blood pressure were well controlled within the guidelines, and he passed his stress test without any problems, but then a few weeks later he died suddenly from a blood clot to his heart (Grady 2008).

The early stages of atherosclerosis are not easily measured by "outcome" data (meaning how many patients actually have a heart attack, stroke, or other poor CVD outcome). Dr. Michael Makover and Dr. Michael Schloss from NYU School of Medicine wrote a convincing article in the *Journal of Clinical Lipidology* expounding on this challenge and defending their stance in support of new treatment approaches to atherosclerosis (Makover and Schloss 2006). They argue that the causes of atherosclerosis are multifaceted among patients, so medical providers cannot effectively manage a patient's risk through simple algorithmic guidelines.

Makover and Schloss explain that: "Medicine is an art-based science. The quality of the science is critical but ineffective unless applied correctly to the unique needs of each patient. It is the application that is the art" (2).

As a physician assistant working in family practice for seventeen years, I have come across various perspectives on how to best treat/prevent heart disease; nonetheless, most medical providers shape their treatment decisions around the current guidelines. This makes sense for a lot of reasons, but the guidelines still have their drawbacks. Let's look at some of the pros and cons surrounding the current paradigms for treating heart disease, and see if we can ascertain what factors ultimately shape a medical provider's treatment decisions.

CULTURE OF MEDICINE AND ACCEPTED NORMS

Medical guidelines help to answer the most critical questions related to clinical practice; they aim to improve the quality of decision-making in medicine by standardizing the approach to care. Today these documents are established by a panel of experts and grounded in evidenced-based medicine. They are typically viewed as the best standard of care, and as new data unfolds, the guidelines change. In addition to evaluating data from randomized clinical trials, the panel of experts also assesses the risks versus benefits of the recommended treatments and the cost-effectiveness of the treatment. In the end, consensus statements on best practice in health care are provided, with a goal to help providers avoid over or under treating a patient's risk factors. Doctors use guidelines to steer their treatment decisions, but the guidelines are not perfect (The National Academies of Sciences, Engineering, Medicine 2011). According to Makover and Schloss (2016):

> Guideline committees are rigidly structured, and more recently, required to rely almost exclusively on randomized clinical trials. Although of great value in testing the effectiveness of specific inter-ventions, they are subject to many flaws, biases, and limitations . . . In most successful preventive efforts, the intervention is focused on treating and controlling the underlying disease process, not simply the clinical manifestations. (3)

The current guidelines, as outlined by the National Lipid Association (NLA), recommend using risk calculators to assess a patient's future risk of heart disease. These risk calculators incorporate a few easily measured characteristics of the patient, and are tested by how well they predict the risk of hard end points (such as a heart attack or stroke), within the next decade. Since atherosclerosis can take decades to develop, and these risk calculators do not take into account factors like genetics, family history, prediabetes, waist circumference, triglycerides, or advanced biomarkers of inflammation, these calculators can underestimate cardiovascular risk in some patients. This is especially the case for younger patients who are at risk, because the calculators are heavily weighted by age (Blumenthal 2014). Sadly, data shows that a majority of middle-aged patients who experienced a first heart attack did not even have a risk factor profile that would have qualified them for preventive medical therapy (Akosah, Schaper, Cogbill, and Schoenfeld 2003).

Risk algorithms may be effective in populations, but they should not be utilized as a prescriptive formula because they are limited in predictive power for individuals (Grundy et al. 2005). For some patients, they can lead to misclassification of true risk (Berman et al. 2004). Instead, such tools should be viewed as a starting point in assessing a patient's cardiovascular risk—a resource to help *guide* the practitioner in their medical decision-making. Even the NLA advises practitioners to take other factors into consideration when making treatment decisions for patients (Bays, Jones, Brown, and Jacobson 2014). In their annual summary of clinical lipidology they state,

> This summary should not be interpreted as rules or directives with regard to the most appropriate care of an individual patient because no set of recommendations or guidelines can have 100% applicability to an individual patient. Thus, evaluation and treatment decisions should be based on individual circumstances. As such, this document should be used in conjunction with, and not a replacement for the preferences of patients with dyslipidemia and the judgment of their treating clinicians. (S3)

Even though guideline committees advise against using their summaries in a strict, algorithmic way, there are providers who still do this. Maybe because adhering to the guidelines is considered a respectable approach—it is not typically questioned by other health care practitioners, or by the legal system in a malpractice lawsuit. On the other hand, providers who stray outside the guidelines sometimes face reproach from peers in their field.

An alternate approach for prevention of cardiovascular disease includes ordering advanced lipid testing on patients. The advanced panels incorporate a more thorough and accurate measurement of the quality (not just the quantity) of cholesterol, and can also include genetic tests, tests for prediabetes, and tests for vascular inflammation; however, the current clinical recommendations do not indicate this is necessary. Even though certain advanced lipid measurements have outperformed basic lipid measurements in predicting CVD, the NLA only suggests checking these advanced lipid markers as an optional secondary treatment target for select patients (Sniderman et al. 2011; Bays, Jones, Brown, and Jacobson 2014, S6).

Many medical providers conclude that if a test or treatment is not included in the current guidelines, which are scrutinized by experts in the field, then it must not be best practice. And since most practitioners do not have the time to read multiple medical studies on their own and sort through the data, they simply defer to the guidelines. But there may be other factors that have also tainted their thoughts regarding advanced lipid testing.

PERSONAL EXPERIENCE/TRAINING

There are many sources of information for medical providers, from the instructors and preceptors in medical school, to the ongoing medical training required to maintain their license. Practitioners actually get to choose the topics and venues in which they obtain their "continuing medical education" credits. Even with standardized credentialing, medical providers have the power to choose which direction to go in medicine, and each one is influenced by their individual training and experiences.

In addition, the weight of the evidence seems to say that interaction with pharmaceutical representatives plays a significant role in the prescribing habits of the medical providers. Exposure to their data and marketing strategies likely affects a provider's choice when prescribing medicine (Gallan 2004). Reputable research organizations like the National Institute of Health do not have a budget to wine and dine physicians in order to share their latest data; only drug companies with a vested interest do this. Ultimately, the medical data that providers are exposed to, whether biased or not, plays a role in their decision making.

Though providers have to be careful not to become narrow minded from their personal experience, anecdotal successes or failures influence their perceptions about treatments. If a provider follows a certain treatment model with success, they will most likely continue to use this model. But if their patients continue to have problems within this model, they may start looking into alternative options.

Medical providers may shift focus and become open to a different medical approach after a disease has personally impacted them. Maybe a family member contracts an illness that mainstream medicine cannot seem to remedy, or a beloved patient has not responded to the prescribed treatments. But what happens when their colleagues practice the same way and do not have the answers? Is there a willingness to go outside the current norms or standards to search for alternative or advanced treatment options for the patient?

LACK OF KNOWLEDGE

Many practitioners are simply uninformed about other approaches to cardio-vascular treatment, and it is important to recognize that ignorance is not the same thing as opposition. How many medical providers are not using a particular mode of testing simply because they are unaware of it? Or maybe they have heard of the testing but do not understand how to interpret and apply the information clinically.

As a new physician assistant out of school, I was uncertain myself. It was years before I realized it was okay for me to practice slightly differently than other medical providers. It took time for me to grow in my clinical judgment and in my confidence to stray beyond the current guidelines. For years, I practiced traditional lipid management because that is all I knew. When I first heard of advanced lipid testing, I wanted to learn more, but I struggled to find local colleagues who had experience in this area. It took effort to search out additional training.

Additionally, as a physician assistant I did not have the authority to order these advanced tests on my patients until my supervising physician agreed to set up an account with one of the advanced laboratories. This lack of autonomy in a medical practice can be a limiting factor to ordering advanced labs for midlevel providers, and also for hospital-owned practices that require their offices to only use in-house laboratories.

TIME WITH PATIENTS

In general I believe most medical providers care about their patient's well-being and want to provide quality medical care to those they treat. However, in order to do this, providers have to overcome several obstacles. One of those obstacles is time.

A study from the 2016 *Annals of Internal Medicine* showed that doctors are not spending their entire fifteen-minute appointment slot on direct patient care. In this study, led by Dr. Christine Sinsky from the American Medical Association, fifty-seven physicians from family practice, internal medicine, orthopedics, or cardiology were observed for 430 hours. Sinsky found that even when the doctor was in the examination room with the patients, he or she only spent 52.9 percent of the time talking to or examining them—37 percent of this time was spent doing paperwork. So that fifteen-minute appointment actually equates to less than eight minutes of direct care (Sinsky et al. 2016).

Insurance companies set the standard for reimbursements and thus shape the time limit for these appointments. Decreased insurance reimbursements and increased expectations with medical documentation have forced medical providers to provide a lower quality of care to their patients. Shorter visits are assumed to equate with reduced health care costs, but this may be a nearsighted way of evaluating cost. These short appointments can lead to higher future costs if medical problems are overlooked and medical errors occur as a result. So are health care companies really benefitting from short appointment times?

A study published in 2003 in the *American Journal of Public Health* demonstrates that physicians do not have enough time to provide all the preventative services recommended by the US Preventative Services Task Force. In the end, less preventative care can mean higher rates of disease over time and increased health care costs as a result (Yarnall et al. 2003).

There are numerous increasing demands for additional chart documentation and coding and extra buttons to press that "prove" certain expected measurements are being done. Though it makes sense to try and hold medical providers to a high standard, and reward those who are providing quality medical care versus substandard care, the additional time it takes to enter these new detailed diagnoses and compliance codes only ends up impeding the quality of care extended to the patient.

There are also time constraints connected to accessing the best treatments for the patient. Insurance companies are placing increasing restrictions on which medications they will cover, and practitioners are forced to prescribe the cheap generic medications, even though this may not be the best treatment available. Preauthorization paperwork can be required if the patient warrants an exception, which takes additional time and resources to complete (Bendix 2013).

In addition to the time limitations related to direct patient care, there are challenges connected with the ability to stay current with the latest medical studies and advances. Doctors are not researchers, so they need sound bites to keep them in the loop. Many will subscribe to newsletters such as "Prescribers Letter" or "Up To Date," where other medical providers have read the most recent data and then abbreviate it into a short synopsis. Resources such as these are typically grounded in evidenced-based medicine and can be extremely helpful; however, they also carry limitations, such as potential author bias. And yet some medical providers view these newsletters like the guidelines, as if they are the final say. I once had a doctor question my use of advanced lipid testing simply because he had not read about it in "Up To Date."

THE ECONOMICS OF MEDICINE

Everyone knows that "time is money," so these two factors overlap in many ways. A three-minute appointment is typically reimbursed the same as a thirty-minute appointment, so the more patients a physician sees in a day, the more money he or she makes. Certainly the ethics of medicine come into play here, because financial gain should not take precedence over what is best for the patient. But this is not a straightforward problem.

We mentioned already that insurance companies could be nearsighted with their cost/benefit analysis. Some insurance companies refuse to pay for advanced lipid testing, because it costs more than a standard lipid panel. Interestingly, an assessment of the long-term benefits of advanced lipid testing demonstrates enormous cost savings. According to a peer-reviewed study in *The Journal of Medical Economics,* routinely ordering inflammation testing in patients can reduce heart attacks and strokes by nearly 10 percent, which would equate to an enormous cost savings for patients and the health care system (Penn et al. 2015). These advanced biomarkers can identify vascular inflammation connected with the risk of a plaque rupture and highlight a patient's hidden cardiovascular risk. If the markers are abnormal, a medical provider could intervene earlier with a more aggressive and strategic treatment plan for these patients.

BELIEF SYSTEMS AND PERSONALITY

As previously stated, some medical providers prefer to be more structured in the way they practice medicine and follow the guidelines as closely as possible. These practitioners tend to wait longer before adopting new ideas or treatments, and are sometimes referred to as late adopters. I tend to view these providers as more "thinkers" than "feelers," because they are less easily swayed by an emotional appeal or anecdotal experience.

Early adopters, on the other hand, tend to be more flexible in their approach to patient care (Lubloy 2014). They get excited about new tests and treatments they can try with their patients, hoping they might stumble upon something better. Their personality tends toward including the patient in the decision making and tailoring treatments individually based on the patient's preference and specific needs.

MAKING SOCIOLOGICAL SENSE

In trying to make sociological sense of the factors that contribute to physician decision making with patients suffering from heart disease, an essential element relates to the culture of medicine and the relationships physicians have with one another. Sociologist Charles Horton Cooley developed the looking-glass self theory to explain how people formulate their identities through a process of socialization that takes into account the interactions with others in the social development of the person. He argues that people shape their self-concepts based on their understanding of how others perceive them.

No matter how much someone might want to claim that they are their own person, meaning they make their decisions independent of what others think or feel about a given topic, much of their identity, beliefs, likes, opinions, and behaviors are a product of the way they think others view them. Cooley says the idea is that people in our close environment serve as the "mirrors" that reflect images of ourselves.

According to Cooley, as we present our social selves to others, we imagine how other people see us. We also imagine how other people evaluate our behavior and social selves. From those imagined evaluations, we develop our own sense of identity and who we are, as well as our behavior, as a result of how we think others see us. At times our assessment is correct, but since much of our identities are based on imagined evaluations and interpretations (we don't know what people actually think of us), at other times we can be wrong. Cooley points out, though, that those perceptions of how others see us are powerful predictors of how we feel about ourselves and shape our self-conceptions (Cooley 1998).

Related to Cooley's theory is the work of sociologist Erving Goffman, who offers important insight into the tendency of people to interact with others on the basis of creating and maintaining a positive impression. He calls this the art of impression management. This involves a series of techniques that people use to manipulate and control the flow of information from the actor to his or her audience, thereby conveying a more positive impression in their minds about the person (Goffman 1969).

Cooley's and Goffman's theories are helpful in understanding how physicians make decisions about patient care. Because they are concerned about how their colleagues might view them, and because physicians, like all professions, use colleagues and coworkers to create and maintain a reputation or social identity, using the feedback they receive about practicing medicine, they are vulnerable to conventional wisdom about certain forms of treatment or the value of protocols. This could be one reason why so many physicians adhere so closely to the industry-created guidelines for treating heart disease, or do not explore innovative testing until the rest of the medical community accepts those practices as valid. In other words, pressures from colleagues and patients to practice a certain way (inside or outside a certain paradigm) will ultimately influence a medical provider's tendencies in treating a patient.

CONCLUSION

There are a variety of factors that influence a medical provider's decision making. Though not an exhaustive list, these factors include: the culture of medicine and accepted norms among peers, personal belief systems and personality, training and knowledge base, time limitations, and profitability. There are sociological implications to why health care providers practice differently, and patients should realize these factors directly affect the care they are receiving. Providers who strictly adhere to the guidelines are practicing population-based medicine, shaping their treatment choices around generalized data from the results of large studies. On the other hand, providers who practice personalized medicine tailor treatments individually to each patient based on their specific risks, needs, and preferences. Since medicine is an art-based science, there are different ways of addressing symptoms, and the best solution can vary among patients.

Bibliography

Akosah, K. O., A. Schaper, C. Cogbill, and P. Schoenfeld. "Preventing Myocardial Infarction in the Young Adult in the First Place: How Do the National Cholesterol Education Panel III Guidelines Perform?" *Journal of the American College of Cardiology* 41, no. 9 (2003): 1475–79.

American Heart Association. "atherosclerosis." *Heart and Stroke Encyclopedia*. http://www.heart.org/HEARTORG/Encyclopedia/Heart-and-Stroke-Encyclopedia_UCM_445084_ContentIndex.jsp?title=atherosclerosis.

Bale, B. and A. Doneen. *Beating the Heart Attack Gene: A Revolutionary Plan to Prevent Heart Disease, Stroke and Diabetes.* New York: John Wiley and Sons, 2014.

Bays, H. E., P. H. Jones, W. V. Brown, and T. A. Jacobson. "National Lipid Association Annual Summary of Clinical Lipidology 2015." *Journal of Clinical Lipidology* 8, no. 6 (2014): Supplement, S1–S36.

Bendix, J. "Curing the Prior Authorization Headache." *Medical Economics*. October 10, 2013. http://medicaleconomics.modernmedicine.com/medical-economics/content/tags/americas-health-insurance-plans/curing-prior-authorization-headache.

Berman, D. S., N. D. Wong, H. Gransar, R. Miranda-Peats, J. Dahlbeck, S. W. Hayes, J. D. Friedman, X. Kang, D. Polk, R. Hachamovitch, L. Shaw, and A. Rozanski. "Relationship Between Stress-Induced Myocardial Ischemia and Atherosclerosis Measured by Coronary Calcium Tomography." *Journal of the American College of Cardiology* 44, no. 4 (2004): 923–30.

Blumenthal, R. "The New CV Prevention Guidelines are Here!" *John Hopkins Medicine*. January 6, 2014. https://www.hopkinsmedicine.org/news/publications/

cardiovascular_report/ cardiovascular_report_winter_2014/the_new_cv_
prevention_guidelines_are_here.

Cheng, H. G., B. S. Patel, S. S. Martin, M. Blaha, A. Doneen, B. Bale, and S. R. Jones. "Effect of Comprehensive Cardiovascular Disease Risk Management on Longitudinal Changes in Carotid Artery Intima-Media Thickness in a Community-Based Prevention Clinic." *Archives of Medical Science* 12, no. 4 (2016): 728–35.

Cooley, Charles Horton. *On Self and Social Organization*. Chicago, Il; University of Chicago Press, 1998.

Falk, E. "Why do Plaques Rupture?" *Circulation* 86, no. 6 (1992): 11130–42.

Gallan, A. "Factors that Influence a Physician's Prescribing of Pharmeceuticals: A Literature Review." *Journal of Pharmaceutical Marketing and Management* 16, no. 4 (2004): 3–46.

Goffman, Erving. *The Presentation of Self in Everyday Life.* New York; Basic Books, 1969.

Grady, Denise. "From a Prominent Death, Some Painful Truths." *The New York Times.* June 24, 2008. http://www.nytimes.com/2008/06/24/health/24hear.html.

Graham, Robin, Michelle Mancher, Dianne Miller Wolman, Sheldon Greenfield, and Earl Steinberg, eds. *Clinical Practice Guidelines We Can Trust.* Washington, D.C.: The National Academies Press, 2011. https://www.nap.edu/read/13058/chapter/1.

Grundy, S. M., J. I. Cleeman, S.R. Daniels, K.A. Donato, R.H. Eckel, B.A. Franklin, D.J. Gordon, R. M. Krauss, P. J. Savage, S. C. Smith, J. A. Spertus, and F. Costa. "Diagnosis and Management of the Metabolic Syndrome: An American Heart Association/ National Heart, Lung, and Blood Institute Scientific Statement." *Circulation* 112, no. 17 (2005): 2735–52.

Harvard Medical School. "The Problem with Plaque: Even Lesser Amounts are Still Risky." *Harvard Heart Letter.* February 2015. https://www.health.harvard.edu/ heart-health/the-problem-with-plaque-even-lesser-amounts-are-still-risky

———. "Cardiac Exercise Stress Testing: What It Can and Cannot Tell You." *Harvard Men's Health Watch.* March 18, 2016. https://www.health.harvard.edu/ heart-disease-overview/cardiac-exercise-stress-testing-what-it-can-and-cannot-tell-you.

Lubloy, A. "Factors Affecting the Uptake of New Medicines: A Systematic Literature Review." *BMC Health Services Research* 14 (2014): 469.

Makover, M. E., and M. Schloss. "The Very High Residual Degree of Death and Disease From Atherosclerosis Needs New Approaches." *Journal of Clinical Lipidology* 10, no. 3 (2016): 466–8.

Mozaffarian, D.; E. J. Benjamin; A. S. Go; D. K. Arnett; M. J. Blaha; M. Cushman; S. de Ferranti ; J. P. Després; H. J. Fullerton; V. J. Howard; M. D. Huffman; S. E. Judd; B. M. Kissela ; D. T. Lackland; J. H. Lichtman; L. D. Lisabeth; S. Liu; R. H. Mackey; D. B. Matchar ; D. K. McGuire; E. R. Mohler, 3rd; C. S. Moy; P. Muntner; M. E.

Mussolino; K. Nasir ; R. W. Neumar; G. Nichol; L. Palaniappan; D. K. Pandey; M. J. Reeves; C. J. Rodriguez ; P. D. Sorlie; J. Stein; A. Towfighi; T. N. Turan; S. S. Virani; J. Z. Willey; D. Woo ; R. W. Yeh; M. B. Turner; and on behalf of the American Heart Association Statistics Committee and Stroke Statistics Subcommittee. "Heart Disease and Stroke Statistics – 2015 Update. A Report from the American Heart Association." *Circulation* 131, (2015): e29–e322.

Penn, M. S.; M. A. Yenikomshian; A. K. G. Cummings; A. Klemes; J. M. Damron; S. Purvis; M. Beidelschies; and H. G. Birnbaum. "The Economic Impact of Implementing a Multiple Inflammatory Biomarker-Based Approach to Identify, Treat, and Reduce Cardiovascular Risk." *Journal of Medical Economics* 18, no. 7 (2015): 483–91.

Sachdeva, A.; C. P. Cannon; P. C. Deedwania; K. A. Labaresh; S. C. Smith Jr.; D. Dai; A. Hernandez; and G. C. Fonarow. "Lipid Levels in Patients Hospitalized with Coronary Artery Disease: An Analysis of 136,905 Hospitalizations in Get with the Guidelines." *American Heart Journal* 157, no. 1 (2009): 111–17.e2.

Sinsky, C.; L. Colligan; L. Li; M. Prgomet; S. Reynolds; L. Goeders; J. Westbrook; M. Tutty ; and G. Blike. "Allocation of Physician Time in Ambulatory Practice: A Time and Motion Study in 4 Specialties." *Annals of Internal Medicine* 165, no. 11 (2016): 753–60.

Sniderman, A. D.; K. J. LaChapelle; N.A. Rachon; and C. D. Furber. "The Necessity for Clinical Reasoning in the Era of Evidence-Based Medicine." *MayoClinic Proceedings* 88, no. 10 (2013) 1108–14.

Sniderman, A. D.; K. William; J. H. Contois; H. M. Monroe; M. J. McQueen; J. de Graa; and C. D. Furberg. "A Meta-Analysis of Low-Density Lipoprotein Cholesterol, Non-High-Density Lipoprotein Cholesterol, and Apolipoprotein B as Markers of Cardiovascular Risk." *Circulation:* Cardiovascular Quality and Outcomes 4, (2011): 337–45.

Texas Heart Institute. "Coronary Artery Disease." https://www.texasheart.org/heart-health/heart-information-center/topics/coronary-artery-disease/.

Yarnall, K. S. H.; K. I. Pollak; T. Ostbye; K. M. Krause; and J. L. Michener. "Primary Care: Is There Enough Time for Prevention?" *American Journal of Public Health* 93, no. 4 (2003): 635–41.

The Sociology of Chiropractic Medicine

Robert McNamara, PhD

A FEW MONTHS ago, I spent the weekend moving several yards of mulch around my front and back yards. By the end of the day, I was tired and sore. I woke up the next morning and realized that my back muscles were in spasm and told my wife that I was "out of alignment." As a medical professional, one who also made semiregular use of a chiropractor, she knew that meant I would be visiting a local chiropractor for an adjustment.

We had made use of several different chiropractors over the years to treat back and neck injuries. My first experience with a chiropractor, who was a friend at the time, involved an initial assessment, complete with x-rays and a consultation, that indicated the curvature of my neck was insufficient and would require several treatments to restore it to normal levels. This, I was told, was causing my occasional back pain. I came back the next day and received my first adjustment.

I remember lying face down on a table and the chiropractor, a Logan University graduate, performed a technique called "basic" on me. This involved the chiropractor finding an area around my buttocks (I later learned there is a nerve that runs through that area), with one hand while the other pressed into the area in spasm. Then he used a series of techniques on me that resulted in loud noises from this strange table that had sections that dropped once he put pressure on that portion of my body. The spasms were alleviated, at least temporarily and some of the pain subsided. Other visits produced similar results, so I would occasionally visit this provider for treatment.

After moving to another part of South Carolina, we found another chiropractor who specialized in sports injuries. This was the provider I visited after my mulching adventure. My experiences with this chiropractor were quite different, however. While there were different techniques used, there were also noticeable "audibles" from the adjustment. These cracking sounds, I later learned, were the release of gases in the body, similar to what is heard when a person cracks their knuckles. Still, it was a bit unsettling, particularly when the adjustment involved my neck. The stiffness and pain relief from these adjustments was considerable though. At times, the muscle spasm would stop almost immediately and the range of motion from the problem area would be restored, while in other cases, when the injury was severe, such as the one from my mulching experience, the problem took a day or two to resolve. I was often sore from these adjustments, and could not tell if the ice pack was to help with the initial injury, the adjustment, or both.

After being treated a few times by this chiropractor, I became curious about exactly what was going on during treatment. These visits were very different from those involving my primary care physician, so I wondered what the chiropractor did that my regular doctor did not. During these treatments, I would allow the chiropractor to gently massage my back and then use his hands to feel along my spine area, and he would invariably find a spot that triggered pain or discomfort. He would leave his finger in that spot and then use it as a marker to manipulate the area, even when I would not offer where my pain was coming from. He would also hold my feet together and bend my knees as if measuring them. That was a bit confusing too. After a few treatments, I asked, "How does this all work? How did you know where the problem was?" He would typically shrug and say, "I don't know, it's all God." Wait, what?

As a Christian, I think he was trying to be humble, but I never really received a complete answer to my question. I trusted this doctor, who also became a friend, and he was making me feel better so I was willing to let it go at first, but my curiosity led me to learn more about chiropractic medicine. I have since learned that these types of comments are not uncommon from some chiropractors, in part because of the philosophy of treatment and the training they receive, and in part because there generally is not a scientific explanation of what occurs.

As it turns out, the religious component of what this particular chiropractor said to me has been the topic of some sociological research. For instance, Meister (2010), using paradigms from the sociology of religion, offered insight into the evangelical nature of chiropractic medicine, where providers used techniques employed by high-profile pastors to convince prospective patients to visit their offices. Meister's subjects also used a form of evangelism to globally distinguish chiropractic from traditional medical treatments by physician, thereby giving it a more divine inspiration. A third technique used by chiropractors in Meister's research involved providers using their own illnesses to serve as a kind of religious testimony, a technique also used by some evangelical pastors. These efforts were successful largely because the patients were familiar with a Christian message, and the techniques established a pastor-like trust with patients. As Meister points out, nothing in the message had anything to do with scientifically validated forms of treatment, but it did provide a platform to distinguish chiropractors from other medical doctors and, especially, from other chiropractors in the area.

The scientific validity of chiropractic treatment is controversial to be sure, and there are many chiropractors who absolutely believe in the science behind the treatments, but a significant challenge for chiropractic medicine centers around the issue of whether there is adequate proof about the effectiveness of chiropractic adjustments, particularly as they compare with other forms of treatment. Some chiropractors scoff at science and other rational forms of verification in favor of the dogmatic belief that what they do, like faith, is beyond scientific inquiry. Many chiropractors from this school of thought point to the fact that patients say they feel better, thereby validating the treatment. However, patient satisfaction or the relief of symptoms is not proof that a technique worked. As critics point out, the power of suggestion and/or a placebo effect can convince a patient that they feel better. Thus these accounts are analogous to customer satisfaction surveys and are not an adequate substitute for scientific validity.

THE PROJECT

This study attempts to explore the life of chiropractors in light of all the historical and current changes taking place within the medical profession. It also seeks to understand the external and internal threats posed to chiropractors, with an eye towards understanding how and in what ways the future of medicine, as well as their visions for the profession in the future, will alter what we currently understand to be chiropractic care. Some providers have noted that either the profession will have to become better organized to establish an identity, find a way to the mainstream with traditional medicine (as more chiropractic colleges appear to be doing), relegate themselves to technicians who perform a limited array of treatments for back and neck pain, but do not really serve as primary health care providers, or disband all together.

A host of issues are generated from any one of these possible scenarios, and there appears to be less optimism within the profession about its future. This is particularly true since many other health care providers, such as physical therapists, osteopathic doctors, and even some types of massage therapists, can often provide a similar type of treatment offered by chiropractors. Despite the concerns and challenges within the profession, according to the US Department of Labor, the chiropractic profession is growing at a much faster trajectory than other professions (US Department of Labor Statistics 2015). Despite this optimism, given the costs involved in completing chiropractic training (which can cost between $150,000–$200,000, as much as medical school) coupled with the low salary (recent data from the US Department of Labor Statistics shows that the median salary for a chiropractor is $64,440 per year and other data indicates that it could be lower), along with the challenges of starting and sustaining an individual practice (with considerable startup costs along with the challenges of generating a large patient base when most chiropractors are operating as solo practitioners), these obstacles are formidable ones.

This is particularly true in light of the recent development of large chiropractic chains such as *the Joint,* that offer spinal and neck adjustments at a fraction of the cost of a traditional provider (McNamara 2017). In light of all these challenges, how are chiropractors coping? What are some of the real and potential consequences of these changes, and how are existing providers, even successful ones, managing these turbulent times? As Medicare requirements increase the amount of documentation and verification required to certify that certain treatments are medically necessary, adding to the workload of providers, and reimbursement rates decline, it is possible that many chiropractors could decide to close their practices. It is also possible that the difficulties of sustaining a practice, along with the competition for patients among providers, could cause some chiropractors to engage in questionable practices and treatments in order to diversify and generate revenue (McNamara 2018). The Office of Inspector General's (2016) recent report about Medicare fraud focuses a great deal of attention on some of these practices by chiropractors.

AN ETHNOGRAPHIC APPROACH

This ethnographic study used classic techniques of systematic observation and unstructured and semistructured interviews with patients (Lecomte and Schensul 2012; Taylor 2002) of South Carolina chiropractors and their staff, to learn more about the nature of chiropractic care and how the proposed changes in health care impact the profession's viability. Time was spent in numerous chiropractic offices learning about the procedures used in operating a practice, observing interactions between staff and patients, as well as examining the role of the chiropractor within the practice. Formal interviews were conducted with staff members, patients, and providers, along with informal conversations that occurred as a normal part of the ethnographic approach. Visits to various chiropractic offices occurred twice a week for approximately eighteen months, with each visit lasting approximately three to four hours, including the interviews.

Some practices focus on certain segments of the patient population, such as pregnant women, sports injuries, pediatrics, or family practices, which involve an entire family seeing the provider for wellness care. Other differences between practices focus on how potential patients are identified, either through referrals, social media, online marketing, or practice-building seminars designed to enhance revenue and the size of the practice. On several occasions, while making observations in waiting rooms, informal conversations with patients occurred, which helped to gauge their understanding of chiropractic medicine, the services offered by the provider, and their overall feelings about the benefits of treatment.

Additionally, phone interviews were conducted with provosts, deans, and faculty at several schools of chiropractic medicine to learn more about the training that students receive. Given that the philosophies of a particular chiropractic college drive the nature of the medical practices of its graduates, it is also important to understand how the various chiropractic colleges and their faculty and staff socialize students to understand what chiropractic care looks like, along with what their professional futures might be in the changing face of medicine in this country.

Interviews were also conducted with members of other related professions, such as physical therapists, osteopathic doctors, and acupuncturists, to learn more about how they understand the role of chiropractors in relation to what they do in their own profession. Interviews were also conducted with medical doctors, including specialists such as orthopedic surgeons, general practitioners/ family practice doctors, and others in the profession who could be likely to refer patients to chiropractors based on the nature of the injury or illness. Their perspective was designed to gain some insight into the nature of how the medical community generally perceives chiropractors and the range of treatments, if any, that they feel chiropractors have to offer.

Finally, in an effort to understand more about the questionable practices of some chiropractors, interviews were conducted with representatives from Medicare concerning the auditing process and efforts to bring some level of accountability to the billing for chiropractic care. This was an important part of the discussion with providers since the penalties derived from audits mean that chiropractors could have to pay back some of the fees for which they were reimbursed. An understanding of the process and the extent of the problem was critical to the project since it has become a central feature of life for most chiropractors.

In sum, face-to-face and telephone interviews were conducted for this project, each lasting approximately one to two hours, and covering a range of activities and issues that span the discussion of chiropractic medicine. Additionally, numerous informal conversations occurred with practitioners and others associated with the medicine over the course of the project. In total, approximately one hundred interviews and conversations occurred from fall 2016 through fall 2017.

CHIROPRACTIC MEDICINE DEFINED

It may be fair to say that most people really do not understand much about chiropractic medicine or exactly what chiropractors do. If you asked an average

American about chiropractic medicine, it is likely to result in an array of questions about it. In addition to the obvious questions, such as what exactly is chiropractic medicine, how does it work, and what type of people make use of this type of care, other questions about comparisons to physicians are inevitable, since that is what most people use as an identifying marker in medicine.

For those who understand a bit about traditional medicine, questions such as what types of people become chiropractors and how are they different from traditional physicians are likely to be asked, along with those that raise concerns about the level of credibility of chiropractors compared to physicians. Other questions could include those about the way chiropractors operate. These are all reasonable questions but, unfortunately, the answers to them are not nearly as straightforward or simple. As we will see, the confusing nature of chiropractic medicine can lead some people to be skeptical about treatments and providers.

In addition to these questions, there are a host of sociological questions about chiropractors and chiropractic medicine, particularly in light of the recent health care reform taking place in the United States.[1] Other issues ripe for sociological discussion include the professional identity and social standing of chiropractors and their efforts to stake a claim as a legitimate provider of various forms of treatment. Also important for consideration are the issues and challenges involved in the training and education of chiropractors, along with the political and social issues stemming from the profession.

Similarly, the interactions and relationships between chiropractors and patients, between chiropractors and physicians, and between chiropractors and the general public, also generate fascinating sociological discussions about the profession. While some of these topics have been explored by other sociologists and researchers in the past, given the numerous changes to the medical landscape in the United States, one of the goals of the present study is to understand the impact of the changes taking place in the current health care environment as they relate to chiropractic medicine.

As one advocate of chiropractic medicine involved in this study noted, there are lots of "warts," or limitations, in medicine and most providers would rather

---

1   As an initial disclaimer, I am not a medical doctor nor a chiropractor, so I cannot claim any level of medical expertise that would allow me to offer insight into the biomechanics or neurophysiology about whether there are in fact misalignments in a person's vertebrae, if the nerves are being impeded, or even if there is such a thing as Innate Intelligence or Vitalism (key components to understanding some versions of chiropractic medicine). The debate and controversy are, by themselves, worthy of sociological observation and I believe there is a role for sociology to play in understanding this profession and its place in medicine.

not discuss or call attention to the ones in their own field (although they may be more willing to expose them in other professions). Similarly, there are those who enter a profession with less than ethical motives and for whom economic greed drives their efforts. To suggest that all chiropractors are quacks or frauds, or to imply that what they do is either a placebo or ineffective is an unfair assessment—traditional medicine or medical doctors struggle with similar criticisms and are not without flaws.

Both professions have "warts," both leave many questions unanswered about patients' health, and both continually need objective assessments of standard practices to ensure providers are offering the best care possible. The main difference between the two is that traditional medicine has continued to attempt to develop scientific explanations for the unknown aspects of medicine and until recently, chiropractic medicine has not. This has set in motion a contest of credibility for chiropractic medicine and providers within the medical community, the public, and in some cases, even each other.

WHAT IS CHIROPRACTIC MEDICINE?

Chiropractic medicine is one type of treatment that falls under the category of Complementary and Alternative Medicine (CAM). This collection of treatments, which include chiropractic medicine, acupuncture, yoga, herbal medicine, and other forms, has become increasingly popular in the United States. According to one estimate, in 1990 about a third of all Americans had used some form of CAM. By 2002 the number had nearly doubled, and the numbers continue to increase even today (McMillen 2011). Chiropractic care is perhaps the most widely known form of CAM, and it too has seen increases in popularity, despite the fact that only a small segment of the population actually knows, uses, and understands it.

According to the American Chiropractic Association, the largest organization within the profession, chiropractic medicine, is defined in the following way:

> Chiropractic is a health care profession that focuses on disorders of the musculoskeletal system and the nervous system, and the effects of these disorders on general health. Doctors of chiropractic—often referred to as DCs, chiropractors or chiropractic physicians—practice a drug-free, hands-on approach to health care that includes patient examination, diagnosis and treatment. In addition to their expertise in spinal manipulation/adjustment, doctors of chiropractic have broad diagnostic skills and are also trained to recommend therapeutic

and rehabilitative exercises, as well as to provide nutritional, dietary and lifestyle counseling. (American Chiropractic Associaion 2017)

From its very beginning, chiropractic medicine has faced challenges about the scientific validity of the treatment and the credibility of its practitioners. Since those early years, many of these criticisms have remained, but legislation, licensure, and litigation have created an environment where chiropractic care is allowed in all fifty states, and licenses are required of all chiropractors who wish to practice medicine. As the data indicates, chiropractic care, while still marginal in terms of popularity, has become more commonplace in recent years as a form of alternative treatment for people, particularly in the United States.

Evidence of the popularity of chiropractic medicine is seen in estimates that it is a $14 billion a year industry, particularly for neck and back injuries (English and Keating 2015). Still, many critics contend that chiropractic care lacks scientific rigor and amounts to quackery, fraud, or simply is no more effective as a form of treatment than traditional remedies. While the medical community is legally prohibited from discriminating against chiropractors, there remains a good deal of controversy and contention about chiropractic care and treatment.

THE PUBLIC'S PERCEPTION OF CHIROPRACTORS

The public seems poorly informed about what chiropractors do and the nature of chiropractic medicine. Surprisingly little data has been collected on the public's perception of chiropractors in the United States. Of what data does exist, many practitioners call attention to recent research that suggests about 14 percent of the population uses a chiropractor, an increase from the 9 percent found in a 2012 study by the National Health Interview Survey.

More recently, according to a 2015 report by Gallup, entitled "Americans' Perceptions of Chiropractic," which was a collaboration between Gallup and the Palmer College of Chiropractic, found that about 14 percent of Americans (approximately thirty-three million people) have visited a chiropractor in the last twelve months (English and Keating 2015). Additionally, about half the population had been seen by a chiropractor. Still, about as many Americans (49 percent) claim to have never seen a chiropractor. This data, in comparison to previous public opinion polls, suggests that the number of people willing to be treated by chiropractors, while still quite small, is increasing.

While this study's findings suggest more people are considering the use of a chiropractor, there are some patterns worth noting, particularly from those people who had never seen one. For instance, among the people surveyed, younger adults (age eighteen to thirty-four) compared to older adults (those thirty-five to forty-nine), are more likely to say they have never been to a chiropractor. Blacks (compared to whites or Hispanics), and men (compared to women), as well as people with higher levels of education and income (compared to those with fewer years of education or lower incomes), are more likely to have never seen a chiropractor (English and Keating 2015).

Among those who have made use of chiropractic treatment, most people average about one visit per month. In the survey, the average number of visits within the past year was eleven. Women are slightly more likely to see their chiropractors than men (with women averaging 11.5 visits compared to men with 9.4 visits in the last year). Older people, those age fifty to sixty-four, and those whose annual household income is between $50,000 and $100,000 report less frequent visits than users in other age and income categories (English and Keating 2015).

While the public generally does not really understand what chiropractors do or how someone becomes a chiropractor, this lack of understanding does not seem to affect people's overall assessment of them. About 50 percent of respondents agree that most chiropractors are trustworthy (39 percent state they did not know or had no opinion about the trustworthiness of members of this profession). Additionally, nearly 64 percent state they believe that most chiropractors have their patients' best interests in mind (28 percent state they did not know or had no opinion on this question). Generally speaking, these findings are consistent with previous research that those who have been treated by chiropractors are more likely to have a positive view of them (English and Keating 2015).

Those who do not use chiropractors, however, offer a different view. About a quarter of respondents think that chiropractic care is dangerous and about a third are unsure about those risks. That uncertainty increases to 47 percent among people who have never been to a chiropractor. That is, even if people have no opinion on the danger of chiropractic treatment, if one has not ever been to a chiropractor, those fears are heightened.

In sum, while the general public tends to look favorably upon the chiropractic profession and its practitioners, they still remain uninformed about exactly what chiropractic medicine is and how chiropractors provide treatment. There remains a good deal of skepticism about the profession, which is undoubtedly related to this lack of understanding as well as the lack of scientific studies that prove chiropractic treatment is an effective way of addressing back and neck pain. The public tends to see chiropractors not as primary care providers, but as providers to see if they have a neck or back problem, after first going to their primary care provider. These findings are an important part of the discussion of how chiropractors see themselves, as well as their understanding of their professional identity and place in medicine.

414 Sociology as Everyday Life

THE MEDICAL COMMUNITY'S PERCEPTION OF CHIROPRACTORS

While the public may offer some confidence and trust in chiropractors and in chiropractic treatments, such confidence is not and has not always been assigned to chiropractors or chiropractic care by the medical community (Ingraham 2016; Long 2013; Magner and Barrett, 1995; Singh and Ernst 2009).

For instance, critics point out that the training chiropractors receive is not on par with medical schools, and the knowledge chiropractors possess to diagnose and treat illness is inadequate. Critics also point to examples of unethical marketing practices, false claims, dangerous techniques, and the exploitation of patients, who cannot adequately discern the difference between medical doctors and chiropractors or understand the science behind chiropractic treatment. However, despite these criticisms, there is some evidence to justify chiropractic treatment as a form of treatment for some types of injuries (Paige et. al 2017).

Doctors are reluctant to refer patients to chiropractors, in part due to a lack of understanding about chiropractic medicine and in part because of the wide range of providers, some of whom engage in questionable treatments. As one doctor pointed out,

> I can't refer patients to a chiropractor because I have no idea what type of treatment they will receive. Some guys know what they are doing in terms of treating some types of neck and back injuries, but a lot of them are way out there and do goofy things that have no basis in science and don't help the patient. In fact, some of these guys could make the injury worse for that patient. I can't let my reputation be affected by that nor do I want patients getting hurt. It's not that I have anything personal against chiropractors, but the only way I am going to refer a patient to one is if I know what this guy is going to do once my patient gets to his office. And since I don't have time to investigate every chiropractor to separate the good ones from the weird ones, I simply can't take that chance.

Another doctor points out that chiropractors think all doctors are out to get them. He says:

> Listen, while there was a lawsuit many years ago because the AMA tried to shut chiropractors down, there remains this feeling that all doctors are against chiropractors or that physicians somehow feel threatened by what they do. I don't feel threatened since they are not going to take away patients from me...some of the things that I do can't be done by chiropractors, and even if they could,

there's no way they are going to be a threat to me—I have more work than I know how to manage as it is. But this perception that the medical community is threatened by chiropractors and so we try to cut them out of the industry is all in their heads. Maybe that's what they do to each other or that's what they might do if they were in our position, but the problem really feels to me like an example of their own inferiority complexes, and they are looking for someone to blame for the fact that they haven't done what they needed to in order for society and other professions to look at them with respect.

This notion that we know what chiropractors do and the only reason we don't refer to them is because we don't want to lose the fee? That's nonsense. If we can find a way to help the patient, why wouldn't we explore that? I refer patients to physical therapists all the time, technically I'm "losing" money on that unless I own that PT practice. So it's not a matter of some conspiracy or we are so economically motivated that we want to cut people out of the business. We just don't know what business they are actually in and aren't able to get good answers when we ask them.

In general, the problem that traditional medicine has with chiropractic care is the absence of any scientific proof that the types of treatments offered actually work. As was noted earlier, a recent article in the *Journal of the American Medical Association* (JAMA) points to the mild effectiveness of some chiropractic treatments in relieving back pain, but the problem for many physicians has been a fundamental lack of effort to validate the treatment or adequately explain the philosophy (Paige et. al 2017). As one chiropractor put it,

One of the things I love about chiropractic is that it's been around for over a hundred years and it hasn't changed. Medicine is always changing; they weren't doing the things they do today fifty years ago, and the things they'll be doing fifty years from now will be different from what they are doing today. Chiropractic principles have stood the test of time. How do I know? If it didn't work, patients wouldn't come to me over and over again.

An orthopedic surgeon who refers patients to chiropractors in his home town, offers this as a testimony to the problem. He says:

Yes, medicine has changed over time; that's because we have continued to strive for scientific answers to problems and illness. We used to put leeches on people because we thought it worked too, but we realized, after investigating further, that this actually made people worse. So our failures are not really evidence of our lack of effectiveness. Our failures are a sign that we are always trying to improve, we are always seeking the best way to treat and to scientifically determine which is the best way to get our patients healthy. Chiropractors don't do that. They fall back on anecdotal patient testimonies or dogmatic ideas that might have held sway a hundred years ago, but science and society has evolved considerably since then.

If they could point to some good research that showed what they do is effective, I think more doctors would be willing to acknowledge that the profession is in need of maturation and more data, but we would at least be able to say there's something in there that shows it works. But many of these guys reject the idea of science, they reject the idea of evidence-based practices, and they reject the criticism levied against them because they don't have an answer. They keep going back to their mantra, that it works, it works, it works, despite any real proof that it does.

They won't accept the idea that relieving symptoms doesn't mean the patient is cured, that they say they feel better is not proof that the treatment worked...AT ALL. And this is where they get into trouble and lose many doctors' confidence in what it is they do. So I would say that most doctors, and I'm in the small minority of people who do refer some patients to chiropractors, but most doctors either think of chiropractors as quacks, as frauds, or as so blindly misguided in their thinking that they can't be trusted, and surely not with one of our patients.

TRADITIONAL MEDICINE AND CHIROPRACTIC CARE

In addition to the skepticism from physicians about chiropractic medicine, including from groups like the American Medical Association, health care reform presents a host of challenges to the profession. Similar to medical doctors who own and operate small general medical practices who are forced to merge with other providers to extract reasonable reimbursement rates from insurance companies, many chiropractic offices, who overwhelmingly remain solo practitioners or consist of practices with less than three providers, struggle to keep up with the outcome and accountability measures as part of the insurance reimbursement protocols. The difference, however, is that unlike the groups created to advocate for doctors or dentists, chiropractors remain decentralized and unable to marshal significant political leverage to address the changing legislative, health care, and insurance landscapes.

The implementation of the Affordable Care Act, also known as Obamacare, has changed the way insurance companies provide reimbursement for services by medical providers. With a greater emphasis on administratively documenting how and in what ways a particular form of treatment actually improves a patient's health, coupled with a greater level of restriction on the types of services medical providers can offer without justification and authorization, many medical providers have had to reexamine the services they provide, and how they operate (AMGA 2016). For chiropractors in particular, who tend to treat patients with a more holistic approach to improve patient health, and who have lingering conflicts with traditional medicine (making it unlikely chiropractors will be included in collaborations with other medical providers), restrictions on the number and types of treatment they can provide have created difficulties within some practices.

SOCIOLOGY AND CHIROPRACTIC MEDICINE

A review of the literature shows a handful of studies about the sociological dimensions of the chiropractic profession or its providers (Wardell 1952, 1955, 1961, 1968, 1976, 1978; McCorkle 1961; Roebuck and Hunter 1972; Lin 1972; Rosenthal 1986; Villanueva-Russell 2005, 2008, 2009; Briggs, Hay, and Mierau 1997; Yealis et. al 1980; Wild 1978; Kelner, Hall, and Coulter 1980), most of which occurred in the 1970s and 1980s. However, very little research has been done since 2000 and none has been conducted about how the changes in medicine, particularly as it relates to health care reform, impacts chiropractors and their practices.

This lack of sociological research is a bit odd, given the many issues and challenges in health care as well as a growing body of literature on alternative medicine. Even the unethical practices of some medical providers, which would likely attract criminologists and those who study deviant behavior, would likely generate some sociological attention, especially given that medical sociology as a subfield is the largest one in the discipline. However, this has not been the case. In fact, a review of medical sociology textbooks shows scant attention devoted to chiropractors and chiropractic medicine, often just a few paragraphs (see for instance Cockerham 2017). Far more attention is paid in these textbooks to faith healers and more obscure practitioners.

The earliest sociological studies on chiropractic medicine were those by Wardell (1950). In his book *A Sociology of Chiropractic*, Rosenthal (1986) pointed out that up until 1950, there were only seven sociological studies on chiropractic medicine.

Much of what had been understood about the profession during a period that spanned almost twenty years was based only on Wardell's work.

These initial sociological explorations of chiropractic medicine were linked to the study of deviant behavior, and this was the framework in which sociology began to examine chiropractic medicine. In the 1950s Walter Wardell offered insight into chiropractic medicine in terms of its marginality. As he described it, marginality as a concept carries with it challenges to legitimacy and credibility, along with questions about competence and inferiority. This marginality comes, according to Wardell, as a result of comparisons to traditional medicine. At the microlevel, Wardell (1952) found a good deal of role ambiguity among chiropractors and role strain in their actual performance.

Rosenthal (1986) attributes the early conceptualization of chiropractic as deviant behavior based to the relationship between sociology and traditional medicine. The political and social climate of traditional medicine, particularly its opposition to chiropractic treatment, resulted in an understanding of chiropractic medicine as being substandard and inferior to what physicians offered patients.

Throughout the 1970s and into the 1980s, the research began to focus less on chiropractic medicine's place in the occupational scheme and more on what chiropractors actually did and how they did it (Rosenthal 1986; Wild 1978; Yealis et. al 1980; Coulter et. al 1980). For instance, in an ethnographic study of chiropractic medicine, Cowie and Roebuck (1975) offer insight into the nature of social interaction within a chiropractic office. Serving as a member of the staff, Cowie was able to observe how and in what ways the front office learned about the patients' needs, interests, and issues, and then relayed them to the doctor prior to receiving their treatment.

Drawing heavily on a Goffmanian framework, particularly as it relates to the notion of impression management and controlling the patient's understanding of the role of the chiropractor, this study offered great insight into how marketing efforts are employed, where staff members routinely encouraged patients to refer their friends and relatives to the office for care. While this may also occur in a traditional physician's office, Cowie and Roebuck point out that there is an intentionality and intensity to this type of self-promotion that can create an uncomfortable atmosphere and cause patients to question the motives of a chiropractor.

Cowie and Roebuck (1975) conclude that there is an element of trust that is created between the patient and the provider, including the office in general, that allows them to thoughtfully consider the advice offered by the chiropractor during their visits. In addition, like the earlier studies, much of the impression management performed by the chiropractor is an effort to manage the stigma of being a member of a "tainted" profession.

Since the 1980s, much of the sociological research on chiropractic medicine has focused on the profession's ability to adapt and respond to the criticisms of the effectiveness of chiropractic treatments. Much of the medical literature during this period focused on evidence-based practices, meaning treatments are given much greater credibility and support when there is clinical research that shows its overall effectiveness. Clearly, this is problematic for chiropractic treatments, since the lack of scientific evidence supporting these treatments has been a consistent criticism. This is particularly true of the identification and proof of the vertebral subluxation, a key element to the justification of chiropractic medicine from its very beginnings.

As guidelines were being developed for evidence-based medicine, all complementary and alternative-based medicines, but particularly chiropractic with its emphasis on concepts such as vitalism and innate intelligence, struggled to find a place in the discussion. Consequently, chiropractic medicine's credibility and professionalism within medicine continued to suffer. The lack of evidence about chiropractic treatment also created challenges within the profession as it related to insurance reimbursement under the managed care model. This lack of understanding or willingness to embrace a scientific approach is not simply a criticism from outside the profession.

It was also during the 1990s and into the early 2000s that many books were written that heavily criticized the profession, particularly those written by chiropractors themselves. While not sociological in scope, and while these authors did not provide sufficient data to document their criticisms against the profession, there were sociological elements and concepts to consider in these texts. For example, in the book entitled *Spin Doctors*, Benedetti and MacPhail (2002), two investigative journalists, offer a scathing overview of the chiropractic profession and its lack of scientific validation. They also dedicate a significant amount of attention to chronicling the fraudulent, questionable, and even dangerous practices performed by chiropractors. Similarly, other accounts offered by chiropractors and scientists provide a platform of criticism of the profession and the lack of proof about chiropractic medicine as a legitimate form of treatment (Long 2013; Magner and Barrett 1995; Singh and Ernst 2008).

The current study, then, takes some of the issues discussed in previous sociological studies and examines them in light of the health care reform that is currently being debated in the United States. The fact that some of the issues continue to plague the profession is important, as are the new issues that are topics of discussion among American chiropractors. Included in this study is a focus on the internal strife within the profession, the impact of a large-scale social problem, health care reform, as well as how and in what way chiropractic colleges are responding to changes in medicine. Included in this discussion is the shift in focus by some chiropractic colleges to train students to become primary care providers instead of traditional chiropractors.

In sum, there are a host of sociological issues to address in the study of chiropractic medicine, particularly since the profession is undergoing significant changes as a result of health care reform in this country. Insurance companies are reluctant to cover chiropractic treatments, largely because they do not think of them as medically necessary or are interested only in reducing costs. The impact on the profession is significant. This is particularly true given that most chiropractors remain solo practitioners, who are limited in the types of treatments they can provide that are reimbursable by insurance companies. In fact, many of the chiropractors interviewed for this study have lamented the changes in health care and their impact on chiropractic medicine. In fact, data collected from the South Carolina Department of Labor Licensure and Regulation shows that nearly 40 percent of chiropractors in South Carolina have not renewed their licenses to practice, indicating they are no longer in business. Others have tried to diversify their businesses by offering weight loss programs or nutritional supplements. Still others have become desperate and engaged in questionable billing practices, particularly through Medicare, in an effort to remain viable.

Bibliography

"Affordable Care Act Implementation and Information." AMGA. 2016. https://amga. org/wcm/advocacy/issues/aca_issues.aspx.

American Chiropractic Association. "Patient Fact Sheet." ACA Today. 2017. https:// www.acatoday.org/Portals/60/Docs/Patients/Patient%20Fact%20Sheets/ HealthyLiving_GetHealthywithChiro.pdf.

Briggs, L., D. Hay, and D. Mierau. "Canadian Chiropractors' Attitudes Towards Chiropractic Philosophy and Scope Of Practice: Implications for the Implementation of Clinical Practice Guidelines." *Journal of Canadian Chiropractic Association* 41, no. 3 (1997): 145–54. https://www.ncbi.nlm.nih.gov/pmc/articles/PMC2485157/ pdf/jcca00027-0019.pdf.

Cockerham, William. *Medical Sociology*, 8th ed. New York: Taylor and Francis, 2017.

Cowie, J. B., and J. Roebuck. *An Ethnographic Study of a Chiropractic Clinic*. New York: The Free Press, 1975.

English, Cynthia, and Elizabeth Keating. "Majority in U.S. Say Chiropractic Works for Neck, Back Pain." Gallup. 2015. http://www.gallup.com/poll/184910/majority-say-chiropractic-works-neck-back-pain.aspx.

Ingraham, P. "Does Chiropractic Work?" *Pain Science*. 2016. http://www.painscience. com/articles/does-chiropractic-work.php.

Kelner, M., O. Hall, and I. Coulter. *Chiropractors: Do They Help?* Toronto: Fitzhenry and Whiteside, 1980.

Lecomte, M. D., and J. J. Schensul. *Designing and Conducting Ethnographic Research.* New York: Rowman and Altimira, 2012.

Lin, P. *The Chiropractor, Chiropractic and Process: A Study of the Sociology of an Occupation.* Unpublished Ph.D. Dissertation, University of Missouri, 1972.

Long, P. H. *Chiropractic Abuse: An Insider's Lament.* New York: American Council on Science and Health, 2013.

Magner, G., and S. Barrett. *Chiropractic: The Victim's Perspective.* New York: Prometheus Books, 1995.

McCorkle, T. "Chiropractic: A Deviant Theory of Disease and Treatment in Contemporary Western Culture." *Human Organization* 20, (1961): 20–2.

McMillen, M. "Complementary and Alternative Medicine on the Rise." WebMD. 2011. https://www.webmd.com/a-to-z-gudies/news/20110201/complementary-and-alternative-medicine-on-the-rise.

McNamara, R. H. "The Joint as a Form of Innovative Disruption in Chiropractic Medicine." *International Journal of Social Science and Business*, 2(5):1–11, 2017.

Meister, A. *Evangelical Ideology in Chiropractic Medicine.* Master's Thesis, University of Pittsburgh, 2010.

Paige, N. M., I. M. Miake-Lye, M. S. Booth, J. M. Beroes, A. S. Mardin, P. Dougherty, R. Branson, B. Tang, S.C. Morton, and P. G. Shekelle. "Association of Spinal Manipulative Therapy with Clinical Benefit and Harm for Acute Low Back Pain, Systematic Review and Meta-Analysis." *Journal of American Medical Association* 317, no. 14 (2017): 1451–60.

Roebuck, J., and B. Hunter. "The Awareness of Healthcare Quackery as Deviant Behavior." *Journal of Health and Social Behavior* 13, (1972): 162–66.

Rosenthal, S. *A Sociology of Chiropractic.* New York: Edwin Mellen, 1986.

Singh, S., and E. Ernst. *Trick or Treatment: The Undeniable Facts About Alternative Medicine.* New York: W. W. Norton and Company, 2009.

Taylor, S. *Ethnographic Research: A Reader.* Belmont, CA: Sage, 2002.

US Department of Labor, Bureau of Labor Statistics. *Occupational Outlook Handbook 2016–2017 Edition*, Chiropractors. 2016. http://www.bls.gov/ooh/healthcare/chiropractors.html.

U.S. Department of Health and Human Services, Office of Inspector General, (2016). *Hundreds of Millions in Medicare Payments for Chiropractic Services did not Comply with Medicare Requirements.* Available at: https://oig.hhs.gov/oas/reports/region9/91402033.pdf

Villanueva-Russell, Y. "Evidence-based Medicine and Its Implications for the Profession of Chiropractic." *Social Science & Medicine* 60, no. 3 (2005): 545–61.

———. "An Ideal-Typical Development of Chiropractic, 1895–1961: Pursuing Professional Ends Through Entrepreneurial Means." *Social Theory & Health* 6, no. 3 (2008): 250–72.

———. "Chiropractors as Folk Devils: Published and Unpublished News Coverage of a Moral Panic." *Deviant Behavior* 30, no. 2 (2009): 175–200.

Wardell, W. I. "A Marginal Professional Role: The Chiropractor." *Social Forces* 30, (1952): 33–348.

———. "The Reduction of Strain in a Marginal Social Role." *American Journal of Sociology* 61, (1955): 16–25.

———. "Public Regulation of Chiropractic." *Journal of the National Medical Association* 53, (1961): 166–72.

———. "Chiropractic Among the Healing Professions." *The ACA Journal of Chiropractic* 5, (1968): 13–19.

———. "Orthodox and Unorthodox Practitioners: Changing Relationships and the Future of Chiropractic." In *Marginal Medicine*, edited by R. Wallis, and P. Morley, 61–73. New York: The Free Press, 1976.

———. "Social Factors in the Survival of Chiropractic: A Comparative View." *Sociological Symposium* 22, (1978): 6–17.

Wild, P. "Social Origins and Ideology of Chiropractors: An Empirical Study of the Socialization of the Chiropractic Student." *Sociological Symposium* 22, (1978): 33–54.

Yealis, C.E., R.B. Wallace, W.P. Fisher, and R. Tolkheim. "Does Chiropractic Utilization Substitute for Less Available Medical Services?" *American Journal of Public Health* 70, (1980): 415–17.

CPSIA information can be obtained
at www.ICGtesting.com
Printed in the USA
BVHW011204290620
582565BV00006B/105